Study Guide

Nile R. Leach

Operations Management

Strategy & Analysis

Fourth Edition

Krajewski/Ritzman

Study Guide

Nile R. Leach

Operations Management

Strategy & Analysis

Fourth Edition

Krajewski/Ritzman

 ADDISON-WESLEY PUBLISHING COMPANY

Reading, Massachusetts • Menlo Park, California • New York
Don Mills, Ontario • Wokingham, England • Amsterdam • Bonn
Sydney • Singapore • Tokyo • Madrid • San Juan • Milan • Paris

Reproduced by Addison-Wesley from camera-ready copy supplied by the author.

ISBN 0-201-60723-9
2 3 4 5 6 7 8 9 10 CRS 99989796

Preface

This study guide is designed to accompany *Operations Management / STRATEGY AND ANALYSIS*, Fourth Edition, by KRAJEWSKI AND RITZMAN ©1996 Addison-Wesley. This study guide may be useful in several ways.

The chapter review section is an overview of topics this author considers to be particularly relevant. *Key points* that should not be lost in the clutter are marked with a small *key* such as the one at the left. The chapter review section may also serve as an outline for lecture notes. If you bring this guide to class, it may save a lot of frantic note taking.

The side bars contain formulas or information that is not in the text. Side bars contain questions and suggestions for additional study, historical perspectives and personal experiences relating theory to practice.

Most of the multiple choice questions have been used in actual testing situations. The answer key appears near the end of each chapter or supplement. Therefore, the guide should be useful in self-checking the level of understanding before you move on to new topics.

The applicable formula usually appears in the column next to the problem statement. All formulas have been checked to assure the symbols match those used in the text. A small amount of space has been provided for writing the student's solutions in the study guide. This should again be useful in keeping the work together and in preparing for tests.

It is important that the student attempt to solve the problems *before* looking at the author's solutions. Solutions appear on pages that immediately follow the problem statements. They have been checked to the best of my ability. Please advise the publisher if you find errors.

Acknowledgments

Authors often state in their acknowledgments that their work could not have been completed without the help of a list of people. I can now appreciate and attest to that fact. Thank you, Kate Morgan, editorial assistant, and Julia Berrisford, senior editor for your patience and skill. This Study Guide could not have been completed without your help.

Nile R. Leach

Nile R. Leach
Corporate Trainer – Manufacturing
J. D. Edwards & Company

Table of Contents

Study Guide

Nile R. Leach

Operations Management

Strategy & Analysis

Fourth Edition

Krajewski/Ritzman

Chapter One, Operations as a Competitive Weapon

Doesn't it seem as though in every class the professor acts like her course is the most important one you will ever take in college? That really bothers me, because *this* is the most important course you will ever take in college!

Only a little humor is intended in that first paragraph. (My wife said that there is no need to worry about anyone thinking there is a lot of humor in it.) Operations management *is* important. *Every* organization has an operations function. Depending on how well it is managed, operations can be a competitive weapon, or it can cause the ruin of the entire organization. The operations function is changing rapidly. These changes have great impact on all other functions of business, including management, marketing, finance, engineering, human resources, and information systems. The degree of success in implementing change in operations will greatly affect the standard of living of all participants in the organization.

In most business colleges, this is the only chance you will have to study the business function that spends most of the budget, uses most of the physical assets, and employs most of the human resources. No matter what you choose as a career, you will work frequently with operations. Operations probably will be the cause of most of your headaches. Doesn't it make sense then, to give the study of operations management a high priority?

What Is Operations Management?

"Today, the term **operations management** refers to the direction and control of the processes that transform inputs into finished goods and services." p. 3

The "Functions" columns added to Fig. 1.1 show operations management communicates and coordinates with these functions in order to obtain the needed input resources and to deal with the outputs of operations.

FIGURE 1.1

The Operations Management System

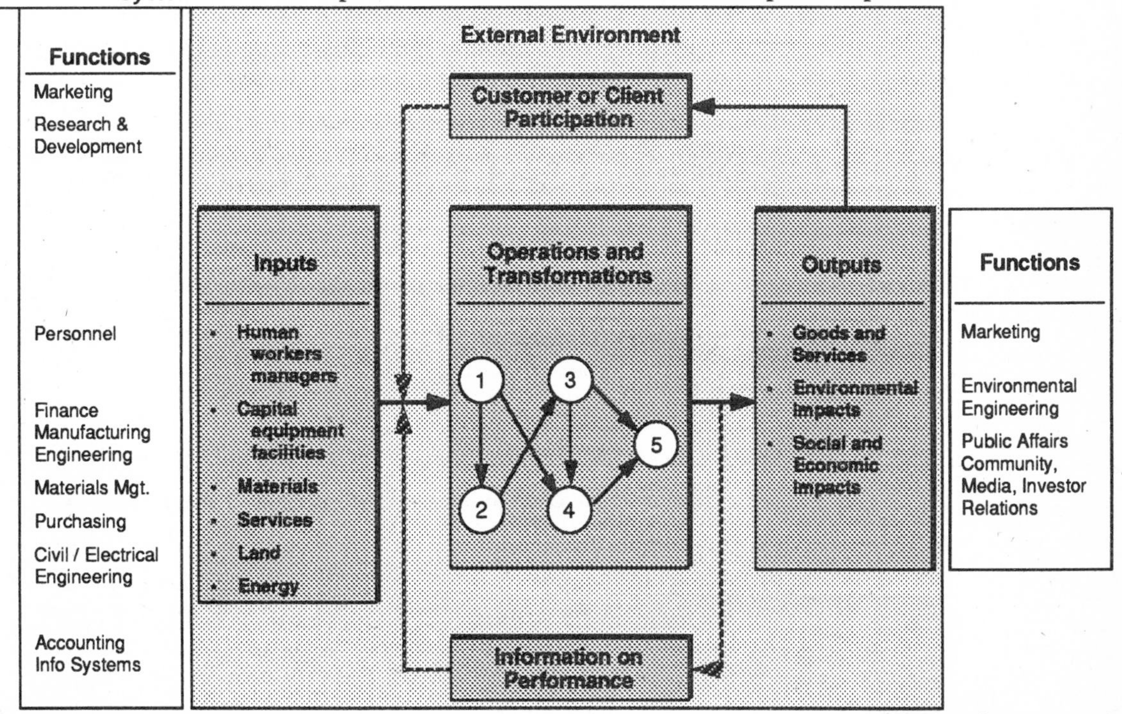

- Inputs
  - human resources
    - . workers
    - . managers
  - capital
    - . equipment
    - . facilities
  - purchased materials and services
  - land
  - energy
- Special inputs
  - customer participation
  - internal and external information

All operations systems have transformation processes.

- Transformation examples
  - manufacturing — physical, chemical
  - airline — locational
  - school — educational
  - hospital — physiological
  - congress — deliberative
- Outputs
  - goods and services
  - environmental impact
  - political and economic impact

Operations produce outputs in addition to goods and services. For example, pollution is a bi-product of many manufacturing processes. Environmental responsibilities include mitigating adverse impacts of operations. Employment opportunities are accompanied by population growth and additional demands for education, public works, recreation, and natural resources. Newcomers may not share the values and political views prevalent in the native population. Community relations and legal affairs deal with these economic and political impacts, but the root cause is operations.

Differences and Similarities Between Manufacturing and Services

FIGURE 1.2

Continuum of Characteristics of Manufacturing and Service Organizations

More Like a Goods Producer ◄——►	More Like a Services Producer
• Physical, durable product	• Intangible, perishable product
• Output can be inventoried	• Output cannot be inventoried
• Low customer contact	• High customer contact
• Long response time	• Short response time
• Regional, national, or international markets	• Local markets
• Large facilities	• Small facilities
• Capital intensive	• Labor intensive
• Quality easily measured	• Quality not easily measured

How do service operations differ from manufacturing operations?

There are some exceptions to these differences. For example, can you think of a service that has a national market? How about a manufacturer that has a short response time? … a capital-intensive service? … a manufacturer with high customer contact?

With regard to services, how would you measure the quality of an operations management lecture?

Measuring service quality: A common method of measuring the quality of services is to use customer surveys. However, individual preferences usually result in a wide range of responses.

"Moreover, individual preferences affect assessments of service quality, making objective measurement difficult." p. 6

Trends in Operations Management

Service Sector Growth

What are the implications of recent employment and productivity trends in the service sector?

Components of the Service Sector

1. Local, state, and federal governments
2. Wholesale and retail sales
3. Transportation, public utilities, communication, health, financial services, real estate, insurance, repair services, business services, and personal service

The growing service sector should not lead you to conclude that manufacturing is becoming an insignificant part of the U.S. economy. Many experts argue convincingly that U.S. firms must keep their mastery over manufacturing.

"… the service and manufacturing sectors of the economy are complementary." p. 8

Productivity Changes

"**Productivity** is the value of outputs (goods and services) produced divided by the values of input resources (wages, cost of equipment, and the like) used." p. 8

EQUATION 1.1

$$\text{Productivity} = \frac{\text{Output}}{\text{Input}}$$

At the national level, productivity typically is measured as:

$$\text{Labor Productivity} = \frac{\text{Dollar value of output}}{\text{unit of labor input}}$$

This result is the *labor* productivity ratio. There is an important difference between labor productivity and *multifactor* productivity. Automation, which is the replacement of labor with capital equipment, nearly always improves labor productivity ratio. However when automation choices are made poorly, the added costs of capital and maintenance may exceed labor savings, so the value of output as a ratio to *multiple* inputs (labor + equipment + capital) could decrease.

"Operations managers play a key role in determining productivity. Their challenge is to increase the value of output relative to the cost of input."

"Productivity is the prime determinant of a nation's standard of living." p. 9

- Productivity of human resources determines employee wages.
- Wage increases that are not a result of improved productivity are inflationary. They do not increase the standard of living at the national level. Such wage increases are consumed by inflation.
- Productivity increases more slowly in services (less than 0.1% per year) in comparison to manufacturing (2.9% per year).

Productivity Exercises:

Labor Productivity.
From Chrysler's 1994 Annual Report to the Stockholders:

	This year	Last year	Year before last
Factory unit sales of cars and trucks	2,762,103	2,475,738	2,175,447
Employment (worldwide)	112,000	113,000	115,000 (estimate)

Only about 5% of Chrysler's Revenues come from financial services and sources other than sales of cars and trucks. Chrysler has an ongoing early retirement program resulting in decreased employment, particularly in financial services. Assuming there was no appreciable change in the inventory levels or number of hours worked per employee, what is the year-to-year percentage change in *labor* productivity at Chrysler?

Solution*:

The annual report does not break out the number of employees involved with cars and trucks as compared to financial services. Since we are just looking for year-to-year percentage changes, and since cars and trucks represent almost all of the revenue, we can use the total employment without introducing significant error.

"Many measures of productivity are possible, and all are rough approximations." p. 8

output / employee 24.66 21.90 18.92

(24.62 - 21.90) / 21.90 = 12.49% (21.90 - 18.92) / 18.92 = 15.75%

Multifactor Productivity.
From Chrysler's 1994 Annual Report to the Stockholders: (Note 2. inventories and cost of sales)

(in millions of dollars)	This Year	Last Year
Sales of manufactured products	$49,363	$40,831
Total manufacturing cost of sales	$39,000	$33,100

Assuming there was no appreciable change in the year-to-year inventory levels (true), what is the year-to-year percentage change in *multifactor* productivity at Chrysler?

Solution*:

productivity 49.363 / 39000 - 40.831 / 33100

= 1.266 = 1.234

(12.66 - 12.34) / 12.34 = 2.6%

---

* To check your solutions to exercises, refer to the last page of the Study Guide chapter (page 12).

What are the causes of recent productivity trends and shifts in shares of world markets?

Some Possible Explanations.

- Unreliable service sector data, difficult to place value on services
- Increased regulation — adds cost, generally doesn't increase value, and therefore depresses productivity ratio.
- Net investment in new equipment is low — when capital/labor ratio increases, labor productivity improves. U.S. managers tend to invest for quick paper profits, e.g., mergers, rather than invest in capital equipment.
- Changing work-force composition and attitudes toward work
- Strong unions can increase labor costs without commensurate increases in output. Productivity ratio decreases.
- Difficult to improve already high productivity — the learning curve (see Supplement D) has become flat.

"However, such explanations are incomplete." p. 11

- Managers and employees can improve productivity, maintain high wages and increase standard of living through careful attention to operations management.

Year-to-year Percentage Changes in Productivity

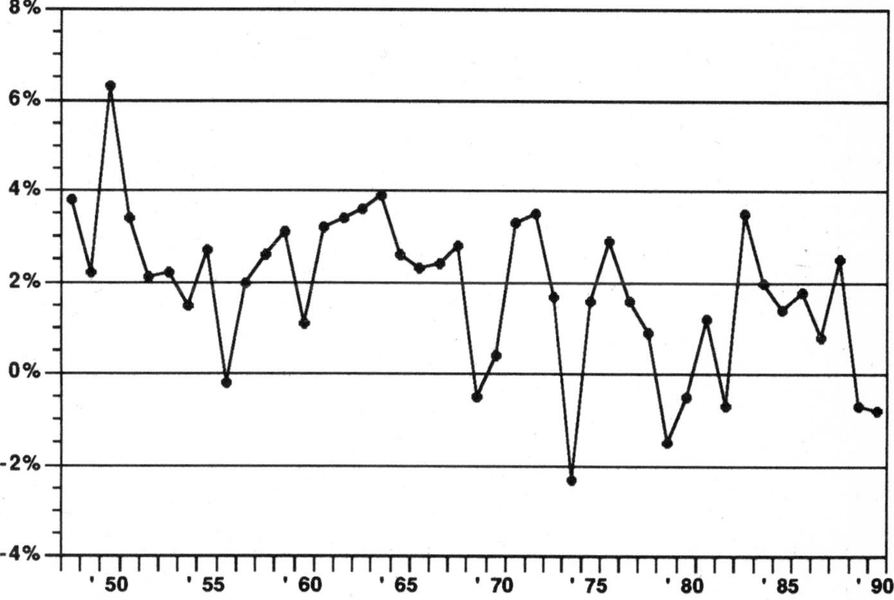

Other causative factors:

- Trend Toward Stronger Service Sector

Services are labor intensive and usually difficult to automate. To produce twice as many haircuts, we need twice as many barbers. Productivity *ratio* does not improve. The general downward trend in productivity might be explained by the coincident increase in the service sector.

- War

Productivity ratio *decreases* at the start of a war. Yes, production output increases, but not as quickly as the cost of inputs. In a war, we increase output at *any* cost. This forces inefficient resources into use, and decreases productivity ratio. Can you locate the beginning of the Korean and Vietnam conflicts on the graph?

This does **not** advocate paying women less than men.

- Trend Toward Two-Income Families

Women receive about 70% of the pay that men receive for equal work. Therefore, the productivity ratio tends to increase as more women enter the work force.

- Scarce Resources, High Interest Rates

These increase costs without increasing value of output. Can you locate the effects on year-to-year productivity associated with the oil embargo of the early 1970s, the high interest rates during the Carter Presidency, reduced regulation during the Reagan Presidency, and the current shortage of entry-level workers?

Global Competition

"Today businesses accept that, to prosper, they must view customers, suppliers, facility locations, and competitors in global terms." p. 11

- Imports as a percent of the total U.S. output have increased.
- East Asian countries achieved remarkable productivity gains.
- Developing countries are future competitors and markets.
- The rise (ECC, NAFTA) and fall of trading blocks (Eastern Europe) change global competition.
- American workers are still more productive, but faster productivity increases in other countries is narrowing the gap.

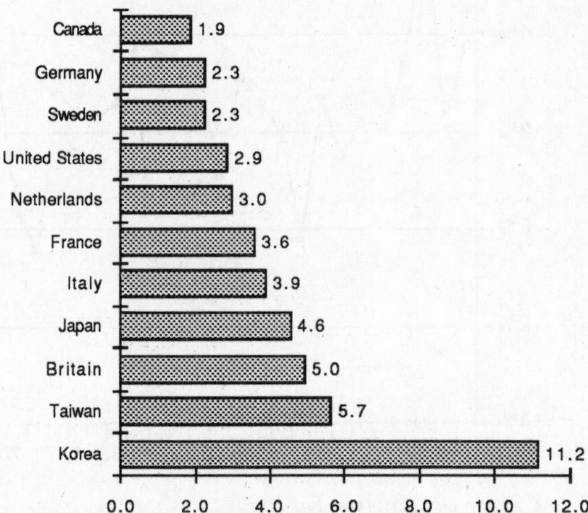

- Toyota and Honda have shown (Managerial Practice 1.1) that American workers can be very productive when managed with the techniques inherent in Japanese management culture.
- Operations management is key to world-class competition.

What can be done to compete better in terms of quality, time, and technology?

Competition Based on Quality, Time, and Technology

- Without quality, a firm loses its ability to compete
- Competing on the basis of time
  - fill orders earlier, shorter lead time than the competition
  - quickly introduce new products or services
- Accelerating technological change

How can operations be continuously improved?

Continuous Improvement

"The philosophy of **continuous improvement** seeks ways to improve operations." p. 13

- Select important performance measures
- Get feedback on current performance
- Set goals for future improvement
- Get everyone involved in the change process

Just-in-time systems

- Driven by continuous improvement
- Focus on customers' needs
  - lower costs
  - improved quality
  - faster delivery (shorter lead time)

To foster a creative, competitive environment

- Restructuring the organization
- Decentralizing responsibilities
- Removing management layers
- Empowering, involving employees in key decisions
- Teams for cross-functional coordination

Horizontal or molecular organization

- Teams represent different functional areas organized around markets
- Replaces pyramid organization and top-down decision making
- Mass customization — closer customer contact

Reengineering — a philosophy that calls for the radical redesign of a company's critical business processes.

- Aims at change
- Focus on business processes rather than functional departments

Environmental, Ethical, and Work-force Diversity Issues

"Soft" Issues in a Fast-Changing Global Marketplace

How do ethics and the environment affect operations?

1. Responsibilities beyond producing goods and services profitably
2. Help solve important social problems
3. Broader constituency than just stockholders
4. Consider impacts beyond marketplace transactions
5. Serve human values that range beyond economic values

Operations Management and the Organization

Operations Management as a Functional Area

• Operations	Transforms inputs into outputs
• Accounting	Collects costs, financial information
• Marketing	Generates demand
• Finance	Secures, invests capital
• Human Resources	Hires, trains employees
• Distribution	Transports inputs and outputs
• Engineering	Product and process designs

Operations as a Profession: During the early 1980s the American Production and Inventory Control Society (APICS) claimed that production and operations management was the "newest profession." Many corporations were only then realizing that meeting global challenges would require managers recruited from the professions.

In another sense, operations management has been claimed as the "oldest profession." One day, an argument broke out among several persons, each claiming to be occupied in the oldest profession. After hearing from the professions that you'd expect, an operations manager said: "You're all wrong. Operations management is the oldest profession and I can prove it." With that he opened a Bible to the book of Genesis and read: "In the beginning there was chaos ..."

Organizations may contract for some of these functions. Common examples include law, accounting, advertising, and training, but may also include public relations and engineering. A small central firm that contracts for the production of goods and services is called a "hollow corporation".

Operations managers use many of the disciplines usually taught in business schools ... see Figure 1.5, p. 15.

- Career path to upper management positions

Operations Management as an Interfunctional Concern

Decisions in Operations.

Basic Steps for Decision Making

1. clearly define/state the problem/decision
2. collect information needed to analyze possible alternatives
3. choose alternative and implement decision

Managers of all types either make decisions or teach others to make decisions … a distinction of operations management can be found in the type of decisions that operations managers make.

Three Categories of Decisions

This list forms the basic outline for our text book.

1. Strategic — affect future decisions
   - Which products or services to offer?
   - What are the competitive priorities?
   - Should resources be organized around products or processes?
   - What are the quality objectives?
   - What methods will be used for control?
2. Design — long-term commitments
   - What system capacity is needed?
   - Where should facilities be located?
   - How should facility layouts be organized?
3. Operating — continuous improvement
   - Which forecasting method is appropriate?
   - How will inventory be managed?
   - What are the options to achieve short-term output increases?
   - What, when, and how many items should be authorized for purchase or production?
   - Would Just-In-Time techniques benefit our organization?
   - Which task should receive top priority?
   - How should resources be scheduled?

Linking Decision Areas.

- Operations decisions compliment corporate strategy — example; inventory decisions are influenced by finance and marketing strategy.
- Plans, policies, and actions within operations are linked and should be mutually supportive — example; inventory decisions affect capacity, production scheduling, and quality.

Note the subtitle of the text.

Strategy and Analysis.

- Concepts and calculation
- Wide variety of analytic techniques available

Cross-functional Coordination.

- Interdependent functions require coordination and understanding across functional boundaries.
- Strongest connection with marketing
  - marketing determines demand for existing and new products
  - operations uses human and capital resources to make products
  - operations locates facilities to serve markets
  - marketing, delivery promises based on operations capabilities
- Accounting provides operations performance feedback (for control and corrective actions) and handles routine financial transactions (customer invoicing, supplier payment).
- Finance influences operation's investment in technology, process improvement, capital expansion, and inventory.
- Human resources recruits and trains personnel for operations work.
- The first few engineering design decisions determine the majority of that product's manufacturing costs. Early coordination ensures the design matches operation's capabilities and that needed components can be purchased.

Achieving Cross-Functional Coordination.

> How can coordination be achieved with other functional areas?

- Unified strategy, department vision
- Redesigned organizational structure
  - promote cross-functional coordination
  - push decision making responsibility lower in the organization
  - group functional areas around markets for product or services
- Reward systems consistent with cross-functional goals
- Decision support information systems designed to boost coordination
- Informal social systems, coffee-break centers, open office arrangements promote better communication and understanding across functional lines.
- Employee selection and promotion based on broad perspectives and achieving common goals.

Operations Management as a Competitive Weapon

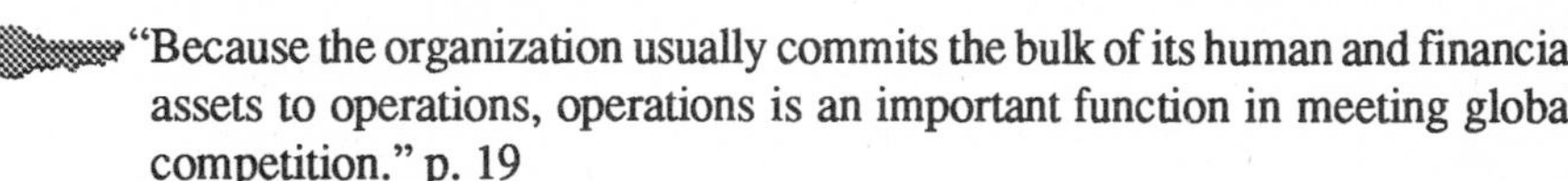
"Because the organization usually commits the bulk of its human and financial assets to operations, operations is an important function in meeting global competition." p. 19

- Operations can be either a competitive weapon or a millstone.

A firm competes by

- Creative marketing
- Skillful finance
- Unique competencies in operations

Meeting the Competitive Challenge

> What are companies doing to make operations a competitive weapon?

Examples include IKEA, Cincinnati Milacron, Inc., Dillard's, and Shenandoah Life. Note that most of these corporations share in common a situation of facing strong challenges. "If it ain't broke don't fix it" is part of our corporate culture. When it comes to motivating change in large American corporations, being in a little trouble can be a luxury. Trouble indicates that the status quo is inadequate, and motivates change.

Multiple-Choice Questions

1. Operations responsibilities are primarily associated with
   A. Manufacturing production
   B. Obtaining needed input resources
   C. Transforming inputs into outputs
   D. Distributing finished goods

2. Which of the following is a "special" type of input?
   A. Capital
   B. Materials
   C. Participation by customers
   D. Workers and managers

3. Which of the following is a characteristic which is more like a services producer than like a goods producer?
   A. Durable product
   B. International markets
   C. Labor intensive
   D. Low customer contact

4. Which of the following would tend to **improve** year-to-year percentage changes in the productivity ratio?
   A. Increased interest rates
   B. Increased regulation
   C. Increased resource availability
   D. Increased union strength

5. Which sector of the U.S. economy employs the most people?
   A. Agriculture
   B. Government
   C. Manufacturing
   D. Services

6. Which of the following is "the prime determinant of a nation's standard of living"?
   A. Abundant natural resources
   B. Capitalism
   C. Infrastructure
   D. Productivity

7. Radical redesign of a company's critical business processes is called
   A. a contract with America
   B. crossfunctional coordination
   C. mass customization
   D. reengineering

8. Which of the following countries currently has the highest value added per hour worked?
   A. France
   B. Germany
   C. Japan
   D. United States

9. Which function has primary responsibility for developing product designs and production methods?
   A. Engineering
   B. Management
   C. Marketing
   D. Operations

10. An important trend is that more firms are competing on the basis of:
    A. Deceptive advertising
    B. Nationalism
    C. Price
    D. Time

11. The plurality of Chief Executive Officers for manufacturing corporations come from which of the following functions?
    A. Finance
    B. Legal
    C. Marketing
    D. Operations

12. Which of the following increases cross-functional coordination?
    A. Departmental lines drawn around areas of specialization
    B. Pushing decision-making responsibility lower in the organization
    C. Pyramid organizational structure
    D. Set goals to reward increased competition between departments

13. Which of the following explains *in general* why productivity is improving more rapidly in some countries than in the U.S.A?
    A. Regulatory environment
    B. Work force attitudes
    C. Unions
    D. Careful attention to operations management

(Multiple-Choice answers are on page 12.)

Problem

Raven Industries annual reports include the following information:

(Dollars in thousands)	Year 0	Year 1	Year 2	Year 3	Year 4
Sales		$85,502	$100,609	$111,214	$121,468
Finished Goods + Work In Progress Inventories	$8,521	$9,425	$9,468	$10,257	$9,917
Employees		1142	1252	1316	1435

Estimate the rate of labor productivity improvements.

Caution: *It is very important to make an honest attempt to solve the exercises before proceeding to the solutions. Tests generally do not provide the solutions to problems, then ask the student to merely check the solutions as to whether the answers seem reasonable. Solved problems should be used to learn which techniques require additional study.*

Solution to Raven Industries

If we assume that the value of output is fairly represented by sales plus the year-to-year change in inventories and assume the amount of labor input is fairly represented by the number of employees, then:

EQUATION 1.1

$$\text{Productivity} = \frac{\text{Output}}{\text{Input}}$$

Labor productivity ratio, Year 1:

$$\frac{\$85{,}502 + (\$9{,}425 - 8{,}521)}{1142 \text{ employees}} = \frac{\$75{,}662}{\text{employee}}$$

Labor productivity ratio, Year 2:

$$\frac{\$100{,}609 + (\$9{,}468 - 9{,}425)}{1252 \text{ employees}} = \frac{\$80{,}393}{\text{employee}}$$

Percent change:

$$\frac{\$80{,}393 - \$75{,}662}{\$75{,}662} = 6.25\%$$

Labor productivity ratio, Year 3:

$$\frac{\$111{,}214 + (\$10{,}257 - 9{,}468)}{1316 \text{ employees}} = \frac{\$85{,}109}{\text{employee}}$$

Percent change:

$$\frac{\$85{,}109 - \$80{,}393}{\$80{,}393} = 5.87\%$$

Labor productivity ratio, Year 4:

$$\frac{\$121{,}468 + (\$9{,}917 - 10{,}257)}{1435 \text{ employees}} = \frac{\$84{,}410}{\text{employee}}$$

Percent change:

$$\frac{\$84{,}410 - \$85{,}109}{\$85{,}109} = -0.08\%$$

The average year-to-year improvement in productivity ratio is:

$(6.25\% + 5.87\% - 0.08\%)/3 = 4.01\%$

Solution to Productivity Exercise — Chrysler

Labor productivity	This year	Last year	Year before last
Output/employee	24.662	21.909	18.917
Productivity improvement (%)	12.56%	15.82%	

Multifactor productivity	This year	Last year
Value of output/input	1.2657	1.2336
Productivity improvement (%)	2.6%	

The multifactor productivity improvement is typical of the U.S. manufacturing sector. Chrysler's labor productivity numbers may be unusually high because of reduction in workforce, increased use of overtime, automation, or increased use of subcontractors (who don't count as Chrysler employees).

MULTIPLE CHOICE ANSWERS

1.	C	8.	D
2.	C	9.	A
3.	C	10.	D
4.	C	11.	D
5.	D	12.	B
6.	D	13.	D
7.	D		

Chapter Two, Operations Strategy

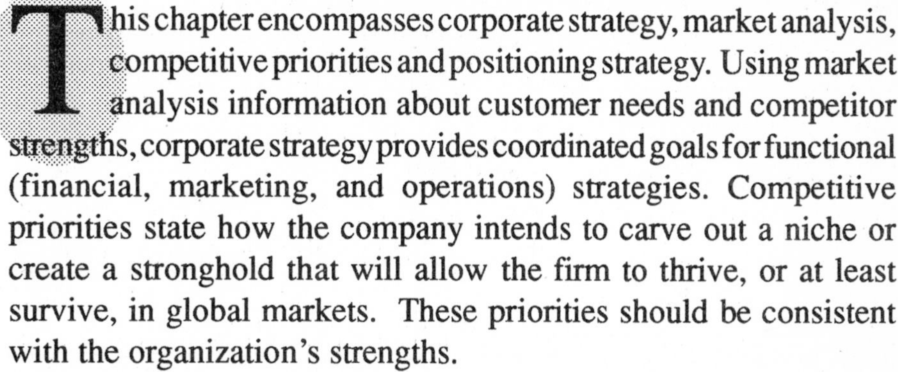

This chapter encompasses corporate strategy, market analysis, competitive priorities and positioning strategy. Using market analysis information about customer needs and competitor strengths, corporate strategy provides coordinated goals for functional (financial, marketing, and operations) strategies. Competitive priorities state how the company intends to carve out a niche or create a stronghold that will allow the firm to thrive, or at least survive, in global markets. These priorities should be consistent with the organization's strengths.

Product life cycles span five stages, starting with "product planning" and ending with "decline." Some organizations find an advantage in shifting competitive priorities at the appropriate point in the product life cycle. Other organizations find that their strengths are limited to a specific band width in the life cycle and that they should not attempt to compete when the product moves to its next life-cycle stage.

It is especially important to understand positioning strategy at this early point in the text. Positioning strategy determines what an organization's strengths will be over the long term. It is always difficult, and often impossible, for a firm to recover from adopting the wrong positioning strategy. All operations decisions as described throughout the remainder of this text must be consistent with the established positioning strategy.

How does operations strategy relate to corporate strategy?

Operations Strategy

"Developing a customer-driven operations strategy begins with a process called market analysis, which categorizes the firm's customers, identifies their needs, and assesses competitor's strengths." p. 28

Market analysis
- Categorize customers
- Identify customer needs
- Assess competitors' strengths

Corporate strategy
- Provides framework of goals for the organization

Competitive priorities
- Operating system capabilities and strengths required to serve customers

Functional strategies
- Goals and long term plans for each of the functional areas (operations, finance, marketing)

The main topic of this chapter is **operations strategy**, a functional area strategy which states how operations will implement the firm's corporate strategy.

"Continuous cross-functional interaction must occur in implementing operations strategy — or any other functional strategy." p. 29

FIGURE 2.1

Linking Corporate Strategy, Market Analysis, and the Environment Through Competitive Priorities

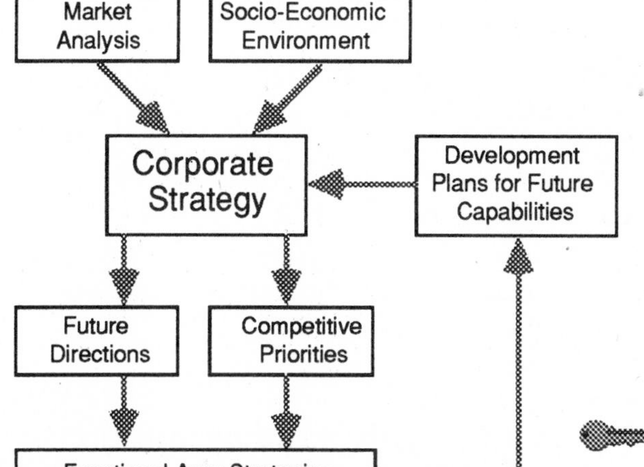

Corporate Strategy

"**Corporate strategy** is an organization's plan that defines the business(es) the company will pursue, new opportunities and threats in the environment, and growth objectives the company should achieve." p. 30

Strategic Choices

- Determine the mission
- Monitor and adjust to changes in the environment
- Identify and develop distinctive competencies

Mission

> Look in the front of your college course catalog or bulletin for a statement of your school's mission. Does it answer these questions?

- What business are we in? Where should we be ten years from now?
- Who are our customers (or clients)?
- What are our basic beliefs?
- How do we measure success? What are the key performance objectives?

Broad or Narrow Mission?

- Too broad — the firm enters businesses in which it has no distinctive competencies. Examples: Westinghouse, Chrysler, and U S WEST all entered the financial services business, and later retreated.
- Too narrow — may miss promising growth opportunities. Examples: Ampex, once the leader in TV studio video recorders, completely missed the home video recorder market. U.S. automakers had no desire to enter the small car market until the opportunity was lost to foreign competitors.

Environment

> How can management identify and deal with environmental change when formulating corporate strategy?

- Environmental scanning: monitor socio-economic trends for potential opportunities or threats.
  - competition may be broadening product lines, improving quality or lowering costs
  - economic trends
  - technological changes
  - political conditions
  - social changes
  - availability of vital resources
  - collective power of customers or suppliers

> The "baby bust" of the 1970s resulted in a shortage of entry-level workers for the growing service sector. Some employers are looking to the semiretired to fill entry-level positions. Others have recognized the need to become more responsible employers.

Distinctive Competencies

"**Distinctive competencies** are the unique resources and strengths that management considers when formulating strategy." p. 31

Some Distinctive Competencies

1. Work force, well-trained and flexible
2. Facilities, well-located and flexible
3. Marketing and financial skill
4. Systems and technology, achieve competitive advantage through innovation

What role does operations play in entering international markets?

Global Strategies

Forms of Strategic Alliances

1. Collaborative effort
2. Joint venture
3. Licensing of technology

Locating Operations in Foreign Countries, Some Differences to Consider

1. Political environment
2. Customer needs
3. Customs
4. Economic situation

Market Analysis

"One key to success in formulating a customer-driven operations strategy for both manufacturing and service firms is understanding what the customer wants and how to provide it better than the competition does." p. 34

Market Segmentation (Step 1)

- Identify customer groups having common characteristics which differentiate them from other market segments.
- Incorporate market segment needs into product or service design and the operations system design.

Dimensions Used to Determine Market Segments

1. Demographic factors
2. Psychological factors
3. Industry factors

"Identifying the key factors in each market segment is the starting point for a customer-driven operations strategy." p. 35

Needs Assessment (Step 2)

"The second step in the market analysis is to make a **needs assessment**, which identifies the needs of each segment and assess how well competitors are addressing those needs." p. 35

Customer benefit package

- Core product or service
- Set of peripheral products or services

"Customers will not be completely satisfied without the entire customer benefit package." p. 35

Four Categories of Market Needs

1. Product/service
2. Delivery system
3. Volume
4. Other

Competitive Priorities

Market analysis identifies market needs for each market segment. Management then determines the important capabilities, or **competitive priorities**, for each of the functional areas as needed to achieve a competitive advantage while meeting market needs.

Should an organization emphasize price, quality, time or flexibility?

Four Groups, Eight Dimensions of Competitive Priorities

- Cost
  1. low price
- Quality
  2. high-performance design
  3. consistent quality
- Time
  4. fast delivery time
  5. on-time delivery
  6. development speed
- Flexibility
  7. customization
  8. volume flexibility

Cost

Cash poor college students immediately think of low cost as a competitive priority. However, lowering per-unit costs usually requires lots of capital. There are other ways to compete.

> "Often, lowering costs requires additional investment in automated facilities and equipment." p. 36

Quality

- High Performance Design — the customer's view of quality
  - superior features
  - close tolerances
  - greater durability
  - available, courteous, knowledgeable service
  - convenient location
  - product safety
- Consistent Quality — the producer's view of quality
  - frequency of conformance to specifications

Time

- Fast Delivery Time — short lead time
- On-Time Delivery — Manufacturers' material management systems possess the ability to plan ahead. In that environment, it is not so important to deliver quickly as it is to deliver as promised.
- Development Speed — getting the product to market first

Time-Based Competition

- Define the steps and time involved to deliver a product.
- Analyze each step to see whether time can be saved without compromising quality.

Reducing Response Time

- Focus on fast delivery time
- Save time in order entry, engineering, pricing, scheduling, manufacturing, and distribution

More Products in Less Time

- Focus on development speed

Flexibility

- Customization — accommodate unique needs of customers
- Volume Flexibility — ability to quickly change production rate

Trade-Offs

Why not compete on all dimensions of the competitive priorities at once?

> "Unfortunately, at some point further improvements on one area require a trade-off with one or more of the others." p. 42

- Sometimes a competitive priority becomes an order qualifier (a prerequisite to entering the market place). Quality and reliability are often order qualifiers.

Shifts in Competitive Priorities

What impact do product life cycles have on competitive priorities?

Product or Service Life Cycles

> "A firm that fails to introduce new products or services periodically will eventually decline." p. 42

Life-Cycle Stages

Most product ideas fail in product planning stages. Of those that survive to introduction, again most fail. Only one in about 60 product ideas are successful.

1. Product Planning
   - product ideas are generated, screened, designed
   - concurrent engineering (see next page)
2. Introduction
   - sales begin
   - first profits
   - evolving operations
   - marketing effort to develop market
   - large profit margin, increasing volume
3. Growth
   - rapid sales growth
   - operations efficiency not as important as keeping up with demand
   - marketing effort to increase market share

Large profit margins attract competition, driving prices toward costs. Only efficient producers survive.

4. Maturity
   - sales level off, per-unit profits decline
   - operations must stress efficiency
   - marketing efforts differentiate the product, delaying onset of decline

Sometimes a low overhead company, perhaps employing retired workers from the original producer, can profitably take over manufacturing or service and warranty obligations of declining products.

5. Decline
   - obsolete
   - demand disappears or shifts to better products
   - firm drops the product

Concurrent engineering.

Most of a product's production costs are determined by the first few product design decisions. Rather than waiting for a completed design to emerge from R&D that calls for components that can not be purchased, production processes that are beyond current capabilities, and design features that are not desired by the customer, concurrent engineering calls for early cross-functional involvement in the design effort.

Buyers — Can these components be purchased?
Manufacturing — Are processes within production capabilities?
Quality — Is quality job one? Will the first units be good ones?
Marketing — Does this design match the customers' needs?

Managing Life Cycles.

Life-cycle audits evaluate whether it is time to eliminate an existing product or introduce new ones. Trends in sales and per-unit profits are good indicators of which stage of the life cycle a particular product is in.

FIGURE 2.2

Life Cycle of a Product or Service

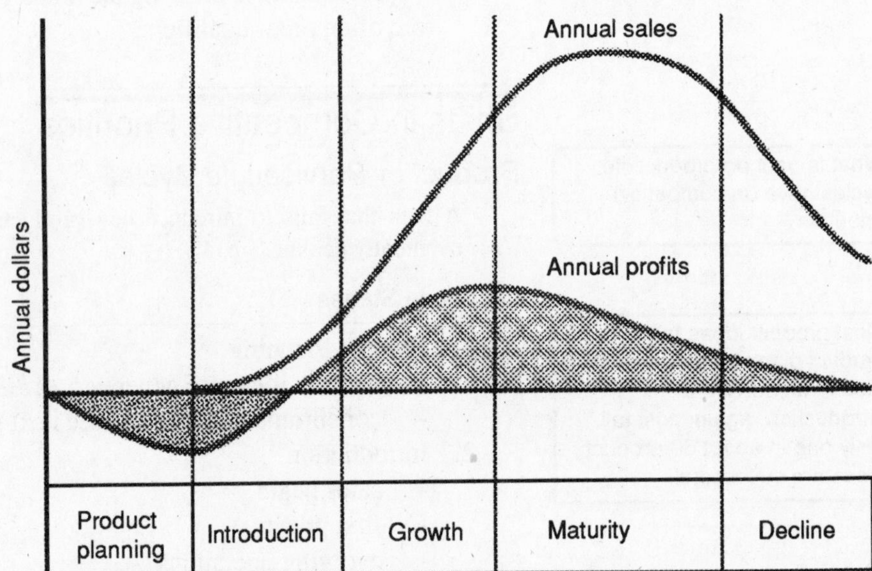

Options upon entering decline

- Stay with it for a few more years ... milk a (dead) cash cow.
- Become a *very* efficient producer ... purchase competitors and gain market share in a shrinking market, for example, Martin Marietta's purchases of several aerospace and defense firms.
- Revise and rejuvenate product ... requires the cooperation of marketing, design, and operations.

Life-cycle Audit Exercise:

Carefully review Example 2.1 *before* proceeding to the solution. In the following exercise, compare trends in sales, price and total profits to Fig. 2.2 to estimate where the product is in its life-cycle.

Product: Swash Buckles (a closure mechanism for ski boots)

Performance Measure	Change Over Last Year	Average Annual Change Over Last Four Years
Annual sales (units)	–2%	+8%
Per-unit price	–8%	–5%
Per-unit profit margin	–3%	–6%
Total profits	–4%	–5%

Solution*:

* Solution check appears on page 22 of this Study Guide.

Entrance-Exit Strategies

As an engineering student I thought, as many people do, that you had to invent the products you produced. In other words, I thought that enter early and exit late was the only strategy available.

Enter Early and Exit Late

Develop a product and grow with it. It is important to note that this strategy has a down side. As the product volume grows, the company must make a costly transition from being a low-volume innovator to a high-volume producer of a standardized product. The Cabbage Patch doll is an often-quoted example. At low volume, parents were literally assaulting each other for the opportunity to throw money at the sales clerks. At high volume, the producer went bankrupt.

Enter Early and Exit Early

An alternative to making the transition to high volume is to "stick to your knitting." That is, a small innovator chooses to stay with what it does well ... innovating and developing markets. When profit margins begin to decline, the rights to the product are sold to more efficient high-volume (often foreign) producers. The innovator is well advised to sell, because the innovator cannot successfully compete at high volume.

Wouldn't patents prevent competitors from entering late? First, most new products are not patentable because they are just new combinations of existing products. Second, minor design changes might get around the original patent protection. Third, whether patents provide any real "protection" is questionable.

Perpetrators usually have few assets, so litigation costs can't be recovered even when judgements are favorable.

When products have short life cycles it might be better to skip the patent process. Why publish your design work for your competitors?

Enter Late and Exit Late

Innovation and market development are both high-risk activities. That risk can be avoided by waiting until the product has been developed and proven to be a winner in the market. When a company's strength is high-volume, efficient operations, it has an advantage when the product matures. For an innovator to continue into the mature stage, the innovator must finance and otherwise struggle with the transition to high-volume efficient production, which is not an innovator's strength. High-volume producers are typically large. When they jump in, they jump in with both feet, using deep pockets, **preemptive pricing,** and in the case of some foreign firms, product "dumping" to drive out the innovators.

To check the effectiveness of the enter late and exit late strategy, find the manufacturer's name (not the marketer's name) on mature products that you own ... television, camera, VCR, bicycle, car, motorcycle. Did that company design the product or develop the market?

Positioning Strategy

What is the best positioning strategy for the operations system?

"Based on the firm's competitive priorities for its products or services, the operations manager must select a **positioning strategy,** which determines how the operations system is organized....

This fundamental decision sets the stage for all operations decisions that follow." p. 47

Note that a company that has a process-focused strategy is *not* a process industry. Process industries make commodities, which are *not* customized products. Nor is a process-focused facility an assembly line. Assembly lines have a product focus.

Process-Focused Strategy

- Equipment and work force are organized around processes.
- Equipment is general purpose.
- Workers have multiple skills.
- Volume is low.
- Routings vary from one order to the next.
- Flow pattern is jumbled.
- The facility (a job shop) can produce a wide range of products.

Process-focused facilities usually make to order. They receive a customer's order *before* they begin work. The customer's order is usually a small quantity of a custom, special, or unique product.

Product-Focused Strategy

- The equipment and work force are organized around a small number of products, or a single product line that offers the customer a choice from a defined list of options.
- Equipment is special purpose.
- Workers have few skills.
- Volume is high.
- Single routing, material may be moved by conveyors.
- The facility (a flow shop) can produce a high volume of just a few products, or a single product line with a near infinite number of combinations of options.

Product-focused facilities usually make standard products to stock. They complete the finished good and place it in inventory (or stock) *before* the customer orders it. When the customer is allowed to choose a combination of options, the flow shop usually assembles to order. That means the facility produces subassemblies to stock then, after the order is received, does only the final assembly for the waiting customer. Product-focused facilities compete on the basis of fast delivery, quality, or cost, but not flexibility.

A Continuum of Strategies

- Positioning strategy can vary by facility, depending on the products and services.
- A continuum of choices exists between the extremes of process focus and product focus.

Intermediate Strategy

- Product volumes are higher than found in job shops.
- Some standardized products are made to stock.
- Some customized products are made to order.
- Flow pattern is jumbled, with some frequently used paths.
- Some equipment may be dedicated to small flow lines to produce popular products made to stock.
- Remainder of equipment is arranged as a job shop.

Manufacturing Strategies Based on Positioning Strategy

Make-to-Stock Strategy

- Finished-goods items held in stock for immediate delivery.
- High volumes, standard products, mass production, flow shop.
- Production based on forecasted demand.
- **Product focus** corresponds with low cost and consistent quality competitive priorities.

Assemble-to-Order Strategy

- Assemblies and components held in stock.
- Final assembly completed after customer selects options.
- A very large number of final configurations is usually possible.
- Forecasting which combination of options will be chosen would be impractical and produce inaccurate results.
- **Intermediate strategy** offers some customization along with fast delivery time.

Make-to-Order Strategy

- Most required materials are ordered after the customer order is received.
- Produce to customer specifications.
- Flexible processes, job shop.
- **Process focus** is consistent with a high degree of customization.
- Mass customization — people, processes, and technologies are reconfigured continually to match customers' changing needs .

Positioning Strategy and Competitive Priorities

Table 2.1 (reproduced below) is a useful summary of several chapter concepts. If we have a business environment and competitive priorities similar to those in the left-hand column, we usually organize operations around processes, and face operations management situations typical of job shops. The right-hand column shows characteristics typical of operations in a flow shop environment.

Table 2.1 *Linking Positioning Strategy with Competitive Priorities*

Positioning Strategy	
Process Focus	**Product Focus**
More customized products and services, with low volumes	More standardized products and services, with high volumes
Shorter life cycles	Longer life cycles
Products and services in earlier stages of life cycle	Products and services in later stages of life cycle
An entrance–exit strategy favoring early exit	An entrance–exit strategy favoring late exit
High-performance design quality	Consistent quality
More emphasis on customization and volume flexibility	More emphasis on low cost
Long delivery times	Short delivery times

Solution to Life-cycle Audit Exercise:

Since competition drives prices towards cost, it is not unusual to see both the per-unit price and per-unit profit margin decline at any point in the life cycle after introduction. Life-cycle stage possibilities are narrowed when we notice that sales units declined slightly last year, while in the past sales had been increasing. Total profits have also been decreasing for some time at an apparently fairly steady rate. This places swash buckles in the late maturity stage. We should expect annual sales units to drop off dramatically in the near future.

Multiple Choice Answers

1. D	8. D
2. B	9. D
3. B	10. C
4. B	11. C
5. D	12. A
6. D	13. C
7. C	14. C

Multiple-Choice Questions

1. Developing a *customer-driven operations strategy* begins with _______.
   A. competitive priorities.
   B. corporate strategy.
   C. functional strategies.
   D. market analysis.

2. Which of the following provides a framework of goals for the organization?
   A. Competitive priorities
   B. Corporate strategy
   C. Functional strategies
   D. Market Analysis

3. Which of the following questions is likely to be answered in the *mission* statement?
   A. How should we schedule the work force?
   B. What are our basic beliefs?
   C. Which orders have highest priority?
   D. Where should we locate our facilities?

4. Which of the following is symptom of a mission that is too broad?
   A. Diseconomies of scale
   B. The firm enters businesses in which it has no distinctive competencies.
   C. The firm is missing promising growth opportunities.
   D. Top management is not doing environmental scanning.

5. Which of the following is a *distinctive competency*?
   A. An accelerated depreciation schedule
   B. An employee stock option plan
   C. Limited liability due to incorporation
   D. Well-located and flexible facilities

6. Which of the following does not refer to a form of global *strategic alliances*?
   A. Collaborative effort
   B. Joint venture
   C. Licensing of technology
   D. Time-based competition

7. Identifying customer groups having common characteristics is called _______.
   A. global strategy.
   B. mass customization.
   C. market segmentation.
   D. product planning.

8. Customers will not be completely satisfied without _______.
   A. a needs assessment.
   B. the core customer benefit package.
   C. the set of peripheral products or services.
   D. B and C

9. A *job shop* is most likely to compete on the basis of _______.
   A. consistent quality.
   B. fast delivery time.
   C. low price.
   D. resource flexibility.

10. At what stage of its life cycle is a product if marketing intensifies efforts to differentiate the product?
    A. Growth
    B. Introduction
    C. Maturity
    D. Product planning

11. What implications does an "enter early and exit late" strategy have for a firm?
    A. Stay in a low-volume, customized business throughout the product life cycle.
    B. Enter the market with an automated, efficient production facility and stay with it.
    C. Evolve from a low-volume, flexible production system into a high-volume, low-cost system.
    D. Enter the market with preemptive pricing, setting prices lower than competitors.

12. Which one of the following is an example of a process-focused facility?
    A. Aerospace machine shop
    B. Automobile final assembly line
    C. Brewery
    D. Central electric power station

13. A manufacturer choosing a product focus is likely to _______.
    A. assemble-to-order.
    B. make-to-order.
    C. make-to-stock.
    D. enter early and exit early in product life cycle.

14. The ultimate use of the make-to-order strategy is _______.
    A. a continuum of strategies.
    B. concurrent engineering.
    C. mass customization.
    D. process focus.

(Multiple-choice answers appear on page 22.)

Supplement A, Decision Making

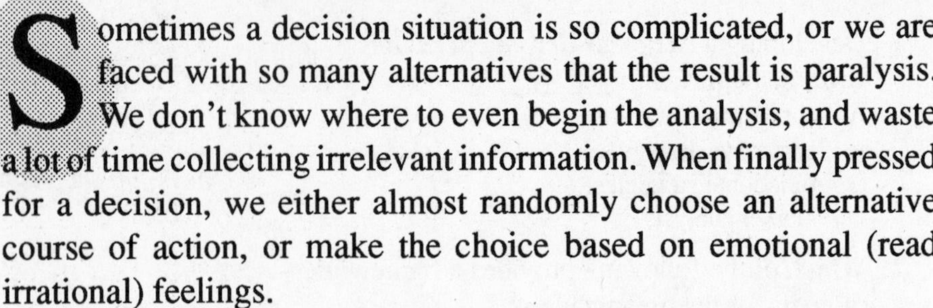

Sometimes a decision situation is so complicated, or we are faced with so many alternatives that the result is paralysis. We don't know where to even begin the analysis, and waste a lot of time collecting irrelevant information. When finally pressed for a decision, we either almost randomly choose an alternative course of action, or make the choice based on emotional (read irrational) feelings.

It can be argued that some decisions, such as marriage, are appropriately made solely on the basis of irrational emotions. Half of the time emotional decisions work out okay (or so they tell me), and half of the time they don't. In a business situation, it would be good for our company (and our career) if we could raise the batting average a bit. Quantitative techniques, some of which are presented here, tend to improve decisions. This chapter also includes a process for decision making which is useful in overcoming the paralysis associated with complex decision situations.

Since I am the only person who is always right, it makes sense that at some point in your career you will make a mistake. If that mistake was the result of an emotional process; "Gee, it felt right," then you're "in trouble." On the other hand, if you can show that you followed a rational process, that anyone making a careful analysis of the available information would have come to the same (but erroneous) conclusion, then you're "experienced."

It is important to point out that it is rarely appropriate to make any significant decision solely on the basis of the numbers. Quantitative analysis provides useful information, but important decisions ultimately hinge on the manager's values, experience, and judgement. In this course we make no attempt to teach values, experience, or judgement.

Decision-Making Steps

1. Recognize and clearly define the decision
2. Collect information, analyze alternative courses of action
3. Choose and implement the most feasible alternative

Break-Even Analysis

"The **break-even point** is the volume at which total revenues equal total costs." p. 72

Evaluating Products or Services

- We assume total costs equals fixed costs; which do not vary with volume, plus variable costs; which vary linearly with volume.

Break-Even Exercise, Evaluating a Service:

Klondike and Snow are twin polar bear cubs born at The Denver Zoo and raised (out of necessity) by humans. Public interest in the pair have substantially increased zoo attendance. Genetics and polar bear culture require that Klondike and Snow be relocated to other zoos by their second birthday. The powerful animals are rapidly outgrowing their temporary quarters. The zoo must decide whether to move them to Sea World in Orlando now, or to build a special enclosure to house them for one more year.

EQUATION A.1

Break-even point, Q

$$Q = \frac{F}{p - c}$$

Total cost $= F + cQ$

Total revenue $= pQ$

<u>Estimated revenue sources, average per person for this attraction</u>:

Gate receipts:	\$4
Concessions:	\$5
Licensed apparel:	\$15

<u>Estimated fixed costs</u>:

Enclosure:	\$2,400,000
Salaries:	\$220,000
Food:	\$30,000

<u>Estimated variable costs, average per person for this attraction</u>:

Concessions:	\$2
Licensed apparel:	\$9

It is predicted that if Klondike and Snow spend the year at the Denver Zoo, attendance will increase by 200,000 patrons.

a. Is the predicted increase in attendance sufficient to break even?

b. How low must the variable cost per patron be to break even, given prices and forecast of attendance?

c. How low must the fixed cost be to break even?

d. At what admission price would the attraction break even?

(Solutions appear on Study Guide page 39.)

Break-Even Analysis: Graphical Solution for Klondike and Snow

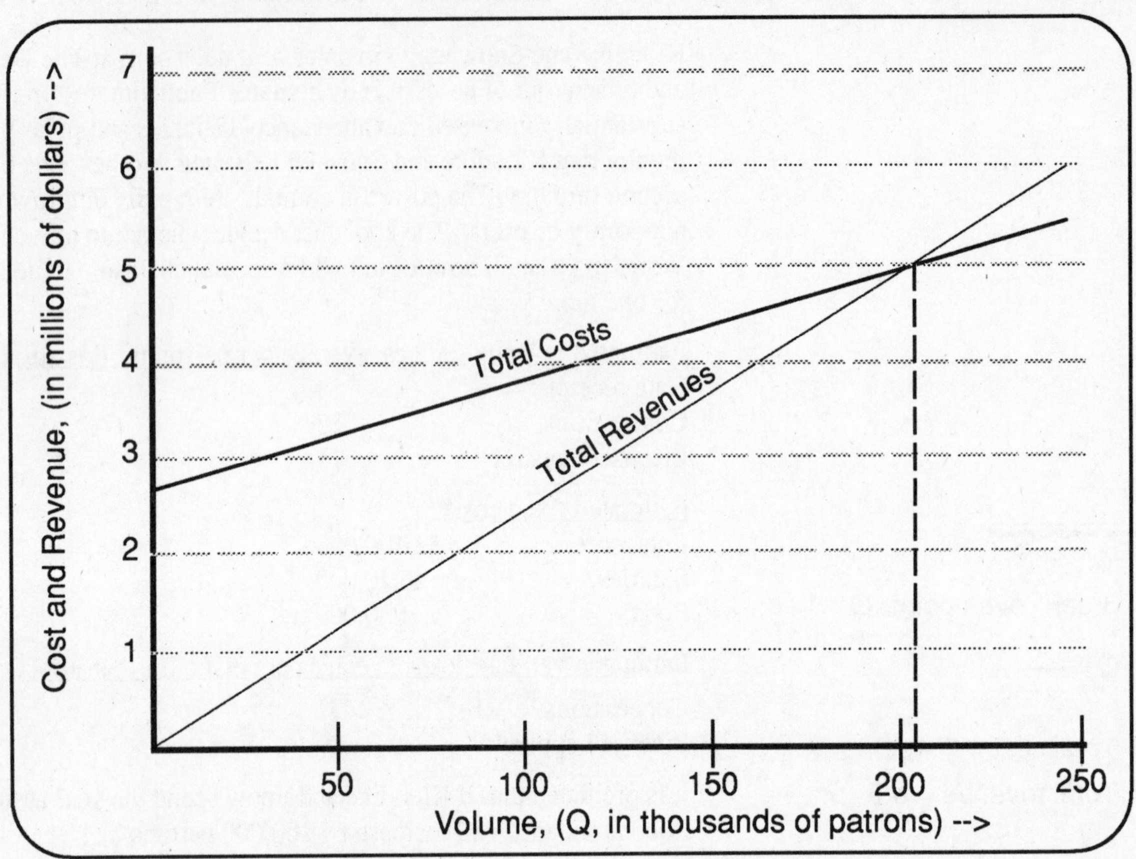

Note that the slope of the total revenue line is the price, *p*. What would happen to the break-even quantity if the price increases? Lay a straightedge along the total revenue line. Anchor the left end at the origin (intersection of the horizontal and vertical axes). Now pivot the right end upward, increasing the slope. Does the intersection of the straightedge with the total cost line move to the left or the right? Left, right? When the price per unit increases, the break-even quantity decreases. What happens if the variable cost per unit decreases?

> "Break-even analysis cannot tell a manager whether to pursue a new product or service idea or drop an existing line." p. 74

Evaluating Processes

- We assume that the make versus buy or process 1 versus process 2 decision does not affect revenues.
- The decision alternative is indicated on the basis of the lowest total costs at the expected volume.

Break-Even Exercise, Alternative Processes:

The Denver Zoo is marketing sweatshirts "bearing" colorful pictures of Klondike and Snow. The garments will sell for $15. If the garments are printed by an outside firm, the cost per unit is $9. If the garments are printed by Zoo employees, the cost per unit is $7. If the zoo chooses to do the work "in-zoo," fixed costs for printing and maintenance will be $300,000. At what volume would the zoo be indifferent between making or buying the sweatshirts?

EQUATION A.2

$$Q = \frac{F_m - F_b}{c_b - c_m}$$

Solution: (see Study Guide page 39)

Preference Matrix

"A **preference matrix** is a table that allows the manager to rate an alternative according to several performance criteria." p. 76

1. Decision Statement — define the decision and the factors that are relevant to that decision. For example in answering the question: "Who shall I marry?", relevant factors may include money, hair, and the desire to upset ones parents.
2. Assign weights to the relevant factors that reflect *how* important each is to your decision. It is nice if the weights add to 100%. Later, we could then say that 40% of the decision to marry Skip was because of money, and 30% was because of the desire to upset our parents.
3. Objectives/assumptions — establish the decision criteria, perhaps a scale from 1 (worst) to 5 (best). *State your assumptions!*
4. Generate alternatives — techniques such as "brainstorming" or research methods may be employed
5. Formulate a matrix — relating the relevant factors (rows) to the alternatives (columns) generated in step 3.

		Alternatives									
Relevant Factor	**Weight**	**John**		**Paul**		**George**		**Ringo**		**Skip**	
Money	40%										
Hair	30%										
Upset	30%										
Total	100%										

6. Evaluate the Alternatives
   a. Compare each alternative to each relevant factor, then assign a score that describes how well that alternative satisfies that factor.

Relevant Factor	Weight	Alternatives									
		John		Paul		George		Ringo		Skip	
Money	40%	4		4		2		1		5	
Hair	30%	2		4		5		5		1	
Upset	30%	3		1		4		5		5	
Total	100%										

   b. Multiply the score times the weight for that factor.
   c. Add the weighted scores in each column to obtain total points.

Relevant Factor	Weight	Alternatives									
		John		Paul		George		Ringo		Skip	
Money	40%	4	1.6	4	1.6	2	0.8	1	0.4	5	2.0
Hair	30%	2	0.6	4	1.2	5	1.5	5	1.5	1	0.3
Upset	30%	3	0.9	1	0.3	4	1.2	5	1.5	5	1.5
Total	100%		3.1		3.1		3.5		3.4		3.8

7. Tentative decision — the alternative that best satisfies the objectives is the one that gets the most points. In this example: John; 3.1, Paul; 3.1, George; 3.5, Ringo; 3.4, and **Skip; 3.8.**
8. Assess adverse consequences/qualitative factors — this is where nonquantitative values come in. We don't want to make decisions based solely on numbers. Example: If I marry Skip, our children may turn out to be just like him!
9. Implement the decision and monitor the results — manage change, look for early warning signals of trouble, mitigate damages, have alternative plans.

Criticism of Preference Matrix

1. Requires the manager to state criterion weights before examining alternatives
2. Allows one very low score to be overridden by high scores on other factors. For example, Skip might have lots of money and really upset your folks, (desirable) but he might have bad hair (compared to John, Paul, George, and Ringo).
3. This approach does take time to analyze, so it would not be useful for trivial situations such as deciding which movie to attend.

Decision Theory

Decision Process

1. List a reasonable number of feasible *alternatives.*
2. List the *events.*
3. Calculate the *payoff* table showing the payoff for each alternative in each event.
4. Estimate the *probability* of occurrence for each event.
5. Select a *decision rule* to evaluate the alternatives

Decision Making Under Certainty

The manager knows which event will occur.

Decision Making Under Uncertainty

The manager can list the possible events but cannot estimate probabilities.

1. Maximin — For those pessimists who tend to believe that the worst possible event will certainly occur, this decision rule chooses the alternative that has the best result, given the worst event will occur.
2. Maximax — For those optimists who tend to believe that the best possible event will certainly occur, this decision rule chooses the alternative that has the best result, given the best event will occur.
3. Laplace — For realists who tend to believe that events tend to even out in the long run, this decision rule places equal weight, or assumes equal probability, for each of the possible events.
4. Minimax Regret — For Monday morning quarterbacks, and those who focus on past mistakes, this decision rule looks to minimize the worst possible negative effect (regrets) associated with making a wrong decision (and ignoring the positive effects of a good decision).

Decision-Making Exercise, Under Uncertainty:

Once upon a time in the old west, Fletcher, Cooper and Wainwright (CF&W) were deciding whether to make arrows, barrels or Conestoga wagons. Fletcher was a realist, known for taking a balanced, direct approach to decision making. Cooper was a pessimist, always looking for the one bad apple at the bottom of the barrel. Wainwright was an optimist, a pioneer looking for new adventures. CF&W understood that demand for products would vary depending on U.S. Government policies concerning the development of travel routes to California. If land routes were chosen and treaties with Native Americans could not be negotiated, there would be a great demand for arrows. Success in those negotiations would favor demand for Conestoga wagons. If the water route was chosen, negotiations with Native Americans would be irrelevant. Instead, many barrels would be needed to contain goods during the long sea voyage around the horn.

Although Fletcher, Cooper and Wainwright were experts in forecasting the effect of policy on their business, they could not estimate the probability of the Government favoring one policy over another.

Policy	Forecasted Demand		
	Arrows	Barrels	Conestoga Wagons
Land, no treaty	9,000,000	300,000	5,000
Land with treaty	5,000,000	200,000	50,000
Sea	2,500,000	500,000	3,000

Price & Costs	Product		
	Arrows	Barrels	Conestoga Wagons
Fixed costs	$60,000	$80,000	$100,000
Variable costs per unit	$0.05	$1.50	$50
Price per unit	$0.15	$3.00	$75

Which product would be favored by Fletcher?

Which product would be favored by Cooper?

Which product would be favored by Wainwright?

(Solutions appear on Study Guide page 40.)

Decision Making Under Risk

The manager can list the possible events and estimate their probabilities.

Value of Perfect Information

"The **value of perfect information** is amount by which the expected payoff will improve if the manager knows which event will occur." p. 80

Expected Value:

$$EV = \sum_{i=1}^{n} P_i X_i$$

1. Identify the best payoff for each event.
2. Calculate the expected value of these best payoffs.
3. Find the difference between expected payoff values with and without perfect information.

This is the maximum one would pay for information.

Decision Trees

- A schematic model of available alternatives and possible consequences
- Useful with probabilistic events and sequential decisions
- Square nodes represent decisions
- Circular nodes represent events
- Events leaving a chance node are collectively exhaustive (probabilities sum to one)
- Conditional payoffs for each possible alternative-event combination shown at the end of each combination
- Draw the decision tree from left to right
- Calculate expected payoff to solve the decision tree from right to left

Decision Making Excercise, Under Risk:

We now assume that Fletcher, Cooper and Wainwright have contributed to the reelection campaign and legal defense fund for the Chair of the House Ways and Means Committee. They learn the probability of the government choosing the sea route is 0.2, the probability of developing the land route and successful treaty negotiations is 0.3, and the probability of the land route and unsuccessful negotiations is 0.5.

a. Draw a decision tree to analyze this situation. Calculate the expected value of each product alternative.

b. The Chair informs Fletcher, Cooper and Wainwright that advance notice of the government's decision is available "for a price." What is the value of perfect information?

(Solutions appear on Study Guide page 41.)

Multiple-Choice Questions

1. In break-even analysis, what is the effect of increasing price?
   A. The break-even quantity increases.
   B. The slope of the total cost function increases.
   C. The slope of the total revenue function increases.
   D. The variable cost per unit increases.

2. In break-even analysis, what is the effect of increasing variable cost per unit?
   A. The break-even quantity decreases.
   B. The slope of the total cost function increases.
   C. The slope of the total revenue function increases.
   D. The price per unit increases.

3. Break-even techniques can be useful in all of the following applications *except*:
   A. To analyze how price levels affect the break-even volume
   B. To compare alternative production methods
   C. To determine whether the predicted sales volume is sufficient to break even
   D. To tell whether to drop an existing product line

4. Which of the following techniques is useful for analyzing qualitative factors?
   A. Break-even
   B. Decision tree
   C. Decision theory
   D. Preference matrix

5. Which of the following shows the amount for each alternative if each event occurs?
   A. Payoff table
   B. Preference matrix
   C. Expected value
   D. All of the above

6. Which one of the following reasons makes the preference matrix approach to decision making attractive?
   A. The criterion weights must be specified before examining the alternatives.
   B. The selection of weights is subjective.
   C. The technique can be applied to a variety of decision making situations.
   D. The technique always indicates the correct decision.

Multiple Choice Answers

1. C
2. B
3. D
4. D
5. A
6. C

Problems

1. Total revenue at a volume of 15,000 units is \$6000.
   Total costs at a volume of 15,000 units are \$3500.
   Total costs at a volume of 20,000 units are \$4000.

   a. What is the best estimate of the variable cost per unit, *c*?
      Hint: *c* is the slope of the total cost line.

EQUATION A.1

Break - even point, Q

$$Q = \frac{F}{p - c}$$

Total cost $= F + cQ$

Total revenue $= pQ$

   b. In the above problem, what is the profit at the break-even point?

2. Use the preference matrix to evaluate the following products.

		Alternatives					
Relevant Factor	**Weight**	**Metric Hammer**		**Metric Screwdriver**		**Metric Crescent Wrench**	
Market Potential	40%	4		2		4	
Profit Margin	20%	3		5		1	
Operations Compatibility	30%	2		1		4	
Investment Requirement	10%	2		5		1	
Total	100%						

3. The Fly-By-Knight Airline company charters flights to Cicely, Alaska. Fixed costs are \$31,500. The price of a ticket to Cicely is \$247.50. Variable costs, including landing fees, luggage handling, and an in-flight dinner are \$22.50.

   a. What is the break-even point quantity?

   b. If Fly-By-Knight estimates demand of 164 tickets to Cicely, what is the total profit contribution?

4. Draw a graph to find the break-even quantity if the price per unit is $1.50, fixed costs are $200 and variable costs per unit are $0.75.

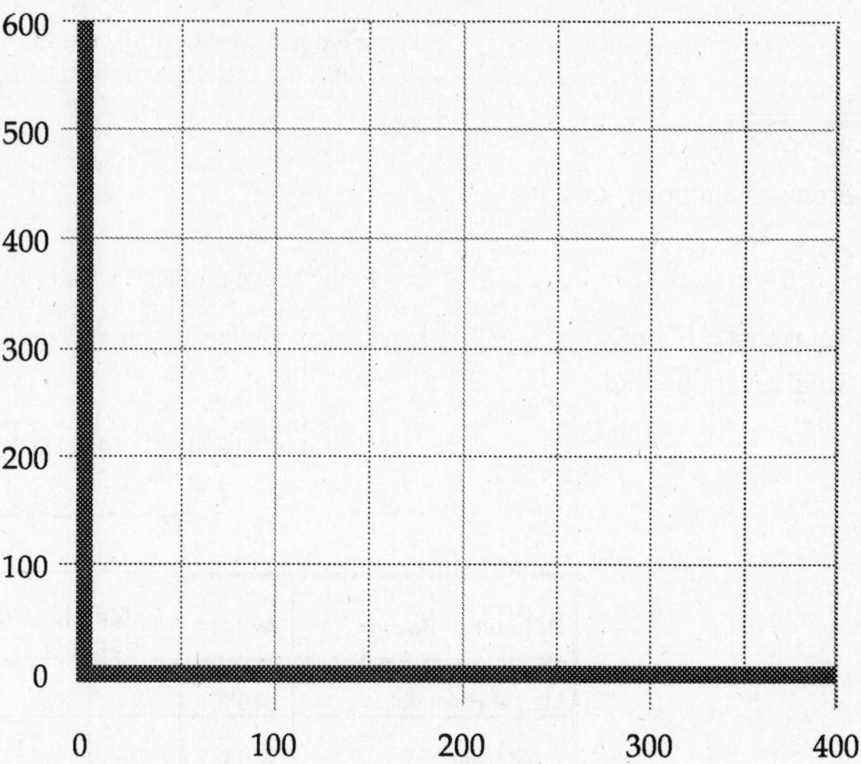

5. The Shreader Pizza Company is considering a potential new market for pizza: pet food for turtles. The company will decide to 1) wait and see, 2) expand at the present site, or 3) build an additional plant at a new location. Regardless of the decision, it is expected that one of three events will occur. The market will be 1) a great success, 2) a moderate success, or 3) a dismal failure. The probabilities of these events are estimated to be 25%, 35%, and 40%, respectively. Although it would be less costly, expansion at the present site is limited by available space, so the company stands to gain less in the event of a wildly successful market. If the company decides to wait and see and the market is either greatly or moderately successful, it could then decide to either expand on site or build a new plant. The wait and see payoffs are diminished because of lost market share and missed opportunities. The payoffs are as shown below:

Initial decision	Event	Payoff (loss)
Additional Plant	Great success	$8,000,000
Additional Plant	Moderate success	$2,000,000
Additional Plant	Dismal failure	($6,000,000)
Expand on Site	Great success	$4,000,000
Expand on Site	Moderate success	$3,571,429
Expand on Site	Dismal failure	($2,000,000)
Wait-and-See	Great success	Subsequent decision
Wait-and-See	Moderate success	Subsequent decision
Wait-and-See	Dismal failure	($200,000)

Subseq. decision	Event	Payoff (loss)
Add Plant	Great success	$ 3,600,000
Add Plant	Moderate success	$ 2,000,000
Expand	Great success	$ 1,600,000
Expand	Moderate success	$ 2,857,143

Draw a decision tree and use expected value to analyze this decision situation.

Solutions

EQUATION A.1

Break - even point, Q

$$Q = \frac{F}{p-c}$$

Total cost $= F + cQ$

Total revenue $= pQ$

1. Total revenue at a volume of 15,000 units is $6000.
   Total costs at a volume of 15,000 units are $3500.
   Total costs at a volume of 20,000 units are $4o00.

   a. What is the best estimate of the variable cost per unit, *c*?
   Hint: *c* is the slope of the total cost line.

   $$c = \frac{\Delta \text{ cost}}{\Delta \text{ quantity}} = \frac{\$4{,}000 - \$3{,}500}{20{,}000 - 15{,}000} = \frac{\$500}{5{,}000 \text{ units}} = \$0.10 / \text{unit}$$

   b. In the above problem, what is the profit at the break-even point?
   By definition, there is no profit at the break-even point.

2. Use the preference matrix to evaluate the following products.

Relevant Factor	Weight	Alternatives: Metric Hammer		Metric Screwdriver		Metric Crescent Wrench	
Market Potential	40%	4	1.6	2	0.8	4	1.6
Profit Margin	20%	3	0.6	5	1.0	1	0.2
Operations Compatibility	30%	2	0.6	1	0.2	4	1.2
Investment Requirement	10%	2	0.2	5	0.5	1	0.2
Total	100%		3.0		2.5		3.2

3. The Fly-By-Knight Airline company charters flights to Cicely, Alaska. Fixed costs are $31,500. The price of a ticket to Cicely is $247.50. Variable costs, including landing fees, luggage handling, and an in-flight dinner are $22.50.

   a. What is the break-even point quantity?

   $$Q = \frac{F}{p-c} = \frac{\$31{,}500}{\$247.50 - \$22.50} = 140 \text{ tickets}$$

   b. If Fly-By-Knight estimates demand of 164 tickets to Cicely, what is the total profit contribution?

   $$\text{Total profit contribution} = \text{Total revenue} - \text{Total cost}$$
   $$= PQ - (F + cQ)$$
   $$= (\$247.50 \times 164) - [\$31{,}500 + (\$22.50 \times 164)] = \$5400$$

4. Draw a graph to find the break-even quantity if the price per unit is $1.50, fixed costs are $200 and variable costs per unit are $0.75.

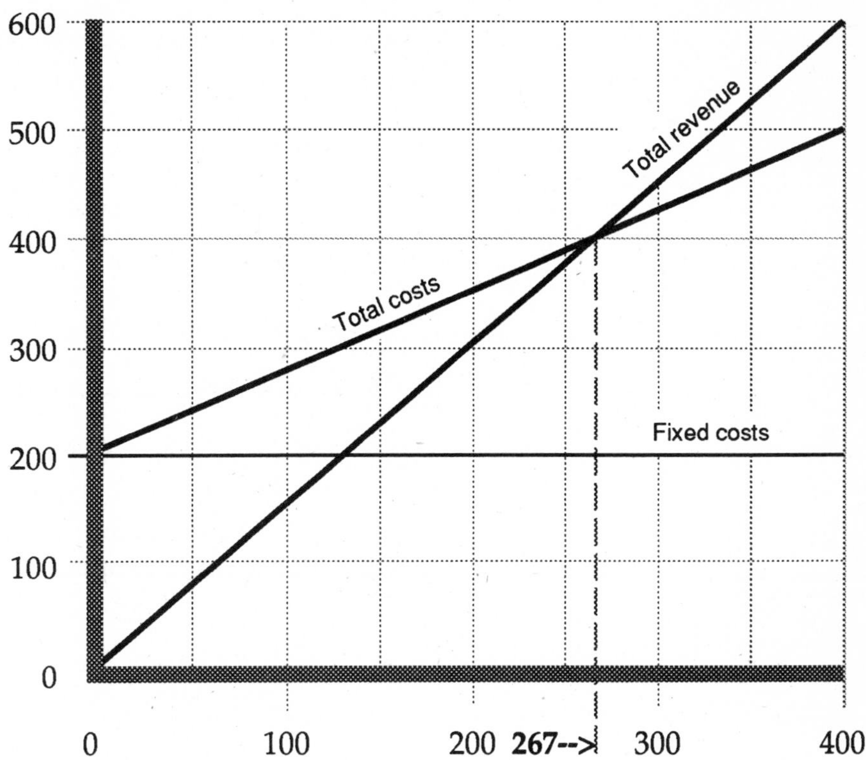

5. The Shreader Pizza Company.

Expected value of adding a new plant:

$$[(0.25 \times \$8{,}000{,}000) + (0.35 \times \$2{,}000{,}000) + (0.40 \times -\$6{,}000{,}000)]$$
$$= \$300{,}000$$

Expected value expanding on site:

$$[(0.25 \times \$4{,}000{,}000) + (0.35 \times \$3{,}571{,}429) + (0.40 \times -\$2{,}000{,}000)]$$
$$= \$1{,}450{,}000$$

Expected value of wait and see:

$$[(0.25 \times \$3{,}600{,}000) + (0.35 \times \$2{,}857{,}143) + (0.40 \times -\$200{,}000)]$$
$$= \$1{,}820{,}000$$

The decision tree indicates we should wait and see if the market develops. If it is a great success, add a new plant. If it is a moderate success, we should expand on site. If it fails, we should do nothing.

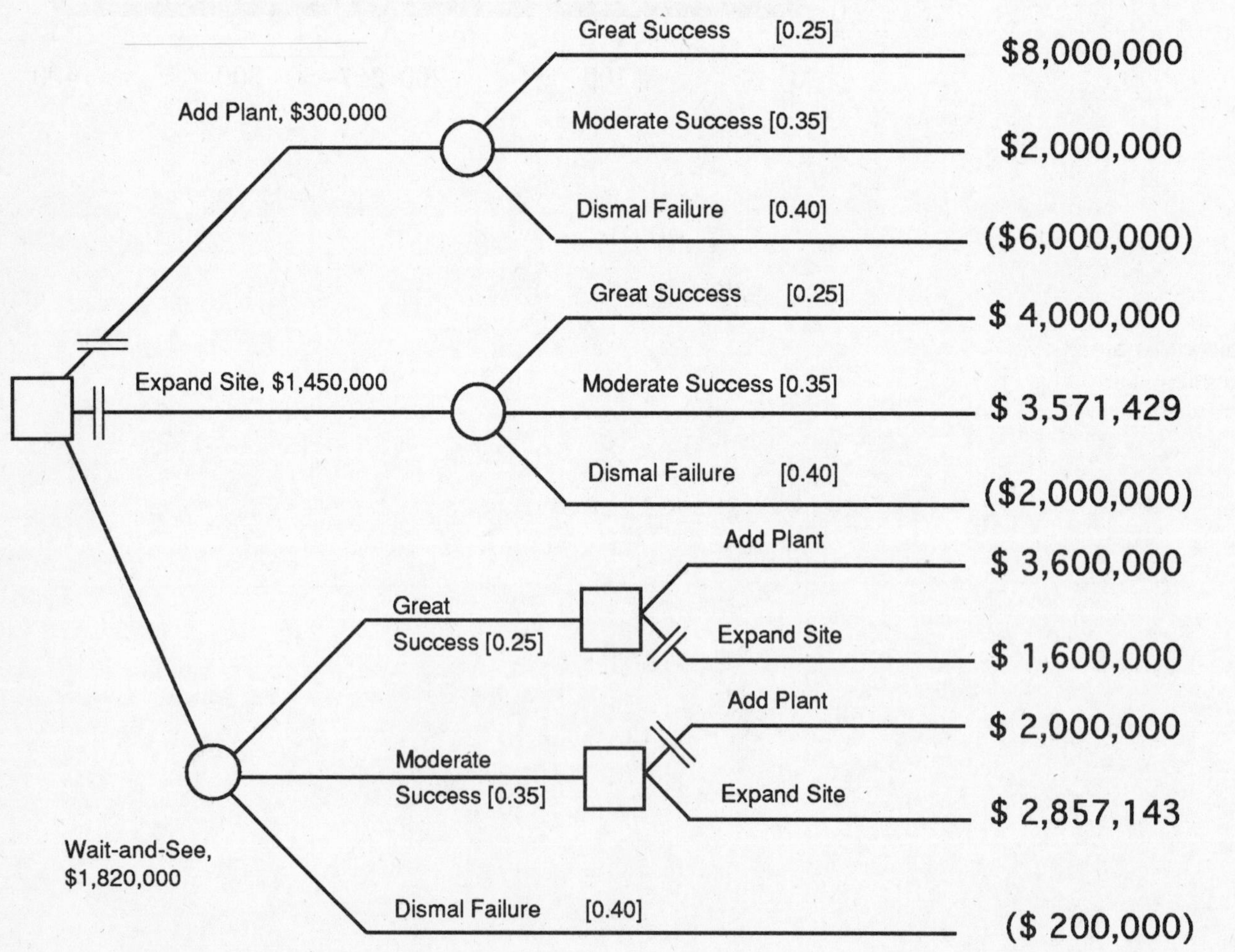

Solution to break-even exercise, evaluating a service

EQUATION A.1

Break-even point, Q

$$Q = \frac{F}{p - c}$$

$$\text{Total cost} = F + cQ$$

$$\text{Total revenue} = pQ$$

Klondike and Snow.

a. The fixed costs are \$2,650,000, the price is \$24, and the variable cost per unit is \$11.

$$Q = \frac{F}{p - c} = \frac{\$2{,}650{,}000}{\$24 - \$11} = 203{,}846$$

The forecasted attendance increase (200,000) is not quite enough to break even.

b. Given Q = 200,000, find c.

$$Q = \frac{F}{p - c}$$

$$p - c = \frac{F}{Q}$$

$$c = p - \frac{F}{Q} = \$24 - \frac{\$2{,}650{,}000}{200{,}000} = \$10.75$$

c. Given Q, p, and c, find F.

$$F = Q(p - c) = 200{,}000(\$24 - \$11)$$

$$F = \$2{,}600{,}000$$

d. Given Q, F, and c, find admission price ("gate").

$$p = \frac{F}{Q} + c = \frac{\$2{,}650{,}000}{200{,}000} + \$11 = \$24.25$$

$$p = \text{gate} + \text{concessions} + \text{apparel} = \$24.25$$

$$p = \text{gate} + \$5 + \$15 = \$24.25$$

$$\text{gate} = \$4.25$$

Solution to break-even exercise, alternative processes

EQUATION A.2

$$Q = \frac{F_m - F_b}{c_b - c_m}$$

Sweatshirt printing.

$$Q = \frac{F_m - F_b}{c_b - c_m}$$

$$= \frac{\$300{,}000 - \$0}{\$9 - \$7}$$

$$= 150{,}000$$

Solution to decision-making exercise, under uncertainty

Fletcher, Cooper, and Wainwright.

The following calculations show the payoffs for each policy-product combination

Policy	Product — Arrows
Land, no treaty	9,000,000($0.15) – [$60,000 + (9,000,000 x $0.05)] = $840,000
Land, with treaty	5,000,000($0.15) – [$60,000 + (5,000,000 x $0.05)] = $440,000
Sea	2,500,000($0.15) – [$60,000 + (2,500,000 x $0.05)] = $190,000

Policy	Product — Barrels
Land, no treaty	300,000($3.00) – [$80,000 + (300,000 x $1.50)] = $370,000
Land, with treaty	200,000($3.00) – [$80,000 + (200,000 x $1.50)] = **$220,000**
Sea	500,000($3.00) – [$80,000 + (500,000 x $1.50)] = $670,000

Policy	Product — Conestoga Wagons
Land, no treaty	5,000 ($75.00) – [$100,000 + (5,000 x $50.00)] = $ 25,000
Land, with treaty	50,000($75.00) – [$100,000 + (50,000 x $50.00)] = **$1,150,000**
Sea	3,000 ($75.00) – [$100,000 + (3,000 x $50.00)] = $–25,000

	Possible Future Policy		
Alternatives	**Land—no treaty**	**Land—w/treaty**	**Sea**
Arrows	$840,000	$440,000	$190,000
Barrels	$370,000	$220,000	$670,000
Conestoga Wagons	$25,000	$1,150,000	($25,000)

a. Laplace — Fletcher, a realist, and would choose to make arrows.

Alternative	Weighted Payoff
Arrows	1/3 ($840,000) + 1/3 ($440,000) + 1/3 ($190,000) = $490,000
Barrels	1/3 ($370,000) + 1/3 ($220,000) + 1/3 ($670,000) = $420,000
Conestoga	1/3 ($25,000) + 1/3 ($1,150,000) + 1/3 ($–25,000) = $383,333

b. Maximin — $220,000 ... Cooper, a pessimist, would make barrels.

c. Maximax — $1,150,000 ... Wainwright, an optimist, would make wagons.

Solution to decision making exercise, under risk

Fletcher, Cooper and Wainwright under risk.

a. Expected Value

Arrows [0.5 ($840,000) + 0.3 ($440,000) + 0.2 ($190,000)]
= $590,000

Barrels [0.5 ($370,000) + 0.3 ($220,000) + 0.2 ($670,000)]
= $385,000

Conestogas [0.5 ($25,000) + 0.3 ($1,150,000) + 0.2 ($–25,000)]
= $352,500

The decision tree is shown in the following illustration.

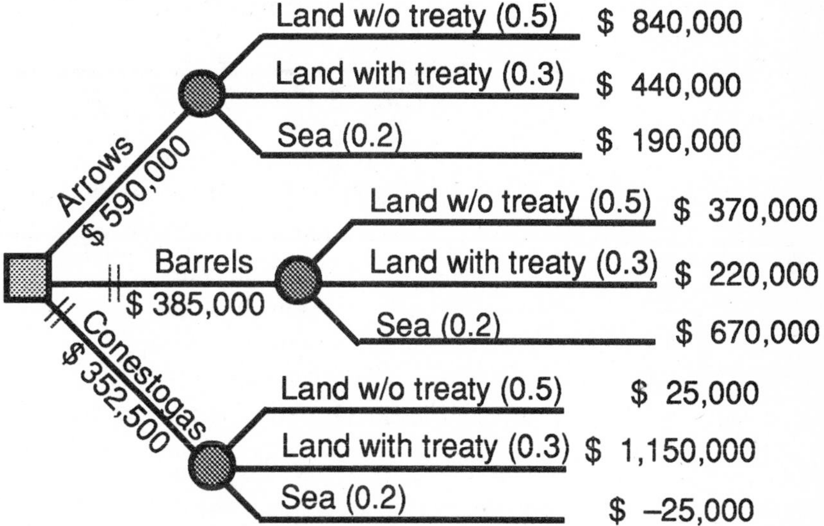

b. Value of perfect information.

Policy	Best Payoff
Land—no treaty	$840,000
Land—with treaty	$1,150,000
Sea	$670,000

$$EV_{perfect} = [(0.5 \times \$840,000) + (0.3 \times \$1,150,000) + (0.2 \times \$670,000)]$$
$$= \$899,000$$
$$EV_{imperfect} = [(0.5 \times \$840,000) + (0.3 \times \$440,000) + (0.2 \times \$190,000)]$$
$$= \$590,000$$

The value of perfect information is $899,000 – $590,000 = $309,000

Chapter Three, Process Management

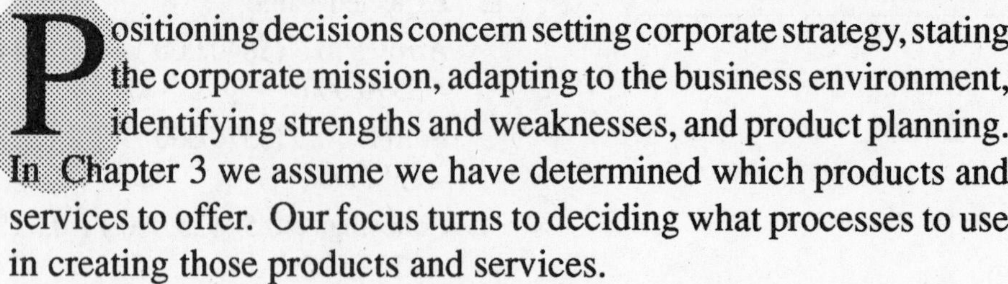

Positioning decisions concern setting corporate strategy, stating the corporate mission, adapting to the business environment, identifying strengths and weaknesses, and product planning. In Chapter 3 we assume we have determined which products and services to offer. Our focus turns to deciding what processes to use in creating those products and services.

"Process decisions are strategic and can affect an organization's ability to compete over the long run." p. 94

What is Process Management?

"**Process management** is the selection of inputs, operations, work flows, and methods for producing goods and services." p. 95

- Input selection, consistent with positioning strategy
  - human skills
  - raw materials
  - outside services
  - equipment
- Operations managers determine
  - work flow
  - transformation processes, methods
  - degree of automation
- Process decisions
  - implement positioning decision (product or process focus)
  - consider quality, capacity, layout, and inventory choices
  - depend on life cycle, competitive priorities, and positioning strategy

When Process Decisions Are Required

1. New or modified product is offered
2. Quality improvement is needed
3. Competitive priorities change
4. Demand volume changes
5. Inadequate current performance
6. Competitors use new technology or a different process
7. Cost of inputs change

In other words, process design decisions are required continuously. It would be very difficult to produce in an environment of continuously changing process design. Fortunately, the response to the above situations is often a decision to not change the current process design.

Major Process Decisions

Five Common Process Decisions

1. Process choice
2. Vertical integration
3. Resource flexibility
4. Customer involvement
5. Capital intensity

Process Choice

Four Basic Choices for Implementing Positioning Strategy

How can a positioning strategy best be implemented?

1. Project process, unique sequence of operations
2. Batch process, shared resources, varied sequence
3. Line process, dedicated resources, repetitive manufacturing
4. Continuous process, commodities, process industry

Vertical Integration

Which services and products should be created in-house?

"**Vertical integration** is the degree to which a firm's own production system handles the entire chain of processes from raw materials to sales and service." p. 95

- Attractive when
  - high input volume
  - firm has the required skills
  - process integration is important to the future of the firm
- Not attractive when
  - a supplier can do the work more efficiently
- Backward integration — a type of vertical integration that acquires more of the supply chain toward raw materials.
- Forward integration — a type of vertical integration that acquires more of the distribution chain toward the customer.

"Increasing vertical integration can reduce resource flexibility if it requires a large investment in facilities and equipment." p. 102

- Hollow corporations
  - rely on other firms for most of their production
    - little backward integration, low capital intensity
    - quickly move in and out of markets
    - effective when life cycles are short
  - vulnerable to vertical integration when volume is high or life cycles are long
    - hollow corporations add little value, investment barriers to competition are low
    - high volume customers can integrate backward to the actual producer, cutting out the hollow corporation
    - manufacturers can integrate forward toward the customer, again cutting out the hollow corporation

Make or Buy

"The decision about whether to implement backward integration is often referred to as the *make-or-buy decision.*" p. 103

- Commonly outsourced services, which are not provided by employees of the firm that needs the service, include
  - payroll
  - security
  - cleaning
  - accounting
  - training
  - legal
  - public relations
  - advertising

Globalization, Information Technology, and Outsourcing Services — Electronic immigration is a recently coined term to describe the situation where foreign workers provide information services which are then telecommunicated across political borders. For example, it is no longer necessary for a worker to physically immigrate into the United States in order to find work there.

Services may be outsourced because the firm doesn't have enough work to employ the service on a full-time basis. Or the corporation may desire to avoid offering an expensive benefit package to blue collar service workers.

- Globalization creates more supplier options.
- Information technology allows competitors to come together as a **virtual corporation** in order to respond to market opportunities.

Own or Lease

Sometimes the IRS tax depreciation schedule shows an unrealistically long expected life for rapidly advancing technological equipment. For example, telecommunications equipment is often obsolete long before it can be depreciated out. There is a tax advantage to leasing such equipment and taking the full deduction for those expenses against current income.

- leased equipment is favored when
  - changes in technology are rapid
  - frequent servicing is required
  - need for equipment is short term

Alternative Processes Exercise:

The Backward Bicycle Company (BBC) is deciding whether to weld bicycle frames manually or to purchase a welding robot. If welded manually, investment costs for equipment are only $10,000. However, welders skilled in making strong joints of thin wall tubing receive high wages. The per-unit cost of manually welding a bicycle frame is $50 per frame. On the other hand, a robot capable of performing the same work costs $400,000. Robot operating costs, plus minimum wage labor to load tubing and remove welded frames, total $20 per frame. At what volume of bicycle frames would the Backward Bicycle Company be indifferent to these alternative methods?

EQUATION A.2

$$Q = \frac{F_m - F_b}{c_b - c_m}$$

(Solution appears on Study Guide page 52.)

Resource Flexibility

> "**Resource flexibility** is the ease with which employees and equipment can handle a wide variety of products, output levels, duties, and functions." pp. 95–96

Product flexibility and volume flexibility are competitive priorities. When humans are replaced by machines, both product flexibility and volume flexibility decrease. Humans are more flexible resources than are machines.

Short life cycles call for general-purpose (flexible) machines and workers having a variety of skills (also flexible). Job shops typically employ those types of resources, so they can produce products with short life cycles. They compete on resource flexibility.

Work Force.

Implications of a flexible work force

- Requires more education and training
- Capable of many tasks
- Alleviates capacity bottlenecks, volume flexibility
- Reliable customer service
- Increased job satisfaction

Volume flexibility and needed skills determine the type of work force.

- Steady volume, high skills — permanent work force
- Variable volume, low skills — part-time or temporary employees to supplement permanent work force. However, there are behavioral problems when there is such a "two-cast" system.
- Variable volume, high skills — trained flexible force that can be moved to produce whatever the market demands

Equipment.

- General purpose

Resource flexibility is crucial to the success of a process-focused positioning strategy.

How much should customers be involved in processes?

Customer Involvement

> "**Customer involvement** reflects the ways in which the customer becomes a part of the production process and the extent of this involvement." p. 96

When a customer chooses a salad from a McDonald's restaurant menu, they make a "product selection" of sorts. But they are not at all involved in product design or specifications. Nor do they participate in any production process. For our purposes here, there is virtually no "customer involvement".

On the other hand, at Wendy's the customer determines much of the size and content of the salad, and completes the final assembly process.

- Self-Service
  - customers do part of the process formerly done by the manufacturer.
- Product Selection
  - product specification and design
- Time and Location
  - by appointment or on demand?
  - at supplier's, location, customer's location, or third-party location?

Customers are unlikely to have the skills required to operate capital intensive equipment. For example, customers have very little to do with the production of electricity or operation of airliners. However, most can handle the implements at a salad bar. Highly capital-intensive services tend to have less customer involvement. There is an inverse relationship between customer involvement and capital intensity.

Capital Intensity

"**Capital intensity** is the mix of equipment and human skills in a production process; the greater the relative cost of equipment, the greater is the capital intensity." p. 96

- Which tasks will be performed by humans and which by machines?
  - more machines means more capital intensity, and less resource flexibility and less customer involvement

How much should one depend on machinery and automated processes?

More capital intensity is not always best.

- Automated (capital intensive) operations must have high utilization. There is increased pressure for using capital-intensive equipment to maximum capacity regardless of demand. This in turn increases materials and finished goods inventory costs.
- Automation may not align with competitive priorities.

Fixed automation.

Favored when

- high demand volume
- stable product design
- long life cycle

Fixed automations maximizes efficiency and minimizes variable cost per unit *when utilization is high.*

Flexible automation.

- Useful in both process-focused and product-focused operations
- Can be quickly set up to make a variety of products in small batches
- Flexible manufacturing systems
  - capital intensive
  - allow more flexibility in the product produced
  - shorter design and manufacturing lead time
  - efficient while producing low-volume, customized products

How should process decisions be coordinated?

Relationships Between Decisions

- An underlying variable creating the relationships is volume.

Low Volume	High Volume
1. Project or batch process	1. Line or continuous process
2. Less vertical integration	2. More vertical integration
3. More resource flexibility	3. Less resource flexibility
4. More customer involvement	4. Less customer involvement
5. Less capital intensity	5. More capital intensity

Should more economies of scope be sought?

Economies of Scope

Until recently, the low production volumes that go along with short life cycles and product flexibility also meant that a firm could not be capital intensive. The result was a strong inverse relationship between resource flexibility and capital intensity.

"...programmable automation breaks this traditional inverse relationship between resource flexibility and capital intensity. ...

Economics of scope reflect the ability to produce multiple products more cheaply in combination than separately." p. 110

- Requires a family of products having enough collective volume to utilize equipment fully

Managing Technological Change

"...we define **technology** as any manual, automated, or mental process used to transform inputs into products or services." p. 110

Linking Technology with Strategy

- Volume is derived from corporate strategy and competitive priorities.
- Volume is an important consideration in determining the amount of automation.

If a firm chooses fixed automation to achieve low variable costs per unit at high volume, and then finds that sales do not materialize, the production system will not have the flexibility required to recover from that mistake.

Finding a Competitive Advantage

- Reduced direct costs for labor and raw materials
- Increased sales
- Improved quality
- Quicker delivery times
- Smaller inventories
- Improved environment

What are some keys to successful technological change?

Some Guidelines

Simplification and Initial Planning

"The *base case* used to justify new automation should be what the current operation *can* achieve, not what it *is* achieving." p. 113

Justification

Operations managers must look beyond the effects of automation on direct costs such as labor (which is now a very small component of total costs). They must consider the impact on competitive priorities such as customer service, delivery times, inventories, and resource flexibility.

Automation often looks good when we compare its costs and benefits against those of the status quo. However, when we make the comparison against the best the firm *could* do with existing resources, the additional investment for automation might not be justified.

If a company doesn't make the full use of their current resources, will they achieve the full benefits of automation?

The Human Side

- Automation affects jobs at all levels.
- Employee involvement in design of new systems is key to successful implementation.

Leadership

- Identify a team representing all affected departments to lead and coordinate automation projects
- Project champion
  - enthusiastic for change
  - respected and experienced
- Operations manager gives ongoing support

Do some of the organization's key processes need reengineering?

Designing Processes

Process Reengineering

"**Reengineering** is the fundamental rethinking and radical redesign of business processes to dramatically improve performance in areas such as cost, quality, service, and speed." p. 114

Critical Processes

- Emphasis is placed on core business processes.
- Processes are broadly defined in terms of costs and customer value.

Strong Leadership

- Top management makes a compelling case for change.

Cross-Functional Teams

- Reengineering works best at high-involvement workplaces.

Information Technology

- Restructuring around information flows can reduce management and work activity.

Clean Slate Philosophy

- Start with the way the customer wants to deal with the company.

Process Analysis

- Understanding current processes can reveal areas where new thinking will provide the biggest payoff.

Process Improvement

"Process improvement is the systematic study of the activities and flows of each process to improve it." p. 116

Can flow diagrams and process charts be used to study and improve operations?

Two Basic Techniques for Analyzing Activities and Flows Within Processes:

1. Process charts
2. Flow diagrams

Characteristics of Operations Having Greatest Payoff Potential

1. Slow in responding to the customer
2. Poor quality
3. Time consuming, costly
4. Bottleneck process, limiting throughput of entire facility
5. Disagreeable or dangerous work, pollution
6. Little value added, waste of materials or effort

Break Process into Detailed Components, Asking Six Questions & *Why*

1. *What* is being done? ... *Why* is it being done?
2. *When* is it being done? ... *Why* at that particular time?
3. *Who* is doing it? ... *Why* have that person or group do it?
4. *Where* is it being done? ... *Why*? Is that the right place?
5. *How long* does it take? ... *Why* does it take that long?
6. *How* is it being done? ... *Why* is it being done that way?

Flow Diagrams

"A **flow diagram** traces the flows of information, customers, employees, equipment, or materials through a process." p. 117

- Plot the path followed by the person, material, or equipment.

Process Charts

"A **process chart** is an organized way of recording all the activities performed by a person, by a machine, at a work station, with a customer, or on materials." p. 118

Five Categories of Activities

1. Operation	●	productive work
2. Transportation	➡	movement of the study's subject
3. Inspection	■	check or verify, but do not change
4. Delay	◗	awaiting operation, transportation, or inspection
5. Storage	▼	put away until later, not a delay

Completing a Process Chart

1. Identify each step performed.
2. Categorize each step ● ➡ ■ ◗ ▼ relative to the subject: person, material, or machine. For example, the person may be waiting, ◗, for a machine to complete an operation, ●.
3. Record distances traveled, ➡, and the time required.
4. Calculate summary data: steps, times, and distance.
5. Ask the what, when, who, where, how long, and how questions, challenging each of the charted process steps (asking why).
6. Plan and implement improvements.

Multiple-Choice Questions

1. Which of the following is true of process management?
   A. Different principles apply to first-time and redesign choices.
   B. It is a one-time activity of choosing a positioning strategy.
   C. It involves the selection of inputs, work flows, and methods for producing goods and services.
   D. It is independent of product life cycle, competitive priorities, and positioning strategy.

2. The five basic decisions about process include all of the following *except*:
   A. Capital intensity
   B. Customer involvement
   C. Resource flexibility
   D. Volume

3. Process design decisions are required
   A. when new products are offered.
   B. when quality must be improved.
   C. when competitors use new technology.
   D. All of the above.

4. ________ is defined as: "The mix of equipment and human skills in a production process."
   A. Capital intensity
   B. Customer involvement
   C. Process choice
   D. Resource flexibility

5. Which of the following positioning strategies tends to be chosen by process industries such as oil refineries, paper mills, and breweries?
   A. Intermediate focus
   B. Process focus
   C. Product focus
   D. Project focus

6. Which of the following is characteristic of a product focus?
   A. Customer involvement
   B. General-purpose equipment
   C. Low volume
   D. Standardized product

7. A company needing resource flexibility to offer custom products and customer involvement
   A. should be vertically integrated.
   B. should be capital intensive.
   C. should have a process focus.
   D. should produce finished goods inventory in advance of receiving orders.

8. Vertical integration is attractive when
   A. a corporation does not currently possess the skills required in the acquired business.
   B. strategy calls for a "hollow" corporation.
   C. suppliers are inefficient.
   D. volume is low.

9. Backward integration
   A. adds distribution to the scope of manufacturing operations functions.
   B. is a pre-automation technique.
   C. is associated with make-or-buy decisions.
   D. is the term for policies that segregate management from labor.

10. Which of the following is true of hollow corporations?
    A. Enter markets early and exit late.
    B. Investment barriers are high.
    C. Products have long life cycles.
    D. Vulnerable to vertical integration.

11. Global competition and information technology have the effect of
    A. discouraging competitors from forming short-term "virtual" corporations.
    B. increasing backward integration.
    C. increasing outsourcing.
    D. reducing supplier options.

12. The lease option is favored when
    A. the equipment frequently needs service.
    B. the equipment is in the mature stage of its life cycle, has a stable product design, and technological advancements are infrequent.
    C. the equipment will be used over long time periods.
    D. the tax code allows the equipment to be depreciated rapidly.

13. One of the best ways to achieve reliable customer service and alleviate capacity bottlenecks is:
    A. Greater worker flexibility
    B. Increased capital intensity
    C. Larger capacity cushions
    D. More fixed automation

14. Operations managers favor fixed automation
    A. when demand volumes are low
    B. when flexibility is crucial to process-focused positioning strategy.
    C. when interest rates are high
    D. when product designs are stable

15. Process choice and the other basic process decisions are tied to
   A. capital budgeting.
   B. flexibility.
   C. training.
   D. volume.

16. Which of the following breaks the traditional inverse relationship between resource flexibility and capital intensity?
   A. Customer involvement
   B. Employee involvement
   C. Programmable automation
   D. Vertical integration

17. The *base case* used to justify new automation should be
   A. what the current operation *can* achieve.
   B. what the current operation *is* achieving.
   C. what the new operation *can* achieve.
   D. the match between the new operation and competitive priorities.

18. Operations having the greatest payoff potential from process analysis have characteristics such as all of the following *except*
   A. the operation introduces quality defects.
   B. the operation involves dangerous or disagreeable work.
   C. the operation is costly or time consuming.
   D. the operation requires creativity or innovation.

19. Which of the following is an organized way of recording all the activities that are performed by the object of a study?
   A. Flow diagram
   B. Process chart
   C. Process design

20. In a process chart, we use the "■" symbol to represent
   A. a delay.
   B. an inspection.
   C. an operation.
   D. transportation.

(Multiple-choice answers appear on page 53.)

Problems

EQUATION A.2

$$Q = \frac{F_m - F_b}{c_b - c_m}$$

1. Joe College is a business student deciding whether to make his own pizzas or simply to purchase them from others. If he buys pizzas in batches of five the cost is $28 per batch (regular price, $12, plus 4 bucks, 4 bucks, 4 bucks, 4 bucks). If he makes his own pizzas, he must purchase a $600 oven for his dorm room. The cost of ingredients is $4.10 per pizza. In either case (make or buy), he will need a $200 refrigerator. If the student expects to consume 50 pizzas during each of his seven years in college, should he make or buy the pizza? Since Joe never intends to clean either the refrigerator or the oven, ignore salvage value. Also ignore the time value of money, inflation, taxes, limited-time promotional offers, and the value of Joe's time, since it is well known that a student's time has no value.

2. and 3.

The Flat Beer Company is deciding whether to make or to buy aluminum cans. The purchase price of cans in high volume is $0.09 per can. If Flat decides to buy, the contract has a "take-or-pay" clause. That is, if Flat purchases less than $90,000 worth of cans per year, they still have to pay $90,000. If Flat produces its own cans, the annual fixed cost is $60,000 and the cost to make cans is $0.06 per can.

EQUATION A.2

$$Q = \frac{F_m - F_b}{c_b - c_m}$$

2. Flat beer has caught the attention of the local college. Forecasted sales of beer for the next three years are 400,000, 1,500,000, and 2,500,000 cans, respectively. Should the company make or buy the cans?

3. Draw a graph for this make-or-buy decision and show the indifference quantity.

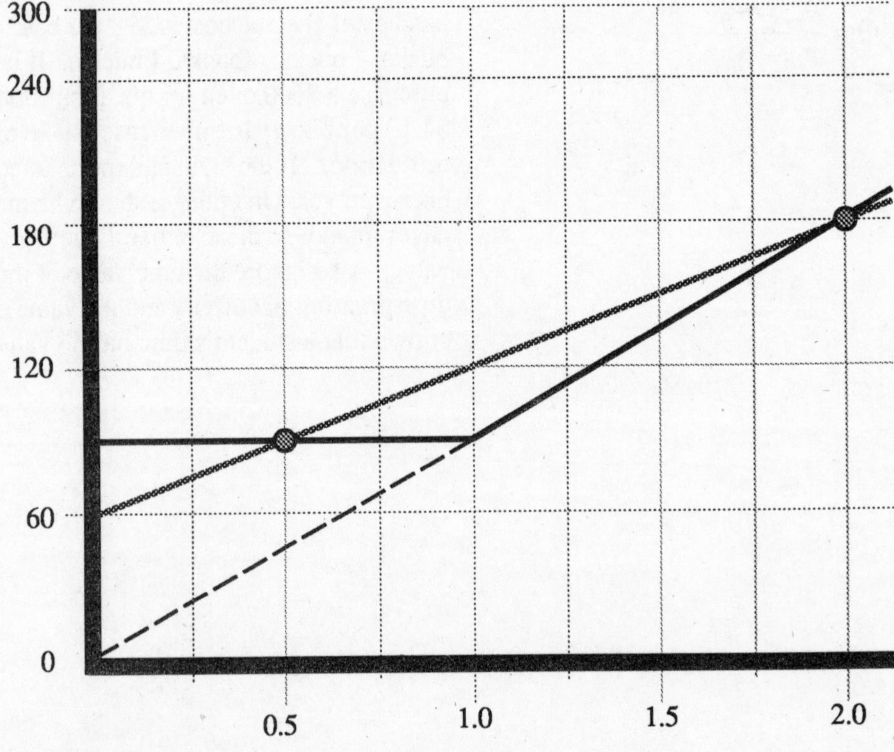

Solutions

EQUATION A.2

$$Q = \frac{F_m - F_b}{c_b - c_m}$$

1. Joe College.

   The average variable cost per pizza when purchased in batches of five is $28/batch divided by 5 pizzas per batch, or $ 5.60 per pizza.

   $$Q = \frac{F_m - F_b}{c_b - c_m} = \frac{\$800 - \$200}{\$5.60 - \$4.10}$$

   $$Q = 400 \text{ pizzas}$$

   Since Joe plans to consume fewer than 400 pizzas, (50 x 7) = 350 pizzas during his seven-year college career, he should **buy** them.
   The cost of making pizza is

   $F_m + c_mQ$ = $800 + ($4.10 * 350) = $ 2,235

   The cost of buying pizza is:

   $F_b + c_bQ$ = $200 + [($28/5) * 350] = **$ 2,160**

2. The Flat Beer Company.
   Ignoring the take-or-pay clause, the indifference quantity is

   $$Q = \frac{F_m - F_b}{c_b - c_m} = \frac{\$90{,}000 - \$0}{\$0.09 - \$0.06}$$

   $$Q = 2{,}000{,}000 \text{ cans}$$

   The take-or-pay clause produces another indifference point where the cost of making the cans crosses the purchase price of $90,000.

   $$F_m + c_mQ = \$90{,}000$$

   $$\$60{,}000 + \$0.06(Q) = \$90{,}000$$

   $$Q = 500{,}000 \text{ cans}$$

Solution to Alternative Processes Exercise:

Backward Bicycle Company. Considering the size of initial investment and the variable cost per unit, the robot alternative is analogous to the "make" alternative, while manually welding the bicycle frames is similar to the "buy" alternative.

$$Q = \frac{F_m - F_b}{c_b - c_m} = \frac{\$400{,}000 - \$10{,}000}{\$50 - \$20}$$

$$Q = 13{,}000 \text{ frames}$$

MULTIPLE CHOICE ANSWERS

1. C	11. C
2. D	12. A
3. D	13. A
4. A	14. D
5. C	15. D
6. D	16. C
7. C	17. A
8. C	18. D
9. C	19. B
10. D	20. B

3. The Flat Beer can solution is easier to see on the graph. Indicated at a volume of zero to 500,000 is "make," from 500,000 to 2,000,000; "buy," and over 2,000,000; we're back to "make." The first year's volume of 400,000 indicates "make." The second year's volume of 1,500,000 falls within the "buy" zone. And the third year's volume of 2,500,000 indicates "make." Since "buy" is the indicated answer over a fairly short time period, the company should probably **make** the cans.

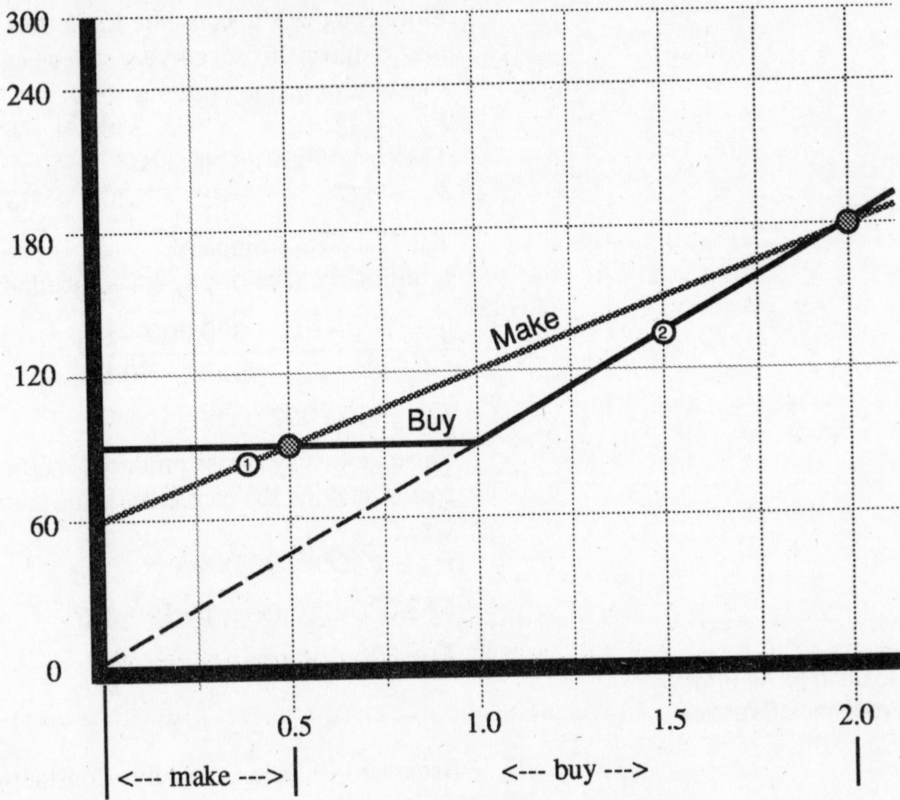

Volume of cans, in millions

Supplement B, Computer-Integrated Manufacturing

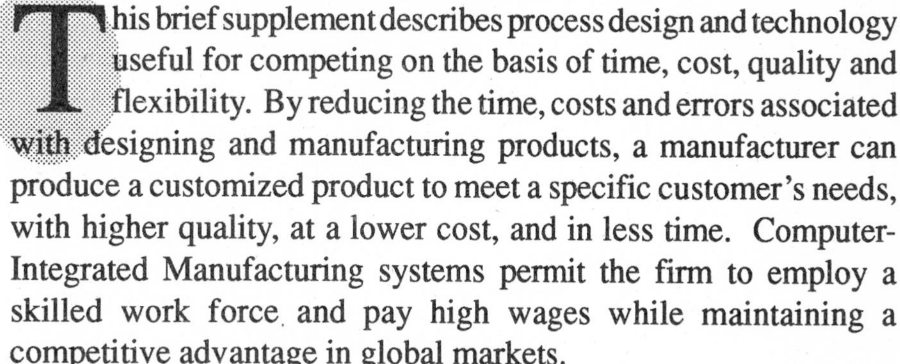

This brief supplement describes process design and technology useful for competing on the basis of time, cost, quality and flexibility. By reducing the time, costs and errors associated with designing and manufacturing products, a manufacturer can produce a customized product to meet a specific customer's needs, with higher quality, at a lower cost, and in less time. Computer-Integrated Manufacturing systems permit the firm to employ a skilled work force and pay high wages while maintaining a competitive advantage in global markets.

"**Computer-integrated manufacturing** (**CIM**) is an umbrella term for the total integration of product design and engineering, process planning, and manufacturing by means of complex computer systems." p. 131

- Computerized integration of all phases of manufacturing
- CIM helps manufacturers with high wage rates remain competitive

Computer-Aided Manufacturing

"The component of CIM that deals directly with manufacturing operations is called **computer-aided manufacturing** (**CAM**)." p. 131

Various types of programmable automation are parts of CAM.

Computers

- Design production processes
- Schedule manufacturing operations
- Track labor costs
- Send instructions to control machine tools
- Direct materials flow

Computer-Aided Design

"**Computer-aided design** (**CAD**) is an electronic system for designing new parts or products or altering existing ones, ..." p. 131

- Replaces drafting by hand
- Computer shows several views as designer creates the drawing
- Stress analysis shows reaction to force, indicating where the design is weak or likely to fail.
- Successful designs are stored, building a library of designs which can be retrieved and reused.

Boeing used computers exclusively to design their new 777 airplane. As part of the testing process, Boeing built, then destructively tested a wing to determine its strength. The wing shattered at exactly the stress predicted by the computer model.

CAD/CAM System.

- Integrates the design and manufacturing function
- Translates the computer drawing or image into code which directs and controls a machine to produce parts

MULTIPLE CHOICE ANSWERS

1. D	4. A
2. B	5. D
3. B	6. A

NC machines used to receive their instructions from a fragile roll of paper tape that had holes punched in it. As the tape fed through a reader, little mechanical fingers would sense the holes. It worked like the old player pianos. The sequence of punched holes programmed the machine.

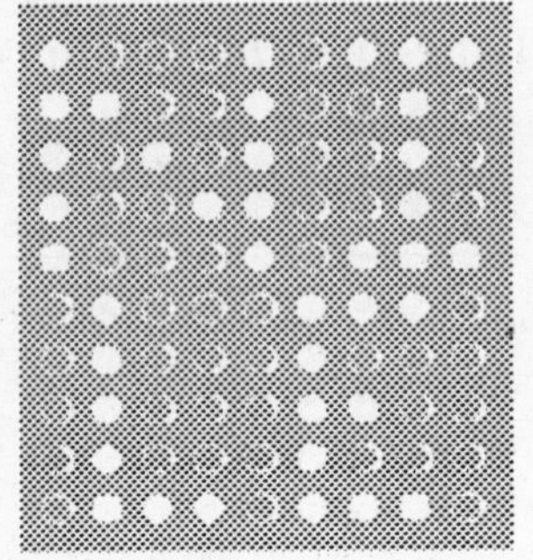

Numerically Controlled Machines

"**Numerically controlled (NC) machines** are large machine tools programmed to produce small- to medium-sized batches of intricate parts." p. 132

- Most commonly used form of flexible automation
  - one machine has many tools and performs many operations, perhaps machining a detailed part from a block of metal
  - receives instructions from external source (tape or computer)

"**Computerized numerically controlled (CNC) machines** are usually stand-alone pieces of equipment, each controlled by its own microcomputer." p. 132

Industrial Robots

"**Industrial robots** are versatile, computer-controlled machines programmed to perform various tasks." p. 132

- Limited reach
  - increased travel or axis of movement rapidly increases price
  - robot must always know where it is relative to the work, precision depends on maintaining a reference point
- Usually sightless
  - tools must be stored in predetermined locations
  - material must always be presented in the same orientation
  - some second generation robots have sensors to simulate touch and sight
- Relatively slow speed (when compared to fixed automation)
  - usually not suitable for high volume standardized production

One of the topics discussed in the Just-in-Time Chapter 15 is "pre-automation." This includes initial planning and simplification, streamlining, bringing operations close together, organizing the work area, and designing standard containers to always contain the same number of parts in the same orientation. All this preliminary organization is necessary before a robot could be programmed to perform the operations.

Automated Materials Handling

"**Materials handling** covers the processes of moving, packaging, and storing a product." p. 133

Materials handling

- Costs time and money
- Adds no value to the product
- Always look for ways to reduce materials handling

Materials handling automation justification depends on positioning strategy

- Process focus, materials handling automation rarely justified
  - job paths vary
  - little repeatability
- Product focus, materials handling automation may be justifiable

Technologies Available for Intermediate Positioning Strategies

1. Automated Guided Vehicle
   - follow cable or optical (paint stripe) path
   - on board or centralized computer control
   - route around transportation bottlenecks
   - just-in-time delivery of parts

"An **automated guided vehicle (AGV)** is a small, driverless, battery-driven truck that moves materials between operations, following instructions from either an on-board or a central computer." p. 134

Companies that perform initial planning and simplification *before* automating with an AS/RS system often find that much of the inventory to be stored and retrieved is not really needed. Once inventory is reduced, investment in the AS/RS system isn't justified. It is not hard to find companies that have installed AS/RS systems first, only later to find they have little use for them.

- AS/RS

"An **automated storage and retrieval system (AS/RS)** is a computer-controlled method of storing and retrieving materials and tools using racks, bins, and stackers." p. 134

Flexible Manufacturing Systems

"A **flexible manufacturing system** (FMS) is a configuration of computer-controlled, semi-independent workstations where materials are automatically handled and machine loaded." p. 134

Characteristics of FMS

1. Large initial investment
2. Little direct labor
3. Routing of operations determined by central computer
4. Short setup times
5. Different machines can perform the same operation

Three Key Components of an FMS

1. Several computer-controlled work stations, CNC machines, or robots that perform a series of operations
2. A computer-controlled transport system
3. Loading and unloading stations

Multiple-Choice Questions

1. An umbrella term for the total integration of product design and engineering, process planning, and manufacturing by means of complex computer systems is:
   A. AS/RS
   B. CAD
   C. CAM
   D. CIM

2. One difference between NC machines and CNC machines is:
   A. CNC machines are more common.
   B. CNC machines have an on-board computer.
   C. CNC machines carry more tools.
   D. NC machines are a form of fixed automation.

3. Which location has the most robots?
   A. Europe
   B. Japan
   C. North America
   D. South America

(Multiple-choice answers appear on page 55.)

4. Which of the following is true of materials handling?
   A. Always look for ways to reduce materials handling.
   B. Materials handling adds value to the product.
   C. Automated materials handling is a difficult to justify in product-focused facilities.
   D. Materials handling includes the process of inspecting the product.

5. Which of the following is *not* a key component of flexible manufacturing systems?
   A. A computer-controlled transport system
   B. Loading and unloading stations
   C. Several computer-controlled work stations, that perform a series of operations
   D. Standard sequence of operations common to each family of parts

6. Which of the following is an advantage of flexible manufacturing systems?
   A. Alternative routings avoid bottlenecks
   B. Low labor costs permit low utilization rate
   C. Low initial cost
   D. Low wage rates for unskilled operators

Chapter Four, Total Quality Management

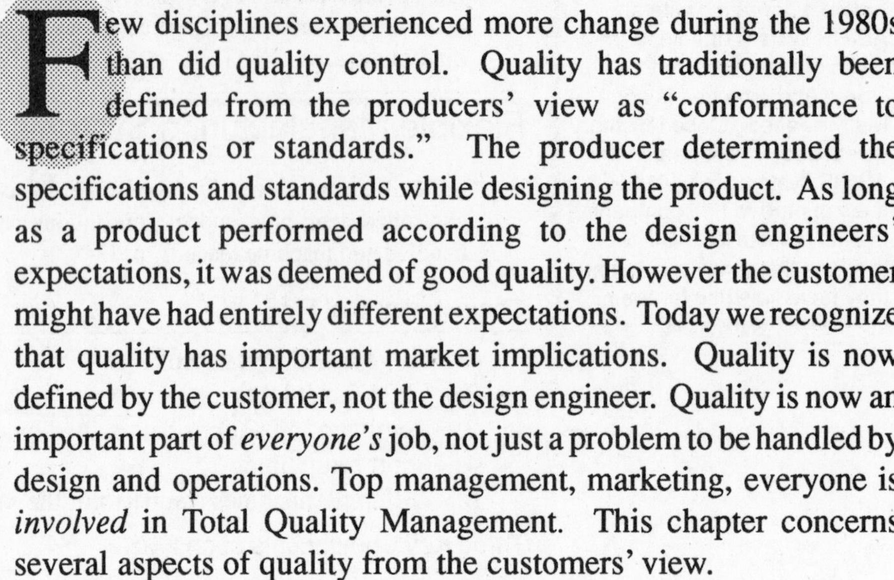

Few disciplines experienced more change during the 1980s than did quality control. Quality has traditionally been defined from the producers' view as "conformance to specifications or standards." The producer determined the specifications and standards while designing the product. As long as a product performed according to the design engineers' expectations, it was deemed of good quality. However the customer might have had entirely different expectations. Today we recognize that quality has important market implications. Quality is now defined by the customer, not the design engineer. Quality is now an important part of *everyone's* job, not just a problem to be handled by design and operations. Top management, marketing, everyone is *involved* in Total Quality Management. This chapter concerns several aspects of quality from the customers' view.

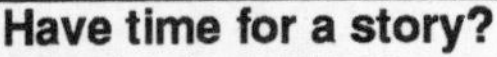

Have time for a story?
At the end of WWII, my parents bought a farm in Nebraska. We had good dirt, but no electric service. One day, they purchased a new electric refrigerator and freezer, even though they knew rural electric service would not be available for another two years! Why? Right after WWII durable goods were in such short supply that consumers bought *any* available goods simply because they didn't know how long it would be until they would have another chance.

During the economic boom of the 1950s, manufacturers learned they could sell just about anything. Witness the 1958 Plymouth. Quantity counted. Quality did not. American businesses promptly forgot the quality lessons Deming had taught them during WWII. Meanwhile, Deming went to Japan, and you know the rest of the story.

How do customers perceive the quality of services?

"**Total quality management** (TQM) stresses three principles: customer satisfaction, employee involvement, and continuous improvements in quality." p. 140

Quality: A Management Philosophy

- Quality was not always a top priority.
- 1980s — U.S. car manufacturers realized need to listen to the customer or lose market share.
  - Ford: "We listen." and "Quality is job one."
  - However, quality is not improved by marketing slogans.

Customer-Driven Definitions of Quality

- Quality has multiple dimensions
- One or more definitions of quality may apply

Definitions of Quality

1. Conformance to Specifications — Does the product or service meet or exceed advertised levels of performance? Does drinking this brand of beer really attract good looking dates?
2. Value — Does the product serve the customers' purposes considering this price? Will cheap beer attract good enough looking dates?
3. Fitness for Use — Appearance, style, durability, reliability, craftsmanship, serviceability ... How well does the product perform its intended purpose? Will drinking this light beer make me as thin as those people I see in the advertisements?
4. Support — Even when the product performs as expected, if service after the sale is poor, the customers' view of quality diminishes. The beer example does not lend itself well to the after-sale experience.
5. Psychological Impressions — Atmosphere, image, or aesthetics. Will drinking this beer improve my image among peers?

Quality as a Competitive Weapon

> "In general, a business's success depends on the accuracy of its perceptions of customer expectations and the ability to bridge the gap between consumer expectations and operating capabilities." p. 143

Students earning high grades will attest that it is just as important for work to look good as it is for work to be good. These students also tend to match their output to preferences expressed by their professors.

In the market

- Perception plays as important a role as does performance
- Producers that can match their operating capabilities with consumer preferences have a competitive advantage.
- Good quality can also pay off in higher profits
  - increased volume
  - increased price
  - *reduced* production cost

It is important to note that when one considers *all* of the costs of poor quality, it actually can be less costly to produce a good product than to produce an inferior one.

Employee Involvement

Cultural Change

- Cultural change must be motivated by top management.
- Everyone is expected to contribute.
- External customers buy the product or service.
- Internal customers are employees in the firm who rely on output of other employees.

An assembly line is a chain of internal customer-supplier relationships, with an external customer purchasing the finished good.

But trainers must be masterful. If a worker is not formally trained, is not a subject matter expert, is not a good teacher, or is more concerned about doing their own job, it is unrealistic to expect that (s)he will give effective instruction.

Individual Development

- On-the-job training programs can improve quality.
- Cross-train on related jobs so people understand how their work affects internal customers' work.
- Managers need to develop teaching skills.

Awards and Incentives

- Tie monetary incentives directly to quality improvements.
- Recognition also an improvement quality.

How can quality improvement teams be developed in a company?

Teamwork

- Worker participation is key to improving quality.

Characteristics of Teams

1. Common commitment to an overarching purpose
2. Shared leadership roles
3. Performance measures reflect collective "work products"
4. Open-ended discussion rather than managerially defined agendas
5. Do the work together rather than delegation to subordinates

> **Quality Circles Fail!**
>
> I invited a manager from a large corporation to be a guest speaker. The topic was to be "Successful quality circles." The manager stated that he would be very happy to speak to my class, but for his firm quality circles had been a miserable failure! Although initial reaction from the work force was overwhelmingly favorable, within a short time the circles began to die out. After a year, only one or two of the several hundred circles initially formed remained in existence. So the manager spoke to the class about why their quality circles failed:
>
> - Management held unrealistic expectations
>   - thought quality circles would quickly solve all quality problems
> - Lack of management support
>   - management did not participate in the groups
>   - autocratic managers felt threatened by democracy inherent to quality circles
>   - withdrew resources when results weren't immediate
>   - managers viewed worker time spent in circles as a waste of resources and tended to punish those who became involved
> - Lack of trained facilitators
>   - group effort not focused on issues group could resolve (85% of quality problems were rooted in management issues)
> - Lack of management action on improvement suggestions
> - Lack of recognition, inappropriate rewards
>   - For example, one "reward" was the opportunity to make an oral presentation to management. One worker became physically ill, terrified at the prospect of public speaking.
>
> Moral: Even the best of theory is vulnerable to poor execution.

The following three approaches to teamwork share in the use of **employee empowerment** to move decision-making responsibility down to those who have the best information — those who are actually doing the job. These approaches lead to **organizational restructuring**, eliminating some supervisors and middle managers.

Problem-Solving Teams, or Quality Circles

- Small groups of supervisors and employees
- Employees shape their work, more pride, involvement
- Quality circles die if management fails to implement suggestions.

Special-Purpose Teams

- Address a specific issue of management concern (Ad hoc team)
- Gives workers a voice in high-level decisions
- Members represent several departments or functions

Self-Managing Teams

- Highest level of worker participation
- Employees design the processes, control their jobs

Some concerns.

- Not everyone wants decision making responsibility or control over their work.
- Supervisor and middle manager resistance to change
  - different skill sets are required
  - organizational restructuring may cost them their jobs

Continuous Improvement

Getting Started With Continuous Improvement

A Process for Instilling a Philosophy of Continuous Improvement

1. SPC training
2. Make SPC a normal aspect of daily operations
3. Build work teams and employee involvement
4. Utilize problem-solving techniques within the work teams
5. Develop operator process ownership

Problem-Solving Process

Deming Wheel

1. Plan — Select a process needing improvement, document process, analyze data, set improvement goals, discuss alternatives, assess benefits and costs, develop a plan and improvement measures
2. Do — Implement plan, monitor improvements
3. Check — Analyze data to evaluate effectiveness of the plan
4. Act — Document and disseminate improved process as a standard operating procedure. Gain leverage on the investment associated with solving this problem by broadly applying the lessons learned to all similar processes.

What are the costs of poor quality?

The Costs of Poor Quality

When managers underestimate the costs of poor quality, it appears that the costs of making quality improvements exceed the costs of living with defects. But when *all* of the costs of poor quality are considered, it is often less costly to produce high quality goods and services than it is to produce inferior ones.

Prevention

Costs in this category include time, effort, and money to:

- Redesign the processes to remove causes of defects
- Redesign the product to make it simpler, easier to produce
- Train employees
- Train suppliers

Appraisal

Costs incurred to identify and assess quality problems

- Inspection
- Quality audits
- Statistical quality control programs

Internal Failure

Costs from defects discovered before the product or service is sold

- Yield losses — The material costs associated with scrap losses.
- Rework — Time, space, and capacity to store then reroute to operations for correcting defects

External Failure

Costs when a defect is discovered after the customer has received the product or service.

- Loss of market share
- Warranty service
- Litigation
- Increased regulation

FIGURE 4.4

The Costs of Detecting a Defect

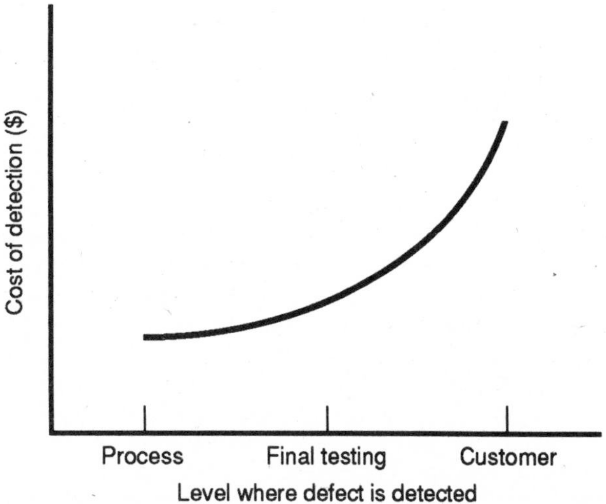

What are the "hidden" costs of internal and external failures?

- More labor
- More machine capacity
- Increased work-in-process inventory
- Extended lead times
- Increased chance of defects reaching the customer
- Increased pressure to produce more to make up for defects
- Reduced employee morale
- More defects

Costs Associated with Quality Management

Cost Category	As Quality Increases, Costs
Prevention	Increase
Appraisal	Decrease
Internal Failure	Decrease
External Failure	Decrease

Improving Quality Through TQM

How good is the company's quality relative to that of competitors?

Benchmarking

"**Benchmarking** is a continuous, systematic process that measures products, services, and practices against those of industry leaders." p. 156

Four Basic Steps of Benchmarking

1. Planning — Identify process, leader, performance measures.
2. Analysis — Measure gap, identify causes.
3. Integration — Establish goals and resource commitments.
4. Action — Develop teams, implement plan, monitor progress, return to Step 1.

What factors in the operations system are causing major quality problems?

Product and Service Design

- Design changes can increase defect rates
- Stable designs reduce quality problems
- Stable designs may become obsolete in the marketplace

"Another dimension of quality related to product design is reliability, which refers to the probability that the product will be functional when used." p. 157

BMW Product Design. For the half-century between 1930 and 1980 BMW produced touring motorcycles that shared the same basic engine design. It was a simple, light weight, air-cooled, horizontally opposed, two cylinder engine. Over the years many improvements were made, but the design changes were evolutionary rather than revolutionary. Because of this stable design, the BMW became known for very reliable performance. But by 1980, the design had become obsolete. Competitors in the touring bike market offered more powerful engines. This required BMW to change their touring engine design. Rather than start anew, BMW applied a proven automobile racing engine design. However to this day BMW continues to use the original engine design for their off-road bikes. In that application, light weight and high reliability are more important than maximum power output.

Reliability Exercise

If a component does not exist, it cannot fail. Therefore simplicity, or fewer parts, increases reliability. (Honda, we make it simple.) On the other hand, nuclear power plants claim to be very safe because of *redundant* safety systems, in other words, *more* parts. This apparent inconsistency is explained by determining whether the parts are in series or in parallel. Additional components *in series* reduce reliability. Additional components *in parallel* improve reliability. For example, in order to start an old car, we need keys, fuel, and a charged battery. Lacking any of these, the car will not start. In order to start a new car, we need keys, fuel, a charged battery, and a computer system that is powerful enough to land a 777. Which is more likely to start?

For our example, say the probability of remembering the keys is 95%, the chances of fuel being in the tank varies inversely with the number of teenagers in the family, but lets say it is 80%, and the probability of a charged battery is 98%. What is the reliability of the old car?

The reliability of a system with *N* components *in series* is equal to the probability of the simultaneous occurrence of independent events.

$$r_S = (r_1)(r_2)(r_3)$$
$$= ?$$

Now let's say the probability of the computer functioning in the new car is 92%. This estimate is very low, but suits the purposes of our example. What is the reliability of starting the new car?

$$r_S = (r_1)(r_2)(r_3)(r_4)$$
$$= ?$$

The answers are 74.48% for the old car and 68.52% for the new car. The addition of a required component *in series* reduces reliability.

FORMULA 4.1

$$r_s = (r_1)(r_2)\ldots(r_n)$$

Old Volkswagens had no gas gauge, but did have a reserve fuel tank *in parallel.* So the VW will start if we have the keys, fuel in *either or both* tanks, and a charged battery. The result is increased reliability, but how is the effect of the redundant fuel tank calculated? Let's say that there is an 80% chance of fuel in the main tank and a 70% chance of fuel in the reserve tank. Now the probability we're completely out of fuel is the simultaneous occurrence of *both* tanks being *empty*: (100% – 80%) (100% – 70%) = 6%. The reserve fuel tank increases fuel reliability from 80% to 94%, and the chance of starting the old car from 74.48% to (.95)(.96)(.98) = 89.38%. The addition of redundant components *in parallel* increases reliability. Critical systems in nuclear power plants have multiple layers of independent and redundant components. It is like wearing a belt and suspenders ... and overalls.

Process Design

- New equipment can overcome quality problems.
- Concurrent engineering ensures that production requirements and process capabilities are synchronized.

Quality Function Deployment

"**Quality function deployment** (QFD) is a means of translating customer requirements into the appropriate technical requirements for each stage of product or service development and production." p. 159

- A way to set targets
- Encourages interfunctional communication

Six Questions for Constructing the "House of Quality" Chart

1. Voice of the customer. What do customers need and want?
2. Competitive analysis. Relative to competitors, how well are we serving customers?
3. Voice of the engineer. What technical measures relate to our customers' needs?
4. Correlations. What are the relationships between the voice of the customer and the voice of the engineer?
5. Technical comparison. How does our product or service performance compare to that of our competition?
6. Trade-offs. What are the potential technical trade-offs?

Purchasing Considerations

"...purchased parts of poor quality can have a devastating effect." p. 161

- Buyer must emphasize quality, delivery, and price.
- Work with the supplier to obtain defect-free parts.
- Specifications must be clear and realistic.
- Allow time to identify qualified suppliers.
- Improve communication between purchasing and engineering, quality control, and other departments.

How can areas for quality improvement be identified?

Tools for Improving Quality

Seven Tools for Organizing and Presenting Data

1. Checklists — record the frequency of occurrence.
2. Histograms — summarizes data measured on a continuous scale.
3. Bar Charts — bar height represents the frequency of occurrence.
4. Pareto Charts — a bar chart organized in decreasing order of frequency.
5 Scatter Diagrams — a plot of two variables showing whether they are related
6. Cause-and-effect, fishbone, or Ishikawa diagram.

A strength of the Ishikawa (or fishbone) diagram is its use in focusing group discussion on potential causes of a problem. Without structure, group discussions tend to wander, wasting time. Simply drawing the diagram often improves understanding of how contributing factors interrelate.

- Graphs — represent data in a variety of pictorial formats, such as line graphs and pie charts.

Prescriptions for Excellence in Quality

W. Edwards Deming: Quality is Management's Responsibility

- Management
  - is responsible for sending the message that quality is valued.
  - must develop statistical tools to manage quality.
- Five-step chain reaction for improving quality
- Fourteen point philosophy for achieving greater quality
- Deming Prize awarded to firms demonstrating excellence in quality

Joseph M. Juran: A Quality Trilogy

- Over 80% of quality defects are caused by factors controllable by management. Blaming American workers for poor workmanship is a popular but invalid excuse. Most quality problems are attributable to management, not labor.
- Trilogy
  - quality planning
    - . select quality level and reliability
    - . link product and service design to process design
  - control
    - . measure, compare to standard, feedback, corrective action
  - improvement
    - . continuous improvement, hands-on management, training

Phillip B. Crosby

- *Quality Is Free*
- Hidden costs of poor quality dwarf the costs of new machines, better materials and training.
- Advocates goal of zero defects

Malcolm Baldrige National Quality Award

- Established in 1987
- Named for Secretary of Commerce Malcolm Baldrige
- Improved quality as a means of reducing the trade deficit
- Learn strengths and weaknesses and find ways to improve operations

From a quality perspective, how can an organization prepare to do business in foreign markets?

International Quality Standards

What is ISO 9000?

"**ISO 9000** is a set of standards governing the requirements for documentation of a quality program." p. 169

- Certified companies are listed in a directory.
- Compliance with ISO 9000 standards indicates only that quality claims can be documented.

Benefits of ISO 9000 Certification

ISO certification is becoming an "order qualifier".

- External — potential sales advantage
- Internal — provides guidance in starting the TQM journey

Multiple-Choice Questions

1. It is three o'clock on Christmas morning and you are *still* trying to decipher unintelligible assembly instructions for a tricycle. Your opinion about this product's quality takes on which of the following definitions?
   A. Conformance to specifications
   B. Value
   C. Fitness for use
   D. Psychological impressions
2. It is seven o'clock on Christmas morning and your child is thrilled with the tricycle. Except the colorful "flaming wheels" and other decals aren't sticking on very well. Your opinion about this product's quality takes on which of the following definitions?
   A. Conformance to specifications
   B. Fitness for use
   C. Support
   D. Psychological impressions
3. It is two o'clock on Christmas afternoon and your child has already worn flat spots on the plastic wheels of the tricycle. Apparently it is great fun to roll down the driveway towards the street and just as Mom screams, lock the wheels and make spiraling skid marks. Your opinion about this product's quality takes on which of the following definitions?
   A. Conformance to specifications
   B. Value
   C. Support
   D. Psychological impressions
4. It is ten o'clock on the day after Christmas and you learn that replacement wheels are not available for the tricycle. Your opinion about this product's quality takes on which of the following definitions?
   A. Conformance to specifications
   B. Value
   C. Fitness for use
   D. Support
5. Viewing quality as a responsibility to be shared by the entire organization is an example of
   A. Continuous Improvement
   B. Cultural change
   C. Individual development
   D. Teamwork
6. Higher quality can pay off in
   A. Increased market share
   B. Higher prices
   C. Lower production costs
   D. All of the above
7. A complete program in employee involvement includes all of the following *except*:
   A. Awards and incentives
   B. Benchmarking
   C. Cultural change
   D. Teamwork
8. A quality circle is one type of
   A. ISO 9000 certification
   B. Problem-solving teams
   C. Self-managing teams
   D. Special-purpose teams
9. Total quality management (TQM)
   A. is a management program designed to get more work from labor.
   B. improves quality by increasing the number of quality control inspectors.
   C. means that employees do not pass defective units to the next operation.
   D. is a supplier development program to improve the quality of purchased materials.
10. A quality circle
   A. should have at least 20 members.
   B. should not include supervisors.
   C. should concentrate on a small number of major quality problems.
   D. requires prompt management response to large numbers of suggestions.
11. In order to improve quality, managers should do all of the following *except*
   A. assume more decision-making responsibility.
   B. foster individual development through training.
   C. instill an awareness of the importance of quality in all employees.
   D. improve their skill in training others.
12. The four parts of the Deming wheel are
   A. Benchmarking, Product design, Process design, Quality function deployment
   B. Cultural change, Individual development, Awards and incentives, Teamwork
   C. Plan, Do, Check, Act
   D. Prevention, Appraisal, Internal Failure, External Failure

13. Organizational restructuring as discussed in this chapter is most often resisted by
    A. Customers
    B. Direct-labor workers
    C. Middle managers
    D. Top managers

14. Which of the following costs of quality usually increases when we invest in improved machines, more training, or purchase better materials to improve quality?
    A. Appraisal
    B. External failure
    C. Internal failure
    D. Prevention

15. Which of the following explains Phillip B. Crosby's statements to the effect that when we invest in improved machines, more training, or purchase better materials that the resulting improvement in quality is free?
    A. Crosby is wrong.
    B. The reduction in the hidden costs of poor quality easily offset these costs.
    C. Since total costs are a function of quality level, a trade-off determines the optimal quality level resulting in minimized total costs.
    D. Quality deployment is not a function of cost.

16. At which location are the costs associated with defects at their lowest?
    A. At the production process
    B. At final product testing
    C. At the distribution warehouse
    D. At the customer

17. All of the following are associated with defective products that cannot be repaired, *except*
    A. increased rework.
    B. increased scrap.
    C. increased work-in-process (WIP) inventory.
    D. increased yield loss.

18. Quality function deployment ______.
    A. is a method of allocating the costs of quality into the four major categories.
    B. is a means of translating customer requirements into technical requirements for product development and production.
    C. is a way for management to assign issues of paramount concern to special-purpose teams.
    D. is the culminating step in Deming's fourteen point philosophy for achieving greater quality.

(Solutions appear on Study Guide page 68.)

Problems

1. A space launch vehicle will only be cleared for take-off when the following conditions occur:
    - Ground Air Temperature $\geq$ 50°F
    - Trajectory Wind Velocity $\leq$ 40 mph
    - Down range cloud cover $\leq$ 20%
    - All systems are operable.
    - No woodpecker damage to fuel tank insulation.

    The weather service says with 80% reliability that weather conditions at the scheduled launch time will be favorable. Engineers have designed each of the 200 required systems to a 99.8% reliability standard. And foresters say there is a 75% probability that placing fake owls around the fuel tank will scare away the woodpeckers. What is the probability of an on-time launch?

2. While registering for the final semester, a college senior majoring in reliability engineering is taking the following three courses with the associated probability of receiving a passing grade:

Operations Management	80%	(required)
Statistical Process Control	90%	(required)
Marriage and the Family	70%	(elective)

    In order to earn enough credits to graduate, the student must pass all three classes.

    a. What are the chances of graduating?

    b. What could this student do to improve the chances of graduating?

3. Al is the owner of Fresco's Sidewalk Coffee Sales of Seattle. Fresco has served the sleepless in Seattle for several years and now desires to become the "official coffee supplier" for an international winter sporting event to be held in Salt Lake City in the year 2002. Fresco estimates the probabilities of winning this honor at 90%, cooperative (coffee drinking) weather at 95%, and public acceptance of his product at 80%. If all three events occur, this success could become the springboard to nationwide franchising. What are the chances Al Fresco will become *the name* for outdoor service?

FORMULA 4.1

$r_s = (r_1)(r_2)\ldots(r_n)$

Solutions

1. Space launch vehicle.

Component		Reliability
Weather		80%
Systems	$(0.998)^{200}$ =	67%
Owls		75%

The probability of an on-time launch is (0.80)(0.67)(0.75) = 0.402, or 40.2%.

2. Graduation.

Component	Reliability
Operations Management	80%
Statistical Process Control	90%
Marriage and the Family	70%

a. The probability of an on-time graduation is (0.80)(0.90)(0.70) = 0.504, or 50.4%.

b. The chances of graduation would increase if the student selected an easier elective, (basketweaving?). This is analogous to increasing the reliability of a component in a system. An alternative method would be to sign up for more than one elective, in effect adding a redundant component *in parallel* to the Marriage and the Family elective. Then the student would not graduate only if (s)he failed *both* electives.

3. Al Fresco's chances of becoming *the name* for outdoor service is:

(0.90)(0.95)(0.80) = 0.684 or 68.4%

MULTIPLE CHOICE ANSWERS

1. C	10. D
2. D	11. A
3. B	12. C
4. D	13. C
5. B	14. D
6. D	15. B
7. B	16. A
8. B	17. A
9. C	18. B

Chapter Five, Statistical Process Control

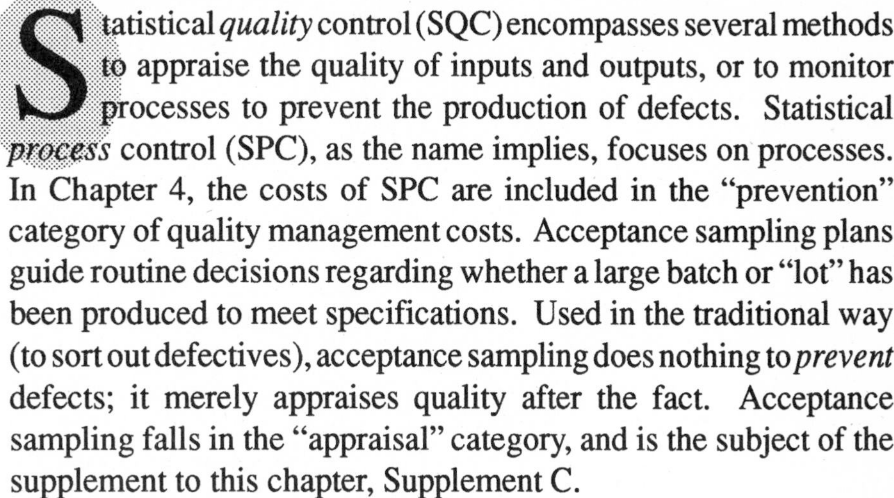

Statistical *quality* control (SQC) encompasses several methods to appraise the quality of inputs and outputs, or to monitor processes to prevent the production of defects. Statistical *process* control (SPC), as the name implies, focuses on processes. In Chapter 4, the costs of SPC are included in the "prevention" category of quality management costs. Acceptance sampling plans guide routine decisions regarding whether a large batch or "lot" has been produced to meet specifications. Used in the traditional way (to sort out defectives), acceptance sampling does nothing to *prevent* defects; it merely appraises quality after the fact. Acceptance sampling falls in the "appraisal" category, and is the subject of the supplement to this chapter, Supplement C.

"**Statistical Process Control** (SPC) is the application of statistical techniques to determine whether the output of a process conforms to the product or service design." p. 181

Examples of Problems Detected by SPC

1. An increase in the proportion of defective components
2. An increase in the average number of service complaints
3. A process frequently fails to conform to design specifications

Upon completing my thrilling lecture on the virtues of statistical process control, I was approached by a student. From previous conversations I knew this student had worked for ten years as a machinist for a large manufacturer.

"We implemented SPC a few years ago, but it doesn't really work."

"Oh ..." I responded, now wishing I had more experience with the technique. "Why not?"

"Well, management got all enthusiastic about SPC and showed us how to plot data. We plastered the walls with control charts, but we didn't show any out-of-control points." At first I didn't understand what he was saying. I couldn't imagine a company that never had processes go out of control. He continued: "Whenever an out-of-control point happened, we just didn't plot it. That kept everyone happy."

Further discussion revealed that when out-of-control points *were* plotted, management would see them on the chart and berate the workers for letting the process drift. Workers soon learned to just not plot incriminating data. Management hailed the SPC program a success. Quality problems had "disappeared."

Sources of Variation

When measured with great precision, in milligrams, nanoseconds, angstroms, ergs, picofarads, coulombs, maxwells, and so forth, we see that the dimensions of all things vary continuously. No two snowflakes are *exactly* alike, nor are any two of anything else. (With the possible exception of DNA found on say, a matching pair of gloves).

All sources of variation can be attributed to one of two source categories: common causes and assignable causes.

Common Causes

- Random, or unavoidable sources of variation within a process

Every variation is potentially explainable. Slight variations in temperature, vibrations from a passing truck, sun spot activity, *something* causes every variation. But the root cause of some variations are never discovered, or when discovered, no practical remedy exits. These "unavoidable" variations are then attributed to "common causes."

Adjustments to a process to compensate for a common cause variation will usually make the process go further out of control. Constant "tweaking" of the process is called "tampering." Since tampering is destructive to quality, one should not respond to a variation if its source is a common cause.

Characteristics of Distributions

1. Mean — the average observation
2. Spread — the dispersion of observations around the mean
3. Shape — whether the observations are symetrical or skewed

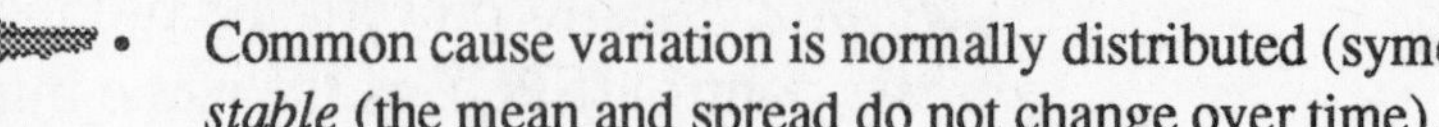

- Common cause variation is normally distributed (symetrical) and *stable* (the mean and spread do not change over time).

Assignable Causes

- Any cause of variation that can be identified and eliminated

Adjustments to a process to compensate for an assignable cause of variation will usually bring the process back into control. So we should respond to variation when its source has an assignable cause. The problem of course is that very often an observed variation looks exactly the same whether its root cause is assignable or common.

Say an Operations student who normally gets test scores in the low 80s instead receives a 78 on one test. Has something gone wrong with this student's learning process? Should we conclude that this student has gone astray and schedule some type of intervention? Should we endeavor to make changes in the way this student studies, sleeps, works, or receives nutrition? Or is this test score variation due to some unavoidable cause? Perhaps the student just wasn't having a good day when taking the test. Or perhaps the instructor wasn't having a good day when writing the test. Or perhaps the graduate assistant wasn't having a good day when grading the test.

If there is an assignable cause, then the student could benefit from a corrective action. If the cause is common, then the student would probably not benefit from investigating and "tampering" with the student's life. But a 78 is a 78. On the basis of this one observation which is only slightly different from the norm, we can not tell whether to act or not to act.

In summary, reaction to common causes is tampering, and that is bad. On the other hand, failure to react to assignable causes is also bad. And finally, based on a single observation one usually can not tell whether to act or not to act. So are we paralyzed? How can we know when taking an action is the right thing to do? We can't know for sure. But we can use a statistical approach to guide our decisions and tip the odds substantially in our favor.

"A process is said to be in statistical control when the dimensions of its distribution don't change over time." p. 183

- *Change* in the mean, spread, or shape of a process distribution is a symptom that an assignable cause of variation has developed.
- *After* a process is in statistical control, SPC is used to detect *significant change*, indicating the need for corrective action.

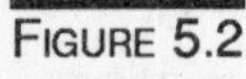

FIGURE 5.2

Effects of Assignable Causes on a Process Distribution

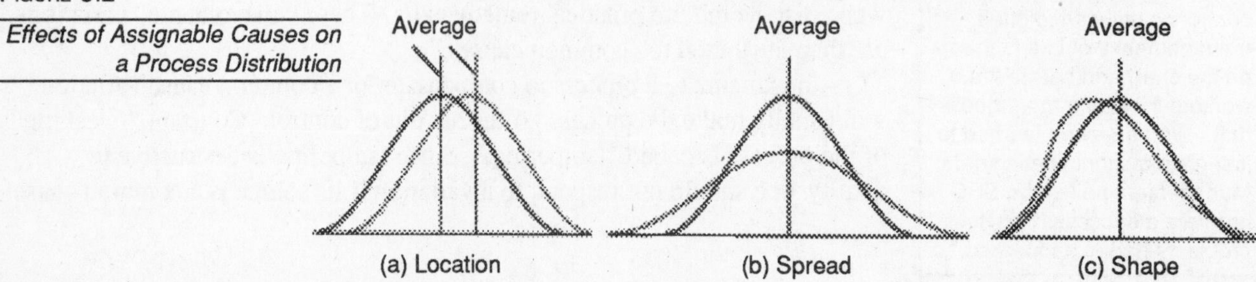

> What trade-offs are involved in using attribute measurements instead of variable measurements of quality?

The Inspection Process

- Use of inspection to simply remove defectives is improper. It does nothing to prevent defects. We can not "inspect" quality into a part.

Quality Measurements

- Variables — a characteristic measured on a continuous scale
  - advantage: if defective, we know by how much — the direction and magnitude of corrections are indicated
  - disadvantage: precise measurements are required
- Attributes — a characteristic counted in discrete units, (yes-no, integer number)
  - used to determine conformance to complex specifications, or when measuring variables is too costly
  - advantages:
    - quickly reveals when quality has changed, provides an integer number of *how many* are defective
    - requires less effort, and fewer resources than measuring variables
  - disadvantages:
    - doesn't show by *how much* they were defective, the direction and magnitude of corrections are not indicated
    - requires more observations, since each observation provides little information

> We will later see that the sample size must be large enough so that on the average, there will be at least one defective found in the sample. The sample size can be small when the incoming quality is poor. Say, $n \approx 50$ if material is 2% defective.
>
> Q: What is the sample size if the incoming materials has only 100 ppm (parts per million) defective?
>
> A: $n \approx 10{,}000$.
>
> Some just-in-time companies do not even attempt to inspect incoming materials. The required sample size is larger than the shipment size. JIT companies instead use SPC and TQM programs, working closely with suppliers to prevent defects and ensure high levels of quality.

Sampling

- Complete inspection
  - used when
    - costs of failure are high relative to costs of inspection
    - inspection is automated
  - some defects are not detected because of
    - inspector fatigue
    - imperfect testing methods
- Inspection sampling
  - used when
    - inspection costs are high
    - inspection destroys the product
  - some defective lots may be purchased and some good lots may be rejected when
    - the sample does not perfectly represent the population
    - testing methods are imperfect
- Sampling plans include
  - sample size, *n* random observations
  - time between successive samples
  - decision rules that determine when action should be taken

Sampling Distributions

- Sample means are usually dispersed about the population mean according to the normal probability distribution (reference the central limit theorum described in statistics texts).

Control Charts

- Used to judge whether action is required
- A sample characteristic measured above the upper contol limit (UCL) or below the lower control limit (LCL) indicates that an assignable cause probably exists.

Other Indicators of Out of Control Conditions

1. A trend in the observations (The process is drifting.)
2. A sudden or step change in the observations
3. A run of five or more observations on the same side of the mean (If we flip a coin and get "heads" five times in a row, we become suspicious of the coin or of the coin flipping process.)
4. Several observations near the control limits (Normally only 1 in 20 observations are more than 2 standard deviations from the mean.)

"Control charts are not perfect tools for detecting shifts in the process distribution because they are based on sampling distributions." p. 188

Two Types of Error Can Result from Sampling

1. Type I error — Good lots are rejected. The producer is harmed.
2. Type II error — Bad lots are accepted. The consumer is harmed.

Note that there is no error associated with either accepting or rejecting mediocre, or what I call "ugly" lots. The consumer is not hurt when accepted material is merely ugly, because it is not really "bad". It's just ugly. On the other hand, the producer is not hurt when ugly material is rejected. The producer should not have shipped ugly material.

Where should inspection stations be put?

Inspection Station Location

- Identify important aspects of quality
  - purchased input materials
    - could use acceptance sampling
  - work in process
    - not after every process
    - before it is covered up
    - before costly, irreversible, or bottleneck operations so that resource is used efficiently
  - finished goods
    - before stocking or shipping to the customer
  - customers often play a major role in final inspection of services

 "...the operations manager must remember that quality can not be inspected into the product;" p. 190

Statistical Process Control Methods

- Measure current quality
- Detect whether the process has changed

Control Charts for Variables

Quality characteristics include variables, which are different from attributes in that variables are measured over a continuum, while attributes have only discrete or integer values.

With variables, we use two types of chart, *R*-charts and *x*-charts. We need two charts because the sample mean doesn't by itself tell us whether the process is in control. A sample mean might fall within the control limits while some of the sample is far too large and some is far too small. In order to detect that situation, we also measure and plot the range of the sample.

Range Charts

- Monitor process variability

In order to use *R*-charts, we must first find and remove the assignable causes of variation until we are assured the process is under control. Then while the process is under control, we collect a history of data to estimate the range of output that commonly occurs while the process is under control. The average of that history is $\overline{R}$. To establish the upper and lower control limits for the *R*-chart, we use Table 5.1, which provides two "magic numbers," D_3 and D_4. These magic numbers establish the UCL_R and LCL_R at three standard deviations above and below $\overline{R}$. The derivation of D_3 and D_4 are thankfully beyond the scope of this course.

EQUATION 5.3.A

$$UCL_R = D_4\overline{R}$$
$$LCL_R = D_3\overline{R}$$

$UCL_R = D_4\overline{R}$

$\overline{R}$ - $\overline{R}$

$LCL_R = D_3\overline{R}$

x-charts

The process average is plotted on the *x*-chart. The upper and lower control limits can be established in two ways. If the standard deviation of the process distribution is known, we could place *UCL* and *LCL* at "z" standard deviations away from the mean, depending on the desired confidence interval. The method shown in the text uses Table 5.1. Again, finding a magic number, A_2, which when multipled by the previously determined $\overline{R}$, places *UCL* and *LCL* three standard deviaitions above and below the mean.

EQUATION 5.3.B

$$UCL_{\overline{x}} = \overline{\overline{x}} + A_2\overline{R}$$
$$LCL_{\overline{x}} = \overline{\overline{x}} - A_2\overline{R}$$

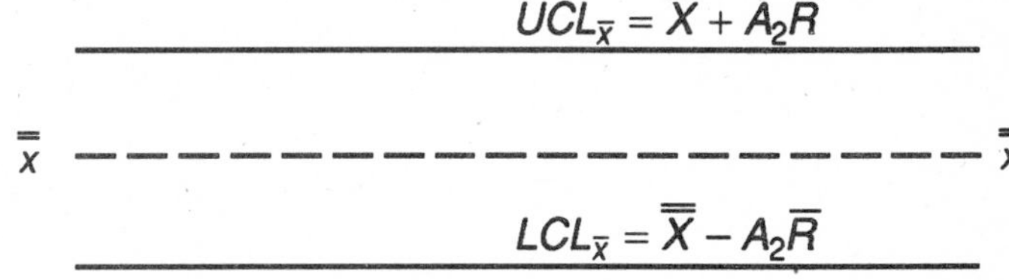

EQUATION 5.3.C

$$UCL_{\overline{x}} = \overline{\overline{x}} + z\sigma_{\overline{x}}$$
$$LCL_{\overline{x}} = \overline{\overline{x}} - z\sigma_{\overline{x}}$$

where

$$\sigma_{\overline{x}} = \frac{\sigma}{\sqrt{n}}$$

Using *x*- and *R*-Charts to Monitor a Process

1. Construct the *R*-chart
2. Compute the range for each sample
3. Plot the ranges on the *R*-chart
4. Construct the *x*-chart
5. Compute the mean for each sample
6. Plot the sample means on the *x*-chart

Exercises

Control Charts for Variables

$UCL_R = D_4\overline{R}$

$LCL_R = D_3\overline{R}$

$UCL_{\overline{x}} = \overline{\overline{x}} + A_2\overline{R}$

$LCL_{\overline{x}} = \overline{\overline{x}} - A_2\overline{R}$

(Solution is on Study Guide page 82.)

1. Webster Chemical Company produces mastics and caulking for the construction industry. The product is blended in large mixers and then pumped into tubes and capped. Webster is concerned whether the filling process for tubes of caulking is in statistical control. The process should be centered on 8 ounces per tube. Several samples of eight tubes are taken and each tube is weighed in ounces.

	Tube Number							
Sample	1	2	3	4	5	6	7	8
1	7.98	8.34	8.02	7.94	8.44	7.68	7.81	8.11
2	8.23	8.12	7.98	8.41	8.31	8.18	7.99	8.06
3	7.89	7.77	7.91	8.04	8.00	7.89	7.93	8.09
4	8.24	8.18	7.83	8.05	7.90	8.16	7.97	8.07
5	7.87	8.13	7.92	7.99	8.10	7.81	8.14	7.88
6	8.13	8.14	8.11	8.13	8.14	8.12	8.13	8.14

a. Assuming that taking only 6 samples is sufficient, use the data in the table to construct *R*-chart control limits. Is the process in statistical control?

b. The process variability for the first and sixth samples appear to be out of control. Webster looks for assignable causes and quickly notes that the weighing scale was gummed up with caulking. Apparently, a tube was not properly capped. The sticky scale did not correctly read the variation in weights for the sixth sample.

Delete that data and recalculate $\overline{R}$, $UCL_{\overline{R}}$, and $LCL_{\overline{R}}$. Is the process in statistical control?

$$UCL_p = \bar{p} + z\sigma_p$$

$$LCL_p = \bar{p} - z\sigma_p$$

$$\sigma_p = \sqrt{\frac{\bar{p}(1-\bar{p})}{n}}$$

Control Charts for Attributes.

(Solutions are on Study Guide page 83).

2. A sticky scale brings Webster's attention to whether caulking tubes are being properly capped. If a significant proportion of the tubes aren't being sealed, Webster is placing their customers in a messy situation. Tubes are packaged in large boxes of 144. Several boxes are inspected and the following number of leaking tubes are found:

Sample	Tubes	Sample	Tubes	Sample	Tubes
1	3	8	6	15	5
2	5	9	4	16	0
3	3	10	9	17	2
4	4	11	2	18	6
5	2	12	6	19	2
6	4	13	5	20	1
7	2	14	1	Total	72

Calculate *p*-chart three-sigma control limits to assess whether the capping process is in statistical control.

$$UCL_c = \bar{c} + z\sigma_c$$

$$LCL_c = \bar{c} - z\sigma_c$$

$$\sigma_c = \sqrt{\bar{c}}$$

3. At Webster Chemical, lumps in the caulking compound could cause difficulties in dispensing a smooth bead from the tube. Even when the process is in control, there will still be an average of 4 lumps per tube of caulk. Testing for the presence of lumps destroys the product, so Webster takes random samples. The following are results of the study:

Tube #	Lumps	Tube #	Lumps	Tube #	Lumps
1	6	5	6	9	5
2	5	6	4	10	0
3	0	7	1	11	9
4	4	8	6	12	2

Determine the *c*-chart two-sigma upper and lower control limits for this process.

Control Charts for Attributes

EQUATION 5.4.A

$$UCL_p = \bar{p} + z\sigma_p$$

$$LCL_p = \bar{p} - z\sigma_p$$

where

$$\sigma_p = \sqrt{\frac{\bar{p}(1-\bar{p})}{n}}$$

p-chart — population proportion defective

1. Take a random sample.
2. Count the number of defectives.
3. Proportion defective = number of defectives ÷ sample size.
4. Plot sample proportion defective on a chart. If it is outside the range between the upper and lower control limits, search for the assignable cause. If cause is found do not use this data to determine the control limits.

$UCL_p = \bar{p} + z\sigma_p$

$LCL_p = \bar{p} - z\sigma_p$

EQUATION 5.4.B

$$UCL_c = \bar{c} + z\sigma_c$$

$$LCL_c = \bar{c} - z\sigma_c$$

where

$$\sigma_c = \sqrt{\bar{c}}$$

c-chart — integer number of defects on one item

1. Take a random sample of one.
2. Inspect the quality attribute.
3. Count the number of defects.
4. Plot the number defective on a chart. If it is outside the range between the upper and lower control limits, search for the assignable cause. If cause is found do not use these data to determine the control limits.

$UCL_c = \bar{c} + z\sigma_c$

$\bar{c}$ – $\bar{c}$

$LCL_c = \bar{c} - z\sigma_c$

The Poisson distribution is used because it fits situations where a large integer number of occurrences are possible but the likely number is small. The Poisson distribution is also nifty because its mean and standard deviation are both described using the same number, $\bar{c}$. The mean is equal to *c*, and the standard deviation is equal to $\sqrt{\bar{c}}$.

We set upper and lower control limits in a manner similar to *p*-charts. Two things to note: (1) The lower control limit cannot be negative. We can never have less than zero defects. (2) When the lower control limit is not zero, and the number of defects is less than the *LCL*, then the system is out of control in a good way. We want to find the assignable cause. Find what was unique about this event that caused things to work out so well. Then change the process so that it is done that way every time.

What are the implications of narrowing the control limits in a process control chart?

What determines whether a process is capable of producing the products or services that customers demand?

Process Capability
Sometimes we remove as many sources of variation from a process as we can, and it still produces too many defectives. Say we are making components of automatic transmissions and no matter how we try, we cannot consistently produce parts that conform to the close tolerances required. There are three choices:

1. Use an entirely different process to produce the components.
2. Redesign the transmission so that it will work even when assembled with the variations produced by the existing process.
3. Change the transmission design so that it does not use these components.

Sample Size Considerations

Economic Implications

- Increased sample size increases sample accuracy and cost.

p-Charts versus *x*-Charts

- *p*-charts — quality attributes are easier to measure
- *p*-charts — sample size must be large enough to detect at least one defective item on the average
- *x*-charts — require smaller sample sizes, because each observation contributes more information
- *x*-charts — unless the variable is very expensive to measure, *x*-charts are usually less expensive to utilize.

Degree of Control

- As the sample size increases, the control limits narrow.
- Larger sample sizes make it more probable to detect a shift in the process average.
- This is another trade-off: cost of sampling versus cost of not detecting a shift in process average.

Homogeneity

- To avoid masking assignable causes, sample should be homogeneous
  - same workers, shift, machine, raw material supplier

Process Capability

- Control limits are based on the mean and variability of the *sampling distribution*, not the design specifications.

"Process capability refers to the ability of the process to meet the design specifications for a product or service." p. 198

Defining Process Capability

A process is capable when

- The specified tolerance width is greater than the range of actual process outputs.

and

- The process is centered near the nominal or target value.

Process Capability Ratio

- Compares the tolerance width (upper spec – lower spec) to the range of actual process outputs. The portion of a distribution within $\pm 3\ \sigma$ of the mean will include the vast majority (99.74%) of the actual process outputs.
- The process is capable when the ratio

$$C_p = \frac{\text{Upper specification} - \text{Lower specification}}{6\sigma} \geq 1.00$$

- Process capability ratios greater than one (say 1.33) allow for some shift in the process distribution before bad output is generated.

Process Capability Index

- Indicates whether the process is sufficiently centered by measuring the distance between the process center and the specification limits and then comparing that to 3σ.
- The process capable index is

$$C_{pk} = \text{Minimum of}\left[\frac{\bar{\bar{x}} - \text{Lower specification}}{3\sigma}, \frac{\text{Upper specification} - \bar{\bar{x}}}{3\sigma}\right]$$

- If the Process capability index is less than one, the process center is too close to one of the specification limits, and will generate too many defects.

Determining the Capability of a Process Using Continuous Improvement

Step 1. Collect data, calculate mean and standard deviation for process.

Step 2. Construct process control charts.

Step 3. Compare random samples to control limits. Eliminate assignable causes and recalculate control limits as appropriate until 20 consecutive random samples fall within the control limits. This indicates that process is in statistical control.

Step 4. Calculate process capability ratio and process capability index. If process is capable, document process and monitor output using control charts. If not capable, eliminate causes of variation and recalculate control limits. Return to step 3.

Process Capability Exercise

(Solution is on Study Guide page 83.)

Webster Chemical's nominal weight for filling tubes of caulk is 8.00 ounces ± 0.60 ounces. The target process capability ratio is 1.33. The current distribution of the filling process is centered on 8.054 ounces with a standard deviation of 0.192 ounces. Compute the process capability ratio and process capability index to assess whether the filling process is capable and set properly.

How can quality engineering help us improve the quality of products and services?

Quality Engineering

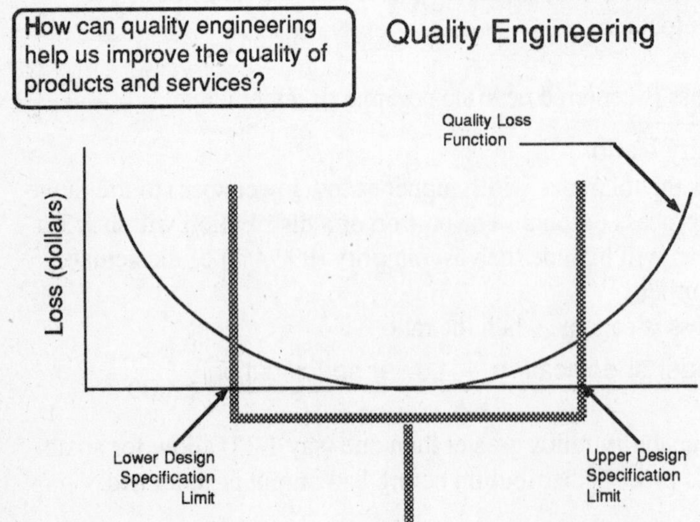

- An approach combining engineering and statistical methods to *optimize* product design and manufacturing processes.
- Before Taguchi, assumed goal was to produce products falling anywhere between design tolerances.
- Quality loss function is optimum (zero) when product is exactly on the target value.
- Continually search for ways to reduce all variablility.

Multiple-Choice Questions

1. Control charts can be useful for evaluating which of the following characteristics of quality?
   A. Conformance to specifications
   B. Psychological impressions
   C. Support
   D. Value

2. Control charts are used primarily to
   A. inspect quality into products and services.
   B. prevent defects.
   C. remove common causes of variation.
   D. weed out defects.

3. A distribution may be characterized by
   A. the mean, spread, and shape.
   B. the process capability ratio.
   C. the total area under the curve.
   D. whether it is a tax-exempt return of capital.

4. Which of the following is true?
   A. Common causes of variation skew the distribution of outputs.
   B. Measuring variables is generally easier than counting attributes.
   C. No two products or services are exactly alike.
   D. The underlying sampling distribution for p-charts is the Poisson distribution.

5. A process is said to be in statistical control when
   A. the dimensions of its distribution don't change over time.
   B. the process capability ratio ≥ 1.0.
   C. the process capability index ≥ 1.0
   D. B and C

6. Which of the following is a quality attribute?
   A. The percentage of oil in potato chips.
   B. The proportion of crumbled potato chips.
   C. The weight of potato chips in a bag.
   D. Several brief speeches honoring a valued employee at her retirement celebration.

7. Inspection stations should be located
   A. after each step in the process.
   B. before costly operations.
   C. as needed to inspect quality into the product.
   D. to rework defectives at the time they occur.

(Multiple-choice answers appear on page 81.)

Questions 8 and 9.

At the end of each semester a professor asks a multiple-choice question to determine whether a large class of students will pass. She takes a random sample of eight student responses to the question. If more than one of these responses are wrong, the class is rejected as a bad lot. One semester Larry, Curly, Shep, and Moe (the Stooge brothers) somehow managed to enroll in the class. As luck would have it, Larry, Curly and Shep are included in the random sample.

8. Which of the following is true?
   A. The quality characteristic examined by the professor is a variable.
   B. The professor is using acceptance sampling to prevent defectives from occurring.
   C. A Type I error will probably occur.
   D. A Type II error will probably occur.

9. Which type of control chart(s) appropriately display the data for the above situation?
   A. a c-chart *or* a p-chart.
   B. an R-chart.
   C. an x-chart.
   D. an R-chart *and* an x-chart.

10. Which of the following, taken by itself, will *increase* the probabilty that a p-chart will detect when a process average has shifted?
    A. Decrease sample size.
    B. Decrease z.
    C. Decrease the frequency of sampling.
    D. None of the above.

11. When a process increases from four-sigma to six-sigma capability, the process center
    A. can shift substantially without being detected.
    B. can shift substantially without producing defectives.
    C. the design specification tolerances narrow.
    D. the design specification tolerances widen.

12. According to Genichi Taguchi, the quality loss function is minimized
    A. when the process capability index equals zero.
    B. when the process capability ratio equals one.
    C. when the product dimensions fall anywhere within the design tolerance.
    D. when the product dimensions fall exactly on the nominal or target value.

Problems

Control Charts for Variables

$UCL_R = D_4\overline{R}$

$LCL_R = D_3\overline{R}$

$UCL_{\overline{x}} = \overline{\overline{x}} + A_2\overline{R}$

$LCL_{\overline{x}} = \overline{\overline{x}} - A_2\overline{R}$

1. The Low-Cal Potato Chip Company makes, as you might guess, reduced calorie potato chips. Low calories are achieved by slicing chips to an average thickness of 500 microns. When the process is in control, the historical average range for a sample size of nine is 100 microns. Low-Cal takes three samples of nine chips, with the following results. Is the process in control?

Sample	Average Thickness	Range	Is the Process in Control?
1	520	157	
2	480	12	
3	490	98	

Control Charts for Attributes

$UCL_p = \overline{p} + z\sigma_p$

$LCL_p = \overline{p} - z\sigma_p$

$\sigma_p = \sqrt{\frac{\overline{p}(1-\overline{p})}{n}}$

2. The Gigantic Electric Company makes light bulbs. The process makes, on the average, 5% defectives. Using SPC *p*-charts, with *UCL* and *LCL* set at three standard deviations from the process mean, and a sample size of 304, Gigantic Electric takes three samples and asks whether the process is under control.

Sample	Number of Defects	Is the Process in Control?
1	18	
2	30	
3	3	

$UCL_c = \overline{c} + z\sigma_c$

$LCL_c = \overline{c} - z\sigma_c$

$\sigma_c = \sqrt{\overline{c}}$

3. The Burl Schwab Company paints automobiles. Burl uses SPC *c*-charts to control the painting process. He counts the number of paint defects on a randomly sampled auto and plots that number on a chart with *UCL* and *LCL* set at three standard deviations. When the process is in statistical control the average number of defects for the painting process is 16. Burl inspected three cars and found the number of defects shown in the table. Is the process still in statistical control?

Auto	Number of Defects	Is the Process in Control?
1	18	
2	30	
3	3	

Solutions

$UCL_R = D_4\overline{R}$

$LCL_R = D_3\overline{R}$

$UCL_{\overline{x}} = \overline{\overline{x}} + A_2\overline{R}$

$LCL_{\overline{x}} = \overline{\overline{x}} - A_2\overline{R}$

1. Low-Cal Potato Chip Company.

$$UCL_{\overline{x}} = \overline{\overline{x}} + A_2\overline{R} = 500 + 0.337(100) = 533.7$$

$$LCL_{\overline{x}} = \overline{\overline{x}} - A_2\overline{R} = 500 - 0.337(100) = 466.3$$

$$UCL_R = D_4\overline{R} = 1.816 \times 100 = 181.6$$

$$UCL_R = D_3\overline{R} = 0.184 \times 100 = 18.4$$

Average Thickness	Range	Average within limits?	Range within limits?
520	157	Yes	Yes
480	12	Yes	**No**
490	98	Yes	Yes

The range in the second sample is smaller than expected. Perhaps the measuring device is not accurately recording potato chip thickness.

$\sigma_p = \sqrt{\dfrac{\overline{p}(1-\overline{p})}{n}}$

$UCL_p = \overline{p} + z\sigma_p$

$LCL_p = \overline{p} - z\sigma_p$

2. The Gigantic Electric Company. $\overline{p} = 5\%$, $n = 304$

$$\sigma_p = \sqrt{\frac{\overline{p}(1-\overline{p})}{n}} = \sqrt{\frac{0.05(0.95)}{304}} = 0.0125$$

$$UCL_p = \overline{p} + z\sigma_p = 0.05 + [3(0.0125)] = 0.0875$$

$$LCL_p = \overline{p} + z\sigma_p = 0.05 - [3(0.0125)] = 0.0125$$

Number of Defects	Proportion Defective	Is Process in Control?
18	0.0592 ie. (18/304)	**Yes**
30	0.0987	**No** (too high)
3	0.0099	**No** (too low!)

$UCL_c = \overline{c} + z\sigma_c$

$LCL_c = \overline{c} - z\sigma_c$

$\sigma_c = \sqrt{\overline{c}}$

3. Burl Schwab Company. $\overline{c} = 16$, $\sqrt{\overline{c}} = 4$.

$$UCL_c = \overline{c} + z\sigma_c = \overline{c} + z\sqrt{\overline{c}}$$
$$= 16 + 3\sqrt{16} = 28$$

$$LCL_c = \overline{c} - z\sigma_c = \overline{c} - z\sqrt{\overline{c}}$$
$$= 16 - 3\sqrt{16} = 4$$

Number of Defects	Is Process in Control?
18	**Yes**
30	**No** (too high)
3	**No** (too low!)

Multiple Choice Answers

1. A	8. C
2. B	9. A
3. A	10. B
4. C	11. B
5. A	12. D
6. B	
7. B	

Solutions to Exercises:

1. Webster Chemical. (control charts for variables)

a. $\overline{\overline{x}} = 8.00,\ \overline{R} = 0.38,\ n = 8$

From Table 5.1:

$$UCL_R = D_4\overline{R} = 1.864(0.38) = 0.708$$
$$LCL_R = D_3\overline{R} = 0.136(0.38) = 0.052$$
$$UCL_{\overline{x}} = \overline{\overline{x}} + A_2\overline{R} = 8.0 + 0.373(0.38) = 8.142$$
$$LCL_{\overline{x}} = \overline{\overline{x}} - A_2\overline{R} = 8.0 - 0.373(0.38) = 7.858$$

Referring to the table, the range for the first observation is above the upper control limit, the range for the sixth observation is below the lower control limit, and the average for the second observation is slightly above the upper control limit.

	Tube Number									
Sample	1	2	3	4	5	6	7	8	Avg.	Range
1	7.98	8.34	8.02	7.94	8.44	7.68	7.81	8.11	8.040	0.76
2	8.23	8.12	7.98	8.41	8.31	8.18	7.99	8.06	8.160	0.43
3	7.89	7.77	7.91	8.04	8.00	7.89	7.93	8.09	7.940	0.32
4	8.24	8.18	7.83	8.05	7.90	8.16	7.97	8.07	8.050	0.41
5	7.87	8.13	7.92	7.99	8.10	7.81	8.14	7.88	7.980	0.33
6	8.13	8.14	8.11	8.13	8.14	8.12	8.13	8.14	8.130	0.03
									8.050	0.38

b. We delete the sixth observation and recalculate the control limits. The ranges, including the range for the first sample are now all within the revised control limits, and the process average for the second sample now falls just inside of the revised control limits. If we had 20 consecutive observations fall within the control limits, we could say that this process is in statistical contol.

$$\overline{R} = \frac{(0.76 + 0.43 + 0.32 + 0.41 + 0.33)}{5} = 0.45$$

$$UCL_R = D_4\overline{R} = 1.864(0.45) = 0.839$$
$$LCL_R = D_3\overline{R} = 0.136(0.45) = 0.061$$
$$UCL_{\overline{x}} = \overline{\overline{x}} + A_2\overline{R} = 8.0 + 0.373(0.45) = 8.168$$
$$LCL_{\overline{x}} = \overline{\overline{x}} - A_2\overline{R} = 8.0 - 0.373(0.45) = 7.832$$

2. Webster Chemical. (p-chart)

$$n = 144,\ \bar{p} = \frac{72}{20(144)} = 0.025$$

$$\sigma_p = \sqrt{\frac{\bar{p}(1-\bar{p})}{n}} = \sqrt{\frac{0.025(1-0.025)}{144}} = 0.013$$

$$UCL_p = \bar{p} + z\sigma_p = 0.025 + 3(0.013) = 0.064$$

$$LCL_p = \bar{p} - z\sigma_p = 0.025 - 3(0.013) = -0.014, \text{ adjusted to zero}$$

The highest proportion of defectives occurs in sample #10, but is still within the control limits.

$p_{10} = 9/144 = 0.0625$

The process is in statistical control.

3. Webster Chemical (*c*-chart)

$$\bar{c} = \frac{(6+5+0+4+6+4+1+6+5+0+9+2)}{12} = 4$$

$$\sigma_c = \sqrt{\bar{c}} = \sqrt{4} = 2$$

$$UCL_c = \bar{c} + z\sigma_c = 4 + (2 \times 2) = 8$$

$$LCL_c = \bar{c} - z\sigma_c = 4 - (2 \times 2) = 0$$

The eleventh tube has too many lumps (9), so the process is probably out of control.

4. Webster Chemical

Process capability ratio:

$$C_p = \frac{\text{Upper specification} - \text{Lower specification}}{6\sigma} = \frac{8.6 - 7.4}{6(0.192)} = 1.0417$$

Process capability index:

$$C_{pk} = \text{minimum of } \frac{x - \text{Lower specification}}{3\sigma},\ \frac{\text{Upper specification} - x}{3\sigma}$$

$$\frac{8.054 - 7.400}{3(0.192)} = 1.135,\quad \frac{8.600 - 8.054}{3(0.192)} = 0.948$$

$$C_{pk} = 0.948$$

The process is not capable. Defectives will be produced even while the process is in statistical control.

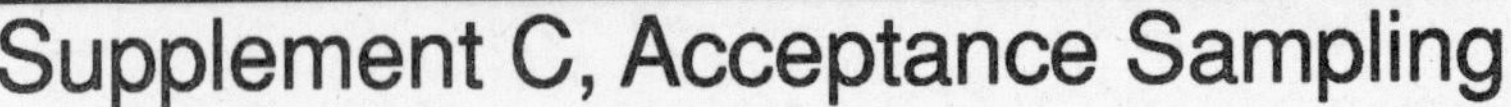

Supplement C, Acceptance Sampling

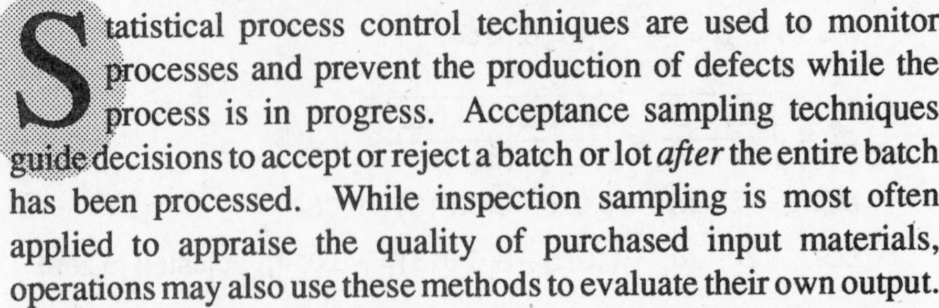

Statistical process control techniques are used to monitor processes and prevent the production of defects while the process is in progress. Acceptance sampling techniques guide decisions to accept or reject a batch or lot *after* the entire batch has been processed. While inspection sampling is most often applied to appraise the quality of purchased input materials, operations may also use these methods to evaluate their own output.

Acceptance sampling is a lose-lose situation brought on by adversarial relationships between producers and consumers. When consumers think of this as a zero-sum (win-lose) game, they may be tempted to specify sampling plans that shift risks onto the producer. However, the producer would undoubtedly retaliate by increasing prices to cover insurance costs for those increased risks. The net effect is increased costs to both parties. Lose-lose.

Remember, "The customer *always* pays." ... and (s)he always pays for *all* costs. Over the long run, producers must recover all costs, or go out of business. Producer's costs include the costs of making defectives (whether or not they are shipped to the customer), and include the costs of making good products that are rejected by poorly designed sampling plans.

Acceptance Plan Decisions

- The consumer, sometimes in cooperation with the producer, specifies the parameters of the acceptance sampling plan.
- The two parameters which completely specify a sampling plan are
  - n, the sample size
  - c, the acceptance number

Definitions

1. Producer, origin of the material, possesses material first.
2. Consumer, destination of the material, possesses it second.
3. Sampling plan, a decision guide to control the risks of the producer and consumer.
4. Acceptable quality level (AQL), a percentage of defects stated by the consumer in the contract, and the aim of the producer.
5. Lot tolerance proportion defective (LTPD), the worst level the customer can tolerate. The customer would not be happy, but probably wouldn't sue.
6. α, the producer's risk. The probability of making a type I error, which is rejecting a good lot.
7. β, the consumer's risk. The probability of making a type II error, which is accepting a bad lot.

Mnemonic: The producer has the material *first*. "α" is the *first* letter of the Greek alphabet. Alpha is the probability of making an error of the *first* type. A *Type I* error results in rejecting good lots, which injures the producer. Everything having to do with the consumer is *second*: β, Type II.

Acceptable Quality Level ?

A student from Japan had some difficulty with our language, but his English was far better than my Japanese. After every class he would stop by my office and we would struggle through the notes until he understood the terminology. He eventually got an "A" in the course, but I don't think he ever grasped the concept of an acceptable quality level greater than zero. Why would customers *desire* to pay for some proportion of defects? My explanations couldn't overcome cultural differences.

There is a story about a Japanese supplier enclosing a separate package of defectives along with an otherwise perfect shipment. "Here are defects you requested, but why do you ask us to destroy these?"

AQL is an old technique. Remember, we used to think that each level of quality had some price. See Crosby, *Quality is Free* reference on text p. 168. So if each quality level has a price (and perfect quality is too costly), what level of quality is the customer willing to pay for? That is AQL.

Quality and Risk Decisions

Acceptable quality level (AQL)

- Quality level *desired* by the consumer (emphasis added)
  - producer's risk, (α) is the probability a shipment having exactly this level of quality (the AQL) will be rejected when the lot is sampled using the specified sampling plan (*n*, *c*).
  - rejecting a good (AQL) lot is a Type I error
- Consumers also desire low producer's risk because sending good materials back to the supplier
  1. disrupts the consumer's production processes due to material shortages
  2. increases lead time
  3. creates poor supplier relations

Lot tolerance proportion defective

- The worst level of quality that the consumer can tolerate.

  "That's all I can stands. I can't stands nomore!" ... Popeye
  - Consumer's risk, (β) is the probability a shipment having exactly this level of quality (the LTPD) will be accepted when the lot is sampled using the specified sampling plan (*n*, *c*).
  - Accepting a bad (LTPD) lot is a Type II error.

Sampling Plans

Single-Sampling Plans (for attributes)

- The plan states the sample size, *n*, and the *acceptable* number of defectives found in that sample, *c*.
- The accept-reject decision is based on the results of one sample.

Single-Sampling Procedure for Determining Whether to Accept a Lot

1. Take a random sample, *n*, from a *large* lot.
2. Measure the quality characteristic.
3. a. If the sample passes the test (defects $\leq c$), accept the lot.
   b. If the sample fails (defects $> c$),
      1. there may be complete inspection of the lot, or
      2. the *entire lot* is rejected.

Samples are not perfectly representative of lots. A good lot could be rejected if the sample happens to include an unusually large number of defects. A bad lot could be accepted if the quality in the sample is better than that of the lot.

Double-sampling plan.

- The double-sampling plan states two sample sizes, (n_1 and n_2), and two acceptance numbers (c_1 and c_2).
- Double-sampling plans reduce costs of inspection for lots with very low or very high proportion defective.

Double-Sampling Procedure for Determining Whether to Accept a Lot

1. Take a random sample of relatively small size n_1, from a *large* lot.
2. Measure the quality characteristic to find the number of defectives in the orignal sample.
3. a. If the sample passes the test (defects $\leq c_1$), accept the lot.
   b. If the sample fails (defects $> c_2$), the *entire lot* is rejected.
   c. If $c_1 <$ defects $\leq c_2$, go to step 4.
4. a. Take a larger second random sample, n_2. Compare the total number of defects found in both samples to c_2.
   b. If the sample passes the test (defects $\leq c_2$), accept the lot.
   c. If the sample fails (defects $> c_2$), the *entire lot* is rejected.

Sequential-Sampling Plan

- A refinement of the double-sampling plan.
- Results of random samples, tested one-by-one, are compared to sequential-sampling chart.
- Chart guides decision to reject, accept, or continue sampling
- Average number of items inspected (ANI) is generally lower with sequential sampling

Operating Characteristic (OC) Curves

- Perfect discrimination between good and bad lots requires 100% inspection.
- Select sample size n and acceptance number c to achieve the level of perfomance specified by the AQL, α, LTPD, and β.

Drawing the OC Curve

- Each item inspected is either defective or not defective (binomial)
- When $n \geq 20$ and $p \leq 0.05$, the Poisson distribution approximates the binomial distribution.
- The Poisson distribution is used to prepare (OC) curves.
- The OC curve shows the probability of *accepting* a lot P_a, as a dependent function of p, the true proportion of defectives in the lot.
- For every possible combination of n and c, there exists a unique operating characteristics curve. (But you will have to draw it.)

Steps for Drawing an Operating Characteristics Curve, Given n and c:

1. Select a value for p, the true proportion of defectives in the lot. Calculate $\lambda = np$. λ is the average number of defectives we would expect to find in samples of size n taken from a lot with p proportion of defectives.
2. Find λ in the left column of the Poisson distribution.
3. Read across that row to the c column specified by the sampling plan.
4. The probability of exactly c or fewer defects occurring in a sample of size n is found at the intersection of the λ row and the c column. Remember, if there are c or fewer defects, we *accept* the lot. We have found P_a, the probability of *accepting* the lot for the selected value of p. Plot this point on a graph with P_a on the vertical axis, and p on the horizontal axis. Return to step 1, selecting a different value for p, and continue this process for a range of p values.

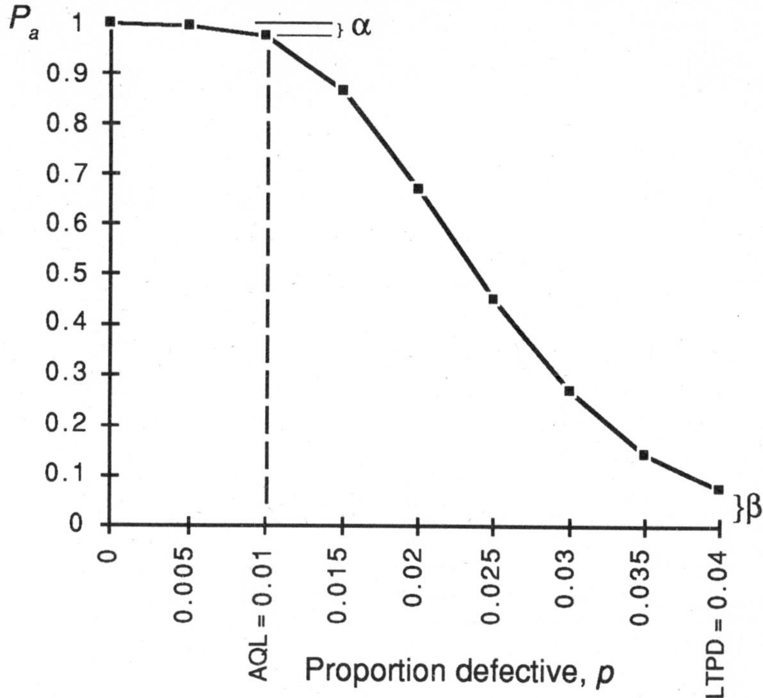

Once we have the OC curve, it is easy to find α and β.

β is the probability of *accepting* the lot when *p* is equal to LTPD. β is found on the OC curve directly above the point on the horizontal axis where *p* equals LTPD. In other words if *p*, the true proportion of defectives in the lot, equals LTPD, the producer sent a bad lot. The consumer doesn't know it because the producer and consumer are adversaries. β is the probability that the customer will find *c* or fewer defects when taking a single random sample of size *n* from that bad lot. And if that happens, the customer will be fooled into accepting the bad lot. The customer would be making a Type II error.

Say the producer has sent a lot with a true proportion of defectives equal to AQL (a good, but not perfect lot). Because they are adversaries, the consumer can not simply take the producer's word that this is a good lot. If the consumer takes a single sample of size *n* from the good lot, and finds more than *c* defects, the customer will *reject* the good lot (making a Type I error). α is the probability of *rejecting* a good (*p* equals AQL) lot. However, the OC curve only shows the probability of *accepting* lots. Therefore, we must first find the probability of accepting a good lot (on the OC curve directly above the point on the horizontal axis where *p* equals AQL). Then we subtract the probability of accepting the good lot from 100% in order to find the probability of rejecting it.

Explaining Changes in the OC Curve

Sample Size Effect

"Increasing *n* while holding *c* constant increases the producer's risk and reduces the consumer's risk." p. 222

Acceptance Level Effect

"Increasing *c* while holding *n* constant decreases the producer's risk and increases the consumer's risk." p. 223

Sampling Plan Changes			OC Curve Changes	
Sample Size, n	Acceptance number, c	Acceptance proportion, c/n	Producer's risk (α)	Consumer's risk (β)
Increases	Unchanged	Decreases	Increases	Decreases
Unchanged	**Increases**	Increases	Decreases	Increases
Increases	**Increases**	Unchanged	Decreases	Decreases

Average Outgoing Quality

- AOQ is the expected (or **A**verage) proportion of defects that a particular sampling plan would allow to pass through (**Q**uality **O**utgoing from) inspection.
- Rectified inspection — defects found during the sampling process are removed and reworked or replaced with conforming material.
- Rejected lots are subjected to 100% inspection.
- Different sampling plans have different *AOQ*'s and *AOQL*'s.

With rectified inspection, the average outgoing quality (*AOQ*) exhibits an interesting phenomenon. When the incoming material is either very good or very bad, the material leaving the inspection area will be very good in *either* case! Very good lots are passed and contain few defects. Very bad lots are likely to fail, and complete inspection replaces the nonconforming material.

However when incoming material is neither good nor bad (just ugly), there is a fair chance the ugly lot will pass the sampling test, and the material leaving the inspection area will be ugly. As incoming material quality varies from good to bad, at some mid-point (ugly) the average outgoing quality will be at its worst. This "worst" level of quality is called the average outgoing quality limit (*AOQL*). The *AOQL* is found by calculating *AOQ* at several values for *p*, then setting *AOQL* equal to the highest occurring *AOQ*.

In the example at left, the AOQL appears to be about 1.2 % when *p* is .02.

EQUATION C.1

$$AOQ = \frac{p(P_a)(N-n)}{N}$$

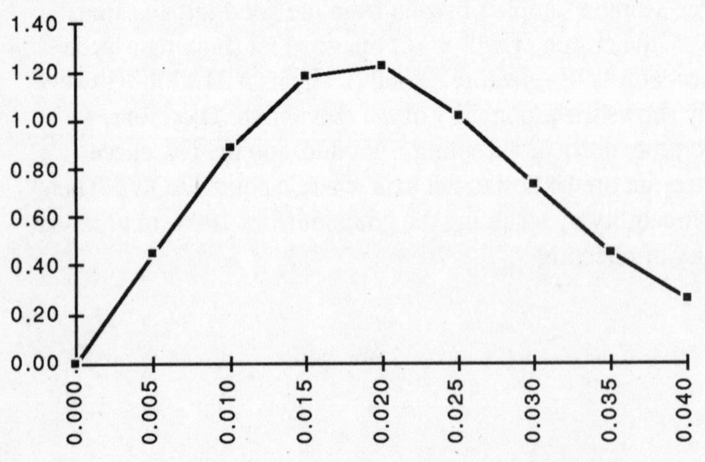

Computers and Statistical Quality Control

- Computers access data and develop control charts, acceptance sampling plans, and frequency diagrams and correlations.

Common Areas of Difficulty in Understanding Quality Control Concepts:

1. Do not confuse the "lot", which is the entire shipment, with the "sample," which is a small subset of the lot.
2. The proportion of defectives found in the sample is *probably not* exactly equal to the proportion of defectives in the lot.
3. Unless we do 100% inspection, we do not learn the value for p, which is the true *but unknown* proportion of defectives in the lot.
4. c is *not* the smallest number of defectives that result in rejecting the lot. When a sampling plan says: "Test 100 light bulbs. If three or more fail, *reject* the lot," $c = 2$, *not 3*. We will *accept* no more than 2 defects. Since we are dealing with attributes, we will never find a fractional number of defects. c is one unit less than the integer number of defects resulting in rejection.
5. When the actual number of defects is exactly equal to the acceptable number of defects c, *accept* the lot.
6. Say $n = 100$ and defects = 2. We make the accept-reject decision by comparing defects to the value of c *only*. Comparisons of defects/n, (0.02), to values for α, AQL, β or LTPD are irrelevant and wrong.
7. Sampling controls risks. It does not eliminate them.
8. If it isn't called by the same name, it isn't referring to the same concept. Concepts students often confuse:
   - α *is not* equal to AQL. They are related (Poisson distribution), and we must know one to find the other, but they are not equal.
   - Similarly, β *is not* equal to LTPD.
   - α is the producer's risk. It is *not* the same as the acceptance proportion, c/n.
   - ***The AQL <u>is not</u> equal to the acceptance proportion, c/n.***
   - α and β *are not* always 5% and 10%, respectively. They *do not* add to 100%.

Multiple-Choice Questions

1. As more firms initiate TQM programs and work closely with suppliers to ensure high levels of quality,
   A. the need for acceptance sampling will decrease.
   B. the need for acceptance sampling will increase.
   C. LTPDs will tend to increase.
   D. acceptance numbers will tend to increase.

2. When the sampling plan is written into a contract or purchase order, the producer of the item strives to achieve
   A. the AOQL.
   B. the AQL.
   C. the LTPD.
   D. zero defects.

3. When a sampling plan results in low consumer's risk and high producer's risk, the consumer can expect which of the following:
   A. decreased lead time.
   B. decreased chances of material shortages.
   C. improved supplier relationships.
   D. higher costs for materials.

4. Two levels of quality are considered in the design of an acceptance sampling plan.
   A. α and β
   B. AQL and LTPD
   C. AOQ and AOQL
   D. n and c

5. Lot tolerance proportion defective (LTPD) can be defined as
   A. the acceptable quality level.
   B. the dividing line between good and bad lots.
   C. the probability of accepting a bad lot.
   D. the worst quality level the consumer can live with (tolerate).

6. It is in the consumer's best interest to minimize
   A. α
   B. β
   C. ANI
   D. the use of sequential-sampling plans.

7. The average outgoing quality is useful
   A. as a goal for the producer.
   B. as a performance check for sampling plans.
   C. to evaluate alternative suppliers.
   D. to level the quality when process centers drift.

8. At the end of each semester a professor asks a multiple-choice question to determine whether a large class of students will pass. She takes a random sample of eight student responses to the question. If two or more responses are wrong, the class is rejected as a bad lot. In this sampling plan, "c" is
   A. eight.
   B. one.
   C. usually the correct answer to multiple choice questions.
   D. two.

9. An operating characteristics curve
   A. describes how well a sampling plan discriminates between good and bad lots.
   B. is drawn using information available from the binomial distribution table.
   C. shows the probability of rejecting a lot for a range of proportions defective.
   D. shows the expected average proportion of defectives after inspection for a range of proportions defective.

10. In attribute sampling, which one of the following, taken by itself, will increase the consumer's risk?
    A. Increase sample size (say from $n = 50$ to 100).
    B. Increase "c" (say from $c = 2$ to $c = 4$).
    C. Increase AQL (say from 1% to 2%).
    D. Increase LTPD (say from 6% to 8%).

11. A single-sampling plan has $n = 300$ and $c = 4$. A sample is taken and four items are found to be defective. What should be done?
    A. "n" and "c" should be increased while maintaining the same acceptance proportion.
    B. The lot should be rejected.
    C. The lot should be accepted.
    D. "c" should be reduced to 3 and another sample taken.

12. ________ defective items found during the inspection process are replaced with conforming material.
    A. Scrap losses decrease when
    B. The AOQ decreases when
    C. The ANI decreases when
    D. With rectified inspection

(Multiple-choice answers appear on page 92.)

Problems

1. Grover supplies cookies to the Cookie Monster in very large lot sizes. Grover and the Cookie Monster want to develop an attribute sampling plan with AQL = 1% and LTPD = 4%. The Count volunteers to be the quality control inspector. He will count 100 of each lot of cookies and will also count crumbled cookies. If the Count finds 3 or more crumbled cookies in the sample of 100, he will reject the lot.

   a. If we were to use the Poisson distribution to calculate the Cookie Monster's risk, we would first have to find λ. Given that $\lambda = np$ and $n = 100$, what is λ?

   b. What is the acceptance proportion, c/n?

   c. Use the Poisson distribution to calculate Cookie Monster's risk.

2. The AQL is 2%. The LTPD is 5%, $c = 4$, $n = 150$. Find the producer's risk.

   a. First calculate $\lambda = np$.

   b. Then use the Poisson curve to find the producer's risk.

3. The lot size is 200 units, the sampling plan is $n = 60$ and $c = 4$,

   a. If the true proportion defective p is 4%, calculate the average outgoing quality, AOQ.

   b. Calculate the AOQ for a range of proportions defective p, and determine the AOQL.

Solutions

1. Grover and the Cookie Monster. This is an attribute sampling plan with AQL = 1%, LTPD = 4%,

   $n = 100$, and **(gottcha!?) c = 2, not 3!**

   "If the Count finds 3 or more crumbled cookies in the sample of 100, he will reject the lot."

   In other words, the most he will *accept* is 2. Therefore $c = 2$.

   a. Calculate the Cookie Monster's risk. Cookie Monster is, true to form, the consumer of cookies. The consumer's risk is β, which is the distance below the OC curve drawn at the LTPD. To find λ, given that $\lambda = np$, and $n = 100$, all we need is p. When finding β, p = LTPD= 4%.

      Therefore:

      $\lambda = np = 100 * 0.04 =$ **4.0.**

   b. What is the acceptance proportion, c/n?

      $c/n = 2 / 100 =$ **0.02**

   c. Use the Poisson distribution to calculate Cookie Monster's risk.

      $\lambda = np =$ **4.0**

      $c = 2$

      Using the Poisson table, move down the left column to $\lambda = np = 4$, read across to the column for $c = 2$. Be careful that you don't wind up in the $c = 1$ column, the table starts with $c = 0$. The probability Cookie will accept a lot as bad as the LTPD is $\beta = 0.238$ or 23.8%.

2. The AQL is 2%. The LTPD is 5%, $c = 4$, $n = 150$. Find the producer's risk.

   a. First calculate $\lambda = np$

      When finding α, p = AQL = 2%. $n = 150$

      $\lambda = np = 150 * 0.02 =$ **3.0**

   b. Then use the Poisson table to find the producer's risk. Using the Poisson table, move down the left column to $\lambda = np = 3$, read across to the column for $c = 4$. Again, be careful that you're in the correct column. The value from the table is 0.815. There is an 81.5% probability of accepting the lot. The probability of *rejecting* a lot as good as the AQL is 1 – 0.815 = 0.185. $\alpha = 0.185$ or 18.5%.

Multiple Choice Answers

1. A	8. B
2. B	9. A
3. D	10. B
4. B	11. C
5. D	12. D
6. C	
7. B	

EQUATION C.1

$$AOQ = \frac{p(P_a)(N-n)}{N}$$

3. The lot size is 200 units, the sampling plan is $n = 60$ and $c = 4$,

   a. If the true proportion defective p is 4%, calculate the average outgoing quality, *AOQ*.

   P_a is found from the Poisson table, $np = (60)(.04) = 2.4$, and $c = 4$.

   $P_a = .904$

$$AOQ = \frac{p(P_a)(N-n)}{N}$$
$$= \frac{0.04(0.904)(200-60)}{200} = .02531$$

   b. To find the AOQL, it is helpful to set up these repetitive calculations in a table format.

p	np	P_a	$(N-n)/N$	AOQ
0.010	0.6	1.000	0.70	0.00700
0.020	1.2	0.992	0.70	0.01389
0.030	1.8	0.964	0.70	0.02024
0.040	2.4	0.904	0.70	0.02531
0.050	3.0	0.815	0.70	0.02853
0.060	3.6	0.706	0.70	**0.02965**
0.070	4.2	0.590	0.70	0.02891
0.080	4.8	0.476	0.70	0.02666
0.090	5.4	0.373	0.70	0.02350
0.100	6.0	0.285	0.70	0.02000

Average Outgoing Quality x 100%

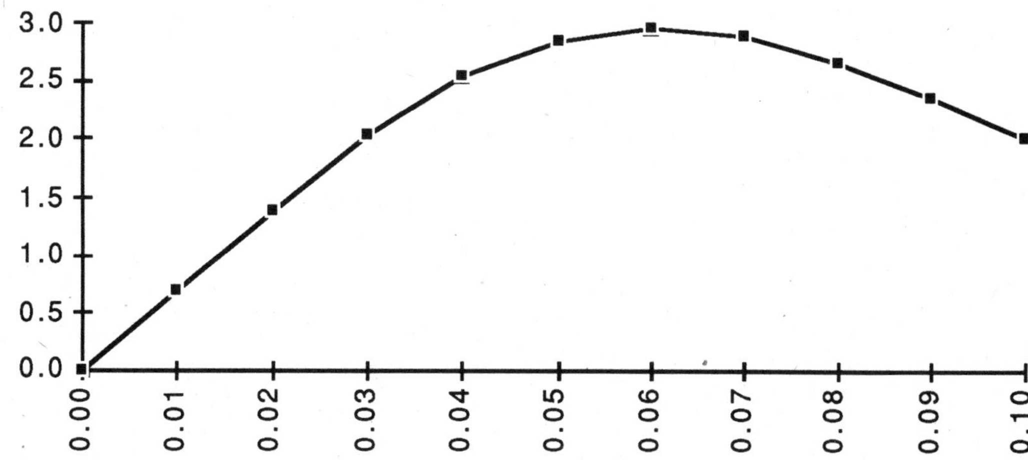

Chapter Six, Work-Force Management

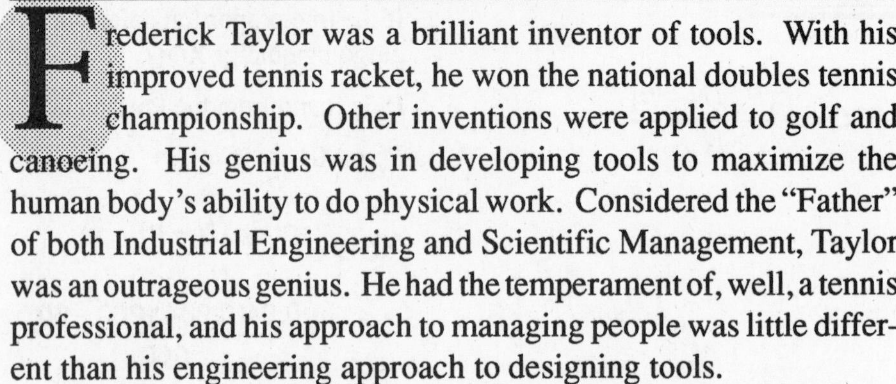
Frederick Taylor was a brilliant inventor of tools. With his improved tennis racket, he won the national doubles tennis championship. Other inventions were applied to golf and canoeing. His genius was in developing tools to maximize the human body's ability to do physical work. Considered the "Father" of both Industrial Engineering and Scientific Management, Taylor was an outrageous genius. He had the temperament of, well, a tennis professional, and his approach to managing people was little different than his engineering approach to designing tools.

Although his intentions were honorable, Taylor's scientific approach to management ignored behavioral considerations. Taylor viewed specialization as a means to efficiency, efficiency as a means to increased production, and increased production as a means to economic gain, which would be shared between management and labor. And except for that last part about sharing economic gain, his views were widely accepted among managers. Laborers generally disagreed with Taylor's proposals.

Under Taylorism, laborers, who Taylor described as "phlegmatic" and "oxen," specialized in physical work. Workers were not allowed to think, take initiative, or make decisions because mental work was reserved as a management specialty. Taylor said: "What I demand of the worker, is not to produce any longer by his own initiative, but to execute punctiliously the orders given, down to their minutest details." When we consider that even basic literacy was uncommon among laborers in Taylor's time, that Taylor was from the wealthy class, and that his genius in technology and physiology did not extend to sociology, we might (without agreeing with him) understand how he arrived at these views. But even in those times workers resented being treated as mere extensions of machines. Animosity rose to the level of a Congressional hearing, which became so raucous the whole proceeding was stricken from the record. Many of today's management-labor problems are rooted in a century of Taylorism, which reserves thinking to managers and actively discourages worker initiative.

Today, firms trying new approaches to work-force management must first overcome distrust caused by a century of management's abuses. And they must dismantle a corporate culture where mental work and physical work are considered to be specialties of management and labor, respectively. New work-force management approaches encourage worker initiative, decentralize decision making, and value generalist rather than specialist skills. New approaches to job design now recognize both the technical and the social aspects of work.

"In this chapter we discuss both new and traditional approaches to work-force management." p. 232

Is a horizontal organization appropriate for the firm?

Organizational Restructuring

Horizontal Organizations

- Hierarchy and functional boundaries are eliminated
- Organization is managed across functional areas by multidisciplinary teams

Seven Key Elements of Horizontal Organizations

1. Organized around processes
2. Flat organizational hierarchy
3. Management teams
4. Customer-driven performance measures
5. Team-oriented rewards
6. Teams (rather than an individual purchasing agent or account manager) maintain supplier and customer relationships
7. Training programs for all employees

Links to Operations Strategy

- Requires major (painful) cultural transformation
- Decide what it takes to be successful in the marketplace
- Decision should be linked to operations strategy
  - traditional (vertical) organization may suit some mass production industries
    - repetitive activities
    - competitive priority is low cost
  - Flexibility of horizontal organizations is useful when competitive priorities include
    - product development speed
    - high-performance design
    - customization and product variety

Should individual-, team-, or group-based incentive plans be used to improve productivity?

The learning curve shows (in Supplement D) that as work methods improve, workers on piece rate compensation will take home more and more pay for the same level of effort. Eventually management says that methods have changed to the extent to justify a new time study. Standards are raised, and piece-rate pay decreases.

"...piecework incentives actually defeat their purpose of increasing worker productivity because employees will have little incentive to improve their work methods." p. 240.

Under this system the worker, for his own protection must resist, even sabotage management's efforts to improve productivity.

Lesson: Managers must design compensation plans that do not pit the worker's interests against the interests of the organization.

Incentive Plans

- Incentives tend to encourage productivity improvements.
- Traditional incentive schemes reward individual behavior rather than team behavior. These are counterproductive in horizontal organizations.

Individual-based plans

Piece rate

"*Piece rate* is a traditional compensation plan based on output: the number of units created or services performed during a day or week." p. 234

- Does not promote team efforts
- Does not encourage high-quality work
  - Note that workers paid by individual incentives are penalized if they momentarily stop their own work to help someone else for the good of the group or organization.

Pay-for-skills plans

- Reward for skills acquired to make workers more valued as team members
- Supports team efforts

Bonus-point plan

- Points for employee involvement (such as participation in quality circles)
- Rewards based on points earned

Team-based plans

- Incentives tied to production/quality goals

Financial rewards for teams rather than individuals

Public recognition rewards intrinsic desire for excellence

Group-Based plans

- Result in higher productivity, value added exceeds costs of plans

Profit sharing

- Paid on profitability levels of the company as a whole

Gain sharing

- Rewards collective performance of a group
- Promotes group efforts to improve productivity

Training Programs

- Emphasis on efficient process and high quality requires employees having a broad base of skills.

General training

- Leadership, communication, project management, problem solving, mathematics, statistical process control methods, critical thinking, remedial English

Administrative training for team leaders

- Employment practices, performance appraisals, and management skills

Technical training

- Increases skills in aspects of a person's job or a related job

Job Design

"**Job design** specifies a job's content, the employee skills and training needed to perform that job, and the degree of specialization appropriate for the job." p. 237

- Improves efficiency through analysis of the job's work elements
- Improves productivity through consideration of technical and human factors
- Increases the quality of the product or service
- Increases worker satisfaction

Scientific management

- Traditional job design
- Any operation can be improved by
  - breaking operation into components
  - studying each component to improve work methods

> Unfortunately, managers often ignored Taylor in this respect. In the history of management it is not at all unusual for well-intentioned theories to be misapplied. Examples of the horrors of Taylorism are nearly all attributable to misuse of Taylor's ideals.

Frederick Taylor

- Sought the most efficient and effective way to perform tasks
- Dealt primarily with the technical aspects of job design
  - best way to reach, grasp, and move objects
  - number of repetitions before rest
  - best physical position for worker
- Management trains workers in new work methods
- Management is responsible for coordinating work
- Stressed the need for teamwork between management and workers
- Method works only if economic benefits are shared

Job Specialization

- Specialization narrows the range of task

Arguments in Favor of Job Specialization

1. Less training time for limited procedures
2. Repetition leads to faster work pace
3. Lower wages paid to unskilled workers

Arguments Against Job Specialization

1. Low morale, high absenteeism, high turnover, low quality
2. More need for managers to coordinate numerous narrow tasks
3. Specialists have little knowledge about the duties of others. The work force has less flexibility, making it difficult to replace workers (see low morale, high turnover above).

Link the degree of specialization to competitive priorities.

- Specialization tends to support product-focused firms.

Alternatives to Specialization

Reasons People Work

1. Economic needs
2. Social needs
3. Individual needs

In Narrowly Defined Jobs There Are Fewer Opportunities to

1. Control the pace of work
2. Receive gratification from the work
3. Advance to a better position
4. Show initiative
5. Communicate with fellow workers

> Do you see the legacy of Taylor here?

Highly Repetitive Jobs Lead to

1. Boredom
2. Poor job performance
   - high turnover rates
   - absenteeism
   - grievances
   - intentional disruption of production
   - incomplete work assignments

Alternatives to (Remedies for) Specialization

1. Job enlargement — horizontal expansion of responsibility
2. Job rotation — workers exchange jobs, no expansion of responsibility
3. Job enrichment — vertical expansion of responsibility

Work Standards

"Creating a commonly accepted basis for comparison requires development of a **work standard**, or the time required for a trained worker to perform a task following a prescribed method with normal effort and skill." pp. 239–240

- Skill, effort, and stamina vary from one employee to another.

"Generally, you cannot use the time per unit observed over a short period of time for one employee as a standard for an extended period of time for all employees." p. 256

Work Standards as a Management Tool

Ways Managers Use Work Standards

How can work standards be used to achieve continuous improvement in operations?

1. Establishing prices and costs
2. Motivating workers
3. Comparing alternative process designs
4. Scheduling
5. Capacity planning
6. Performance appraisal

Most management problems associated with work standards stem from using them for performance appraisals.

Areas of Controversy

- Standards set "too high" or "too low"

"Some managers believe that employees need to be involved in determining work standards, that time studies dehumanize workers, and that the costs of large industrial engineering staffs and the hidden costs of labor-management conflicts outweigh the benefits of elaborate standards." p. 258

"Eliminate work standards on the shop floor. Substitute leadership."

"I have yet to see a work standard that includes any trace of a system which would help anyone do a better job." ...W. Edwards Deming

- Use of work standards for piecework incentives
  - may defeat their purpose of increased productivity because workers become secretive about work methods devised to increase output
  - workers may increase quantity at the expense of quality

Methods of Work Measurement

 "The key to creating a work standard is defining *normal* performance." p. 241

"**Work measurement** is the process of creating labor standards based on the judgment of skilled observers.

How can time standards be obtained to compare alternative process designs or project future capacity requirements?

Methods of Work Measurement

1. Time study method
2. Elemental standard data
3. Predetermined data approach
4. Work sampling method

The choice of work measurement method depends on which of the six uses the manager has in mind for the information.

Time Study Method

This is the method used by Taylor.

- Time study is the method used most often for setting time standards.
  - Select a repetitive job to be studied which may be
    . bottlenecks
    . time consuming
    . dangerous
    . physically exhausting
    . causing quality problems
  - Obtain the cooperation of the workers.
  - Divide the job into smaller work elements.
  - Using a stopwatch, perform a pilot study.
  - Based on the pilot study, determine whether additional observations are required for the desired precision and confidence level.
  - If necessary, make additional observations.
  - Develop a time standard using performance ratings and allowances for fatigue.

Because of its history, bringing a stop watch onto a production floor is akin to inciting to riot. If the subject is comfortable with a video camera, it is easier and more accurate to tape the observations. The analyst can later determine the work element times from the video, viewing it frame-by-frame if necessary. When an improved work method is developed, the tape can be used as a training aid.

Steps in a Time Study

Step 1. Selecting work elements — each should have definite starting and stopping points. Separate incidental operations from the repetitive work.

Step 2. Timing the elements — Use either the continuous or snap-back method. Irregular occurrences should not be included in calculating the average time.

Step 3. Determining sample size — varies with confidence, precision, and variability of the work element times.

Step 4. Setting the standard — Apply subjective performance rating factor, calculate normal times, normal time for the cycle, and adjust for allowances.

Time Study Exercise

(Solution check appears on Study Guide Page 110.)

Lucy and Ethel have repetitive jobs at the candy factory. Management desires to establish a time standard for this work for which they can be 95% confident to be within ± 6% of the true mean. There are three work elements involved:

Step 1: Selecting Work Elements.

#1: Pick up wrapper paper and wrap once piece of candy.
#2: Put candy in a box, one at a time.
#3: When the box is full (4 pieces), close it and place on conveyor.

Step 2: Timing the Elements.

Select an *average* trained worker: Lucy will have to suffice.

EQUATION 6.2

$$NT = \bar{t}(F)(RF)$$

	Initial Observation Cycle Number, minutes									Select
Element	#1	#2	#3	#4	#5	#6	#7	#8	#9	Time, $\bar{t}$
Wrap #1:	.10	.08	.08	.12	.10	.10	.12	.09	.11	___
Pack #2:	.10	.08	.08	.11	.06	.98*	.17	.11	.09	___
Close #3:	.27	----	----	----	.34	----	----	----	.29	___

* Lucy had some rare and unusual difficulties, don't use this data.

Step 3: Determine Sample Size. Assuming a 95% confidence interval, $z = 1.96$. The precision interval of ± 6% of the true mean implies $p = 0.06$. We have calculated $\bar{t}$ for each element in Step 2.

Since z and p are set by the specified confidence level and precision interval, inspection of the sample size formula reveals that the work element having the largest ratio of $(\sigma/\bar{t})$ will require the largest sample size ***n***.

EQUATION 6.1

$$n = \left[\left(\frac{z}{p}\right)\left(\frac{\sigma}{\bar{t}}\right)\right]^2$$

Subtract the number of observations already made in the initial study from this total to determine how many additional observations are required to provide the specified confidence level and precision interval.

Step 4: Setting the Standard.

4a. The analyst *subjectively* assigns a rating factor. (shown below)

4b. Determine the normal time (NT) for each work element.

Element	Select Time, $\bar{t}$	Frequency	Rating Factor	Normal Time
Wrap #1:	0.10 min.	1.00	1.2	___
Pack #2:	0.10 min.	1.00	0.9	___
Close #3:	0.30 min.	0.25	0.8	___

For the third element, the frequency is 0.25 because closing the box occurs only once every four cycles. It is possible that some common work element, such as tightening a bolt, might occur several times during one cycle. In that situation, the frequency is the number of times the element occurs per cycle.

EQUATION 6.3

$$NTC = \sum NT$$

4c. Determine the normal time for the cycle.

EQUATION 6.4

$$ST = NTC(1 + A)$$

4d. *Subjectively* determine the proportion of the normal time to be added for allowance, then calculate standard time, *ST*. Say the allowances are 18.5% of the normal time, then

Judgment in Time Study

- Where should we set the starting and stopping points to define the work elements without making them too long or too short?
- Should we include time for infrequent events?
- Should we eliminate data for unusual events. In other words, is it really unusual for Lucy to have difficulty?
- What is the appropriate amount for allowances?
- Requiring the greatest amount of judgment is the performance rating. Was Lucy really slacking off, working at 90% of her normal speed while packing? How could you prove it was 90%, and not 95%?

Overall Assessment of Time Study

\+ Most frequently used method for setting time standards.

\+ Qualified analysts can typically set reasonable standards.

\- Not appropriate for "thinking" jobs.

\- Not appropriate for nonrepetitive jobs.

\- Inexperienced persons should not conduct time studies because errors in recording information or in selecting work elements can result in unreasonable standards.

\- Workers may object to judgment and subjectivity involved.

Elemental Standard Data Approach

- Useful when a high degree of similarity exists.
- Time standards are developed for common work elements.
- Study results are stored in a database for later use in establishing standards for jobs requiring those elements.
- Allowances must still be added.
- An equation may be used to account for the effect on time required by certain variable characteristics of the jobs.
- Specifying job variables for use in the equation is difficult and may not produce good estimates.
- This approach reduces the number of time studies needed, but does not eliminate time studies.

Predetermined Data Approach

1. Break each work element into micromotions: reach, move, disengage, apply pressure, grasp, position, release, and turn.
2. Find tabular value of time for each micromotion, accounting for mitigating factors: weight, distance, size, degree of difficulty.
3. Normal times of micromotions are added for the task.
4. Adjust for allowances to arrive at the standard time.

Advantages of Predetermined Data Approach

1. Standards can be set for new jobs
2. Work methods can be compared without a time study
3. Greater consistency of results, variation due to recording errors and difference between workers is removed
4. Defuses objections to biased judgment in performance rating

Disadvantages of Predetermined Data Approach

1. Impractical for jobs with low repeatability
2. Data may not reflect the actual situation in a specific plant
3. Performance time variations can result from many factors
4. Actual time may depend on the specific sequence of motions
5. Considerable skill is required to achieve good standards

How can the amount of time that employees spend on unproductive activities be estimated?

Work Sampling Method

1. Results in a proportion of time spent doing an activity, rather than a standard time for the work
2. Requires a *large* number of instantaneous, random observations spread over the length of the study
3. Proportion of observations in which the activity occurs is assumed to be the proportion of time spent on the activity in general

Work Sampling Exercise

(Solution check appears on Study Guide Page 112.)

Major League Baseball (MLB) is concerned about excessive game duration. Batters now spend a lot of time between pitches when they leave the box to check signals with coaches, and then go through a lengthy routine including stretching, spitting, and a variety of other actions inconsistent with family entertainment. Pitching routines are similarly elaborate. In order to speed up the game, it has been proposed to prohibit batters from leaving the box and to prohibit pitchers from leaving the mound after called balls and strikes. MLB estimates the proportion of time spent in these delays to be 20% of the total game time. Before they institute a rules change, MLB would like to be 95% confident that the result of a study will show a proportion of time wasted that is accurate within ± 4% of the true proportion.

Work Sampling Procedure

Step 1. Define the activities.

- Batters
  - acceptable delay
    - foul ball
    - bail out for brush-back pitch
    - receiving signals
  - unacceptable delay
    - leaving batter's box
    - spitting, scratching
    - arguing calls
- Pitchers
  - acceptable delay
    - new ball preparation
    - wild pitch
    - receiving signals
  - unacceptable delay
    - leaving mound
    - spitting, scratching
    - arguing calls

2. Design the observation form.

	Play or Acceptable Delay	Unacceptable Delay	Total
Pitchers			
Batters			

3. Determine the length of the study: 32 hours (ten games)
4. Determine the initial sample size.

$$n = \left(\frac{z}{e}\right)^2 \hat{p}(1-\hat{p})$$

5. Select random observation times.

6. Determine the observer schedule. Use the random number table and the procedure described in Simulation Supplement F, p. 326 to establish a random observation schedule. If the observer has to move around the plant to make observations for several studies, a travel itinerary would have to be prepared.

EQUATION 6.5

$$n = \left(\frac{z}{e}\right)^2 \hat{p}(1-\hat{p})$$

where

$$e = z\sqrt{\frac{\hat{p}(1-\hat{p})}{n}}$$

7. Observe the activities and record the data.

	Play or Acceptable Delay	Unacceptable Delay	Total
Pitchers	289	96	385
Batters	339	46	385

8. Check to see whether additional sampling is required.

EQUATION 6.5

$$n = \left(\frac{z}{e}\right)^2 \hat{p}(1-\hat{p})$$

where

$$e = z\sqrt{\frac{\hat{p}(1-\hat{p})}{n}}$$

Overall Assessment of Work Sampling

- \+ No special training required of observers
- \+ Several studies can be conducted simultaneously
- \+ More economical for jobs having long cycle times, since the observer need not be present for the entire duration.
- \+ Workers prefer this method to time studies
- \- A large number of observations are required
- \- Usually not used for repetitive, well-defined jobs

Managerial Considerations in Work Measurement

Total Quality Management

"Traditional work measurement techniques seem repressive and not applicable to TQM or continuous improvement." p. 253

- However, these techniques *can* be used in the spirit of continuous improvement (provided management earns cooperation of labor).

The nature of worker fatigue is shifting from physical to mental fatigue. The emphasis of work measurement is shifting from measuring strength and dexterity to measuring knowledge and communication.

Increased Automation

- There is less need to observe and rate worker performance, because work is machine paced.
- Work sampling may be electronically monitored.

Multiple-Choice Questions

1. Putting up artificial boundaries that thwart the creativeness and problem-solving abilities of employees is a characteristic of
   A. government.
   B. horizontal organizations.
   C. reengineering.
   D. vertical organizations.

2. Piece rate is
   A. a group-based incentive plan.
   B. an individual-based incentive plan.
   C. a team-based incentive plan.
   D. the per-unit production cost.

3. A college course in operations management is an example of
   A. administrative training.
   B. general training.
   C. specialist training.
   D. technical training.

4. Frederick Taylor's methods dealt primarily with
   A. behavioral aspects of managing people.
   B. job enlargement, rotation, and enrichment.
   C. organizational restructuring.
   D. technical aspects of job design.

5. Which of the following tends to overcome boredom in highly repetitive jobs?
   A. Higher wages
   B. Job enlargement, rotation, and enrichment
   C. Scientific management
   D. Valium

6. Which of the following is true of narrowly defined (specialized) jobs?
   A. High repetition tends to improve quality.
   B. They are more prevalent in process-focused industries (than product-focused).
   C. They tend to increase job satisfaction.
   D. Workers need less time to learn highly specialized procedures.

7. Job enlargement is associated with
   A. available time.
   B. higher production rates.
   C. horizontal expansion of responsibility.
   D. vertical expansion of responsibility.

(Multiple-choice answers appear on page 111.)

8. Managers use work standards in a variety of ways. Which of the following uses is most controversial?
   A. Basis for pay
   B. Capacity planning and scheduling
   C. Comparing alternative process designs
   D. Establishing prices and costs

9. Which of the following work measurement methods is used most often for setting time standards?
   A. Elemental standard data
   B. Predetermined data
   C. Time study
   D. Work sampling

10. When making time standards studies for a task,
    A. observations are made at random intervals.
    B. observed times are modified subjectively for intangible factors.
    C. the subject worker should be the fastest of those available at doing the task.
    D. the subject worker should be timed without her knowledge of being observed.

11. Which aspect of time study requires the greatest amount of judgment?
    A. Defining work elements
    B. Determining the amount of allowances
    C. Eliminating some observed times
    D. Setting performance ratings

12. Time studies are inappropriate for jobs having which of the following characteristics?
    A. A "bottleneck" operation
    B. Cause of defects or poor quality
    C. Creative work
    D. Dangerous or disagreeable work

13. Which of these is an **advantage** of the predetermined data approach?
    A. The specific sequence of motions are disregarded.
    B. It is useful for firms with a process focus.
    C. Little training is required for good results.
    D. Standards can be set before production begins.

14. Work sampling observations
    A. require highly trained observers.
    B. should be conducted over a representative period of time.
    C. should be made at equally spaced intervals.
    D. should be made at the same time every day.

Problems

1. R. Faircity Recycling Company provides a trash collection service. Calculate the required sample size for 90% confidence that the results of a time study will be within ± 3% of the true mean.

Step 1: Selecting Work Elements
#1. Walk to next customer's home
#2. Empty trash into truck
#3. Crush trash can, throw lid
#4. Compress trash

Step 2: Timing the Elements.

Element	Initial Observation Cycle Number, minutes #1	#2	#3	#4	#5	#6	#7	#8	#9	Select	σ
Walk:	.25	.28	.22	.25	.24	.40	.25	.32	.31	____	.0557
Empty trash:	.25	.22	.26	.15	.19	.20	.24	.18	.29	____	.0442
Throw lid:	.08	.11	.08	.85*	.09	.08	.13	.11	.12	____	.0200
Compress trash:	----	----	.29	----	----	.31	----	----	.30	____	.0100

* Chased by rottweiler (don't use this data).

Step 3: Determine Sample Size.
Sample size is determined by the work element having the highest ratio of σ/t.

$$n = \left[\left(\frac{z}{p}\right)\left(\frac{\sigma}{\bar{t}}\right)\right]^2$$

2. Continue problem # 1 to set a time standard. Use the given performance ratings. Allowances are 20%.

Step 4: Setting the Standard.
Determine the normal time for each work element:

Element	Select Time	Frequency	Performance Rating	Normal Time
Walk:	___ min.	1.0	1.25	____ min.
Empty trash:	___ min.	1.0	1.00	____ min.
Throw lid:	___ min.	1.0	0.90	____ min.
Compress trash:	___ min.	0.333	0.90	____ min.

Determine the normal time for the cycle, *NTC* = ____ min.

Adjust for allowances, the standard time, *ST* =____ min.

3. Based on an educated guess, a professor estimates that students spend about 40% of the available time during a test pursuing the wrong solution methodology. He sets out to make a work sampling study to get a better estimate. The professor wants to be 95% confident his results will be within ± 5% of the true percentage. How many work sampling observations should be made in the initial study?

$$n = \left(\frac{z}{e}\right)^2 \hat{p}(1-\hat{p})$$

4. A college is making a time study of the application approval process. (Frequency = one.) The following are the results, in minutes:

	Observation #											
	1	2	3	4	5	6	7	8	9	10	$\bar{t}$	RF
Credit check	3	7	5	5	6	8	4	3	2	7	___	0.8
Recommendations	1	1	2	1	2	2	1	2	1	2	___	1.0
Tests and records	2	4	3	5	2	2	4	3	3	2	___	0.9

a. What is the observed normal cycle time?

$$NT = \bar{t}(F)(RF)$$

$$NTC = \sum NT$$

b. The clerk cannot process applications all day long at this pace. Allowances are set at 22%. What is the standard time?

$$ST = NTC(1+A)$$

c. The school desires 98% confidence that the study results are within ± 5% of the true mean. Have enough observations been made?

$$n = \left[\left(\frac{z}{p}\right)\left(\frac{\sigma}{\bar{t}}\right)\right]^2$$

Solutions

1. R. Faircity Recycling Company provides a trash collection service. Calculate the required sample size for 90% confidence that the results of a time study will be within ± 3% of the true mean.

Step 1: Selecting Work Elements
#1. Walk to next customer's home
#2. Empty trash into truck
#3. Crush trash can, throw lid
#4. Compress trash

Step 2: Timing the Elements.

Element	Initial Observation Cycle Number, minutes #1	#2	#3	#4	#5	#6	#7	#8	#9	Select	σ
Walk:	.25	.28	.22	.25	.24	.40	.25	.32	.31	.28	.0557
Empty trash:	.25	.22	.26	.15	.19	.20	.24	.18	.29	.22	.0442
Throw lid:	.08	.11	.08	.85*	.09	.08	.13	.11	.12	.10	.0200
Compress trash:	----	----	.29	----	----	.31	----	----	.30	.30	.0100

* Chased by rottweiler (don't use this data).

Step 3: Determine Sample Size.
The ratio of σ/t is greatest for the second work element.

$$n = \left[\left(\frac{z}{p}\right)\left(\frac{\sigma}{t}\right)\right]^2 = \left[\left(\frac{1.65}{.03}\right)\left(\frac{.0442}{0.22}\right)\right]^2$$

$= 122.1$ or 123 observations

2. Continue problem # 1 to set a time standard. Use the given performance ratings. Allowances are 20%.

Step 4: Setting the Standard.
Determine the normal time for each work element:

Element	Select Time	Frequency	Performance Rating	Normal Time
Walk:	0.28 min	1.0	1.25	0.35 min.
Empty trash:	0.22 min	1.0	1.00	0.22 min.
Throw lid:	0.10 min	1.0	0.90	0.09 min.
Compress trash:	0.30 min	0.333	0.90	0.09 min.

Determine the normal time for the cycle, $NTC = (0.35 + 0.22 + 0.09 + 0.09) = 0.75$ min.

Adjust for allowances, the standard time, $ST = 1.2(0.75) = 0.90$ min.

3. Based on an educated guess, a professor estimates that students spend about 40% of the available time during tests pursuing the wrong solution methodology. He sets out to make a work sampling study to get a better estimate. The professor wants to be 95% confident her results will be within ± 5% of the true percentage. How many work sampling observations should be made in the initial study?

$$n=\left(\frac{z}{e}\right)^2\hat{p}(1-\hat{p})$$

$$n=\left(\frac{z}{e}\right)^2\hat{p}(1-\hat{p})=\left(\frac{1.96}{0.05}\right)^2(0.4)(1-0.4)$$

$= 368.8$ or 369 observations

4. A college is making a time study of the application approval process. (Frequency = one.) The following are the results, in minutes:

	Observation #											
	1	2	3	4	5	6	7	8	9	10	$\bar{t}$	RF
Credit check	3	7	5	5	6	8	4	3	2	7	5.0	0.8
Recommendations	1	1	2	1	2	2	1	2	1	2	1.5	1.0
Tests and records	2	4	3	5	2	2	4	3	3	2	3.0	0.9

a. What is the observed normal cycle time?

$$NT=\bar{t}(F)(RF)$$

NT1 = 5.0 (0.8) = 4.0
NT2 = 1.5 (1.0) = 1.5
NT3 = 3.0 (0.9) = 2.7
NTC = 8.2

$$NTC=\sum NT$$

b. The clerk cannot process applications all day long at this pace. Allowances are set at 22%. What is the standard time?

$$ST=NTC(1+A)$$

ST = 8.2 (1.22) = 10 minutes

c. The school desires 98% confidence that the study results are within ± 5% of the true mean. Have enough observations been made?

Work Element	Ratio of σ/t
Credit check	2.0/5.0 = 0.40
Recommendations	0.527/1.5 = 0.35
Tests and records	1.0541/3.0 = 0.35

$$n=\left[\left(\frac{z}{p}\right)\left(\frac{\sigma}{\bar{t}}\right)\right]^2$$

$$n=\left[\left(\frac{z}{p}\right)\left(\frac{\sigma}{\bar{t}}\right)\right]^2=\left[\left(\frac{2.33}{0.05}\right)\left(\frac{2.0}{5.0}\right)\right]^2$$

$= 347.45$ or 348 observations

Solution to Time Study Exercise

Lucy and Ethel have repetitive jobs at the candy factory. Management desires to establish a time standard for this work for which they can be 95% confident to be within ± 6% of the true mean.

Step 1: Selecting Work Elements.

#1: Pick up wrapper paper and wrap once piece of candy.
#2: Put candy in a box, one at a time.
#3: When the box is full (4 pieces), close it and place on conveyor.

Step 2: Timing the Elements.

Select an *average* trained worker: Lucy will have to suffice.

	Initial Observation Cycle Number, minutes									Select
Element	#1	#2	#3	#4	#5	#6	#7	#8	#9	Time, $\bar{t}$
Wrap #1:	.10	.08	.08	.12	.10	.10	.12	.09	.11	0.10 min.
Pack #2:	.10	.08	.08	.11	.06	.98*	.17	.11	.09	0.10 min.
Close #3:	.27	----	----	----	.34	----	----	----	.29	0.30 min.

EQUATION 6.2

$$NT = \bar{t}(F)(RF)$$

* Lucy had some rare and unusual difficulties, don't use this data.

Calculating the "select" or average time:
For element # 1, the sum of the 9 observations is 0.90 minutes.
The average is **0.10** minutes.
For element # 2, the sum of the 8 usable observations is 0.80 minutes.
The average is **0.10** minutes.
For element #3, the sum of the 3 observations is 0.90 minutes.
The average is **0.30** minutes.

Step 3: Determine Sample Size. Assuming a 95% confidence interval, $z = 1.96$. The precision interval of ± 6% of the true mean implies $p = 0.06$. We have calculated $\bar{t}$ for each element in Step 2.

The second work element has the largest ratio of $(\sigma/\bar{t})$ and will require the largest sample size *n*.

$$\frac{\sigma_1}{t_1} = \frac{0.015}{0.1} = 0.15$$

$$\frac{\sigma_2}{t_2} = \frac{0.03295}{0.1} = 0.3295$$

$$\frac{\sigma_3}{t_3} = \frac{0.03606}{0.3} = 0.1202$$

EQUATION 6.1

$$n = \left[\left(\frac{z}{p}\right)\left(\frac{\sigma}{\bar{t}}\right)\right]^2$$

$$n = \left[\left(\frac{z}{p}\right)\left(\frac{\sigma}{\bar{t}}\right)\right]^2$$

$$= \left[\left(\frac{1.96}{0.06}\right)\left(\frac{0.03295}{0.1}\right)\right]^2$$

$$= (10.76)^2 = 115.86 \text{ or } 116 \text{ observations}$$

Subtract the number of observations already made in the initial study from this total to determine how many additional observations are required to provide the specified confidence level and precision interval.

108 (116 – 8) more observations are required.

Step 4: Setting the Standard.

4a. Determine the normal time (NT) for each work element.

4b. The analyst *subjectively* assigns a rating factor.

Element	Select Time, $\bar{t}$	Frequency	Rating Factor	Normal Time
Wrap #1:	0.10 min.	1.00	1.2	0.12 min.
Pack #2:	0.10 min.	1.00	0.9	0.09 min.
Close #3:	0.30 min.	0.25	0.8	0.06 min.

For the third element the frequency is 0.25 because closing the box occurs only once every four cycles. It is possible that some common work element, such as tightening a bolt, might occur several times during one cycle. In that situation, the frequency is the number of times the element occurs per cycle.

EQUATION 6.3

$NTC = \sum NT$

4c. Determine the normal time for the cycle.

$$NTC = \sum NT$$
$$= .12 + .09 + .06 = 0.27 \text{ minutes}$$

EQUATION 6.4

$ST = NTC(1 + A)$

4d. *Subjectively* determine the proportion of the normal time to be added for allowance, then calculate standard time, *ST*. Say the allowances are 18.5% of the normal time, then

$$ST = NTC(1 + A)$$
$$= 0.27(1.185) = 0.32 \text{ minutes}$$

MULTIPLE CHOICE ANSWERS

1. D	8. A
2. B	9. C
3. B	10. B
4. D	11. D
5. B	12. C
6. D	13. D
7. C	14. B

Solution to Work Sampling Exercise

Major League Baseball (MLB) is concerned about excessive game duration. Batters now spend a lot of time between pitches when they leave the box to check signals with coaches, and then go through a lengthy routine including stretching, spitting, and a variety of other actions inconsistent with family entertainment. Pitching routines are similarly elaborate. In order to speed up the game, it has been proposed to prohibit batters from leaving the box and to prohibit pitchers from leaving the mound after called balls and strikes. MLB estimates the proportion of time spent in these delays to be 20% of the total game time. Before they institute a rules change, MLB would like to be 95% confident that the result of a study will show a proportion of time wasted that is accurate within ± 4% of the true proportion.

EQUATION 6.5

$$n=\left(\frac{z}{e}\right)^2 \hat{p}(1-\hat{p})$$

4. Determine the initial sample size.

$$n=\left(\frac{z}{e}\right)^2 \hat{p}(1-\hat{p})=\left(\frac{1.96}{.04}\right)^2 (0.2)(1-0.8)$$

$$= 384.16 \text{ or } 385 \text{ observations}$$

5. Select random observation times.
   In order to make 385 observations in 32 hours, observations would need to be made on the average of one every 5 minutes (12 per hour).
6. Determine the observer schedule. Use the random number table and the procedure described in Simulation Supplement F, p. 326 to establish an observation schedule with an average of 5 minutes between random observations.
7. Observe the activities and record the data.

	Play or Acceptable Delay	Unacceptable Delay	Total
Pitchers	289	96	385
Batters	339	46	385

8. Check to see whether additional sampling is required.
   With regard to the pitchers, $p = 0.25$, a total of 450 observations, or 66 more observations, are required.

$$n=\left(\frac{z}{e}\right)^2 \hat{p}(1-\hat{p})=\left(\frac{1.96}{0.04}\right)^2 (0.25)(0.75)=450$$

   With regard to the batters, $p = 0.18$. The total number of observations is 254. We have already observed more than that.

Supplement D, Learning Curves

While no one will confuse learning curves with rocket science, learning curves often do provide surprisingly accurate forecasts for the duration of repetitive tasks. Human organizations exhibit a learning effect which is similar to that characteristic found in human individuals. Just as individuals have traits that affect their learning rate, organizations have cultures that influence the rate of organizational learning. Once established, individual traits and organizational cultures tend to remain constant over time. So for a particular subject matter or product line, once the learning rate is known it can be projected quite a long way into the future, with surprisingly accurate results.

A number of organizational characteristics contribute to reducing direct labor requirements as cumulative production increases (the learning effect). These characteristics include rates of capital investment and automation, how aggressively product and process improvements are pursued, the degree of investment in training personnel, and whether management tends to take risks or tends to maintain the status quo.

> "**Organizational learning** involves gaining experience with products and processes, achieving greater efficiency through automation and other capital investments, and making other improvements in administrative methods or personnel." p. 263

Two Types of Learning

1. Individual — with instruction and repetition, workers learn to perform their jobs more efficiently.
2. Organizational
   - experience in product and process design
   - automation, capital investment
   - methods changes

The Learning Effect

> "The learning effect can be represented by a line called a **learning curve**, which displays the relationship between the total direct labor per unit and the cumulative quantity of a product or service produced." p. 263

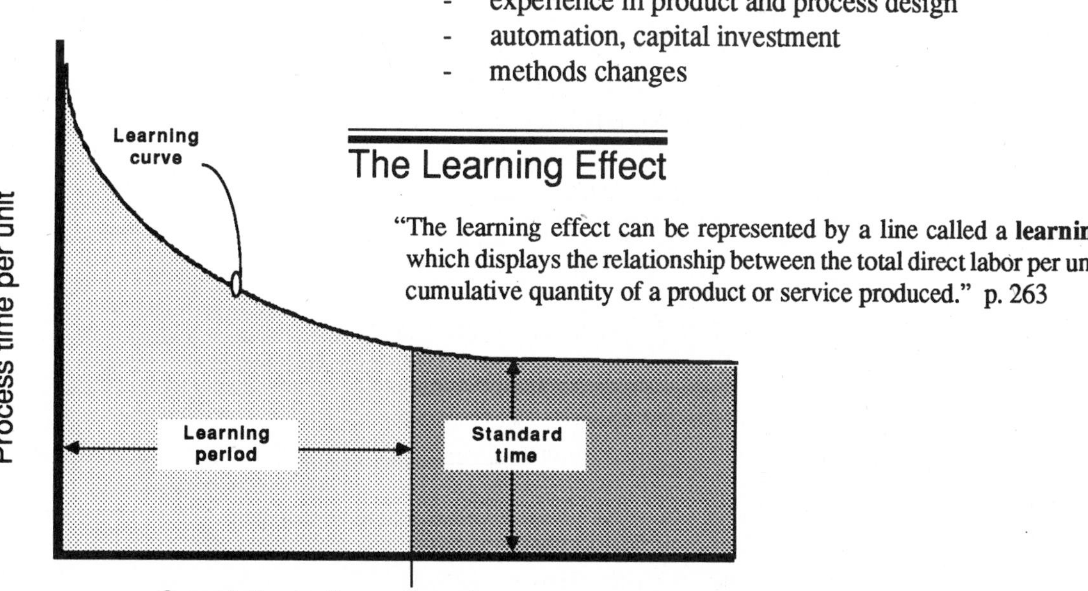

Background

- First developed in aircraft industry
- Each doubling of quantity reduced per-unit production time by 20%
- Rate of learning may be different for different products and different companies

Learning Curves and Competitive Strategy

- Learning curves enable managers to project the manufacturing cost per unit for a given cumulative production quantity.
- Product design changes disrupt the learning effect.
- Firms making standardized products compete on low cost, and use high volume to quickly move costs down the learning curve. Low costs discourage competitors from entering the market.

Developing Learning Curves

The direct labor required for the *n*th unit k_n, is

$$k_n = k_1 n^b$$

where

$$b = \frac{\log r}{\log 2}$$

Estimating the Rate of Learning

The learning rate, *r*, is

$$r = 10^{(b \log 2)}$$

where

$$b = \frac{\log\left(\frac{k_n}{k_1}\right)}{\log n}$$

Table D.1, p. 266, shows conversion factors for the cumulative average number of direct labor hours per unit.

Using Learning Curves

Bid Preparation

- Use learning curve to estimate labor cost
- Add material costs and profit to obtain bid amount

Financial Planning

- Use learning curve to estimate cash needed to finance operations

Labor Requirement Estimation

- Estimate training requirements
- Develop hiring plans

Managerial Considerations in the Use of Learning Curves

- It may be difficult to obtain a good estimate of the learning rate for an organization.
- The simpler the product, the less the learning rate.
- The entire learning curve is based on the time required for the first unit, which may itself be the result of an estimation process.
- Learning curves are used to greatest advantage in the early stages of new product or service production.
- Implementing team approaches change organizational learning rates.
- Learning curves are only approximations.

Learning rate is affected by culture, and team orientation is a major cultural change.

Multiple-Choice Questions

1. We use the term learning curve to depict reductions in
   A. total direct labor per unit.
   B. total value-added costs per unit.
   C. Both A and B
   D. Neither A nor B

2. The learning curve was first developed
   A. as a part of Taylor's Scientific Management methods.
   B. for use in normalizing test scores.
   C. in baseball.
   D. in the aircraft industry.

3. If the third unit takes 100 hours, an 80% learning curve estimates
   A. the second unit will take 80 hours.
   B. the fourth unit will take 80 hours.
   C. the fifth unit will take 64 hours.
   D. the sixth unit will take 80 hours.

4. The learning curve is applied to all of the following **except**
   A. bid preparation.
   B. estimating labor requirements.
   C. financial planning.
   D. standardized test scores.

5. Which of the following is true of learning effects?
   A. Frequent product design changes enhance benefits from the learning effect.
   B. Implementing team approaches tends to change the organizational learning curve rate.
   C. Learning curves can be used to the greatest advantage in the maturity stage of product development.
   D. Simple tasks exhibit stronger learning effects than do complex tasks.

6. Which of the following is a competitive advantage for a company that succeeds in moving down the learning curve before competition enters the market?
   A. Newcomers will initially suffer large losses.
   B. Product design changes will be less disruptive.
   C. The company will have a faster learning rate (compared to that of the competition).
   D. The learning effect becomes stronger as the product moves from early stages to the mature stage of its life cycle.

(Multiple-choice answers are on Study Guide page 117.)

Problems

1. Use the 80% learning curve to estimate how long it will take to produce the seventh unit if the first unit takes 40 hours.

   $$k_n = k_1 n^b$$

2. Use Table D.1 to determine *average* time per unit required for the first seven units in Problem 1.

3. What is the *total* time required to produce all seven units in Problem 1?

4. Use the 90% learning curve to estimate how long it will take to produce the ninth unit if the first unit takes 60 hours.

5. Use Table D.1 to determine the *average* time per unit required for the first nine units in Problem 4.

6. Working backwards, if the fourth unit required 10,000 hours and the learning rate is 81%, estimate how many hours were required for the first unit.

7. Estimate the learning rate when the first unit required 800 hours, and the fifth unit required 600 hours.

Solutions

1. Use the 80% learning curve to estimate how long it will take to produce the seventh unit if the first unit takes 40 hours.

$$b = \frac{\log r}{\log 2} = \frac{\log 0.8}{\log 2} = -0.3219281$$

$$k_n = k_1 n^b = 40(7)^{-0.321928} = 40(0.5345) = 21.38 \text{ or about 21 hours}$$

2. Use Table D.1 to determine *average* time per unit required for the first seven units in Problem 1.

   The conversion factor from the 80% learning curve table where $n = 7$ is 0.69056. The average time per unit is:

   (40 hours)(0.69056) = 27.6224 or about 28 hours

3. What is the *total* time required to produce all seven units in Problem 1?

   The average time per unit (27.6224) times 7 results in the total time required. (27.6224 hours/unit) (7 units) = 193.3568 or about 193 hours.

4. Use the 90% learning curve to estimate how long it will take to produce the ninth unit if the first unit takes 60 hours.

$$b = \frac{\log r}{\log 2} = \frac{\log 0.9}{\log 2} = -0.152$$

$$k_n = k_1 n^b = 60(9)^{-0.152} = 60(0.7161) = 42.9642 \text{ or about 43 hours}$$

5. Use Table D.1 to determine the *average* time per unit required for the first nine units in Problem 4.

   The conversion factor from the 90% learning curve table where $n = 9$ is 0.80998. The average time per unit is:

   (60 hours)(0.80998) = 48.5988 or about 49 hours

6. Working backwards, if the fourth unit required 10,000 hours and the learning rate is 90%, estimate how many hours were required for the first unit.

$$k_n = k_1 n^b$$

$$b = \frac{\log r}{\log 2} = \frac{-0.0457575}{0.30103} = -0.152$$

$$k_1 = \frac{k_n}{n^b} = \frac{10{,}000}{4^{-0.152}} = \frac{10{,}000}{0.81} = 12{,}345.6789$$

7. Estimate the learning rate when the first unit required 800 hours, and the fifth unit required 600 hours.

$$b = \frac{\log(k_n/k_1)}{\log n} = \frac{\log(600/800)}{\log 5} = \frac{-0.12494}{0.69897} = -0.17875$$

$$r = 10^{(b\log 2)} = 10^{(-0.17875\times 0.30103)} = 10^{-0.0538} = 0.88347$$

   The learning rate is about 88%.

Multiple Choice Answers

1. C
2. D
3. D
4. D
5. B
6. A

Chapter Seven, Capacity

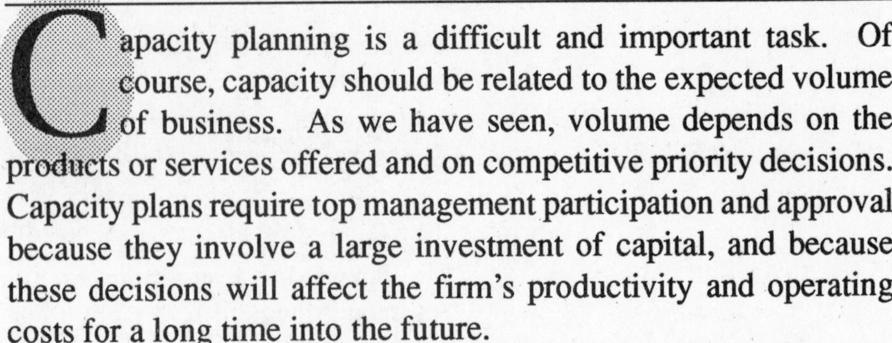

Capacity planning is a difficult and important task. Of course, capacity should be related to the expected volume of business. As we have seen, volume depends on the products or services offered and on competitive priority decisions. Capacity plans require top management participation and approval because they involve a large investment of capital, and because these decisions will affect the firm's productivity and operating costs for a long time into the future.

Given the weight of these decisions, it is particularly disturbing that capacity plans must be based upon long-range forecasts of demand. Long-range forecasting techniques utilize a considerable degree of subjective analysis based upon experience and judgment. Long-range forecasts are notoriously inaccurate, so capacity planning activities are risky.

Capacity plans are made at two levels. This chapter deals with long-term investments in new facilities and equipment. Short-term capacity options such as scheduling overtime, changing work-force size, and adjusting inventory level are discussed in production planning (Chapter 13).

Capacity Planning

- This activity is central to the long-term success of an organization.
- The agony of too much or too little capacity.
  - too much — overhead costs of long-term investment in facilities and equipment consume profits
  - too little — costs of short-term options; subcontracting, overtime, expediting, and lost sales, consume profits

Three Questions Common to All Planning Activities

1. **Where are we now?** A situation analysis to determine the current environment, and the strengths and weaknesses of current resources.
2. **Where do we want to be at some time in the future?** This activity depends on a long-range forecast of demand, which in turn depends on the productivity, competition, technology, and social environment of the distant future. This forecast will be inaccurate.
3. **How are we going to get there?** ...How do we plan to fill the gap between the answer to question #1 and the answer to question #2? What contingent plans would mitigate the adverse effects of inaccurate long-range forecasts?

Career planning considers these three questions with respect to preparing for an occupation. Material plans consider them with respect to input components. Capacity plans consider these three questions with respect to productive resources. What is our current capacity? What capacity will we need in the future? How will we make the adjustment between what we have now and the capacity resources we will need for the future?

Capacity planning considers questions such as

- Should we have one large facility or several small ones?
- Should we expand capacity before the demand is there or wait until demand is more certain?

"A systematic approach is needed in order to answer these and similar questions and to develop a capacity strategy appropriate for each situation." p. 276

How should the maximum rate of output be measured?

Measuring Capacity

- No single capacity measure is universally applicable.
- Capacity can be expressed in terms of outputs or inputs.
  - output measures — the usual choice of product-focused firms
    - low amount of customization
    - product mix becomes an issue when the output is not uniform in work content
  - input measures — used by process-focused firms
    - high amount of customization
    - output varies in work content, a measure of total units produced is meaningless
    - output is converted to some critical homogeneous input, such as labor hours or machine hours

Utilization

- Average utilization rate, expressed as a percentage:

$$\text{Utilization} = \frac{\text{Average output rate}}{\text{Maximum capacity}} \times 100\%$$

- The average output rate and the capacity must be measured in the same terms.

Design Capacity

Some equipment, such as gas turbines, have two nameplate ratings: peak capacity; which burns fuel excessively and causes increased wear, and sustainable capacity.

- Design (or peak) capacity
  - calling for extraordinary effort under ideal conditions which are not sustainable
  - nameplate-rated capacity, engineering design

Effective Capacity

- Economically sustainable under normal conditions

"For this reason, the Census Bureau defines *capacity* as the greatest level of output that the firm can *reasonably sustain* using realistic employee work schedules and the equipment currently in place." p. 277

Having too little capacity is the worst of both worlds. While working very hard, the firm is taking losses. I'd rather be on vacation.

Note that the equipment currently in place may include high-cost, inefficient resources. It may be possible to operate these inefficient resources, such as obsolete equipment or less skilled workers, in a sustainable way. However, it is not profitable to do so. Review Managerial Practice 7.1 and the comments concerning Cummins Engine Company on p. 278. Most organizations are more profitable when their high cost, inefficient resources are idle.

Increasing Maximum Capacity

- The effective capacities of multiple operations within the same facility are different.

"A **bottleneck** is an operation that has the lowest effective capacity of any operation in the facility and thus limits the system's output." p. 279

- Expansion of a facility's capacity occurs only when bottleneck capacity is increased.
- Process-focused facilities may have floating bottlenecks due to widely varying work loads on different operations at different times.
- Job shops have low equipment utilization rates.

Job shops are process-focused facilities that typically have more machines than there are people to run them. So at all times, several machines in the facility are idle. Each production worker is skilled in the operation of a variety of machines. As the work load varies, the flexible work force shifts to the operations where they are most needed. Excess machine capacity at those workstations is then utilized to absorb surges in demand.

What is the maximum reasonable size for a facility?

Economies of Scale

- **Economies of scale:** Increasing a facility's size decreases the average unit cost.

Spreading Fixed Costs

- As the facility utilization rate increases, the average unit cost drops because fixed costs are spread over more units.*
- Increments of capacity are often rather large.

Reducing Construction Costs

- Costs for permits, environmental studies, utility hookup fees and the like are often independent of facility size.
- Doubling facility size usually does not double costs.

Electric utilities often form joint ventures for the purpose of building very large central electric power stations. Large plants are more fuel efficient and are less costly to build than if each utility built its own small power station.

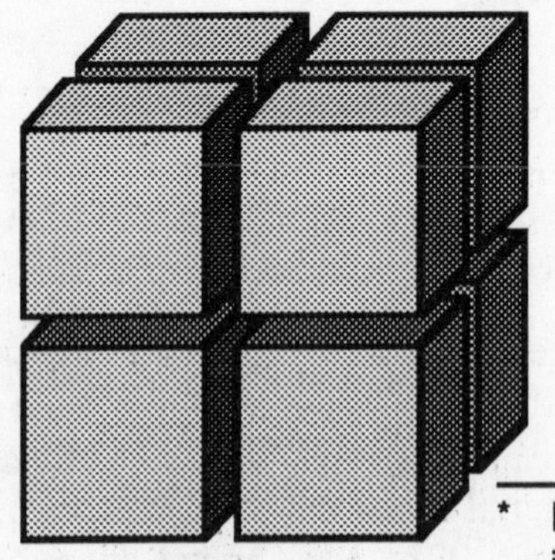

Volume = 8
Surface = 24
Ratio = 1: 3

Volume = 1
Surface = 8
Ratio = 1: 6

Average per-unit construction costs usually decrease with increased size if for no other reason than the fact that volume increases twice as fast as does surface area. The boxes on the left contain eight times the volume, but have only four times the exposed surface area as the one box at the right (24 versus 6).

* Investments in capital equipment are sunk costs. Sunk costs are irrelevant to operating decisions. Increasing production just to spread depreciation over more units *appears* to decrease unit costs, but the actual result is reduced profit. When output exceeds demand we create inventory. Inventory *appears* to be an asset, but actually consumes cash and increases costs. Moral: Never make operating decisions based on anything you learned in cost accounting. Refer to *The Goal* by Goldratt and Cox, © 1992, Published by the North River Press.

Cutting Costs of Purchased Materials

- Higher volumes give the purchaser more bargaining power and the opportunity for quantity discounts.

Finding Process Advantages

- As volume increases, processes shift toward a product focus.
- High volume may justify investment in more efficient technology.
- Benefits of dedicated resources include reduced inventory, reduced setups, enhanced learning effects, and process improvements.

The equipment required for some processes is so costly that doing the work in small volume can't be justified. For example, it would be very costly to produce just one sheet of glass, one gallon of fuel, or one sheet of paper. Process industries do things in a big way because of the economies of scale.

Diseconomies of Scale

- Excessive size can bring complexity, loss of focus, and inefficiencies which raise the average unit cost.
- Characterized by loss of agility, less innovation, risk avoidance, and excessive analysis and planning at the expense of action.
- Nonlinear growth of overhead leads to employee ceilings

As a facility grows in employment, at some point the overhead staff required to coordinate the efforts of the work force begins to increase as a proportion of the total work force.

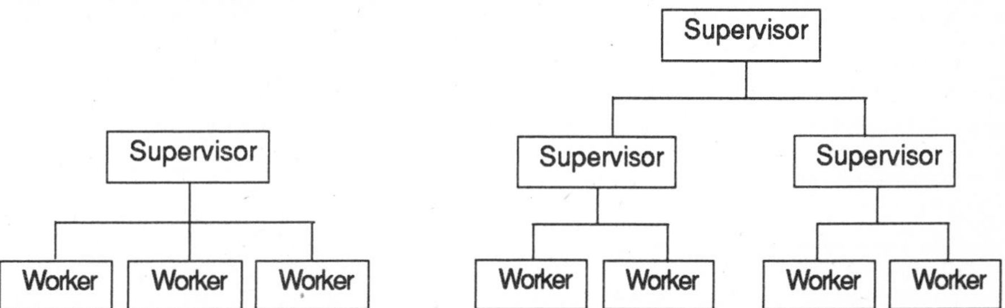

For this (extreme) example, the span of control of a supervisor is limited to three workers. When direct labor increases by one third, direct supervision doubles, and a new organizational layer is required to coordinate the activities of the supervisors. The growth of overhead is disproportionate to the growth in direct labor; a diseconomy of scale.

- Scarce local resources — Large facilities consume critical human or material resources in the locality. Continued growth in that location means greater cost to bring those resources in from further distances.
- Environmental impact — Smaller facilities have less adverse impact on the local environment. Local toxic effects are reduced by dispersing several small plants over large geographic areas. However, the total amount of pollution released to the globe will be the same or even greater than that of a single large point source.
- Social impact — Very large facilities can become too important to a community. A decision to cut back or close a facility is then complicated by a dependent community.
- Loss of Focus; see Focused Facilities.

Is there enough focus in the facilities?

Focused Factories

- Diseconomies of scale, increased demand for high quality, and customized products with short life cycles lead to focused factories.

Examples

- Product plants specializing in a product line
- Plants specializing according to functions, such as
  - a job shop layout for fabricating components and
  - a flow shop arrangement for final assembly
- Plants within plants — different positioning strategies under the same roof

How much capacity cushion is best for various processes?

Capacity Strategy

Sizing Capacity Cushions

- Average utilization rates near 100% indicate
  - need to increase capacity
  - poor customer service or declining productivity
- Utilization rates tend to be higher in capital-intensive industries.

Factors Leading to Large Capacity Cushions

1. When demand is variable, uncertain, or product mix changes
2. When finished goods inventory cannot be stored
   - Services require large capacity cushions.
3. When customer service is important
   - Electric utilities must maintain capacity cushions, called spinning reserve, just in case some facilities malfunction.
4. When capacity comes in large increments
5. When supply of material or human resources is uncertain

Factors Leading to Small Capacity Cushions

Should an expansionist or a wait-and-see strategy be followed?

1. Unused capacity costs money.
2. Large cushions hide inefficiencies, absenteeism, unreliable material supply.
3. When subcontractors are available to handle demand peaks

Timing and Sizing of Expansion

- Expansionist strategy
  - keeps ahead of demand, maintains a capacity cushion
  - large, infrequent jumps in capacity
  - higher financial risk
  - lower risk of losing market share
  - economies of scale may reduce fixed cost per unit
  - may increase learning and help compete on price
  - preemptive marketing

"By making a large capacity expansion or announcing that one is imminent, the firm uses capacity to preempt expansion by other firms. These other firms must sacrifice some of their market share or risk burdening the industry with overcapacity. To be successful, however, the preempting firm must have the credibility to convince the competition that it will carry out its plans — and must signal its plans before the competition can act." p. 286

"**Keystone Trips Gate on 20-year Plan** ... Keystone Resort yesterday unveiled plans for a 20-year expansion that will double the size of the resort, starting with a two-year, $28 million expansion of its ski mountain operation. The expansion will be financed by the Ralston Purina Company, which owns Keystone."
... *The Denver Post*, September 28, 1990.
This strategy preempted expansion at other nearby ski areas. Later, Ralston Purina purchased Breckenridge, and now dominates the Summit County skiing market.

- Wait-and-see strategy
  - lags behind demand, relying on short-term peak capacity options (overtime, subcontractors) to meet demand
  - lower financial risk associated with optimistic demand forecasts
  - lower risk of a technological advancement making a newly built facility obsolete
  - higher risk of losing market share
- Follow-the-leader strategy
  - an intermediate strategy of copying competitors' actions
  - tends to prevent anyone from gaining a competitive advantage

How should capacity and competitive priorities be linked? Capacity and other types of decisions?

Linking Capacity and Other Decisions

- Capacity cushions, resource flexibility, inventory, and longer lead times all serve as buffers against uncertainty.
- A change in one area may affect decisions in the other areas.

Examples of Links With Capacity

1. Competitive priorities—fast delivery requires large capacity cushions
2. Quality management — higher quality reduces uncertainty
3. Capital intensity — increases pressure for high utilization and lower capacity cushions
4. Resource flexibility — a buffer to be balanced with capacity cushion
5. Inventory — another form of buffer, lower investment in inventory generally requires higher investments in capacity
6. Scheduling — stability reduces uncertainty, allows smaller cushions
7. Location — new facilities require suitable locations
8. Other functional areas — Marketing provides demand forecasts, finance provides capital, human resources recruits and trains the work force

How can capacity plans be systematically developed?

A Systematic Approach To Capacity Decisions

(Step 0: Determine Current Capacity of Existing Resources)

Step 1: Estimate (Future) Capacity Requirements

- Begin with a long-range forecast of demand, productivity, competition, and technological change.
- Long-range forecast errors will be large.
- Convert demand into comparable units of capacity.

Converting Demand Rate to the Number of Machines Required

Step 1. Find the number of machine hours required per year by summing the processing times and setup times required for all products.

Step 2. Calculate N, the annual hours of capacity provided per machine.

Step 3. Multiply N by $[1 - (C/100)]$ to account for capacity cushion C.

The ratio of step 1 ÷ step 3 is M, the required number of machines.

$$M = \frac{\left[Dp + \left(\frac{D}{Q}\right)s\right]_{\text{product 1}} + \left[Dp + \left(\frac{D}{Q}\right)s\right]_{\text{product 2}} + \ldots + \left[Dp + \left(\frac{D}{Q}\right)s\right]_{\text{product n}}}{N\left[1 - \left(\frac{C}{100}\right)\right]}$$

As international supplier activity increases, for more and more U.S. companies the bottleneck operation is not anywhere to be found on the production floor. Instead, the bottleneck is in the purchasing department. The correct measure of capacity for these firms is not units produced, nor labor hours, nor machine hours. The correct measure of capacity is the number of purchase orders issued.

It is also possible for the bottleneck to take the form of corporate policies, attitudes, or culture. In that case, capacity expansion requires investment in education, rather than in capital equipment or facilities.

Step 2: Identify Gaps

- This is the difference between projected demand and current capacity (Step 1 minus Step 0).
- Use the correct capacity measure. The correct measure is determined by what is critical to the bottleneck operation.
- Capacity can be expanded only if the bottleneck is one of the expanded operations. Otherwise, expansion just increases idle time.
- Multiple operations and inputs add complexity because floating bottlenecks could change the dimensions of the capacity measure.

Step 3: Develop Alternatives

- Base case ... do nothing
- Alternative timing and size of capacity additions/closings
  - expansionist strategy
  - wait-and-see strategy
  - expand at a different location
  - use short-term options
    - overtime
    - temporary workers
    - subcontracting

Step 4: Evaluate the Alternatives

Qualitative concerns

- fit with overall capacity strategy
- uncertainties in demand, competitive reaction, technological change, and cost estimates

Quantitative concerns

- Net present value of after-tax cash flows

What tools can help in planning capacities?

Tools for Capacity Planning

> "Long-term capacity planning requires demand forecasts for an extended period of time. Unfortunately, forecast accuracy declines as the forecasting horizon lengthens." p. 292

- Unevenly distributed demand necessitates capacity cushions.

Waiting Line Models

> "Waiting line models use probability distributions to provide estimates of average customer delay time, average length of waiting lines, and utilization of the work center." p. 292

Reasons Waiting Lines (or Queues) Form

1. Variable times between successive jobs or customer arrivals
2. Variable processing or service times

A waiting line will form whenever the instantaneous arrival rate exceeds the instantaneous service rate. Supplement E introduces formulas for estimating important characteristics of simple waiting line situations. Analysis of complex waiting line problems requires simulation (refer to Supplement F).

Decision Trees

- Can be applied to a wide range of decisions
- Valuable for capacity decisions when demand is uncertain and when sequential decisions are involved

A decision tree is a schematic model of alternatives available, and their possible consequences, to the decision maker. It consists of a number of nodes with emanating *branches* and should be read from left to right. Refer to Supplement A, Decision Making.

For example, a person can decide whether or not to gamble, but cannot decide to win. That is an event.

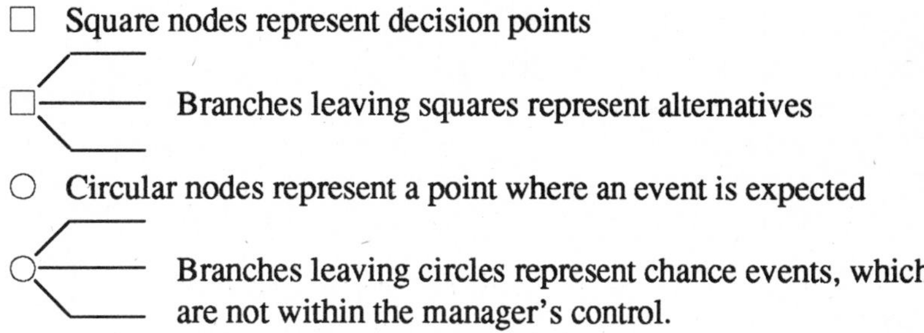

Multiple-Choice Questions

1. The Census Bureau defines capacity as the greatest level of output while including
   A. existing obsolete equipment.
   B. overtime.
   C. reduced maintenance activities.
   D. subcontracting.

2. Managers of process-focused facilities with low volume, flexible production capability tend to express capacity in terms of
   A. average utilization rate.
   B. input measures.
   C. manufacturing efficiency.
   D. output measures.

3. True expansion of a facility's capacity occurs only when
   A. bottleneck capacity is increased.
   B. demand also increases.
   C. investment is made in capital equipment.
   D. investment is made in work-force training.

4. Which one of the following is generally associated with economies of scale (as opposed to diseconomies of scale)?
   A. Agility and innovation
   B. Employee ceilings
   C. Focused factories
   D. Spreading fixed costs

5. Which of the following is generally associated with diseconomies of scale?
   A. Construction costs
   B. Focused factories
   C. Process advantages
   D. Quantity discounts

6. For services and for all but the very capital-intensive industries, an average utilization rate around 95% would be considered
   A. very high and desirable.
   B. very high and undesirable.
   C. about right and desirable.
   D. too low and undesirable.

7. Which one of the following usually results in smaller capacity cushions?
   A. Shorter product shelf life
   B. Higher capital intensity
   C. Increased sales variation or seasonality
   D. Higher customer service requirements

8. Which one of the following statements about capacity expansion is true?
   A. The expansionist strategy lags behind demand, and relies on short-term capacity options.
   B. The expansionist strategy tends to reduce capital investment risks.
   C. The timing and sizing of expansion are related.
   D. The wait-and-see strategy tends to increase market share.

9. A wait-and-see capacity strategy is best characterized by
   A. making large infrequent jumps in capacity expansions.
   B. reducing the risks of facility obsolescence due to technological advancements.
   C. aggressively increasing market share.
   D. using capacity as a competitive weapon.

10. In order for the expansionist strategy to succeed as a form of preemptive marketing,
    A. the capacity expansion should be announced to the competition.
    B. the capacity expansion should occur in several small steps.
    C. the preempting firm should do whatever the competition does.
    D. the preempting firm should keep the competition guessing as to whether it will carry out its expansion plans.

11. When analyzing alternatives to fill the gap between present resources and future capacity needs, which of the following is *most likely* to be qualitatively evaluated on the basis of experience and judgment?
    A. Competitive reaction
    B. Demand fluctuation
    C. Escalating costs
    D. Net present value of cash flows

12. An electric utility requires ten years to build electrical generation capacity. This firm is likely to
    A. maintain a small capacity cushion.
    B. make large infrequent jumps in capacity expansions.
    C. use a wait-and-see strategy.
    D. use overtime to temporarily increase capacity.

(Multiple-Choice answers are on Study Guide page 130.)

Problems

1. All Square, Inc. makes hypodermic needles and dental drill bits of various sizes. The firm works two shifts of nine hours each, four days per week, 48 weeks per year. Assume that setups cannot be avoided by dedicating machines to work on only one product.

Product	Annual Demand, D	Processing Time, p	Lot Size, Q	Setup Time, s
Drill bits	40,000	0.25 hours	250	6 hours
Needles	90,000	0.02 hours	500	8 hours

   a. What are the total machine hours required per year?

   b. If All Square maintains a 20% capacity cushion, how many hours are available annually per machine?

   c. How many machines are needed?

2. If the machines in the All Square needle problem are very expensive, what alternatives would you suggest to reduce the number required to five machines?

3. The Tiny Screen theater has ten auditoriums, each seating 250 customers. A new movie is being released for the Christmas season entitled *Gratuitous Sex and Senseless Violence.* It will play at this theater for one Friday evening and Saturday only ... a total of 20 hours of prime movie viewing. The show runs for one hour and 45 minutes. There is a fifteen-minute delay between showings to change audiences and to apply a fresh layer of sticky goo on the floor. Forecasted demand is 5,000 tickets but is not evenly distributed. The theater accounts for variation in demand with a 25% capacity cushion. How many of the ten theaters should be scheduled to show this movie? *Hint:* The numerator must be expressed in same dimensions as the denominator. The correct measure of capacity is auditorium hours.

EQUATION 7.3

$$M = \frac{Dp}{N\left[1 - \left(C/100\right)\right]}$$

4. A student has listed required courses in decreasing order of priority for graduation. During a semester, a student will receive homework assignments as shown. Each assignment requires reading and preparation before the actual work begins. If a student has 400 hours per semester for doing this work and allows a 20% capacity cushion, for which courses should the student register?

Course	Homework, D	Processing Time, p	Lot Size, Q	Setup Time, s
Operations	20	2.0 hours	1	1.00 hour
Marketing	5	0.5 hours	1	0.25 hours
Accounting	25	3.0 hours	1	4.00 hours
Computer Sci.	3	20.0 hours	1	2.00 hours
Finance	10	1.5 hours	1	1.50 hours
Statistics	5	1.0 hours	1	2.00 hours

Solutions

1. All Square, Inc. makes hypodermic needles and dental drill bits of various sizes. The firm works two shifts of nine hours each, four days per week, 48 weeks per year. Assume that setups cannot be avoided by dedicating machines to work on only one product.

Product	Annual Demand, D	Processing Time, p	Lot Size, Q	Setup Time, s
Drill bits	40,000	0.25 hours	250	6 hours
Needles	90,000	0.02 hours	500	8 hours

a. What are the total machine hours required per year?

$$= \left[Dp + \left(D/Q\, s\right)_{\text{product 1}}\right] + \left[Dp + \left(D/Q\, s\right)_{\text{product 2}}\right]$$

$$= \left[40{,}000(0.25) + \left(40{,}000/250\right)6\right] + \left[90{,}000(0.02) + \left(90{,}000/500\right)8\right]$$

$$= (10{,}000 + 960) + (1{,}800 + 1{,}440)$$

$$= 14{,}200 \text{ hours per year}$$

b. If All Square maintains a 20% capacity cushion, how many hours are available annually per machine?

$$N = 2\frac{\text{shifts}}{\text{day}} \times 9\frac{\text{hours}}{\text{shift}} \times 4\frac{\text{days}}{\text{week}} \times 48\frac{\text{weeks}}{\text{year}} = 3{,}456\frac{\text{hours}}{\text{year}}$$

$$N\left[1 - \left(C/100\right)\right] = 3{,}456\frac{\text{hours}}{\text{year}}\left[1 - \left(20/100\right)\right] = 2{,}764.8\frac{\text{hours}}{\text{year}}$$

c. How many machines are needed?

$$M = \frac{14{,}200 \text{ hours/year}}{2{,}764.8 \text{ hours/machine - year}} = 5.136 \text{ or } 6 \text{ machines}$$

Note that for this type of problem, we always round up.

2. What alternatives would you suggest to reduce the number required to five machines?

- The 0.136 machine could *almost* be removed by working 49 weeks per year instead of 48.
- Change the capacity cushion to 17.824% instead of 20%.
- Rather than increase work hours, or live with a smaller capacity cushion, a less obvious and perhaps better solution is to increase lot sizes by 20% to 300 and 600, respectively. Time saved by doing fewer setups reduced total hours required to 13,800 hours per year. Dividing by 2,764.8 hours per machine-year yields 4.99 (or 5) machines.

$$M = \frac{Dp}{N\left[1-\left(C/100\right)\right]}$$

3. The Tiny Screen theater. First convert the measure of demand (tickets) into the measure of capacity (auditorium hours).

$$M = \frac{Dp}{N\left[1-\left(C/100\right)\right]} = \frac{\left[\dfrac{(5000 \text{ tickets})\left(\dfrac{1 \text{ seat}}{\text{ticket}}\right)}{\left(\dfrac{250 \text{ seats}}{\text{theater}}\right)}\right](1.75 \text{ hours} + 0.25 \text{ hours})}{20 \text{ theater-hours}\left[1-\left(25/100\right)\right]}$$

$= 2.667$ or 3 theaters

4. Which courses should the student take?

Adjusting for the capacity cushion, the student has 400 * 0.8 or 320 hours available for homework and preparation per semester.

Course	*D*	Time, *p*	Time, *s*	Total Time	Cum. Total
Operations	20	2.0 hours	1.00 hours	60.00 hours	60.00 hours
Marketing	5	0.5 hours	0.25 hours	3.75 hours	63.75 hours
Accounting	25	3.0 hours	4.00 hours	175.00 hours	238.75 hours
Computer Sci.	3	20.0 hours	2.00 hours	66.00 hours	304.75 hours
Finance	10	1.5 hours	1.50 hours	30.00 hours	334.75 hours
Statistics	5	1.0 hours	2.00 hours	15.00 hours	349.75 hours

The student would take the four courses above the dotted line. Taking Finance would overload the "work center." If the student takes Statistics instead of Finance; then the work load would total 319.75 hours would closely match capacity.

MULTIPLE CHOICE ANSWERS

1. A
2. B
3. A
4. D
5. B
6. B
7. B
8. C
9. B
10. A
11. A
12. B

Supplement E, Waiting Line Models

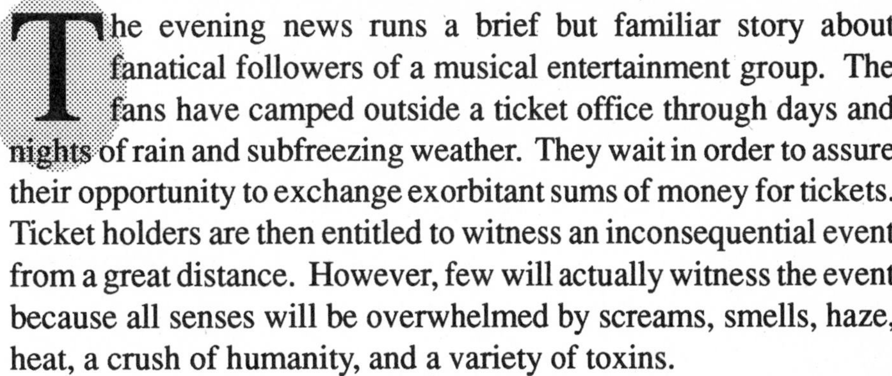

The evening news runs a brief but familiar story about fanatical followers of a musical entertainment group. The fans have camped outside a ticket office through days and nights of rain and subfreezing weather. They wait in order to assure their opportunity to exchange exorbitant sums of money for tickets. Ticket holders are then entitled to witness an inconsequential event from a great distance. However, few will actually witness the event because all senses will be overwhelmed by screams, smells, haze, heat, a crush of humanity, and a variety of toxins.

News reports aberrant behavior. Normal customers would not patronize such an operation. Rational managers are concerned that their operations system capacity is large enough to avoid long waiting lines and yet small enough to avoid excessive idle time. Even when average capacity is much higher than average demand, waiting lines can still develop. This chapter provides formulas for predicting characteristics of waiting line situations.

> "The analysis of waiting lines is of concern to managers because it affects design, capacity planning, layout planning, inventory management, and scheduling." p. 303

Why Waiting Lines Form

- When current demand temporarily exceeds current service rates
- If both demand and service rates are constant, no waiting line forms.

Use of Waiting Line Theory

- Applies to many service or manufacturing situations
- Service is the act of processing a customer (or manufacturing job).

Structure of Waiting Line Problems

Customer Population

- The source of input to the service system
- Whether the input source is *finite* or *infinite* will have an affect on the waiting line characteristics.
    - When several customers from a finite source are already in the waiting line, the chances of new customer arrivals is reduced.
    - When the input source is infinite, customers already in the waiting line do not affect probability of another arrival.
- Whether the customers are *patient* or *impatient* also affects measures of waiting line characteristics
    - Patient customers wait until served (regardless of hostility).
    - Impatient customer arrivals either *balk* at long lines (leave immediately), or join the line and *renege* (leave after becoming discouraged with slow progress).

The Service System

Number of Lines

- Single-line arrangement is favored when multiple servers are each capable of general service.
  - keeps servers uniformly busy
  - levels waiting times among customers, gives sense of fairness
- Multiple-line arrangement favored when servers provide a limited set of services
  - customers wait in the appropriate line for a particular service

Arrangement of Service Facilities

- Single-channel, single-phase — customers form one line, all services performed by a single-server facility

  → Service facility 1

- Single-channel, multiple-phase — servers specialize in one part of service

- Multiple-channel, single-phase —

  First available server / Customers stay in line first joined

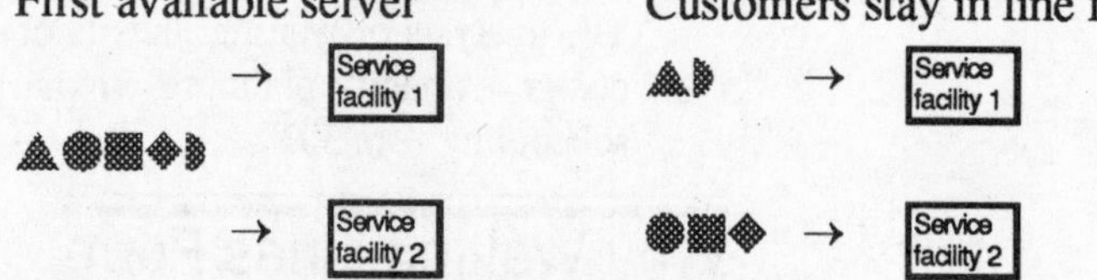

- Multiple-channel, multiple-phase

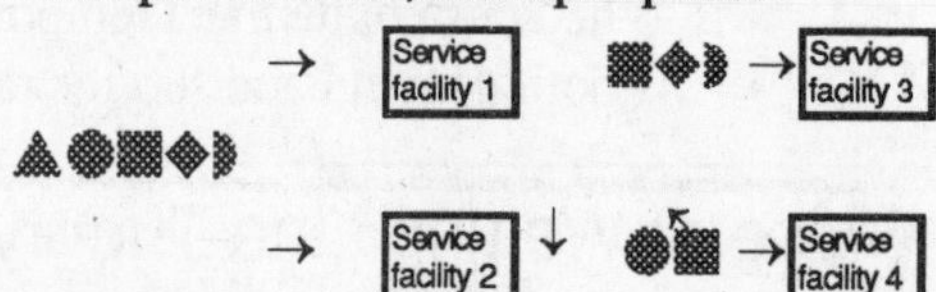

- Mixed arranged, unique services, services can't be described neatly in phases

Priority Rule

- First-come, First-served (FCFS) priority discipline is assumed
- Other rules, [earliest due date (EDD), shortest processing time (SPT)] are discussed in Chapter 16.
- Preemptive discipline — allows a high priority customer to be served ahead of another who would have been served first according to the normal priority discipline (such as FCFS).

Probability Distributions

Arrival Distribution

- Customer arrivals often can be described by the Poisson distribution.
- Arrival rate: the probability of *n* arrivals in *T* time periods:

$$P(n)=\frac{(\lambda T)^n}{n!}e^{\lambda T}$$

- Interarrival times, the average time between arrivals: the probability that the next customer will arrive in the next *T* time periods.

Service Time Distribution

$P(t \leq T) = 1 - e^{-\mu T}$

- Service time: Probability that the service time will be no more than *T* time periods can be described by the exponential distribution.
- The exponential distribution assumes that each service time is independent of those that preceded it.
  - does not account for learning effect
  - very short and very long service times exhibited in the exponential distribution might not ever actually occur

Using Waiting Line Models to Analyze Operations

- Balance costs against benefits of improving service system
- Also consider the costs of *not* making improvements

Waiting Line Operating Characteristics

1. Line length — long lines indicate poor customer service, inefficient service, or inadequate capacity
2. Number of customers in system — a large number causes congestion and dissatisfaction
3. Waiting time in line — long waits are associated with poor service
4. Total time in system — may indicate problems with customers, server efficiency, or capacity
5. Service facility utilization — control costs without unacceptable reduction in service

Single-Server Model

Assumptions		Formulas
Number of servers:	1	$\rho = \frac{\lambda}{\mu}$
Number of phases:	1	$P_n = (1-\rho)\rho^n$
Waiting line:	single line; unlimited length	$L = \frac{\lambda}{\mu - \lambda}$
Input source:	infinite; no balking or reneging	$L_q = \rho L$
Arrival distribution:	Poisson; mean arrival rate = λ	$W = \frac{1}{\mu - \lambda}$
Service distribution:	exponential; mean service time = 1/μ	$W_q = \rho W$
Priority rule:	first-come, first served	

Multiple-Server Model

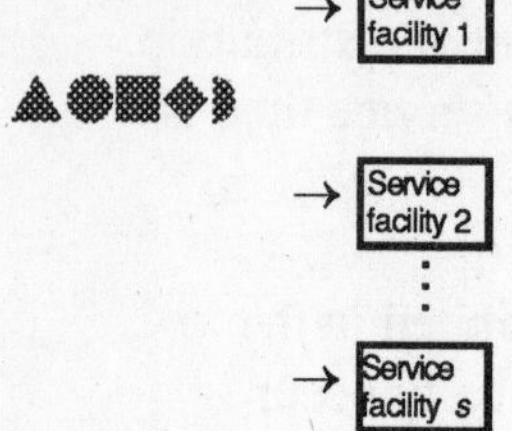

Assumptions		Formulas
Number of servers:	s	$\rho = \frac{\lambda}{s\mu}$
Number of phases:	1	$P_0 = \left[\sum_{n=0}^{s-1} \frac{(\lambda/\mu)^n}{n!} + \frac{(\lambda/\mu)^s}{s!}\left(\frac{1}{1-\rho}\right)\right]^{-1}$
Waiting line:	single line; unlimited length	$P_n = \begin{cases} \frac{(\lambda/\mu)^n}{n!} P_0 & 0 < n < s \\ \frac{(\lambda/\mu)^n}{s! s^{n-s}} P_0 & n \geq s \end{cases}$
Input source:	infinite; patient, no balking or reneging	
Arrival distribution:	Poisson; mean arrival rate = λ	$L_q = \frac{P_0 (\lambda/\mu)^s \rho}{s!(1-\rho)^2}$
Service distribution:	exponential; mean service time = $1/\mu$	$W_q = \frac{L_q}{\lambda}$
Priority rule:	first-come, first served	$W = W_q + \frac{1}{\mu}$
		$L = \lambda W$

Finite Source Model

Assumptions		Formulas
Input source:	finite; equal to N customers	$P_0 = \left[\sum_{n=0}^{N} \frac{N!}{(N-n)!}\left(\frac{\lambda}{\mu}\right)^n\right]^{-1}$
Number of servers:	1	$\rho = 1 - P_0$
Number of phases:	1	$L_q = N - \frac{\lambda + \mu}{\lambda}(1 - P_0)$
Waiting line:	single line; limited to no more than N - 1	$L = N - \frac{\mu}{\lambda}(1 - P_0)$
Arrival distribution:	exponential interarrival times; mean = $1/\lambda$	$W_q = L_q[(N - L)\lambda]^{-1}$
Service distribution:	exponential; mean service time = $1/\mu$	$W = L[(N - L)\lambda]^{-1}$
Priority rule:	first-come, first served	

Decision Areas for Management

1. Arrival rates — adjust through advertising, promotions, pricing, appointments
2. Number of service facilities — adjust service system capacity
3. Number of phases — consider splitting service tasks
4. Number of servers per facility — work force size
5. Server efficiency — training, incentives, work methods, capital investment
6. Priority rule — decide whether to allow preemption
7. Line arrangement — single or multiple lines

Other Waiting Line Models and Simulation

- Models for some other waiting line situations have been developed
- Formula complexity increases rapidly
- All models assume steady state conditions
- Simulation can be used to model the characteristics of waiting lines with a variety of distributions and non steady-state conditions.

Multiple-Choice Questions

1. The arrival rate is Poisson distributed around an average of 15 customers per hour. The service time is exponentially distributed around an average of 3 minutes per customer. Would waiting lines form?
   A. Yes, because the arrival rate would temporarily exceed the service rate.
   B. Yes, because the average service time is longer than the average time between arrivals.
   C. Yes, because the exponential distribution is more variable than the Poisson distribution.
   D. No.
2. The equations in this chapter assume
   A. customers are patient.
   B. multiple-phase service.
   C. the priority rule is earliest due date.
   D. waiting line length is limited.
3. Which of the following instills a sense of fairness?
   A. Multiple waiting lines
   B. Multiple servers
   C. Our judicial system
   D. Single waiting lines
4. When we say that the customer population is infinite we can conclude that
   A. business is very good.
   B. the customers are very patient.
   C. the number of customers in the system has no affect on the distribution of subsequent arrivals.
   D. the waiting line length is unlimited.
5. Advertising and special promotions affect
   A. λ
   B. μ
   C. n
   D. s
6. Which of the following could improve average customer *service* time?
   A. Increasing service facility utilization
   B. Increasing the number of service phases
   C. Increasing the number of waiting lines
   D. Limiting waiting line length
7. The checkout arrangement at your local Target store is approximated by
   A. single-channel, single phase
   B. single-channel, multiple phase
   C. multiple-channel, single-phase
   D. multiple-channel, multiple-phase

Problems

1. The Hilltop Produce store is staffed by one checkout clerk. The average checkout time is exponentially distributed around an average of two minutes per customer. An average of 20 customers arrive per hour.
   a. What is the average utilization rate?
   b. What is the probability that three or more customers will be in the checkout area?
   c. What is the average number of customers in the waiting line?
   d. If the customers spend an average of 10 minutes shopping for produce, what is the average time customers spend in the store?
2. The Lucky U wedding chapel offers wedding ceremonies ranging from a just few essential words to elaborate rituals. Customers arrive at an average rate of 8 customers per hour (four weddings). Lucky has two staffed chapels at the same facility. Each chapel can perform an average of 3 weddings per hour, Poisson distributed of course.
   a. What is the average utilization rate?
   b. What is the probability that three or more wedding parties will be in the facility?
   c. What is the average number of wedding parties in the waiting line?
   d. What is the average time a wedding party will spend in the facility?
3. The Shade Tree Mechanic uses one service bay for electrical repairs on Austin Healeys, MGs, and Triumphs. The total of these British sports cars in this remote desert community totals only 7, and none of these marques have been in production for many years. It is quite rare to see one passing through. These cars were not reliable even when new, and the average time between breakdowns is 40 days, exponentially distributed. Shade Tree can service an average of 0.5 cars per day (Poisson distributed).
   a. What is the average utilization rate?
   b. What is the average number of cars in the waiting line?
   c. What is the average time in the shop?

(Multiple-choice answers are on Study Guide page 138.)

Solutions

1. The Hilltop Produce. λ=20, μ=30.
   a. What is the average utilization rate?

$$\rho = \frac{\lambda}{\mu} = \frac{20}{30} = 66.7\%$$

   b. What is the probability that three or more customers will be in the checkout area?

$$P_0 = (1-\rho)\rho^n = (0.333)(0.667)^0 = 0.333$$

$$P_1 = (0.333)(0.667)^1 = 0.222$$

$$P_2 = (0.333)(0.667)^2 = 0.111$$

   Probability of 3 or more = 1 – (0.333+0.222+0.111) = 0.334

   c. What is the average number of customers in the waiting line?

$$L_q = \rho L = \rho \frac{\lambda}{\mu - \lambda} = (0.667)\left(\frac{20}{30-20}\right) = 1.333$$

   d. If the customers spend an average of 10 minutes shopping for produce, what is the average time customers spend in the store?

$$W = \frac{1}{\mu - \lambda} = \frac{1}{30-20} = 0.1 \text{ hours} \times \frac{60 \text{ min}}{\text{hour}} = 6 \text{ minutes}$$

   10 minutes shopping plus 6 minutes in checkout are = 16 minutes in the store.

2. The Lucky U wedding chapel. λ=4, μ=3, s = 2.
   a. What is the average utilization rate?

$$\rho = \frac{\lambda}{s\mu} = \frac{4}{2 \times 3} = 0.667$$

   b. What is the probability that three or more wedding parties will be in the facility?

$$P_0 = \left[\sum_{n=0}^{1} \frac{(\lambda/\mu)^n}{n!} + \frac{(\lambda/\mu)^s}{s!}\left(\frac{1}{1-\rho}\right)\right]^{-1}$$

$$= \frac{1}{\left[\frac{(4/3)^0}{0!} + \frac{(4/3)^1}{1!} + \frac{(4/3)^2}{2!}\left(\frac{1}{1-0.667}\right)\right]}$$

$$= \frac{1}{\left[\frac{4}{3} + \frac{4}{3} + \frac{(4/3)^2}{2}(3)\right]} = \frac{1}{\left[\frac{8}{6} + \frac{16}{18}(3)\right]} = \frac{6}{24}$$

$$P_0 = 0.25$$

c. What is the average number of wedding parties in the waiting line?

$$P_1 = \frac{\left(\lambda/\mu\right)^n}{n!} P_0 = \frac{\left(4/3\right)^1}{1!}(0.25)$$

$$P_1 = 0.333$$

$$P_2 = \frac{\left(\lambda/\mu\right)^n}{s!s^{n-s}} P_0 = \frac{\left(4/3\right)^2}{2!(2)^{2-2}}(0.25)$$

$$= 0.222$$

Probability of 3 or more = 1 – (0.250+0.333+0.222) = 0.194

d. What is the average time a wedding party will spend in the facility?

$$W = W_q + \frac{1}{\mu} = \frac{L_q}{\lambda} + \frac{1}{\mu} = \frac{\dfrac{P_0\left(\lambda/\mu\right)^n}{s!(1-\rho)^2}}{\lambda} + \frac{1}{\mu} = \frac{\dfrac{0.25\left(4/3\right)^1}{2!(1-0.667)^2}}{4} + \frac{1}{4}$$

$$= \frac{\dfrac{0.333}{2(0.333)^2}}{4} + \frac{1}{4} = \frac{2.5}{4} = 6.25 \text{ hours}$$

3. The Shade Tree Mechanic. λ=0.04, μ=0.5

$$P_0 = \frac{1}{\left[\sum_{n=0}^{N} \frac{N!}{(N-n)!}\left(\frac{\lambda}{\mu}\right)^n\right]} = \frac{1}{\left[\sum_{n=0}^{5} \frac{7!}{(7-n)!}\left(\frac{0.025}{0.5}\right)^n\right]}$$

$$= \frac{1}{1(0.08)^0 + 7(0.08)^1 + 42(0.08)^2 + 210(0.08)^3 + 840(0.08)^4 + 2{,}520(0.08)^5 + 5{,}040(0.08)^6 + 5{,}040(0.05)^7}$$

$$= \frac{1}{1 + 0.56 + 0.26880 + 0.10752 + 0.03441 + 0.00826 + 0.00132 + 0.00011} = \frac{1}{1.98042}$$

$$= 0.50494$$

a. What is the average utilization rate?

$$\rho = 1 - P_0 = 1 - 0.50494 = 0.49506$$

b. What is the average number of cars in the waiting line?

$$L_q = N - \frac{\lambda + \mu}{\lambda}(1 - P_0) = 7 - \left[\frac{0.04 + 0.5}{0.04}(0.49506)\right] = 0.31669 \text{ cars}$$

c. What is the average time in the shop?

$$L = N - \frac{\mu}{\lambda}(1 - P_0) = 7 - \frac{0.5}{0.04}(0.49506) = 0.81175$$

$$W = \frac{1}{L(N-L)\lambda} = \frac{1}{0.81175(7 - 0.81175)0.04} = \frac{1}{0.20094} = 4.9768 \text{ days}$$

MULTIPLE CHOICE ANSWERS

1. A
2. A
3. D
4. C
5. A
6. B
7. C

Supplement F, Simulation Analysis

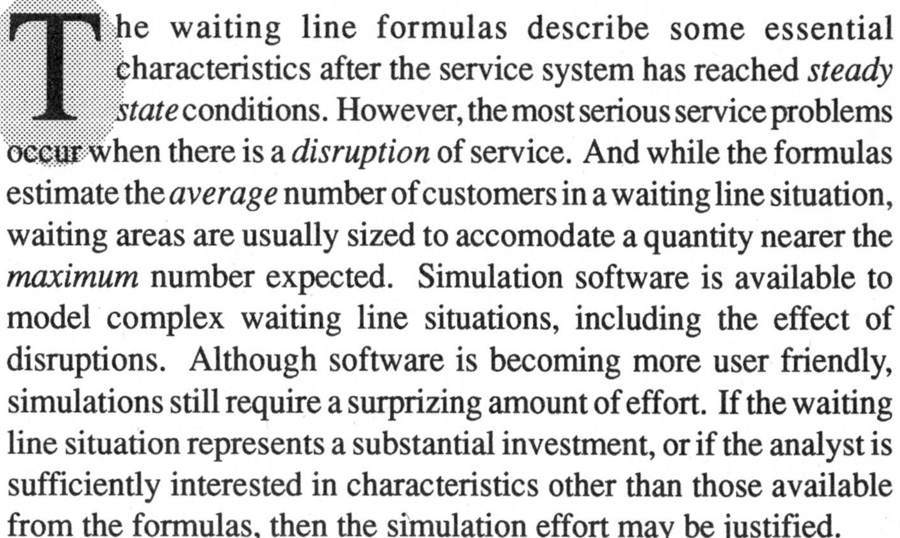

The waiting line formulas describe some essential characteristics after the service system has reached *steady state* conditions. However, the most serious service problems occur when there is a *disruption* of service. And while the formulas estimate the *average* number of customers in a waiting line situation, waiting areas are usually sized to accomodate a quantity nearer the *maximum* number expected. Simulation software is available to model complex waiting line situations, including the effect of disruptions. Although software is becoming more user friendly, simulations still require a surprizing amount of effort. If the waiting line situation represents a substantial investment, or if the analyst is sufficiently interested in characteristics other than those available from the formulas, then the simulation effort may be justified.

> Part of my graduate studies included a simulation of coal mine operations. I felt quite fortunate to have a sponsor pay me $2,000 for this work. Two birds (credit and money) with one stone! By the time I had completed the project, I think I earned about $2 per hour. Most situations are more difficult to simulate than they first appear.

"Spending thousands of hours on programming and debugging complex models is not uncommon." p. 324

- Model describes operating characteristics of interest
- Simulation model samples probability distributions to
  - generate customer arrivals
  - generate service times
  - generate disruptions, and duration of disruptions
- Simulation model collects data
  - waiting times
  - maximum number waiting
- Simulation model calculates
  - average waiting, service times,
  - utilization rate
  - total time of disruptions

Reasons for Using Simulation

- When the relationship between variables is nonlinear, or when the waiting line situation is too complex
- Alternatives can be tried without disrupting existing operations
- Simulation models compress time, obtain results in less time than that required to observe the waiting line in real time
- To sharpen managerial decision-making skills through gaming

The Simulation Process

- Monte Carlo simulation used random numbers to generate the simulation events.

Data Collection

Two Approaches to Gather Data Required for Simulation

1. Statistical sampling procedures when cost of collecting data is high
2. Historical search when data are available

Random-Number Assignment

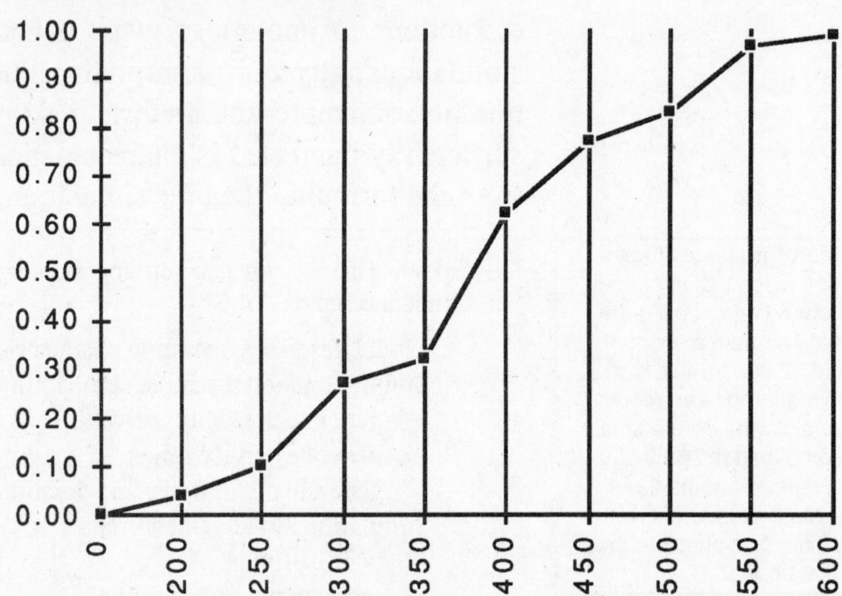

The above graph depicts the same situation as shown in the text Table F.1. The simulator selects a random number from 00 to 99 located on the vertical axis, proceeds horizontally to the curved line, and drops vertically down to the horizontal axis to find the simulated weekly demand.

Model Formulation

Specifies the relationships among variables

- *Decision variables,* such as number of service channels, are controlled by the decision maker
- *Uncontrollable variables*, such as breakdowns, are random events
- *Dependent variables*, such as idle time reflect values for decision variables and uncontrollable variables
- Simulation languages such as GPSS, SIMSCRIPT, and SLAM, simplify model formulation and simulation

Analysis

- Compare simulation results for different sets of decision variables
- Statistically significant differences between simulated situations may not be managerially significant.

Multiple-Choice Questions

1. Waiting line simulation models
   A. require Poisson distributed arrival rates.
   B. require either constant or exponentially distributed service times.
   C. A and B.
   D. Neither A nor B.

2. Simulation models
   A. are useful when the relationship between variables is nonlinear.
   B. calculate averages and variances of dependent variables before each simulation run.
   C. require little data gathering in order to simulate real systems.
   D. use equations to describe the operating characteristics of systems.

3. Simulation models can be used for all of the following *except* to:
   A. conduct experiments without disrupting work.
   B. obtain estimates of operating characteristics in less time than would be required to gather the same data from a real system.
   C. prescribe alternative solutions to problems.
   D. sharpen managerial decision-making skills through gaming.

4. Monte Carlo simulation refers to which of the following?
   A. a training device for driver's education.
   B. data collection, random number assignment, model formulation, analysis
   C. sharpening managerial decision-making skills through gaming.
   D. use of computer simulation software.

5. The average number of customers in a waiting line is
   A. a decision variable.
   B. a dependent variable.
   C. a contollable variable.
   D. an uncontrollable variable.

6. Time compression refers to
   A. dynamic changes in the probability distributions for uncontrollable variables.
   B. obtaining estimates of operating characteristics in less time than would be required to gather the same data from a real system.
   C. preparing detailed analysis of characteristics for small increments of time.
   D. the phenomenon observed when approaching the speed of light.

Problems

1. Famous Chamois is an automated car wash, and has a *constant* service time of 6 minutes per car. Chamois advertises that your car also deserves 15 minutes of fame. The time until the next car arrival is described by the following distribution:

Minutes	Probability	Minutes	Probability
1	0.01	8	0.12
2	0.03	9	0.10
3	0.06	10	0.07
4	0.09	11	0.05
5	0.12	12	0.04
6	0.14	13	0.03
7	0.14		1.00

There is enough room in the driveway to accommodate a maximum of two cars in the waiting line (and one being washed). Simulate this system for three hours of operation to determine whether the driveway is large enough to accomodate all arriving customers, and whether any arrivals will spend more than 15 minutes in the system. Start the simulation on the third row of the random number table.

(Multiple-choice answers are on Study Guide page 142.)

Solution

Multiple Choice Answers
1. D
2. A
3. C
4. B
5. B
6. B

1. Fifteen-Minute Car Wash.

Random Number	Time Until Next Arrival
00 — 00	1
01 — 03	2
04 — 09	3
10 — 18	4
19 — 30	5
31 — 44	6
45 — 58	7
59 — 70	8
71 — 80	9
81 — 87	10
88 — 92	11
93 — 96	12
97 — 99	13

Simulation: Near the end of the simulation, the cars in the driveway and the waiting times exceed limits.

Random Number	Time to Arrival	Arrival Time	Max No. In Drive	Service Begins	Departure Time	Minutes in System
50	7	0:07	0	0:07	0:13	6
63	8	0:15	0	0:15	0:21	6
95	12	0:27	0	0:27	0:33	6
49	7	0:34	0	0:34	0:40	6
68	8	0:42	0	0:42	0:48	6
11	4	0:46	1	0:48	0:54	8
40	6	0:52	1	0:54	1:00	8
93	12	1:04	0	1:04	1:10	6
61	8	1:12	0	1:12	1:18	6
48	7	1:19	0	1:19	1:25	6
82	10	1:29	0	1:29	1:35	6
09	3	1:32	1	1:35	1:41	9
08	3	1:35	1	1:41	1:47	12
72	9	1:44	1	1:47	1:53	9
98	13	1:57	0	1:57	2:03	6
41	6	2:03	0	2:03	2:09	6
39	6	2:09	0	2:09	2:15	6
67	8	2:17	0	2:17	2:23	6
11	4	2:21	1	2:23	2:29	8
11	4	2:25	1	2:29	2:35	10
00	1	2:26	2	2:35	2:41	15
07	3	2:29	2	2:41	2:47	**18**
66	8	2:37	2	2:47	2:53	**16**
00	1	2:38	**3**	2:53	2:59	**21**
29	5	2:43	**3**	2:59	3:05	**22**

Location decisions, like capacity planning decisions, involve a significant investment of capital and affect operating costs and productivity of the firm for a long time into the future. Fortunately, we do not have to find the one optimal location among infinite possibilities. Business can thrive in any of several good locations. The decision methods presented in this chapter seek to identify good locations and to insure against making big mistakes. Services usually must be provided in the presence of customers, so location is one of the three keys to success. The other two are location and location.

Should facilities be opened overseas?

Globalization and Geographic Dispersion of Operations

- Tendency to concentrate operations of a similar nature in one geographic area is lessening
- Exception is JIT manufacturing, which relys on supplier proximity
- Trend toward foreign businesses building facilities in this country

Reasons for Globalization

Four Developments Spurring Globalization

1. Improved transportation and communication technologies
2. Reduced regulations on financial systems
3. Increased demand for imported goods
4. Lowered international trade barriers

Disadvantages of Overseas Manufacturing

1. Giving away proprietary technology
2. Threat of nationalization
3. Alienation of U.S. customers
4. Increased response times
5. Increased training requirements

Where is global economic activity particularly visible?

Hot Spots of Global Activity

Mexico

- Maquiladoras build facilities to client specifications and help foreign firms recruit, train, and pay Mexican employees.
  - \+ save about $15,000 per employee per year
  - \- lower productivity
  - \- less work-force stability
  - \- problematic transportation and utility infrastructure
  - \- considerable training requirements

European Community

- EC corporations trade freely, avoid quotas and duties
- EC corporations manufacture core parts within the EC
- Japanese multinationals are investing in EC to manufacture autos and other durable goods

East Europe and Former Soviet Union

- Uncertain pace of growth
- Population about double that of the U.S.

East Asia

- Increasingly important role in the world economy
- Rapidly industrializing nations

Globalization of Services

- Services represented 20% of total world trade in 1990
- Airlines, education, consulting, and restaurants are globally active services

How should global operations be managed, and what are their biggest challenges?

Managing Global Operations

- International operations require a global view of market opportunities
- New standards of quality and fast delivery

Challenges of Managing Multinational Operations

1. Other Languages — competitors are fluent in several languages
2. Different Norms and Customs — shape business values
3. Work-Force Management — different management styles
4. Unfamiliar Laws and Regulations — affect policies and practices
5. Unexpected Cost Mix — the most efficient mix of labor, capital, and material costs depends on their relative costs, which change with location
6. To what degree should corporate production methods be transplanted overseas?
7. How much control should be centralized at the home office?

Four Approaches to Managing International Operations

1. A *global* firm relies on its home offices for strategic direction and is more centralized.
2. *International* firms are more decentralized, but still depend heavily on the abilities of the home office.
3. *Multinational* firms are highly decentralized, with each company subsidiary operating relatively autonomously.
4. *Transitional* firms have a worldwide vision, but allow for local differences. These are highly decentralized organizations with a wide mix of product strategies, cultures, and consumer needs.

Which factors are dominant in picking a new location?

Factors Affecting Location Decisions

"**Facility location** is the process of determining a geographic site for a firm's operations. Managers must weigh many factors when assessing the desirability of a particular site." p. 346

- Use comprehensive checklist of factors for which the degree of achievement is sensitive to location, or is significant to the decision.
- Divide location factors into dominant factors derived from competitive priorities and secondary factors.

Dominant Factors in Manufacturing
(in decreasing order of importance)

When the Bell system was broken up AT&T retained ownership of Bell Labs. The "Baby Bells" then needed to develop their own research facilities. USWEST sought a suitable research facility location within the 14 large western states it serves.

The facility was eventually located in Boulder, Colorado because of proximity to research universities, and because of outstanding recreational opportunities. Also cited were community attitudes embracing the wide variety of cultures and life-styles found among highly educated research personnel.

Favorable Labor Climate
- Wage rates
- Training requirements
- Attitudes toward work
- Worker productivity
- Union strength

Proximity to Markets
- Particularly important when outbound transportation rates are high

Quality of Life
- High quality of life is required to attract technically skilled workers.
  - Good schools ...educated workers are interested in educating their children
  - Low crime ...skilled workers desire to retain their possessions.
  - Recreation ...local recreational opportunities are important to professionals who have discretionary income, but scarce time.

Proximity to Suppliers and Resources
- Important to industries dependent on bulky or heavy raw materials
  - breweries near sources of water
  - electric utilities near water and coal
  - saw mills near trees
  - food processors near produce farms

Proximity to the Parent Company's Facilities
- Important to plants that supply parts to other facilities or frequently rely on other facilities for coordination and communication

Utilities, Taxes and Real Estate Costs
- Costs and availability of utilities vary by location. Electricity is costly in California and the Northeast, water is precious in the Southwest, and telephone service may be inadequate in rural areas.
- Local governments may provide tax relief, training subsidy, debt financing, and other incentives.
- A square mile of farm land can be purchased for the same price as an acre of land in some major cities.

Other Factors
- Room for expansion
- Accessibility to alternative modes of transportation
- Relocation costs
- Community attitudes toward growth, education, regulations
- Work force education and skills
- Condition of local infrastructure (future tax liability)
- Avoiding import quotas, tariffs
- Image ...Would you rather buy picante sauce made in San Antonio or made in New York City?

How does the location decision for service facilities differ from that for manufacturing facilities?

Dominant Factors in Services

Proximity to Customers

- Location is a key factor in determining customer convenience.

Transportation Costs and Proximity to Markets

- Important to warehousing and distribution operations
- Delivery time can be a competitive advantage.

Should a firm be a leader or a follower in picking locations for new retail outlets?

Location of Competitors

- Estimating the impact of competitors is complicated.
  - anticipate competitors reaction
  - avoiding established competition often pays
  - exception is **critical mass**

Critical mass is a follow-the-leader strategy used by car dealers, furniture showrooms, and fast-food chains. The cluster of competitors attracts a larger total number of customers than would occur if the stores were scattered. Rather than making location decisions to wrestle a bigger piece of the pie from competitors, this strategy increases the size of the pie for all.

Site-Specific Factors

- Level of retail activity
- Residential density, discretionary income level
- Traffic flow and visibility

Locating a Single Facility

(assuming no interdependence with other existing facilities)

Should a firm expand on site, add a new facility, or relocate the existing facility?

Selecting On-Site Expansion, New Location, or Relocation

- On-site expansion
  - \+ keeps management together
  - \+ reduces construction time and costs
  - \+ avoids splitting up operations
  - \- diseconomies of scale
  - \- poor materials handling
  - \- increasingly complex production control
  - \- lack of space at the present site
- Building a new plant
  - \+ in the event of strike, fire, or natural disaster, does not have to rely on production from a single plant
  - \+ escape unproductive labor
  - \+ modernize with all new technology
  - \+ reduce transportation costs
- Relocate (move out of existing facility)
  - . tend to be small
  - . don't move very far
  - . single-plant companies needing space and needing to redesign their production processes and layouts

However, the root cause of unproductive labor is usually poor management. If the firm moves but does not improve management, it is only a matter of time until productivity problems reappear.

Firms using an enter-early, exit-late strategy may time the relocation to coincide with the time their product enters the growth stage of the life cycle. At this time, a change from low-volume job-shop production to a high-volume flow-shop arrangement is advantageous.

Comparing Several Sites

A Systematic Site Selection Process

1. Identify important location factors, categorize them into dominant and secondary categories
2. Consider alternatives, narrow choices
3. Collect data
4. Analyze data quantitatively, transportation costs, taxes
5. Evaluate qualitative factors

Should a firm locate near its suppliers, work force, or customers?

Applying the Load-Distance Method

- Proximity to markets, suppliers, resources and other company facilities are related directly to distance.
- Objective: minimize the total weighted loads moving into and out of the facility.

Distance Measures

- **Euclidean* distance** is the straight-line, shortest distance between two points ... as the crow flies, so to speak.
- **Rectilinear distance** assumes that the trip between two points is made with a series of 90° turns.

Use of rectilinear distance is often appropriate for land travel. For example, roads in our flat western states are laid out on a north-south, east-west grid. Many roads are absolutely straight except for "county line jogs" in north-south roads at county borders. Just as it is difficult to wallpaper a bowling ball, these "jogs" are wrinkles caused by man's attempt to subdivide the globe into absolutely square miles. In facility layout (Chapter 9), travel within a facility is often similarly constrained to rectilinear paths. One usually cannot travel diagonally through departments, which have been arranged in rows and columns like a checkerboard.

---

* Euclid was a Greek mathematician who lived in 300 B.C. His *Elements* was a basic work in geometry. The Euclidean distance formula combines three elements of math and geometry. First is the Pythagorean theorem ($c^2 = a^2 + b^2$), which preceded Euclid by some three hundred years. Second, a rectangular "x,y" coordinate system, called a "Cartesian" coordinate system. "Cartesian" is taken from Cartesius, the Latinized name of Descartes, a 17th century French philosopher and mathematician. Third is algebra. I don't know who we can "thank" for algebra, but apparently the ancient Greeks did not use it. The first use of algebra in connection with geometry occurred two *thousand* years later, and led to what is now called analytic geometry. That was the work of the aforementioned René Descartes and Pierre de Fermat in the first half of the 17th century. This "soon" (second half of 17th century) led Newton and Leibniz to the root of all evil: calculus.

I have included this history for two reasons: First, it is my first opportunity to use something from my calculus text book (© 1959), and second, students often erroneously attribute the rule for calculating Euclidean distance to the scarecrow in *The Wizard of Oz*. Upon receiving his "THD" (Doctor of Thinkology) from the Wizard, the scarecrow pronounced: "The sum of the square roots of any two sides of an isosceles triangle is equal to the square root of the remaining side." Which incidentally, is not true.

Calculating a Load-Distance Score

- Multiply each load (weight or trips per time period) between facilities times the distance (Euclidean or rectilinear) the load travels. The load-distance score is the sum of the products.
- Compare load-distance scores for alternative locations. Locations that generate big loads going short distances reduce *ld*. Of the points investigated, the location minimizing *ld* is the tentative best location.
- Other factors, price of land, zoning, suitability of land for building, etc. may require consideration of other sites.

$$x^* = \frac{\sum_i l_i x_i}{\sum_i l_i}$$

$$y^* = \frac{\sum_i l_i y_i}{\sum_i l_i}$$

Patterned Search

1. Start at the *x,y* coordinates of center of gravity.
2. Investigate the impact on *ld* for locations which are a short distance in each of the four directions from the center.
3. If an improvement is found, start another iteration from that point. If not, stop.

- This process is not guaranteed to always find the optimal location.

How does the expected output level of the facility affect location choice?

Using Break-Even Analysis

- Break-even is discussed in Supplement A

Basic Steps

1. Estimate fixed and variable costs for each alternative location
2. Plot total cost lines
3. Approximate the ranges for which each location has lowest cost
4. Solve algebraically for break-even points

$$F_3 + c_3Q = F_2 + c_2Q$$

$$Q_E = \frac{F_2 - F_3}{c_3 - c_2}$$

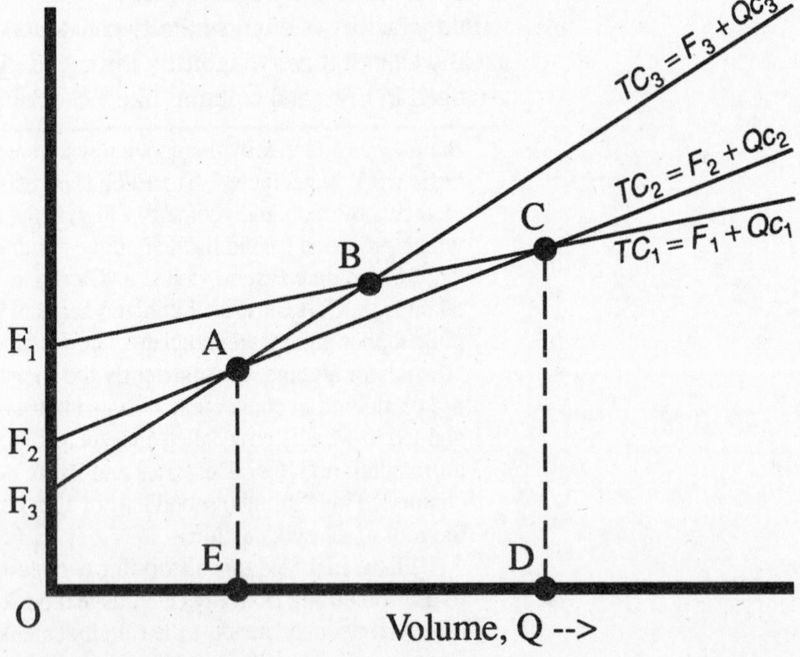

$$F_2 + c_2Q = F_1 + c_1Q$$

$$Q_D = \frac{F_1 - F_2}{c_2 - c_1}$$

The intersection between total costs for Locations 1 and 3 occurring at point B is not relevant. Neither location enjoys the lowest cost at that volume. Location 3 has the lowest total costs at volumes below point E. Location 2 is best between points E and D. Location 1 is preferred at volumes above D.

Location Break-even Exercise

(Solution check appears on Study Guide page 159.)

By chance, The Atlantic City Community Chest has to close temporarily for general repairs. They are considering four temporary office locations:

Property Address	Move-in Costs	Monthly Rent
Boardwalk	$400	$50
Marvin Gardens	$280	$24
St. Charles Place	$350	$10
Baltic Avenue	$ 60	$60

For what length of lease would each location be favored? Hint: in this problem, lease length is analogous to volume.

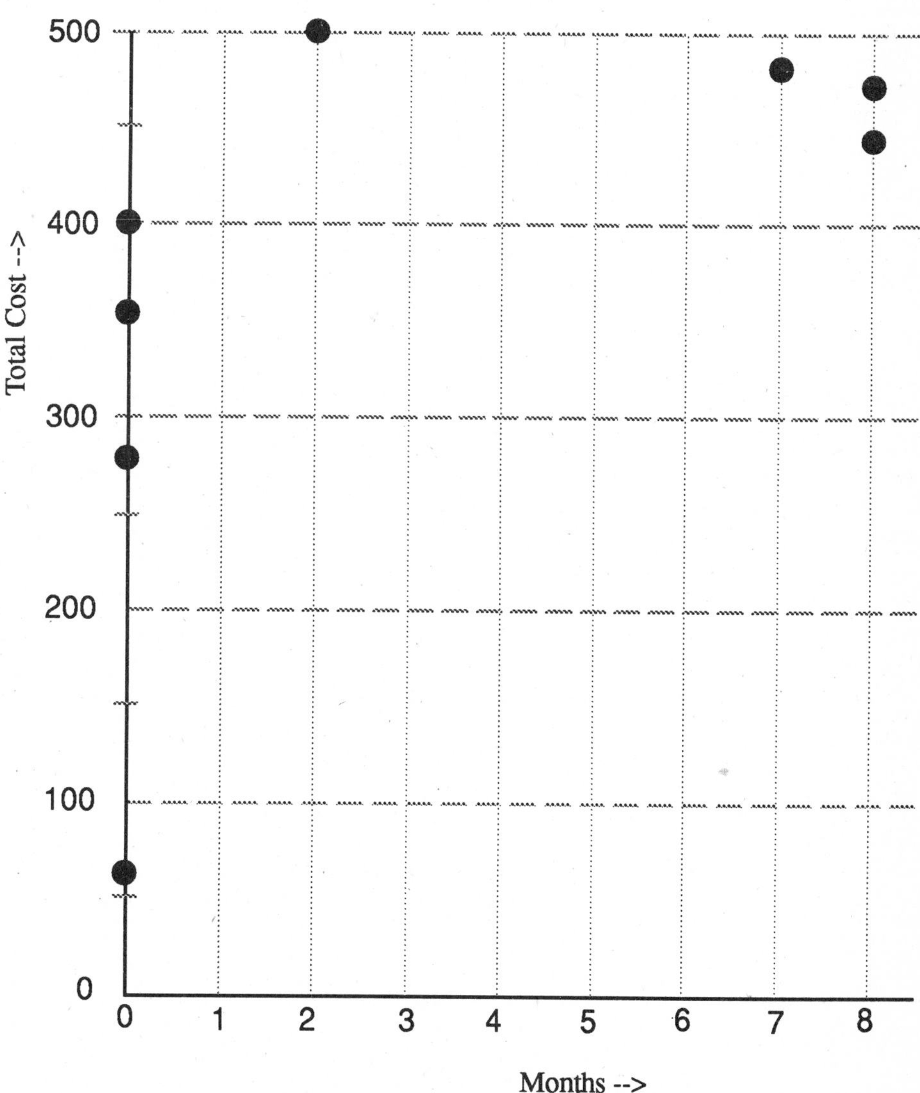

Locating Within a Network of Facilities

(assuming interdependence with other existing facilities)

Three Dimensions of Multiple-facility Location Problems

Location — What is the best location for new facilities?
Allocation — How much work should be assigned to each facility?
Capacity — What is the best capacity for each facility?

Manufacturing or Distribution Systems

- Divide the total market into regions, use a single-facility location technique to locate one facility in each region
- Since each facility serves only its one region, capacity and allocation decisions are straightforward

Service or Retail Systems

- Select some tentative facility locations
- Based on assumptions about how customers select specific locations, obtain allocation and capacity estimates for each location.
- Evaluate solutions obtained, test other reasonable solutions

What is the best way to partition work among various facilities?

The Transportation Method

- Determines the allocation pattern that minimizes transportation costs from multiple sources to multiple destinations
- The method does not consider other facets of the multiple-facility location problem, such as community attitudes or work force skills.

Setting Up the Initial Tableau.

1. Create a matrix with one row for each source (origin or plant) and one column for each sink (destination or warehouse)
2. Make an additional column at the right for plant capacities and an additional row at the bottom for warehouse demands.
3. Insert the transportation cost per unit from each plant to each warehouse in the upper right-hand corner of each cell.

In the example shown below, it costs $3 to ship one unit from Plentywood to Nowood.

	Destinations			
Sources	Nowood, Wyoming	Sundown, Texas	Phoenix, Arizona	Capacity
Plentywood, Montana	$3	$7	$6	6,000
Aurora, Illinois	$8	$5	$9	7,000
Ashland, Nebraska	$7	$6	$4	9,000
Demand	4,000	8,000	10,000	22,000

Finding a Solution

- The least-cost allocation pattern that satisfies all demands and exhausts all capacities is found by using the transportation method (see Supplement G).

Sources	Destinations			Capacity
	Nowood, Wyoming	Sundown, Texas	Phoenix, Arizona	
Plentywood, Montana	$3 4,000	$7 1,000	$6 1,000	6,000
Aurora, Illinois	$8	$5 7,000	$9	7,000
Ashland, Nebraska	$7	$6	$4 9,000	9,000
Demand	4,000	8,000	10,000	22,000

This optimal solution may be interpreted as follows:

Ship 4000 units from Plentywood to Nowood, @ $3 ea. = $12,000.

Ship 7000 units from Aurora to Sundown @ $5 ea. = $35,000.

Ship 9000 units from Ashland to Phoenix @ $4 ea. = $36,000.

Ship 1000 units from Plentywood to Sundown @ $7 ea. = $ 7,000.

Ship 1000 units from Plentywood to Phoenix @ $6 ea. = $ 6,000.

Minimum transportation costs = $96,000.

Note : When considering several locations for a new plant, the transportation method considers only one location alternative at a time. It finds the lowest cost shipping pattern, assuming the new plant will be located as input to the model. The analyst then replaces the first alternative location with the next one, and solves the problem again. An entirely different shipping pattern may result, affecting not only the new location but existing locations as well. Of course, transportation costs also change. The *total* transportation costs of the first location are compared to the *total* for the second, and the lower of the two is generally preferable. Several alternatives are tried, and the one that works best as a part of the system with the existing plants will have the lowest *total* transportation costs. This *does not* say that the transportation costs from the chosen new location will be lower than the transportation costs from any of the other alternatives. What we desire, and what the method identifies, is the location that minimizes transportation costs of the *total* system. Of course, the method can evaluate only the locations that are input to the model by the analyst.

The Larger Solution Process.

"Other costs and various qualitative factors also must be considered as additional parts of a complete evaluation." p. 362

Other Methods of Location Analysis

- Many location analysis problems are complex.
- Analysis of complex location situations involves extensive calculations.
- Three basic computer models have been developed for this purpose.

Heuristics

"Solution guidelines, or rules of thumb, that find feasible — but not necessarily the best solutions to problems are called **heuristics**." p. 362

- Heuristics efficiently handle general views of a problem.

Simulation

- Simulation models evaluate location alternatives by trial and error.

Optimization

- These procedures find the "best" answer, but it is the best answer to a simplified and less realistic view of the problem.

Note that the word "best" is in quotes. Considering the infinity of choices, it is doubtful whether the truly best set of alternatives have been input to the optimization model for consideration. For example, the transportation model optimizes the shipping pattern from a given set of sources, but there is no guarantee that the set of sources are placed in the optimal locations nor is it guaranteed that the sources have optimal capacities.

Multiple-Choice Questions

1. Which of the following is true?
   A. Geography and distance are becoming increasingly important in location decisions.
   B. Just-in-time manufacturing has spurred the trend toward separating operations.
   C. Producing goods or services in the country where the customers live circumvents import quotas.
   D. Regional trading blocks make trade between countries more difficult.

2. What is the primary reason for locating in a maquiladora?
   A. Better utility infrastructure
   B. Higher work force stability
   C. Lower training costs
   D. Lower wages

3. The largest automobile market is
   A. East Asia
   B. Eastern Europe and the Former Soviet Union
   C. European Community
   D. United States of America

4. Which of the following is not usually of prime importance in location decisions, but becomes very important when locating facilities that require good engineering staffs?
   A. Favorable labor climate
   B. Proximity to markets
   C. Proximity to suppliers and material resources
   D. Quality of life

5. Which one of the following factors is much more important for service industries than for manufacturing companies in making location decisions?
   A. Favorable labor climate
   B. Proximity to company's other facilities
   C. Proximity to markets
   D. Proximity to suppliers and resources

6. Which of the following is an advantage of on-site expansion?
   A. Avoidance of unproductive labor
   B. Increased facility focus
   C. Reduced construction time and costs
   D. Reduced outbound transportation costs

7. A small firm of 10 employees in Boulder has designed and introduced a successful new product. The firm is currently paying high rent for a small space on the downtown Pearl Street Mall. Demand has grown to the point where high volume processes are justified, and additional manufacturing space is needed. This firm would be well advised to
   A. build an additional facility in downtown Aspen.
   B. do nothing.
   C. expand at the present site.
   D. relocate everyone to the outskirts of Boulder.

8. A company is more likely to build an additional facility (as opposed to expanding at the present site or relocating) if
   A. it chooses an enter-early, exit-early market strategy.
   B. it desires to avoid splitting up operations.
   C. it desires to reduce transportation costs.
   D. it is small (number of employees around 10).

9. When using break-even to analyze a single facility location, we assume
   A. fixed costs are equal at all locations.
   B. sales volume and price will vary depending on the choice of location.
   C. there is no interdependence with facilities at other locations.
   D. variable costs are nonlinear.

10. In making location decisions, the systematic selection process begins with
    A. bringing the qualitative factors pertaining to each site into the evaluation.
    B. comparing operating costs at alternative locations.
    C. identifing the important location factors.
    D. minimizing transportation costs.

11. The transportation method of linear programming
    A. is a heuristic.
    B. is an optimization technique.
    C. is a simulation modeling technique.
    D. minimizes outbound transportation costs from the new production facility.

(Multiple-choice answers on Study Guide page 156.)

Problems

1. Biff and Sully are considering three potential locations for a new cookie factory and have assigned the scores shown to the relevant factors on a 0 to 10 basis (10 is best). Using the preference matrix, which location would be indicated as the tentative location decision?

Location Factor	Weight	The Neighborhood	Sesame Street	Peewee's Playhouse
Material Supply	0.1	5	9	8
Quality of Life	0.2	9	8	4
Mild Climate	0.3	10*	6	8
Labor Skills	0.4	3	4	7

* It's always a beautiful day in The Neighborhood.

2. The Daryl and Daryl Bros. school of elocution desires to find a central location for providing this service. Business forecasts indicate travel from the central location to New York City on 20 occasions per year. Similarly, there will be 15 trips to Boston, and 30 trips to New Orleans. Using Euclidean distance, what is the load-distance score associated with locating in Chicago?

$$d_{AB} = \sqrt{(x_A - x_B)^2 + (y_A - y_B)^2}$$

$$ld = \sum_i l_i d_i$$

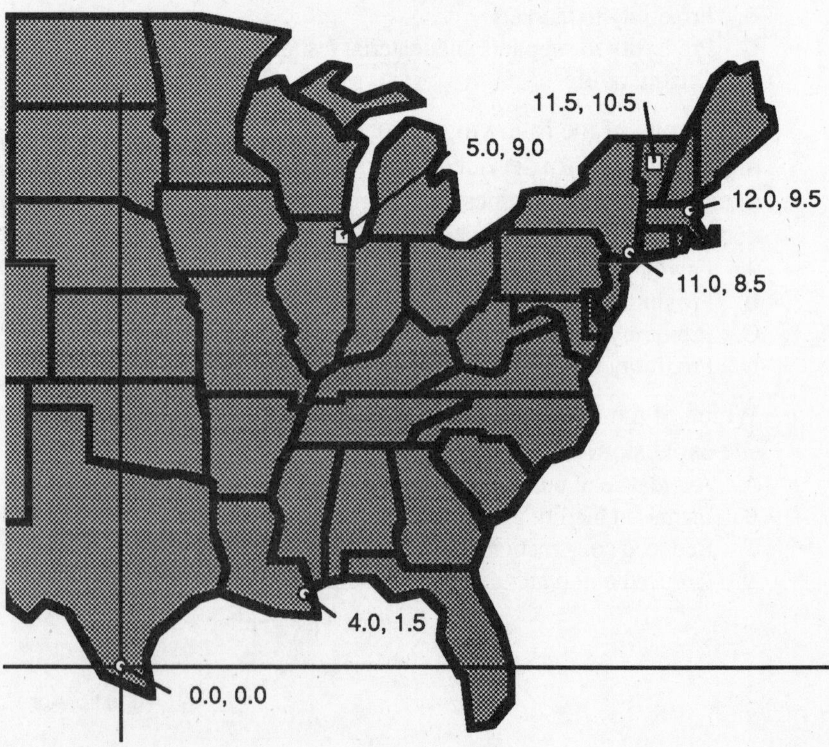

3. In the Daryl and Daryl Bros. problem, using rectilinear distance, what is the load-distance score associated with locating in Vermont?

$$d_{AB} = |x_A - x_B| + |y_A - y_B|$$

$$ld = \sum_i l_i d_i$$

4. What is the center of gravity of the three demand locations?

$$x^* = \frac{\sum_i l_i x_i}{\sum_i l_i}$$

$$y^* = \frac{\sum_i l_i y_i}{\sum_i l_i}$$

5. A brewer is considering whether to add a 4000 barrel per day facility in Omaha or Fort Collins. Compare the two solved linear programming tableaus. Which results in the lower *total* transportation costs?

	Destinations			
Sources	Chicago	Denver	Nashville	Capacity
Boston	$5.00 2,000	$6.00	$5.50	2,000
Seattle	$7.00	$4.00 5,000	$7.00 1,000	6,000
Miami	$5.00	$7.00	$3.00 5,000	5,000
Omaha	$4.00 4,000	$3.00	$5.00	4,000
Demand	6,000	5,000	6,000	17,000

	Destinations			
Sources	Chicago	Denver	Nashville	Capacity
Boston	$5.00 2,000	$6.00	$5.50	2,000
Seattle	$7.00 4,000	$4.00 1,000	$7.00 1,000	6,000
Miami	$5.00	$7.00	$3.00 5,000	5,000
Ft. Collins	$5.50	$1.20 4,000	$8.00	4,000
Demand	6,000	5,000	6,000	17,000

Solutions

1. Biff and Sully. Which location would be indicated as the tentative location decision?

Location Factor	Weight	The Neighborhood		Sesame Street		Peewee's Playhouse	
Material Supply	0.1	5	**0.5**	9	**0.9**	8	**0.8**
Quality of Life	0.2	9	**1.8**	8	**1.6**	4	**0.8**
Mild Climate	0.3	10*	**3.0**	6	**1.8**	8	**2.4**
Labor Skills	0.4	3	**1.2**	4	**1.6**	7	**2.8**
			6.5		**5.9**		**6.8**

Peewee's Playhouse is the indicated location.

2. The Daryl and Daryl Bros. school of elocution. Travel from Chicago to New York City on 20 occasions per year, 15 trips to Boston, and 30 trips to New Orleans. Using Euclidean distance, what is the load-distance score?

New York — Chicago	$= \sqrt{[(11.0-5.0)^2 + (8.5-9.0)^2]}$	= 6.021
Boston — Chicago	$= \sqrt{[(12.0-5.0)^2 + (9.5-9.0)^2]}$	= 7.018
New Orleans — Chicago	$= \sqrt{[(4.0-5.0)^2 + (1.5-9.0)^2]}$	= 7.566

$$ld = \sum l_i d_i = [(6.021 \times 20 \times 2) + (7.018 \times 15 \times 2) + (7.566 \times 30 \times 2)]$$
$$= 905.34$$

Assuming round trips and scale = 250 miles : 1 unit, total ld = 226,335 miles.

$$d_{AB} = \sqrt{(x_A - x_B)^2 + (y_A - y_B)^2}$$

$$ld = \sum_i l_i d_i$$

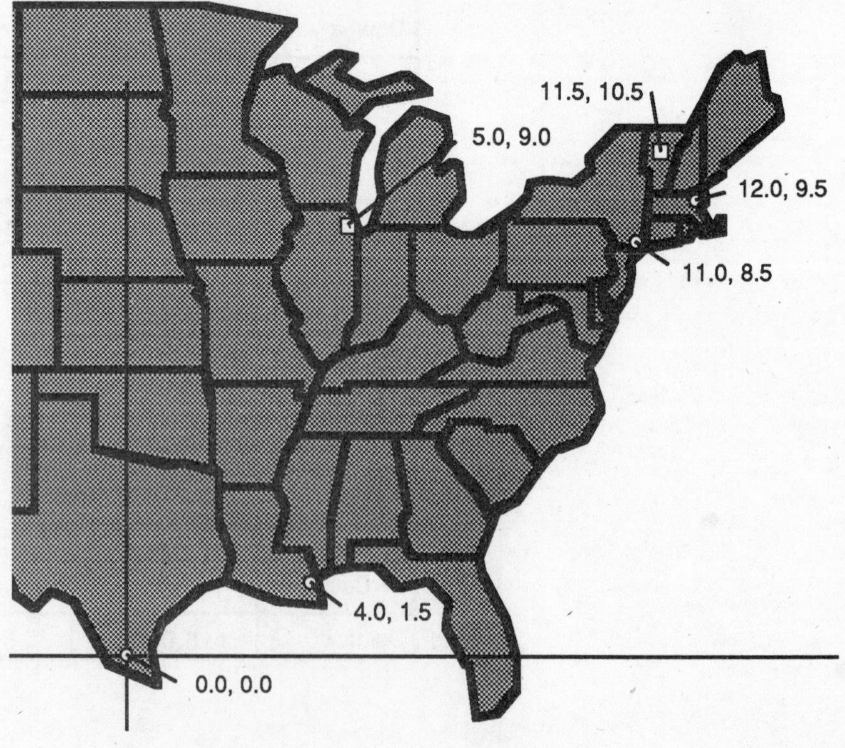

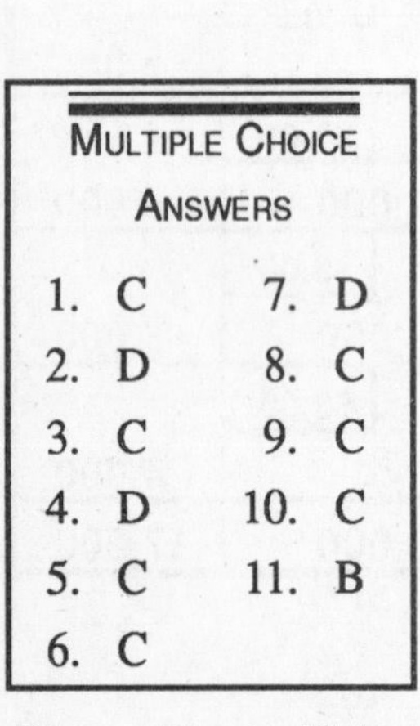

MULTIPLE CHOICE ANSWERS

1. C
2. D
3. C
4. D
5. C
6. C
7. D
8. C
9. C
10. C
11. B

$d_{AB} = |x_A - x_B| + |y_A - y_B|$

$ld = \sum_i l_i d_i$

$x^* = \frac{\sum_i l_i x_i}{\sum_i l_i}$

$y^* = \frac{\sum_i l_i y_i}{\sum_i l_i}$

3. In the Daryl and Daryl Bros. problem, using rectilinear distance, what is the load-distance score associated with locating in Vermont?

New York — Vermont	= I (11.0–5.0) I + I (8.5–9.0) I	= 2.5
Boston — Chicago	= I (12.0–5.0) I + I (9.5–9.0) I	= 1.5
New Orleans — Chicago	= I (4.0–5.0) I + I (1.5–9.0) I	= 16.5

$$ld = \sum l_i d_i = [(2.5 \times 20 \times 2) + (1.5 \times 15 \times 2) + (16.5 \times 30 \times 2)]$$
$$= 1135$$

Assuming round trips and scale = 250 miles : 1 unit, total *ld* = 283,750 miles.

4. What is the center of gravity of the three demand locations?

$$x^* = \frac{\sum_i l_i x_i}{\sum_i l_i} = \frac{[(20 \times 11) + (15 \times 12) + (30 \times 4)]}{65} = 8.0$$

$$y^* = \frac{\sum_i l_i y_i}{\sum_i l_i} = \frac{[(20 \times 8.5) + (15 \times 9.5) + (30 \times 1.5)]}{65} = 5.5$$

Boston, New York, and New Orleans all appear on this map to be located near a straight line running northeast and southwest. The coordinates of the center of gravity (weighted by the number of trips) also falls on this line at 5.5, 8.0. That is a position just north of Charlotte, North Carolina.

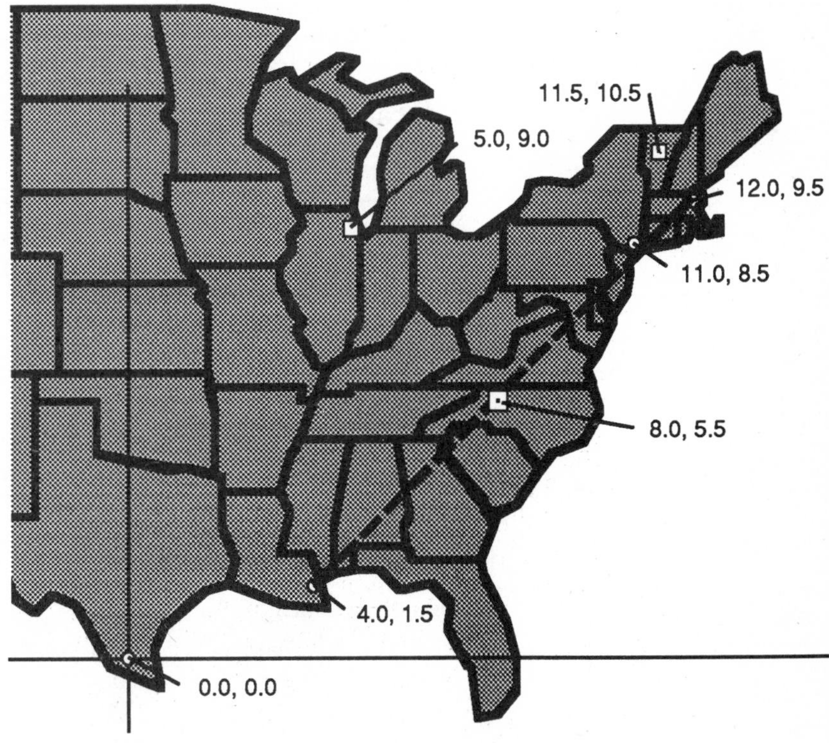

Note that even though the transportation costs from Omaha to Chicago are much higher than the transportation costs from Fort Collins to Denver, Omaha is still the preferred location. The *total* costs of the *system* are lower when the new plant is located in Omaha.

5. A brewer is considering whether to add a 4000 barrel per day facility in Omaha or Fort Collins. Compare the two solved linear programming tableaus. Which results in the lower *total* transportation costs?

Sources	Chicago	Denver	Nashville	Capacity
Boston	$5.00 2,000	$6.00	$5.50	2,000
Seattle	$7.00	$4.00 5,000	$7.00 1,000	6,000
Miami	$5.00	$7.00	$3.00 5,000	5,000
Omaha	$4.00 4,000	$3.00	$5.00	4,000
Demand	6,000	5,000	6,000	17,000

Locating in Omaha:

Shipment	Quantity	Unit Cost	Cost of Shipment
Boston to Chicago	2,000	$ 5.00	$ 10,000
Seattle to Denver	5,000	$ 4.00	$ 20,000
Seattle to Nashville	1,000	$ 7.00	$ 7,000
Miami to Nashville	5,000	$ 3.00	$ 15,000
Omaha to Chicago	4,000	$ 4.00	$ 16,000
		Total Transportation Costs	**$ 68,000**

Sources	Chicago	Denver	Nashville	Capacity
Boston	$5.00 2,000	$6.00	$5.50	2,000
Seattle	$7.00 4,000	$4.00 1,000	$7.00 1,000	6,000
Miami	$5.00	$7.00	$3.00 5,000	5,000
Ft. Collins	$5.50	$1.20 4,000	$8.00	4,000
Demand	6,000	5,000	6,000	17,000

Locating in Fort Collins:

Shipment	Quantity	Unit Cost	Cost of Shipment
Boston to Chicago	2,000	$ 5.00	$ 10,000
Seattle to Chicago	4,000	$ 7.00	$ 28,000
Seattle to Denver	1,000	$ 4.00	$ 4,000
Seattle to Nashville	1,000	$ 7.00	$ 7,000
Miami to Nashville	5,000	$ 3.00	$ 15,000
Ft. Collins to Denver	4,000	$ 1.20	$ 4,800
		Total Transportation Costs	**$ 68,800**

Solution to Location Break-even Exercise

By chance, The Atlantic City Community Chest has to close temporarily for general repairs. They are considering four temporary office locations:

Property Address	Move-in Costs	Monthly Rent
Boardwalk	$400	$50
Marvin Gardens	$280	$24
St. Charles Place	$360	$10
Baltic Avenue	$ 60	$60

For what length of lease would each location be favored?

Solution:

Baltic Avenue would be favored for up to six months, and St. Charles Place is less costly for all longer durations. Neither Boardwalk nor Marvin Gardens is indicated at any lease duration.

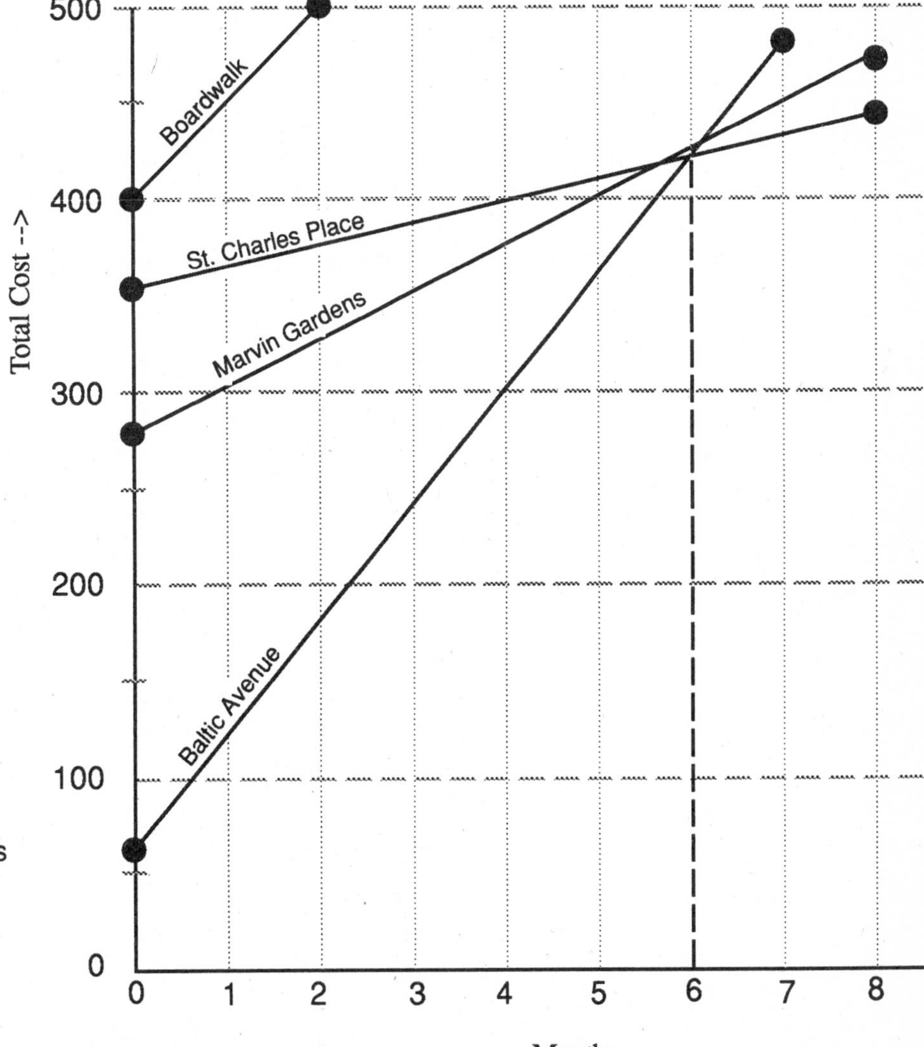

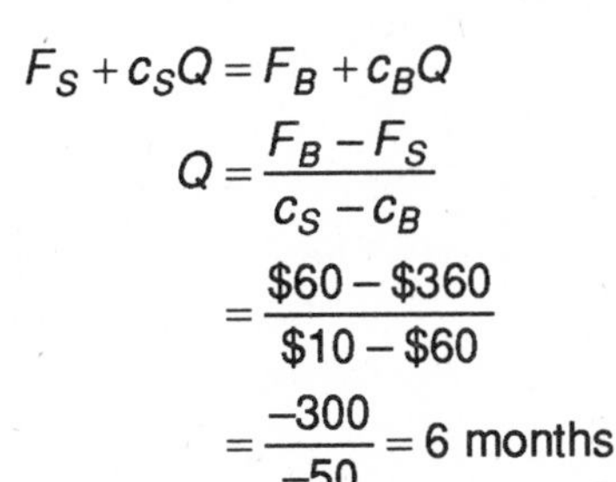

$$F_S + c_S Q = F_B + c_B Q$$

$$Q = \frac{F_B - F_S}{c_S - c_B}$$

$$= \frac{\$60 - \$360}{\$10 - \$60}$$

$$= \frac{-300}{-50} = 6 \text{ months}$$

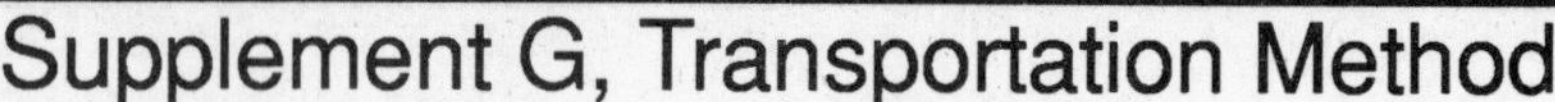

Supplement G, Transportation Method

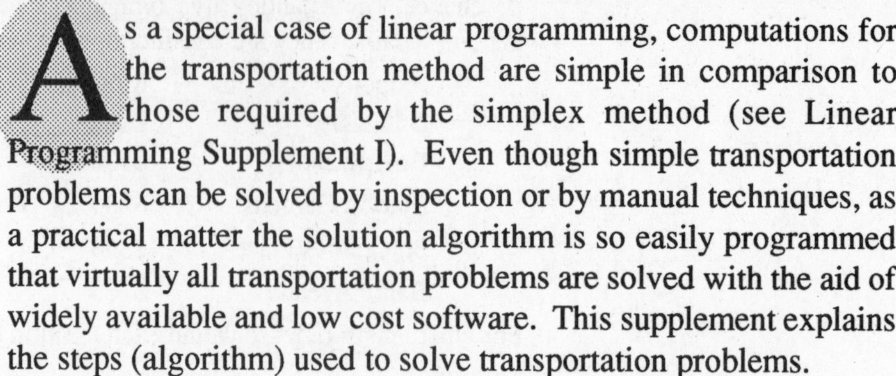

As a special case of linear programming, computations for the transportation method are simple in comparison to those required by the simplex method (see Linear Programming Supplement I). Even though simple transportation problems can be solved by inspection or by manual techniques, as a practical matter the solution algorithm is so easily programmed that virtually all transportation problems are solved with the aid of widely available and low cost software. This supplement explains the steps (algorithm) used to solve transportation problems.

In this text, transportation models are applied to two situations; facility location decisions and aggregate production planning. In location decisions (Chapter 8), this technique allocates shipments from sources to destinations in order to minimize total transportation costs, subject to the assumption that per-unit transportation costs are constant regardless of volume. Other costs which may vary with location, such as wage rates or taxes, are not directly considered within the model.

The transportation method may also be used to find the minimum cost production plan (Chapter 13), subject to the assumption that the variable cost per unit is constant regardless of volume. Other relevant costs, such as the costs of re-sizing the work force, are not directly considered within the model.

Solving Transportation Problems

Four Basic Steps

1. Translate the problem into a tableau.
2. Generate an initial feasible solution.
3. Use the solution algorithm to improve the solution at each iteration until no further improvement is possible.
4. Interpret and evaluate the final (optimal) solution.

1. The Initial Tableau

- Each row represents a supply source, such as picante sauce production plants in San Antonio and in New York City!
- Each column represents a demand destination, such as grocery distribution warehouses at Atlanta, Omaha, and Seattle
- Each cell in the matrix represents a shipping (transportation) route from a source to a demand. For example, the shaded cell will record the number of cases of picante sauce shipped from San Antonio to Omaha (if any).

	Destinations		
Sources	Atlanta	Omaha	Seattle
San Antonio			
New York City!			

- At the upper-right corner of each cell insert the transportation cost per-unit for that shipping route. For example, the cost to move one case of picante sauce from New York City to Seattle is $9.

	Destinations		
Sources	Atlanta	Omaha	Seattle
San Antonio	$4	$5	$6
New York City!	$3	$7	$9

- Add a column at the right side of the matrix to record the capacity of each source. The capacity of the San Antonio plant is 12,000 cases per time period. Add a row at the bottom of the matrix to represent the total demand required at each destination. For example, the demand at Atlanta is 8,000 cases per time period.

	Destinations			
Sources	Atlanta	Omaha	Seattle	**Capacity**
San Antonio	$4	$5	$6	12,000
New York City!	$3	$7	$9	10,000
Demand	8,000	6,000	5,000	

- If the total capacity of all sources exactly matches the total demand for all destinations, go to Step 2.
- If the total capacity of all sources exceeds the total demand of all destinations, insert a (dummy) column between the matrix and the capacity column to absorb the unused (idle) capacity. The transportation cost for each dummy cell is zero. (This is shown below.) Go to Step 2.

	Destinations			**Dummy**	
Sources	Atlanta	Omaha	Seattle	**Unused**	**Capacity**
San Antonio	$4	$5	$6	$0	12,000
New York City!	$3	$7	$9	$0	10,000
Demand	8,000	6,000	5,000	3,000	22,000

- If the total capacity of all sources is less than the total demand of all destinations, insert a (dummy) row between the matrix and the demand row to represent unsatisfied demand. The transportation cost for each cell is zero. Go to Step 2.

2. Generating an Initial Solution

a. Northwest-Corner Method

Sources	Destinations			Dummy	Capacity
	Atlanta	Omaha	Seattle	Unused	
San Antonio	$4 8,000	$5 4,000	$6	$0	12,000
New York City!	$3	$7 2,000	$9 5,000	$0 3,000	10,000
Demand	8,000	6,000	5,000	3,000	22,000

b. Vogel's Approximation Method

- Requires more work than the northwest-corner method
- Provides an initial solution that is much closer to the optimal solution

Penalty cost for San Antonio row = $4 – $0 = $4. <-- largest
Penalty cost for New York City! row = $3 – $0 = $3.
Penalty cost for Atlanta column = $4 – $3 = $1.
Penalty cost for Omaha column = $7 – $5 = $2.
Penalty cost for Seattle column = $9 – $6 = $3.
Penalty cost for Dummy column = $0 – $0 = $0.

Sources	Destinations			Dummy	Capacity
	Atlanta	Omaha	Seattle	Unused	
San Antonio	$4	$5	$6	$0 3,000	12,000
New York City!	$3	$7	$9	$0	10,000
Demand	8,000	6,000	5,000	3,000	22,000

Penalty cost for San Antonio row = $5 – $4 = $1.
Penalty cost for New York City! row = $7 – $3 = $4. <-- largest
Penalty cost for Atlanta column = $4 – $3 = $1.
Penalty cost for Omaha column = $7 – $5 = $2.
Penalty cost for Seattle column = $9 – $6 = $3.

Sources	Destinations			Dummy	Capacity
	Atlanta	Omaha	Seattle	Unused	
San Antonio	$4	$5	$6	$0 3,000	12,000
New York City!	$3 8,000	$7	$9	$0	10,000
Demand	8,000	6,000	5,000	3,000	22,000

Penalty cost for San Antonio row = $6 – $5 = $1.
Penalty cost for New York City! row = $9 – $7 = $2.
Penalty cost for Omaha column = $7 – $5 = $2.
Penalty cost for Seattle column = $9 – $6 = $3. <-- largest

Sources	Destinations Atlanta	Omaha	Seattle	Dummy Unused	Capacity
San Antonio	$4	$5	$6 5,000	$0 3,000	12,000
New York City!	$3 8,000	$7	$9	$0	10,000
Demand	8,000	6,000	5,000	3,000	22,000

The shipments to Omaha satisfying the capacity and demand (rim) conditions are shown below:

Sources	Destinations Atlanta	Omaha	Seattle	Dummy Unused	Capacity
San Antonio	$4	$5 4,000	$6 5,000	$0 3,000	12,000
New York City!	$3 8,000	$7 2,000	$9	$0	10,000
Demand	8,000	6,000	5,000	3,000	22,000

3. Improving the Solution, Iteration by Iteration

(Stepping Stone Method)

a. Select the Entering Route — First Iteration

Sources	Destinations Atlanta	Omaha	Seattle	Dummy Unused	Capacity
San Antonio	$4 ●	$5 ✻	$6 ✻	$0 ✻	12,000
New York City!	$3 ✻	$7 ✻	$9 ▲	$0 ■	10,000
Demand	8,000	6,000	5,000	3,000	22,000

●	San Antonio — Atlanta	+4 –5 +7 –3 = +3
▲	New York City! — Seattle	+9 –7 +5 –6 = +1
■ — —	New York City! — Dummy	+0 –0 +5 –7 = –2

The only entering route offering a savings is the New York City! to Dummy route ■.

b. Select the Exiting Route — First Iteration

The exiting route is the 2,000 units originally planned to be shipped from New York City! to Omaha. The result of this iteration is shown below:

Sources	Destinations Atlanta	Omaha	Seattle	Dummy Unused	Capacity
San Antonio	$4	$5 6,000	$6 5,000	$0 1,000	12,000
New York City!	$3 8,000	$7 —	$9	$0 2,000	10,000
Demand	8,000	6,000	5,000	3,000	22,000

c. Select the Entering Route — Second Iteration

Sources	Destinations: Atlanta	Omaha	Seattle	Dummy Unused	Capacity
San Antonio	$4 ●	$5 ✻	$6 ✻	$0 ✻	12,000
New York City!	$3 ✻	$7 ■	$9 ▲	$0 ✻	10,000
Demand	8,000	6,000	5,000	3,000	22,000

● . . . . San Antonio – Atlanta +4 –0 +0 –3 = +1

▲ . . . . New York City – Seattle +9 –0 +0 –6 = +3

■ — — — — New York City – Omaha +7 –5 +0 –0 = +2

Since no entering route offers the possibility of reducing costs, we have already found the optimal solution.

4. Identifying and Evaluating the Final Solution

Sources	Destinations: Atlanta	Omaha	Seattle	Dummy Unused	Capacity
San Antonio	$4	$5 6,000	$6 5,000	$0 1,000	12,000
New York City!	$3 8,000	$7 —	$9	$0 2,000	10,000
Demand	8,000	6,000	5,000	3,000	22,000

Since Vogel's Approximation Method started us out with such a good initial feasible solution, it required only one iteration to find the optimal transportation plan:

Move 6,000 cases from San Antonio to Omaha @ $5 = $30,000.
Move 5,000 cases from San Antonio to Seattle @ $6 = $30,000.
Move 8,000 cases from New York City! to Atlanta @3 = $24,000.
Minimum Transportation Cost = $84,000.

The San Antonio plant will have 1,000 cases of capacity cushion.
The New York City plant will have 2,000 cases of idle capacity.

Degeneracy

"Degeneracy can occur in the derivation of an initial solution when we satisfy a row constraint and a column constraint simultaneously with one allocation, or when we introduce a new route into the solution and more than one negative cell in the loop has the same minimum allocation." p. 387

- Allocate an infinitesimal quantity, ε
  - to nonallocated cells having loops that cannot be formed without the ε allocation.
  - to bring the total number of allocated cells to $m + n - 1$.
- Since ε is so small, bringing this quantity into the solution will not affect total transportation costs.

Multiple-Choice Questions

1. Which of the following basic steps of the transportation method must always be done by a person (rather than a computer)?
   A. Translate the decision situation into the standard format of a transportation problem.
   B. Generate an initial feasible solution.
   C. Incrementally improve the solutions until no further improvements are possible
   D. Identify and evaluate the final solution.

2. The standard format of a transportation method linear programming problem is called a
   A. matrix
   B. spreadsheet
   C. table
   D. tableau

3. The quickest way to arrive at an initial feasible solution is
   A. the modified-distribution method
   B. the northwest-corner method
   C. the stepping-stone method
   D. Vogel's approximation method (VAM)

4. The optimal solution will never need more than ___ cells
   A. m, the number of rows in the tableau
   B. n, the number of columns in the tableau
   C. $m + n - 1$
   D. $m + n$

5. When applied to a plant facility location decision, the transportation method results in the optimal location with respect to
   A. lowest inbound transportation costs at the new source.
   B. lowest outbound transportation costs at the new source.
   C. lowest total outbound transportation costs for the network of sources.
   D. lowest total of relevant costs for the network of sources.

6. In a *maximization* problem
   A. the entering route has the most negative net contribution of all the nonallocated cells.
   B. the exiting route is the one with the greatest transportation quantity.
   C. the optimal solution is indicated when the net contributions of all nonallocated cells are 0 or negative.
   D. the optimal solution is indicated when all cells have been allocated.

7. When the transportation method is used to optimize *costs of production*
   A. rows represent production locations.
   B. rows represent sources of production.
   C. columns represent demand locations.
   D. use the maximization techniques.

8. Degeneracy refers to
   A. when one iteration is succeeded by the next iteration.
   B. when the number of routes in a tableau are less than $m + n - 1$.
   C. when the succeeding iteration is inferior to the preceeding iteration.
   D. when the transportation method fails to identify the optimal solution.

9. The optimization process demonstrated in this supplement is called
   A. the modified-distribution method
   B. the northwest-corner method
   C. the stepping-stone method
   D. Vogel's approximation method (VAM)

10. An advantage of VAM over the Northwest-corner method is:
    A. Decreased iterations required to solve the problem
    B. It can be used for location decisions in other parts of the country.
    C. Less time is required to establish an initial feasible solution.
    D. VAM finds a better optimal solution.

Multiple Choice Answers

1. A	7. B
2. D	8. B
3. C	9. C
4. C	10. A
5. C	
6. C	

Chapter Nine, Layout

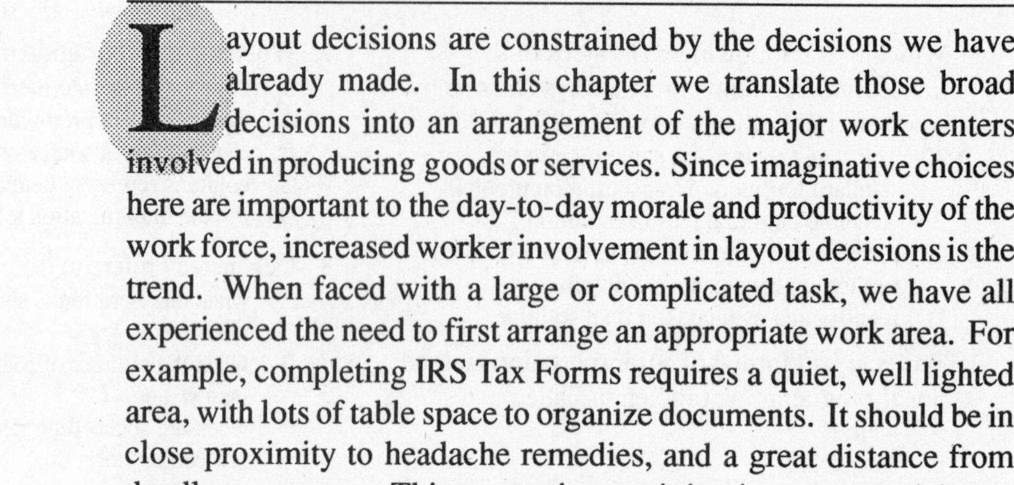

Layout decisions are constrained by the decisions we have already made. In this chapter we translate those broad decisions into an arrangement of the major work centers involved in producing goods or services. Since imaginative choices here are important to the day-to-day morale and productivity of the work force, increased worker involvement in layout decisions is the trend. When faced with a large or complicated task, we have all experienced the need to first arrange an appropriate work area. For example, completing IRS Tax Forms requires a quiet, well lighted area, with lots of table space to organize documents. It should be in close proximity to headache remedies, and a great distance from deadly weapons. This arranging activity is a prerequisite to effectively and efficiently completing work.

What is Layout Planning?

What are some key layout questions that need to be addressed?

"**Layout planning** involves decisions about the physical arrangement of economic activity centers within a facility." p. 398

- The goal is to allow resources to work effectively.

Four Physical Arrangement Questions

1. What centers should the layout include?
   The centers should
   - reflect the process decisions
   - maximize productivity
2. How much space and capacity does each center need?
   Inadequate space can
   - reduce productivity
   - reduce privacy
   - create health and safety hazards

   Too much space can
   - reduce productivity
   - isolate employees
   - increase costs
3. How should each center's space be configured?
   - The amount of space, its shape, and the elements in an activity center are all interrelated.
4. Where should each center be located?
   - Significant effect on productivity
   - Frequent communication calls for close proximity

FIGURE 9.1

Frozen foods	Dry Groceries	Meats
Bread		Vegetables

Meats	Dry Groceries	Frozen foods
Vegetables		Bread

Alternative arrangements of activity centers may have identical relative locations but different absolute locations. For example, if two arrangements of activity centers are mirror images of each other, the centers will have different absolute locations, yet they will have the same neighbors. Relative location is usually the most important issue with respect to material handling cost and communication effectiveness. It usually doesn't matter whether you're traveling east or west when moving materials or communicating. On the other hand, absolute location can be important. Artists may prefer a northern exposure; west-facing offices command a premium in Denver; and if you're in a showdown at the OK corral, you want the sun at your back.

How should layout reflect competitive priorities?

Strategic Issues

- Layout requirements are determined by the type of operation.

Upon reaching the door to the plant, our tour guide stopped to check that we had put on our protective glasses and said: "I'm not sure what we will find on the other side of this door. If the workers decide that a different arrangement might improve things, they just do it."

Layout Choices

1. Plan for current or current plus future needs
2. Single-story or multi-story designs
3. Whether to include employees in the planning process
4. Layout type
5. Which layout performance criteria are important?

Should a layout be process, product, hybrid, or fixed position?

Layout Types

Process Layout

- Organizes resources around the process and groups work stations or departments according to function
- Intermittent, low volume, high-variety production
- Advantages
  - \+ general purpose, flexible resources are less capital intensive
  - \+ less vulnerable to changes in product mix or new market strategies
  - \+ general purpose resources are not dedicated to one product line
- Disadvantages
  - \- slower processing rates
  - \- lost production time during setups
  - \- more capital and more floor space tied up with inventory
  - \- longer manufacturing lead times
  - \- costly materials handling
  - \- complex production planning and control

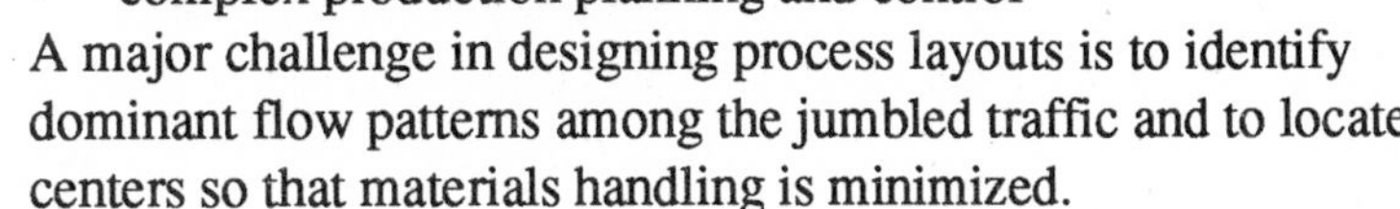

- A major challenge in designing process layouts is to identify dominant flow patterns among the jumbled traffic and to locate centers so that materials handling is minimized.

Product Layout

- Resources dedicated to a product or closely related product family
- Repetitive, continuous production
- Special-purpose equipment arranged in a single path, which is consistent with the routing sequence of the product
- Advantages
  - + faster processing rates
  - + lower inventories
  - + infrequent setups
- Disadvantages
  - for short product life-cycles, the layout might have to be redesigned frequently
  - specialized resources are vulnerable to changes in market
  - for low volume, dedicated resources have low utilization

- Challenge in designing product layouts
  - minimize resources used to achieve desired output rate
  - balance tasks, equalize the workload assigned to resources

The arrangement of work centers in product-focused facilities is an almost trivial task. Arrangement is dictated by the product routing sequence. In comparison to process layout, there are very few viable alternatives.

Hybrid Layout

- Combines elements of both a product and process focus
- Group technology cell
  - identify product families having similar processing steps
  - if the product family volume justifies it, resources are dedicated to making only that product family
  - the equipment is arranged in a production line, matching the process sequence for the family
  - products with insufficient volume to justify dedicated resources are produced in a process layout area of the facility
- Other hybrid layouts
  - flexible manufacturing systems (FMS)
  - one worker-multiple machine (OWMM) stations
  - focused facilities with component fabrication assigned to a job shop (process layout) and assembly accomplished in flow lines (product layout)
  - retail

Fixed-Position Layout

- Product is fixed in place
- Human, material, and capital resources come to the product
- Minimizes number of times product must be moved
- High travel cost, low volume, high wages for multi-skilled workers, uncontrolled environment, and few opportunities for automation combine to result in very low productivity
- Used for
  - very large products, roads, power plants, airplanes
  - service of fragile or bulky items

What performance criteria should be emphasized?

Performance Criteria

Capital Investment

- Process focus
  - + lower investment in equipment and space for equipment
  - - higher investment in inventory and space for inventory

Materials Handling

- More important in process focus, where materials handling is difficult to automate
- Job shops arranged to recognize dominant flows and minimize material handling costs

Flexibility

"**Layout flexibility** means either that the facility remains desirable after significant changes occur or that it can be easily and inexpensively adapted in response to them." p. 405

Other Criteria

- Labor productivity
- Equipment maintenance
- Work environment
- Organizational structure

Can some miniature product layouts be created in a facility?

Creating Hybrid Layouts

One Worker, Multiple Machines

"If volumes aren't sufficient to keep several workers busy on one production line, the manager might set up a line small enough to keep one worker busy." p. 406

- One worker operates several *different* machines simultaneously, to achieve line flow.
- The machines operate on their own for much of the cycle.
- The worker interacts with the machines as required, performing loading, unloading, or other operations that have not been automated.
- Benefits are similar to those of flow lines:
  - + lower WIP inventory
  - + reduced frequency of setup
  - + simplified materials handling
  - + reduced cycle time through overlapped operations
- Costs are associated with the isolation of the worker
  - - job dissatisfaction
  - - high suicide rate

Group Technology

- Group parts into families that have identical processing steps.
- Changeover from producing one part to another requires only minor setup adjustments.
- Product family volume justifies dedication of machines, which are arranged into flow lines called *cells*.

In group technology, when a part is produced it is always sent to the GT cell dedicated to its family. The cell is likely to have only one of each type of machine required for the processing steps. Therefore, the part is always processed on the same set of machines every time it is produced.

In a process layout, there are several similar machines in each work center. The part may be sent to whichever machine in the work center that happens to be available. Although the machines in a work center may appear to be identical, they are not. They differ in wear and in other small ways that may show up as slight variations in the critical dimensions of a part.

Advantages of Group Technology

- \+ less set-up time
- \+ lower WIP
- \+ less materials handling
- \+ reduced cycle time
- \+ increased opportunities for automation
- \+ reduced variation

How can a better process layout be found for a facility?

Designing Process Layouts

Recall that a major challenge in designing process layouts is to identify dominant flow patterns among the jumbled traffic and to locate centers so that materials handling is minimized.

Step 1: Gather Information

Space Requirements by Center

- Tie space requirements to capacity plans.
- Add "circulation" space, that is, aisles wide enough to move materials to and from the center, and space to access the machines for maintenance or disassembly.
  - Recall that process layouts have higher WIP. Provide queue space for that inventory at each center.
  - Also recall that rework requires space.

Department	Square feet
Inspection	600
Operations	2,400
Purchasing	1,200
Reception	600
Engineering & Development	1,200
Shipping & Receiving	1,200

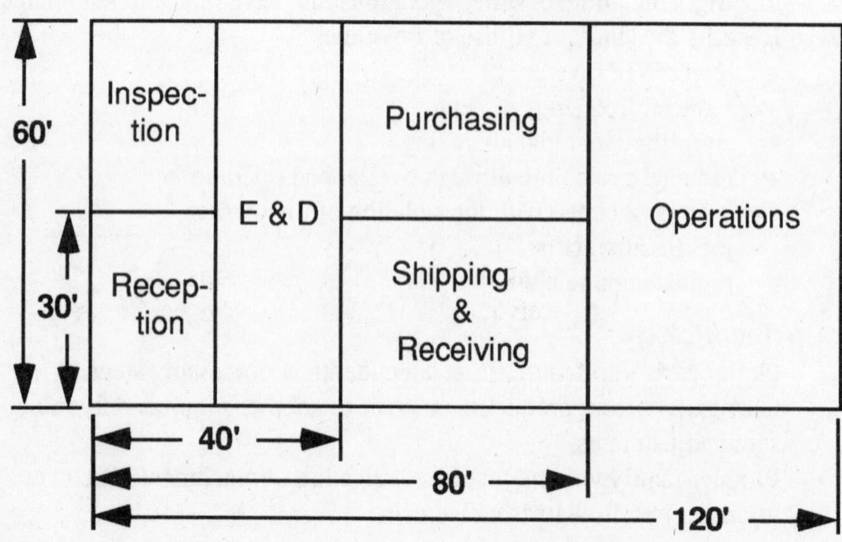

Available Space

- Make a drawing to scale of the exterior walls. Within the walls, make a **block plan** that *roughly* shows the space for each center and its present absolute locations.

Closeness Ratings

- Which items need to be close to each other, and which should not be close to each other?
- From-to matrix

From-to Matrix (trips per day)						
From and To	**1**	**2**	**3**	**4**	**5**	**6**
1. Inspection	—	60	20			90
2. Operations		—	40		50	70
3. Purchasing			—	80	20	
4. Reception				—	20	
5. Engineering and Design					—	
6. Shipping and Receiving						—

- REL (relationship) chart

From the REL chart we see that it is undesirable (x) to have the reception area near engineering and design. We want to prevent the engineers from talking to salespersons without the presence of purchasing. We will place the purchasing department between engineering and the reception area. Because of high traffic it is absolutely necessary (a) that inspection be near shipping and receiving, and that purchasing be near the reception area. It is especially important (e) for operations to be near shipping and receiving, and it is important (i) to have operations near engineering and design. It is of ordinary importance (o) to have inspection near operations. Because of noise and chaos, it is undesirable to have operations near the reception area.

	Closeness Rating Between Departments					
Department	1	2	3	4	5	6
1. Inspection	—		O (1)			A (1)
2. Operations		—		X (5)	I (2)	E (1,4)
3. Purchasing			—	A (1)		
4. Reception				—	X (3)	
5. Engineering & Design					—	
6. Shipping & Receiving						—

Closeness Ratings

Rating	Definition
A	Absolutely necessary
E	Especially important
I	Important
O	Ordinary closeness
U	Unimportant
X	Undesirable

Explanation Codes

Code	Meaning
1	Traffic
2	Shared personnel
3	Security
4	Space utilization
5	Noise
6	Employee preference

Other considerations associated with absolute locations

- The shipping and receiving area should be near the exterior of the building.
- The foundation in operations should be strong enough to support heavy equipment and be isolated from the rest of the plant to reduce noise and vibration.
- Access to electricity, drains, waste treatment, heating, ventilation, and air conditioning and fire protection required for computers.

Step 2: Develop a Block Plan

This example uses rectilinear distance between the *middle* of work centers. For example, in the current arrangement travel between inspection and operations requires moving 90 feet east-west and 15 feet north-south, for a total of 105 feet. From the reception area to purchasing is 50 feet east and 30 feet north, for a total of 80 feet.

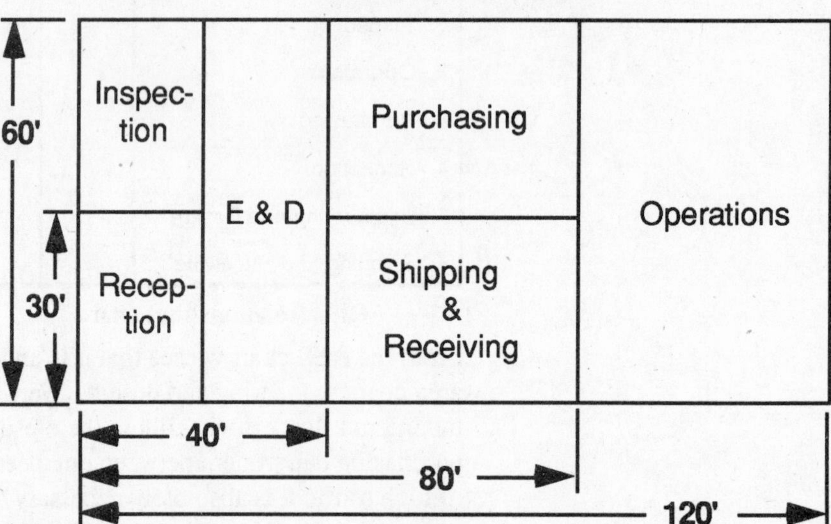

The load distance score for the **current plan** is:

Departments	Trips	Distance	Total
Inspection - Operations	60	105	6,300
Inspection - Purchasing	20	50	1,000
Inspection - Shipping & Receiving	90	80	7,200
Operations - Purchasing	40	55	2,200
Operations - Engineering & Design	50	70	3,500
Operations - Shipping & Receiving	70	55	3,850
Purchasing - Reception	80	80	6,400
Purchasing - Engineering & Design	20	45	900
Reception - Engineering & Design	20	35	700
		Total Load-Distance Score =	**32,050**

The load distance score for the **proposed plan** is:

Departments	Trips	Distance	Total
Inspection - Operations	60	83	4,980
Inspection - Purchasing	20	48	960
Inspection - Shipping & Receiving	90	23	2,070
Operations - Purchasing	40	50	2,000
Operations - Engineering & Design	50	50	2,500
Operations - Shipping & Receiving	70	60	4,200
Purchasing - Reception	80	48	3,840
Purchasing - Engineering & Design	20	40	800
Reception - Engineering & Design	20	88	1,760
		Total Load-Distance Score =	**23,110**

The proposed plan meets all of the criteria and reduces distances traveled by about 28%.

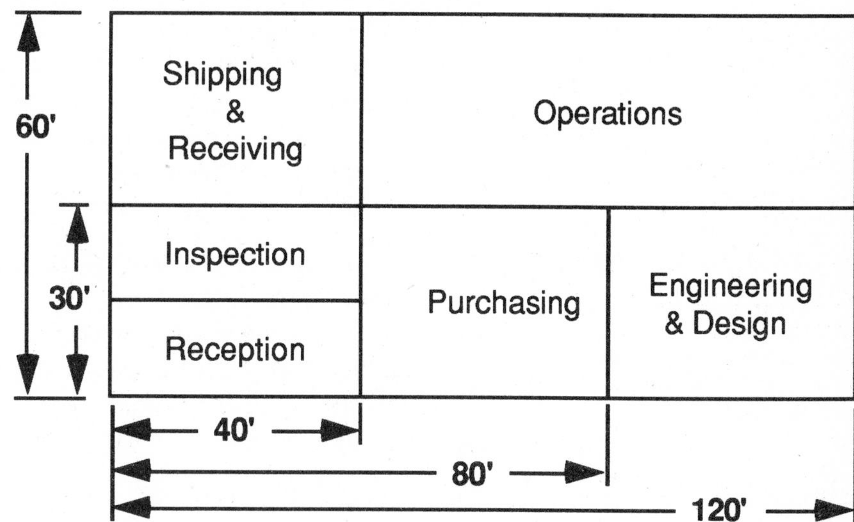

Step 3: Design a Detailed Layout

- Translate block plan into a detailed plan
  - show exact size and shape of each center
  - aisles, stairs, machines, desks, etc.
- Visual models may be used to check the feasibility and appropriate sequence of moving large objects

Aids for Process Layout Decisions

Automated Layout Design Program (ALDEP)

Computerized Relative Allocation of Facilities Technique (CRAFT)

What type of layout pattern makes sense for a warehouse?

Warehouse Layouts

A Layout Solution

- When all travel is direct from dock to storage area and back (no travel between storage areas), this approach finds an optimal solution

Decision Rule

1. Equal areas. Place the most frequent destination closest.
2. Unequal areas. Place the destination with the largest ratio of trip frequency to block space closest.

Additional Layout Options

- Seasonal items may be stored near the dock during peak demand, then replaced by other items as the seasons change.
- Increased stockpicking productivity may offset the higher rack and equipment costs of high-ceilinged warehouses.
- The route collection system, batch picking system, and zone system are alternatives to the out-and-back pattern which may reduce total travel distances.

What is the best trade-off between proximity and privacy for an office layout?

Sometimes called cubies (or "prairie dog villages" because workers duck below office partitions when supervisors approach), acceptance of open office concepts are generally higher among those who won't actually be working in one themselves.

Some supervisors prohibit decorating cubies with plants, pictures or any other expressions of individuality. "The plants disrupt my view of the mountains." "Don't place books on the top shelf of your cubie. They stick up above the partitions." "Don't hang anything on the walls, they've just been painted." or "Put everything away. The client is coming for a tour."

Size of office, partition height, size of desk, desk overhang, depth of carpet pile, a WOWO (write on, wipe off) board, number and style of chairs, a lamp and/or water pitcher on the desk, even the size of the trash can, are specified according to organizational heirarchy status.

A worker who brings in his own desk lamp or heaven forbid, a larger trash can, is viewed as assuming unearned status and will be disciplined. For grins (after you've secured other employment) watch the reaction after you bring in your own office chair!

As Dave Barry would say: "I'm not making this up!" All of the above are actual events.

Office Layouts

Proximity and privacy are conflicting goals in office layouts.

Proximity — open offices with no doors or real walls

- Better communication
- Enhanced teamwork
- Unimaginative checkerboard arrangements adversely affect morale
  - feeling lost in the crowd
  - loss of individual value
  - feeling of being constantly supervised

Privacy — completely enclosed offices

- Fewer distractions
- Better security for proprietary information
- Strong link between privacy and satisfaction with one's supervisor
  - \+ correcting errors need not embarrass the worker in front of peers
  - \+ individual can express creativity within his or her "space"

Options in Office Layout

"Providing both proximity and privacy for employees poses a dilemma for management." p. 422

Four Approaches to Office Layout

1. Traditional
   - Closed offices for management, human resources purchasing, and others which require confidential conversations
   - Open offices for all others
   - Strong status congruence
2. Office Landscaping
   - Plants, screens, and portable partitions which increase privacy and form clusters or work groups.
   - Difficult to concentrate or hold sensitive discussions
3. Activity Settings
   - Employees move from one activity setting to the next as their work changes.
   - Each employee gets a small home base.
   - This is sometimes called a "cave and court." Work that requires concentration is done in the "cave." Communication and coordination is done in the "court."
4. Electronic Cottages
   - They are a modern-day version of cottage industry.
   - The person working at home gets tagged with handling all sorts of errands and crises. The family disruptions can affect productive time greatly.
   - It is difficult to build relationships, so communication with supervisors can become strained.

How can a better product layout for a facility be determined?

Designing Product Layouts

Recall that the major challenge in product layouts is to minimize the number of work stations while balancing the work assigned to the stations. If done properly, the work will flow along a production line at the desired rate.

Line Balancing

"**Line balancing** is the assignment of work to stations in a line so as to achieve the desired output rate with the smallest number of work stations." p. 424

- Lines may be rebalanced
  - when initially set up
  - when the output rate is changed
  - when a work element time standard is changed

Steps in Assembly Line Balancing

1. Begin by breaking the work to be done into *work elements.*
2. Obtain a *labor standard* for each work element.
3. Identify the *immediate predecessors* for each work element.
4. Complete the *precedence diagram.*
5. Convert the *desired output rate* into a *cycle time.*
6. Calculate the *theoretical minimum* number of work stations.
7. Use a *heuristic* to assign work elements to work stations.
8. Calculate the *idle time, efficiency, and balance delay.*
9. Optional: use trial-and-error to seek improved balance, using idle time, efficiency, and balance delay as performance measures.

Precedence Diagram

- Circles (or nodes) denote work elements.
- Arrows indicate precedence relationships. Each arrow leads from an immediate predecessor work element and points to the next work element. Several arrows may emanate from or terminate upon a node. For example, element 2 is the immediate predecessor of work elements 4, 5, and 6. Element 8 is preceded by elements 3 and 7.

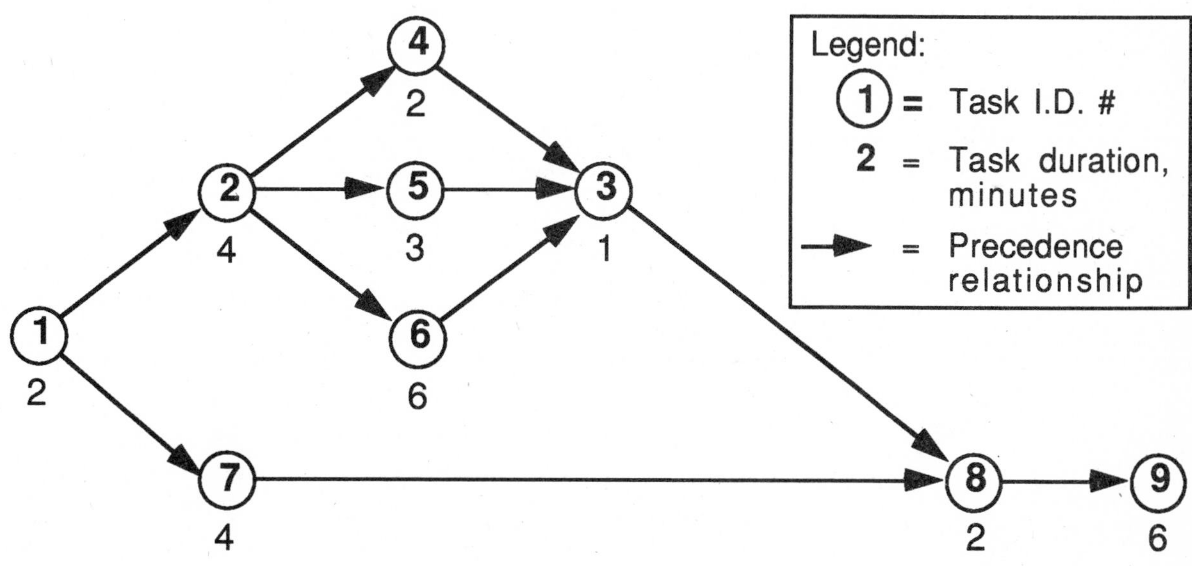

What should be a line's output rate?

Desired Output Rate

- Usually close to the demand rate
- May be held constant for a month at a time, to avoid daily rebalancing, reassigning, and retraining workers
- Multiple shifts increase equipment utilization
- As output rate increases, the number of stations increases and work becomes more specialized. Using multiple lines to produce the same product allows reduced cycle time and job enlargement.

For this example, assume that the desired output rate is 48 units during a single eight-hour shift.

Cycle Time

> "A line's **cycle time** is the maximum time allowed for work on a unit at each station. ... The target cycle time is the reciprocal of the desired output rate." p. 426

Note: Many students confuse cycle time with production rate. Look at the dimensions. Cycle *time* has a measure of time, seconds, minutes, hours, etc. in the numerator. Production *rate*, as is true of all rates, has the measure of time in the denominator. A production rate of 40 units in seven hours and 20 minutes results in a cycle time of 11 minutes per unit.

$$c = \frac{1}{r} = \frac{1}{40 \text{ units}/7.33 \text{ hours}} = \frac{7.33 \text{ hours}}{40 \text{ units}} \times \frac{60 \text{ minutes}}{\text{hour}} = 11\frac{\text{minutes}}{\text{unit}}$$

Theoretical Minimum

Note: This number is always rounded up. Even then, the actual required number of work stations may be higher than the theoretical minimum. Precedence relationships limit the choice of work elements assigned to a work center. If the total time for these elements does not closely match the cycle time, additional work centers may have to be established. In this example, the total productive time is 32 minutes per unit.

$$TM = \frac{\sum t}{c} = \frac{32}{11} = 2.91 \text{ or } 3 \text{ work stations}$$

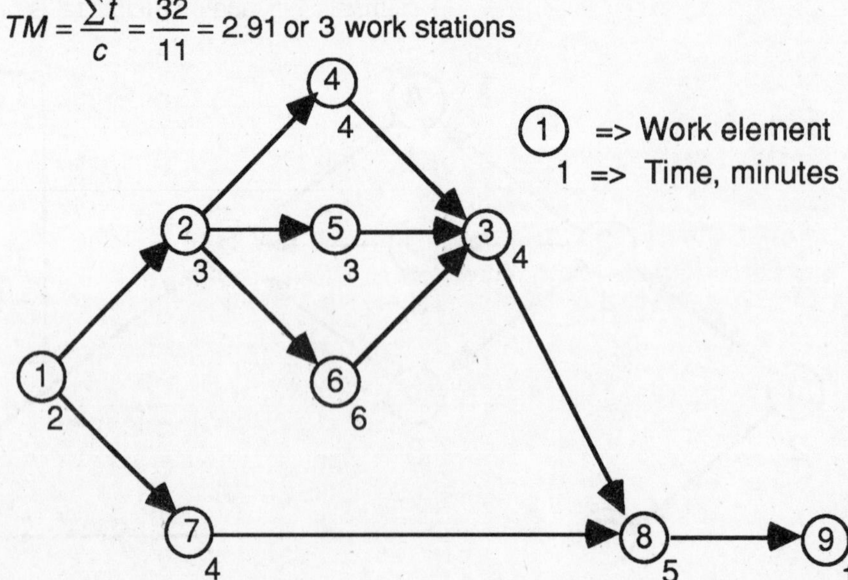

Idle Time, Efficiency, and Balance Delay

Idle Time

In this (contrived) example, the heuristic used for the solution on the next page does not result in the theoretical minimum number of work stations. Four stations are each paid for 11 minutes in order to accomplish 32 minutes worth of work. Idle time $= nc - t = 43 - 32 = 12$ minutes.

Efficiency

The time spent producing as a ratio to the total paid time is:

Efficiency $= (t/nc) * 100\% = (32/44) * 100\% = 73\%$

Balance Delay

The percentage of time lost due to the inability to assign work to the centers to match the cycle time is:

$100\% - \text{Efficiency} = 100\% - 73\% = 27\%$

Finding a Solution

Solution Procedure

$k = 0$

1. $k = k + 1$. Begin work assignments to a new work center, k.
2. Make a list (called the *available list*) of candidate work elements to assign to station k. These work elements meet *all* of the following conditions, and so are available to be assigned:
   a. The work element has not already been assigned.
   b. All of the work element's immediate predecessors have been assigned.
   c. The work element's standard time, when added together with the standard times of the other work elements already assigned to this (k) work station, does not exceed the cycle time.†

   If no work elements remain to be assigned, go to Step 5. If work elements remain to be assigned, but none meet these requirements, go to step 1. Otherwise, continue to Step 3.
3. Assign a work element to the work station from the available list according to decision heuristic "Rule a" or "Rule b".
   (We will use "Rule a" in the example on the following page.)
   Rule a: Pick the candidate work element having the longest duration work element from the available list.
   Rule b: Pick the candidate having the largest number of followers.
4. Determine the available time remaining at the work center by subtracting the cumulative time of all elements so far assigned to this station from the cycle time. Return to step 2.
5. Stop. You have completed the solution.

"Rule a" is an iterative (and easily programmed) routine. Note that a candidate work element does not necessarily remain a candidate on every subsequent iteration. The assignment of a rival task could comsume enough of a work station's cycle time so that the remaining unused time drops below that required to perform the candidate task. If so, on the next pass this task will be rejected from the available list. Not to worry. When we start assignments for the next work station, the task will be reinstated to the available list.

† Special case: When the standard time for a work element is longer than the cycle time, and the work element cannot be broken into smaller elements, two (or more) work stations must be assigned to do the work simultaneously *in parallel*. The production line is split. As work arrives it is alternately diverted to the parallel stations, where they accomplish the long duration work element and return the work to the line.

For those of us who have difficulty thinking like a computer, let's work though the example. We have so far determined we need at least three work stations. What should we assign to the first one?

Station	Time Available	Available List	Element Assigned	Time Remaining
One	11 minutes	#1	#1 2 min.	9 minutes
	9 minutes	#2, 7	#7 4 min.	5 minutes
	5 minutes	#2	#2 3 min.	2 minutes
	2 minutes	...		

Station	Time Available	Available List	Element Assigned	Time Remaining
Two	11 minutes	#4, 5, 6	#6 6 min.	5 minutes
	5 minutes	#4, 5	#4 4 min.	1 minute
	1 minute	...		

Station	Time Available	Available List	Element Assigned	Time Remaining
Three	11 minutes	#5	#5 3 min.	8 minutes
	8 minutes	#3	#3 4 min.	4 minutes
	4 minutes	...		

Station	Time Available	Available List	Element Assigned	Time Remaining
Four	11 minutes	#8	#8 5 min.	6 minutes
	6 minutes	#9	#9 1 min.	5 minutes

Well, the heuristic didn't come up with a solution requiring the theoretical minimum of three work stations. It is a *heuristic*, and is not guaranteed to find the optimal solution. I did contrive the numbers in this example to point out this flaw. This heuristic will usually find a pretty good solution.

By inspection, the theoretical minimum number of work stations can be achieved by:

assigning work elements 1, 2, & 6 to Station One = 11 min.
assigning work elements 4, 5, & 3 to Station Two = 11 min.
assigning work elements 7, 8, & 9 to Station Three = 10 min.

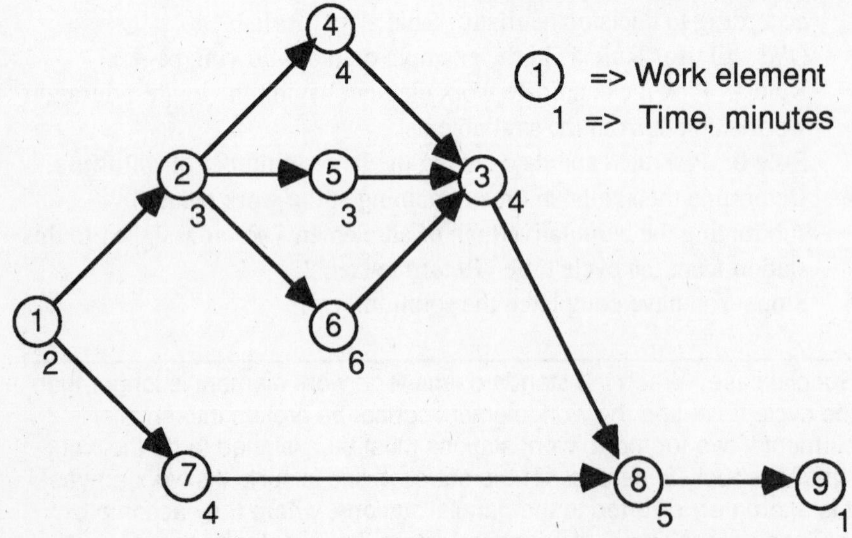

However as the number of work elements increases, the number of permutations of possible assignments quickly becomes astronomical. One could never find the optimal solution to a realistic problem by inspection. Fortunately, we only need a "pretty good" solution to achieve an effective line balance.

Other Considerations

Pacing

"The movement of product from one station to the next after the cycle time has elapsed is called **pacing.**" p. 408

- Paced lines have no buffer inventory
  - susceptible to temporary capacity losses and variability in work-element times
- Unpaced lines require inventory storage areas between stations to absorb temporary capacity losses and variability in work-element times
  - increase space requirements and inventory cost

Machine-paced lines are stressful to workers. One only needs to recall the *I Love Lucy* episode where Lucy and Ethel try to keep up with the candy conveyor.

Just-in-Time lines are unpaced lines, however they also have the advantage of low inventory costs and efficient use of floor space. Workers signal the need for (or pull) materials from the preceding operation only when they are ready for it. In comparison to machine-paced lines, stress is lower, job satisfaction is higher, and quality is vastly improved.

Behavioral Factors

- Product layouts are associated with
  - absenteeism
  - turnover
  - grievances
  - low job satisfaction
- Humanizing assembly lines
  - reduce specialization
  - involve worker groups
  - facilitate social interaction

What can be done to humanize product layouts?

Number of Models Produced

- **Mixed-model lines** produce several items belonging to the same family
  - \+ high volume and product flexibility
  - complicated scheduling
  - increased need for coordinating material flow

Cycle Times

- Maximum efficiency varies with the cycle time. If the cycle time in the example problem is changed from 11 minutes to 10 minutes, the efficiency of the optimal solution would decrease

  from $\frac{32}{3 \times 11}(100\%) = 97\%$ to $\frac{32}{4 \times 10}(100\%) = 80\%$
- Rebalance line periodically to change cycle time so that production rate roughly matches demand rate.

Multiple-Choice Questions

1. Which one of the following statements on layout is best?
   A. Firms producing one-of-a-kind products in low volumes tend to choose product layouts.
   B. Group technology calls for hybrid layouts, which increase repeatability.
   C. Layout planning is deciding the best city in which to locate a new facility.
   D. A product layout requires variable path materials-handling devices because each product has its own routing.

2. Which one of the following statements about layout is true?
   A. A process layout tends to have less work in-process inventory than does a product layout.
   B. A product layout tends to rely more on general-purpose equipment than does a process layout.
   C. A process layout tends to allow higher product flexibility than does a product layout.
   D. Product layouts tend to have higher materials-handling costs than process layouts have.

3. Layout choices must be closely tied to positioning strategy. Which one of the following firms is most likely to select a process layout?
   A. An automobile final assembly plant
   B. An automated car wash
   C. A custom machine tool manufacturer
   D. An oil refinery

4. Which of the following performance criteria is most important to product layouts?
   A. Capital investment
   B. Closeness rating
   C. Flexibility
   D. Minimal materials-handling costs

5. One worker, multiple machines
   A. is a group technology concept.
   B. is a process in which one worker operates several identical machines.
   C. is used when volume is not high enough to keep several workers busy.
   D. increases opportunities for social interaction among workers.

6. Which one of the following statements on office layouts is true with respect to the open office setting typical of high-rise steel and glass office towers?
   A. Communication is an important consideration in open office layouts.
   B. Most employees prefer to be in visual contact with their supervisors.
   C. Protecting proprietary (secret) information is a key benefit of open office design.
   D. The notion of status congruence, by which office accommodations improve with one's position in the organization, is an approach developed in Germany during the late 1950s.

7. Which of the following is a relatively new concept for achieving both proximity and privacy in offices?
   A. Activity settings
   B. Block plans
   C. Electronic cottages
   D. Office landscaping

8. A production line's output rate is determined by
   A. its input rate.
   B. the average output of the work stations.
   C. the slowest work station on the line.
   D. the fastest work station on the line.

9. An objective in line balancing is to
   A. find the center of gravity.
   B. maximize output rate.
   C. minimize the number of work stations.
   D. minimize cycle time.

10. In a precedence diagram, the arrows
    A. denote the work elements.
    B. indicate where the production line splits into parallel lines.
    C. indicate precedence relationships.
    D. terminate at immediate predecessor work elements.

11. The assembly line balancing heuristic finds a solution that
    A. maximizes efficiency.
    B. minimizes materials handling.
    C. assigns work to the theoretical minimum number of work stations.
    D. usually is fairly good.

(Multiple-choice answers are on Study Guide page 184.)

Problems

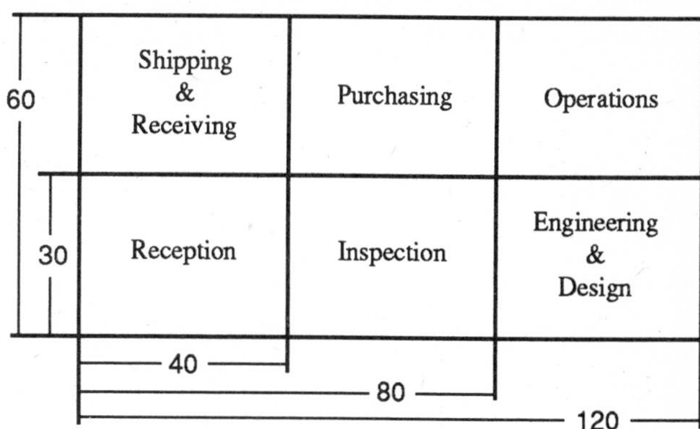

From-to Matrix (trips per day)						
From and To	**1**	**2**	**3**	**4**	**5**	**6**
1. Inspection	—	40				70
2. Operations		—			50	30
3. Purchasing			—	60	20	
4. Reception				—	10	
5. Engineering and Design					—	
6. Shipping and Receiving						—

1. Use rectilinear distance between mid-points of the work centers to compute the load-distance score for the above arrangement.

Departments	Trips	Distance	Total
Inspection - Operations	40	70	
Inspection - Shipping & Receiving	70		
Operations - Engineering & Design			
Operations - Shipping & Receiving			
Purchasing - Reception			
Purchasing - Engineering & Design			
Reception - Engineering & Design			

Total *ld* Score =

2. Use Euclidean distance between mid-points of the work centers to compute the load-distance score for this same arrangement.

Departments	Trips	Distance	Total
Inspection - Operations	40	50	
Inspection - Shipping & Receiving	70		
Operations - Engineering & Design			
Operations - Shipping & Receiving			
Purchasing - Reception			
Purchasing - Engineering & Design			
Reception - Engineering & Design			

Total *ld* Score =

3a. Complete the REL chart to show it is absolutely necessary (a) to have inspection near shipping and receiving, especially important (e) to have operations near engineering & design, important (i) to have purchasing near reception, of ordinary importance (o) to have operations near inspection, unimportant (u) to have reception near shipping and receiving, and undesirable (x) to have engineering near the reception area.

	Closeness Rating Between Departments					
Department	**1**	**2**	**3**	**4**	**5**	**6**
1. Inspection	—					
2. Operations		—				
3. Purchasing			—			
4. Reception				—		
5. Engineering & Design					—	
6. Shipping & Receiving						—

Closeness Ratings

Rating	Definition
A	Absolutely necessary
E	Especially important
I	Important
O	Ordinary closeness
U	Unimportant
X	Undesirable

Explanation Codes

Code	Meaning
1	Traffic
2	Shared personnel
3	Security
4	Space utilization
5	Noise
6	Employee preference

3b. Complete the block plan so that it meets *all* of the above criteria.

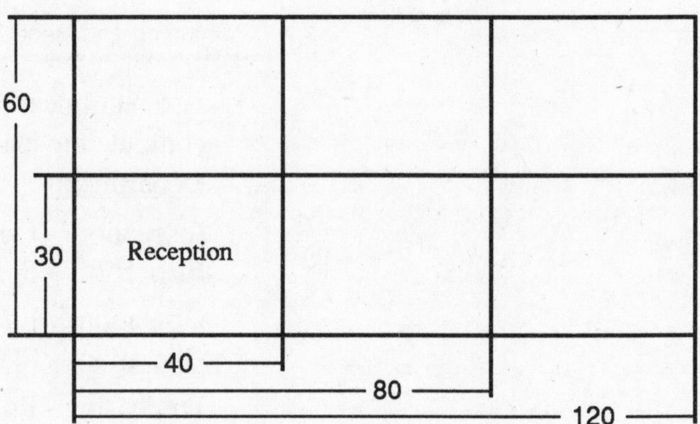

4a. An "enterprise" uses an assembly line to produce dilithium crystals. Determine the cycle time required to make 450 dilithium crystals in a seven-hour workday.

Cycle time

$$c = \frac{1}{r}$$

4b. What is the theoretical minimum number of work stations required to produce these crystals at the desired output rate if the total productive time per unit, *t* is 255 seconds?

Theoretical Minimum Number of Work Stations

$$TM = \frac{\Sigma t}{c}$$

5a. Use the longest work element heuristic (see Rule a) to assign these work elements so that 450 can be completed in a seven-hour workday. Work element times are in seconds.

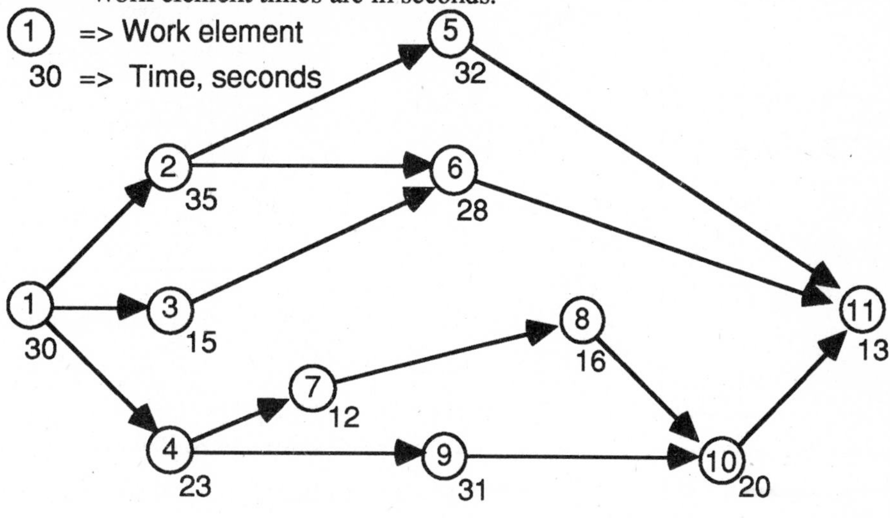

Station	Time Available	Available List	Element Assigned	Time Remaining
One				
Two				
Three				
Four				
Five				
Six				

5b. Calculate the idle time, efficiency, and balance delay.

Idle time
$= nc - t$

Efficiency
$= \frac{t}{nc}(100\%)$

Balance delay
$= 100\% - \text{Efficiency } \%$

Solutions

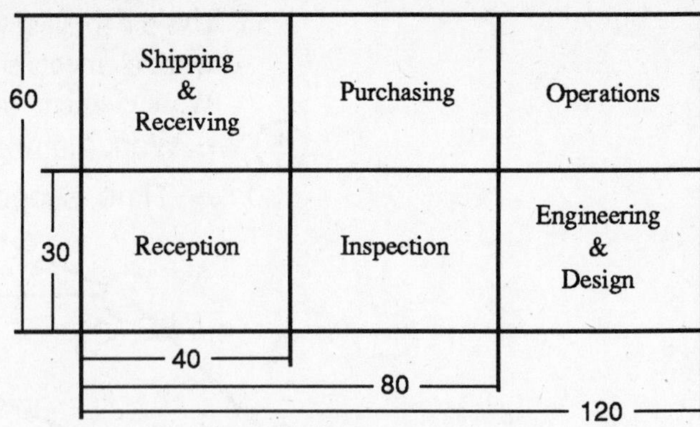

Multiple Choice Answers

1. B	6. C
2. C	7. A
3. C	8. C
4. A	9. C
5. C	10. C
	11. D

1. Use rectilinear distance to compute the load-distance score.

Departments	Trips	Distance	Total
Inspection - Operations	40	70	2,800
Inspection - Shipping & Receiving	70	70	4,900
Operations - Engineering & Design	50	30	1,500
Operations - Shipping & Receiving	30	80	2,400
Purchasing - Reception	60	70	4,200
Purchasing - Engineering & Design	20	70	1,400
Reception - Engineering & Design	10	80	800
		Total Load-Distance Score =	**18,000**

2. Use Euclidean distance to compute the load-distance score.

Departments	Trips	Distance	Total
Inspection - Operations	40	50	2,000
Inspection - Shipping & Receiving	70	50	3,500
Operations - Engineering & Design	50	30	1,500
Operations - Shipping & Receiving	30	80	2,400
Purchasing - Reception	60	50	3,000
Purchasing - Engineering & Design	20	50	1,000
Reception - Engineering & Design	10	80	800
		Total Load-Distance Score =	**14,200**

3a. Complete the REL chart to show

(a) absolutely necessary that inspection be near shipping & receiving,
(e) especially important that operations be near engineering & design,
(i) important to have purchasing near reception,
(o) of ordinary importance that operations be near inspection,
(u) unimportant that reception be near shipping & receiving,
(x) undesirable to have engineering near reception area.

	Closeness Rating Between Departments					
Department	1	2	3	4	5	6
1. Inspection	—	O				A
2. Operations		—			E	
3. Purchasing			—	I		
4. Reception				—	X	U
5. Engineering & Design					—	
6. Shipping & Receiving						—

Closeness Ratings

Rating	Definition
A	Absolutely necessary
E	Especially important
I	Important
O	Ordinary closeness
U	Unimportant
X	Undesirable

Explanation Codes

Code	Meaning
1	Traffic
2	Shared personnel
3	Security
4	Space utilization
5	Noise
6	Employee preference

3b. Complete the block plan so that it meets *all* of the above criteria.

Purchasing	Shipping & Receiving	Engineering & Design
Reception	Inspection	Operations

4a. An "enterprise" uses an assembly line to produce dilithium crystals. Determine the cycle time required to make 450 dilithium cry in a seven-hour workday.

$$c = \frac{1}{r} = \frac{1}{\dfrac{450 \text{ crystals}}{7 \text{ hours}}} = \frac{7 \text{ hours}}{450 \text{ crystals}} \times \frac{60 \text{ min}}{\text{hour}} \times \frac{60 \text{ sec}}{\text{min}}$$

$$= 56 \frac{\text{seconds}}{\text{crystal}}$$

4b. What is the theoretical minimum number of work stations required to produce these crystals at the desired output rate if the total productive time per unit, *t* is 255 seconds?

$$TM = \frac{\sum t}{c} = \frac{255}{56} = 4.55 \text{ or } 5 \text{ work stations}$$

5a. Use the longest work element heuristic (see Rule 1) to assign these work elements so that 450 can be completed in a seven-hour workday.

Station	Time Available	Available List	Element Assigned	Time Remaining
One	56 sec	#1	#1	26 sec
	26 sec	#3, 4	#4	3 sec
Two	56 sec	#2, 3, 7	#2	21 sec
	21 sec	#3, 7	#3	6 sec
Three	56 sec	#5, 6, 7	#5	24 sec
	24 sec	#7	#7	12 sec
Four	56 sec	#6, 8, 9	#9	25 sec
	25 sec	#8	#8	9 sec
Five	56 sec	#6, 10	#6	28 sec
	28 sec	#10	#10	8 sec
Six	56 sec	#11	#11	43 sec

The heuristic is unable to identify a solution that results in the theoretical minimum number of work stations.

5b. Calculate idle time, efficiency, and balance delay.

Idle time:

$$= nc - t = (6 \times 56) - 255$$

$$= 81 \text{ seconds}$$

Efficiency, %:

$$= \frac{\sum t}{nc} = \frac{255}{(6 \times 56)}(100\%) = 75.9\%$$

Balance delay:

$$= 100\% - \text{Efficiency}\% = 100\% - 75.9\%$$

$$= 24.1\%$$

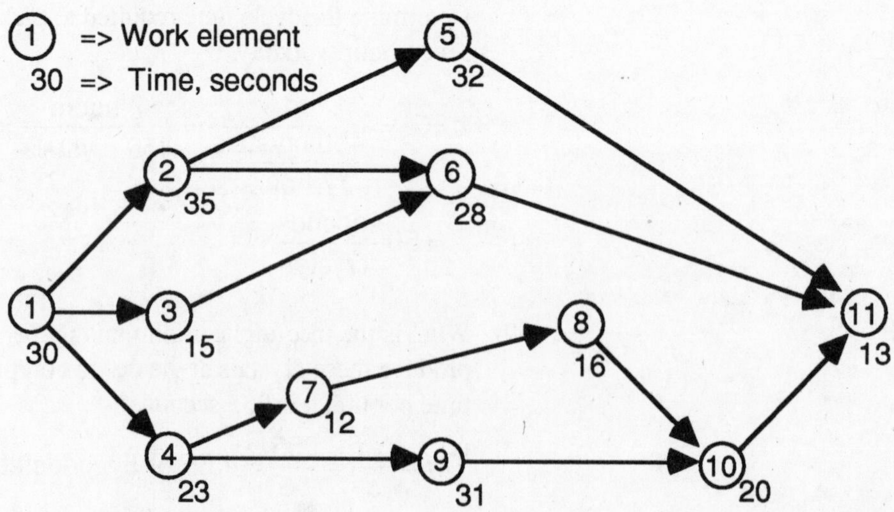

Chapter Ten, Forecasting

Why is forecasting important?

Forecasts are always wrong. Unfortunately the only alternative to "forecasting" is "not forecasting," and that is worse. Forecasting is essential to planning. Without forecasts, one can only react to changes as they occur. Such reaction can be very expensive in terms of employee morale, material management costs, capital equipment utilization, and customer service. Since we do a variety of planning, we need a variety of forecasts ... not just demand forecasts, but technological and environmental forecasts as well. Strategic, operating, and tactical plans require forecasts covering long-, medium-, and short-range horizons.

Demand Characteristics

- Many factors cause demand to vary.

Components of Demand

Five Basic Components of Demand Time Series

1. Average ... the level of demand.
2. Trend ... an upward or downward slope.
3. Seasonal influence ... usually an annually repeating pattern.
4. Cyclical movement. Business cycles often span 4 to 8 years, while life cycles vary widely in duration. It is difficult to quantitatively address this component, because a sufficient data history is rarely available.
5. Random error. By definition, this component can never be forecast using statistical processes. If an identifiable pattern in the errors exists, they are not random.

"Random error is the component of demand that makes every forecast wrong." p. 455

FIGURE 10.1

Components of Demand: a) average (b) trend (c) seasonal (d) cyclical

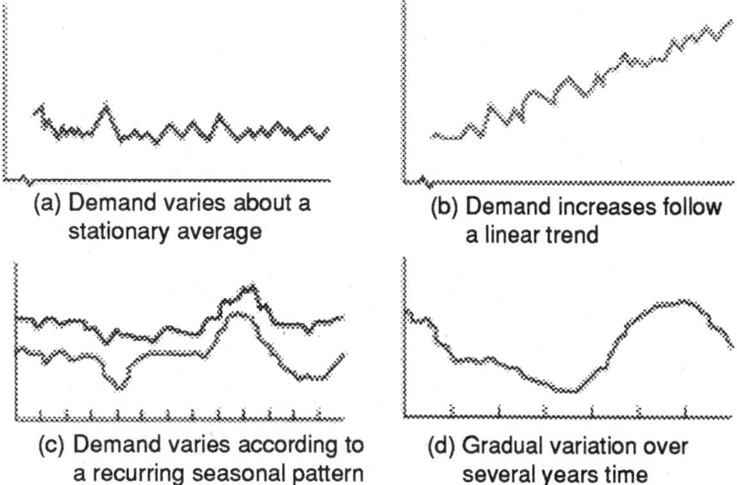

Factors Affecting Demand

External Factors

- Management cannot directly control external factors.
- An external factor may positively affect one product while reducing the demand for another.

Three Basic Types of External Demand Indicators

1. Leading indicators
2. Coincident indicators
3. Lagging indicators

These are so named because their turning points tend to precede, coincide, or follow the peaks and valleys of the general business cycle.

How can demand be influenced?

Internal Factors

In the production planning chapter, aggressive alternatives include influencing the timing and volume of demand, while reactive alternatives adapt to the undesirable effects of unchangeable demand.

"The term **demand management** describes the process of influencing the timing and volume of demand or adapting to the undesirable effects of unchangeable demand patterns." p. 456

- The timing of demand is important to efficient utilization of resources and production capacity.
- Advertising and promotions encourage customers to make purchases during off-peak demand periods.
- Developing products that have different seasonal peak demands tends to level production resource requirements.
- Appointments match demand for services to schedules of available capacity. When demand exceeds capacity, the appointment lead time lengthens until customers balk.

Designing the Forecasting System

What makes a forecasting system best for a particular situation?

Manager Must Determine

1. What to forecast
2. What type of forecasting technique to use
3. What computer assistance is appropriate

Deciding What to Forecast

Level of Aggregation

- Two-tier forecasting

A misapplication of this principle would lead one to believe that a 52-week forecast would be more accurate than a 4-week forecast because of compensating errors. There are compensating errors, but they do not completely counter the effect of long-range uncertainty. The error of a forecast generally increases as the square root of its horizon.

Aggregate forecasts for product families are likely to be more accurate because of compensating errors. Overestimated sales for one member of the group may be partially canceled by underestimated sales of another member. Therefore the forecast for the group is more accurate than the forecasts for individual members of the group. Rather than forecast individual members and sum to find the total for the group, this method forecasts the total, then breaks that total down for each member as a percentage of the total. These percentages are sometimes called "planning factors." As demand shifts among the members, the planning factors are changed, resulting in changed product mix within the group.

Units of Measurement

- Prices fluctuate, masking changes in demand for units of output.
- Forecasting units of *output* may not be possible in process-focused manufacturing or in custom services. Instead, forecast in terms of critical *input* resources such as labor hours.

Choosing the Type of Forecasting Technique

Three General Types of Forecasts

1. **Judgemental methods** translate opinion and judgement into quantitative estimates. These methods recognize that the effect of an important event may not be shown in the patterns and trends of historical demand data. The event may not have ever happened before, or the effect of an historical event may have been obscured by the simultaneous occurrence of several other events in history.
2. **Causal methods** base forecasts on statistically identified trends and patterns present in historical data for external factors. External factors are items *other than* the one being forecast. Causal methods must establish that there is a reliable relationship or correlation between the historical variation of selected external factors and the variation in the item being forecast.
3. **Time series analysis** forecasts base projections on statistically identified trends and patterns present in historical data for the item being forecast.

TABLE 10.1 / Demand Forecast Applications

	Time Horizon		
Application	Short Term (0-3 months)	Medium Term (3 months - 2 years)	Long Term (more than 2 years)
Forecast quantity	Individual products or services	Total sales Groups or families of products or services	Total sales
Decision area	Inventory management Final assembly scheduling Work-force scheduling Master production scheduling	Staff planning Production planning Master production scheduling Purchasing Distribution	Facility location Capacity planning Process management
Forecasting technique	Time series Causal Judgement	Causal Judgement	Causal Judgement

Short Term

- Time series methods are the most often used in the short term.
  - + inexpensive to generate large numbers of forecasts
  - + good quality (small errors) for short-term forecasts
- Causal models not used as extensively
  - + usually more accurate than time series forecasts
  - - more time to develop
  - - more time consuming to compute
  - - less likely to be understood and used
  - - more training required
- Judgement methods are used only on a rare exception basis. They are too costly to apply to thousands of routine short-term forecasts.

Medium Term

- Time series should not be used

  Time series are useful in quickly generating a large number of forecasts. However a relatively small number of forecasts are required to make projections by product family.
  - - unlikely that existing patterns will continue very far into future
  - - poor results
- Causal models are most often used in the medium term
  - + better at identifying turning points in trends
- Judgement methods
  - + also can identify turning points
  - + used when historical data not available
  - – still very costly

Long Term

- Aggregate demand for a product family expressed in homogeneous units, such as dollars of sales, tons of steel
- Causal models adjusted for judgement
- Judgement methods

Forecasting with Computers

- Forecasting software packages are widely available
- Package selection depends on
  1. fit with musts and wants
  2. cost of the package
  3. level of clerical support required
  4. amount of programmer maintenance required

Judgement Methods

How can reasonable forecasts be obtained when no historical information is available?

Sales Force Estimates

- Sales force provides personal estimates of future demands.
- Advantages
  - + Sales force should have good information about customer's purchasing plans.
  - + Forecasts are separated by district or region.
  - + Forecasts are easily aggregated to any level of detail.

- Disadvantages
  - Forecasts may be biased. When incentives, contests, or bonuses are based on sales volume, the sales force has a self-interest in assuring there is always plenty of inventory to sell. Overestimated sales cause overproduction, which results in increased inventory and minimized risk of lost sales.
  - The sales force may not be able to tell the true intentions of their customers. Sales negotiations often turn this into an adversarial relationship. Customers may gain by deceiving the sales force with respect to their plans.
  - When an individual's sales are compared to the sales forecasts as a performance measure, the sales force wins this game by underestimating sales. Not enough units are produced. This causes poor customer service and reduced market share, while profits are consumed with unplanned overtime in operations.

Executive Opinion

- Opinions of a group of executives are summarized
- May be used to modify an existing forecast to account for unusual circumstances
- Disadvantages
  - consumes expensive executive time
  - executives may independently modify forecasts based on individual opinion and treacherous gamesmanship

Market Research

- A systematic approach to creating and testing hypotheses about the market
- Data usually are gathered by survey
- Pitfalls
  - accuracy decreases as projections increase into the long term
  - numerous hedges and qualifications in the findings
  - low response rate to surveys
  - respondents may not be representative of the market

> For example, if one uses a survey to measure a product's acceptance in a target market of busy executives, most of the responses will actually come from idle executives.

Activities for Designing and Conducting a Market Research Study

1. Design a questionnaire
   - requests economic and demographic information
   - asks interest in product
2. Decide method of administering survey
   - telephone
   - mail
   - personal interview
3. Select a representative population to survey
4. Collect, then analyze data
   - interpreting responses
   - poor response rate may skew the data

Delphi Method

- A process of gaining consensus from a group of experts while maintaining anonymity
- Anonymity is important so that a respected guru doesn't dominate the results
- Used for technological forecasting
- Pitfalls
  - the process can take a long time
  - anonymity might also produce irresponsible opinions
  - all forecasts (regardless of method) are wrong
  - results are sensitive to questionnaire design

Forecasting for electric power companies used to be an easy task. From the end of WWII until the mid 1970s demand grew at a steady 6% pace. It did not take very long to build additional capacity, so the forecasts projected usage just a few years into the future. *Time series* methods were used with accurate results.

Then in the 1970s the combined effects of the EPA and the oil embargo increased both facility construction time and the price of energy by a factor of four. Due to rapidly inflating price, the demand for electricity promptly leveled off.

As you know, time series methods are ineffective over the long term because they are poor at identifying turning points in demand. Electric facility planners missed this turning point altogether. Based on the long history of steady growth, they invested billions of dollars in new capacity to satisfy a 6% growth rate projected over an *extended* (15 year) horizon. That demand never materialized.

One utility bankrupted after losing several *billion* dollars in constructing five unneeded nuclear plants. The utility's initials, WPPSS, became the pronounced acronym: "whoops!"

Today, most utilities use *causal* forecasting methods based on price, population, new uses for electricity, and technological advancements in lighting and appliances.

Steps in the Delphi Method

1. Questions about progress in a technological field are sent to a group of experts who are developing that technology.
2. Experts respond, arguing in support of their responses.
3. A report that summarizes the responses is prepared.
4. The report is returned to the experts for another round.
5. Experts modify or reassert their responses.
6. Process repeats two to four times to achieve some form of consensus.

Causal Methods: Linear Regression

- Used when historical data show a relationship between the factor to be forecast and other external or internal factors
- Best for predicting turning points and preparing long-range forecasts

"In **linear regression**, one variable, called a **dependent variable**, is related to one or more **independent variables** by a linear equation." p. 464

- Variations in a dependent variable, such as demand for electric power, are explained or caused by variations in independent variables, such as price and population.
- We use the simplest model, in which the dependent variable is a function of only one independent variable.

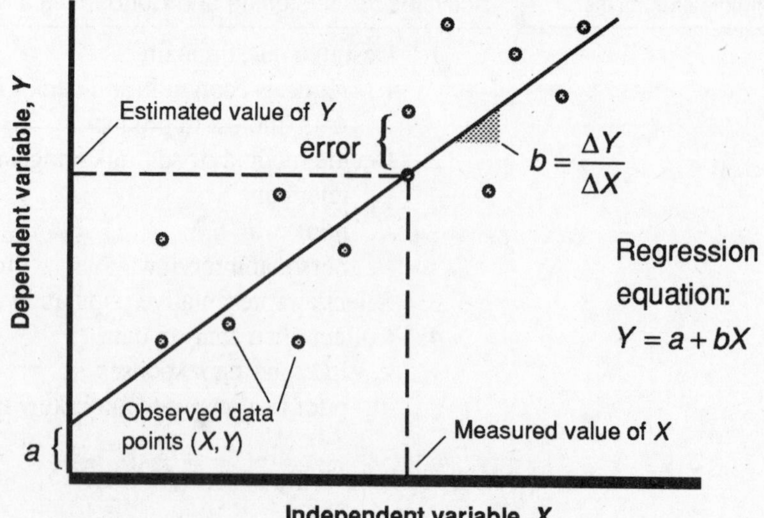

Linear Regression

The equation of the straight line that minimizes the mean of the squares of the errors (MSE) is:

$$Y = a + bX$$

where

$$a = \overline{Y} - b\overline{X}$$

$$b = \frac{\sum XY - n\overline{X}\overline{Y}}{\sum X^2 - n\overline{X}^2}$$

and where

$$\overline{X} = \frac{\sum X}{n}, \quad \overline{Y} = \frac{\sum Y}{n}$$

This approach will always show a straight line relationship between the dependent and independent variable. In reality, the relationship may not be linear, or it may not even exist. For example, one could plot the Dow Jones Industrial Average as a dependent linear function of women's skirt length, but that does not mean that there is really is a relationship between the two.

"The **correlation coefficient** measures the direction and strength of the linear relationship between the independent variable and the dependent variable." p. 465

$$r = \frac{n\sum XY - \sum X \sum Y}{\sqrt{\left[n\sum X - \left(\sum X^2\right)\right]\left[n\sum Y^2 - \left(\sum Y\right)^2\right]}}$$

We are investigating how changes in *one* independent variable reflect in variations of the dependent variable. If several factors can affect the dependent variable, we don't expect just one independent variable to explain all of the fluctuations in the dependent variable. For example, there probably are several causes of variation in the Dow Jones Industrial Average besides changes in the length of women's skirts.

"The coefficient of determination measures the amount of variation in the dependent variable about its mean that is explained by the regression line." p. 465

$$r^2 = \frac{a\sum Y + b\sum XY - \sum X \sum Y}{\sum Y^2 - nY^2}$$

"Finally, the standard error of the estimate measures how closely the data on the dependent variable cluster around the regression line." p. 465

$$\sigma_{YX} = \sqrt{\frac{\sum Y^2 - a\sum Y - b\sum XY}{n-2}}$$

Since forecasting is an imprecise art/science, when *n* is large, one sometimes sees the standard error of the estimate approximated by the more easily calculated:

$$\sigma_{YX} \cong \sqrt{MSE}$$

Time Series Analysis

A time series is a historical record of data organized in time sequence. All time series forecasting methods treat a dependent variable (such as demand) as a function of the independent variable: *time*. It is assumed that historical trends and patterns of variation will continue into the future. We project these historical trends and patterns, and (naively) hope future variations in the dependent variable will continue to be explainable by the passage of time. Many methods of time series analysis have been developed, but they differ in only two respects: 1) the manner in which they ferret out trends and patterns existing in time series data, and 2) the way trends and patterns are projected.

- Focus on average, trend, and seasonal influence components
- Rarely enough data history to identify cyclical influences
- Make no attempt to adjust for random component of demand

Naive Forecast

Some subscripted equations are included here for those who find that equations can more succinctly express relationships than can text. The bullet just above this equation expresses exactly the same relationship as does the equation.

- The forecast for the next period equals the demand for the current period.

  $F_{t+1} = D_t$

- Taking into account a demand trend, the increase (or decrease) in demand observed between the last two periods is used to adjust the current demand to arrive at a forecast.

  $F_{t+1} = D_t + (D_t - D_{t-1}) = (2D_t) - D_{t-1}$

Estimating the Average

We begin with the simplest case in which the historical data are stationary. In other words, there are a level of demand and random variations around the average, but no trend or seasonal pattern exists in the historical data.

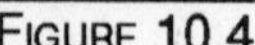

FIGURE 10.4

Weekly Patient Arrivals at a Medical Clinic

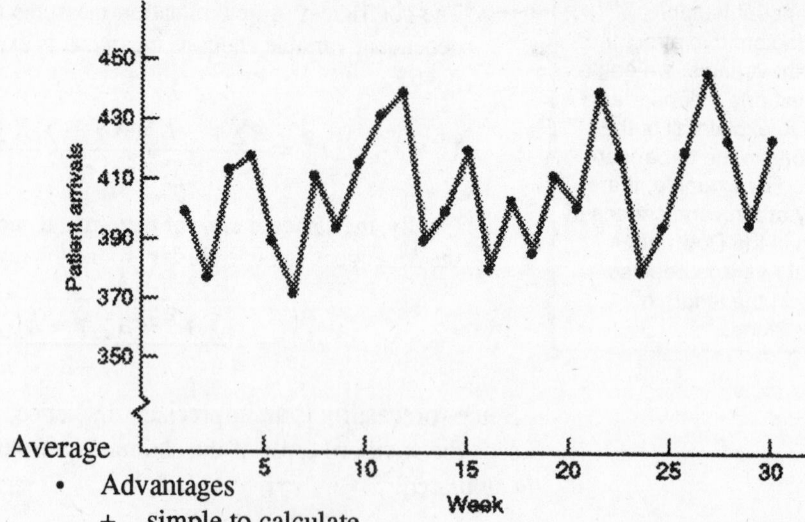

Average

- Advantages
  + simple to calculate
  + commonly understood
- Disadvantages
  - calculation requires input of entire history of data
  - too stable, changes in level of demand are masked by a long history of obsolete data

Simple Moving Averages

- The forecast for the next period is the average of demand for the previous *n* periods.

$$A_t = \frac{\text{Sum of last } n \text{ demands}}{n}$$

$$= \frac{D_t + D_{t-1} + D_{t-2} + \ldots + D_{t-n+1}}{n}$$

$$F_{t+1} = A_t$$

- Advantages
  - \+ simple to calculate
  - \+ reduced amount of data to input and store
  - \+ obsolete data have no effect on results
  - \+ can be used in combination with other techniques to expose underlying trends in the data
- Disadvantages
  - \- all of the data used have equal weight
  - \- can be overly influenced by a few extreme values
  - \- may result in biased forecasts when trends exist in the data

The plot of the three-week moving average from Fig. 10.5 has been removed to better show that the historical data have a very slight trend. The linear regression (dashed) line superimposed on the historical data shows that a trend exists. It has a positive slope of 0.4765. Note that the six-week moving average line (the bolder and smoother of the two jagged lines) is biased. It lags behind the trend and is usually too low.

FIGURE 10.5

Comparison of Six-Week Moving Average Forecast to Actual Patient Arrivals

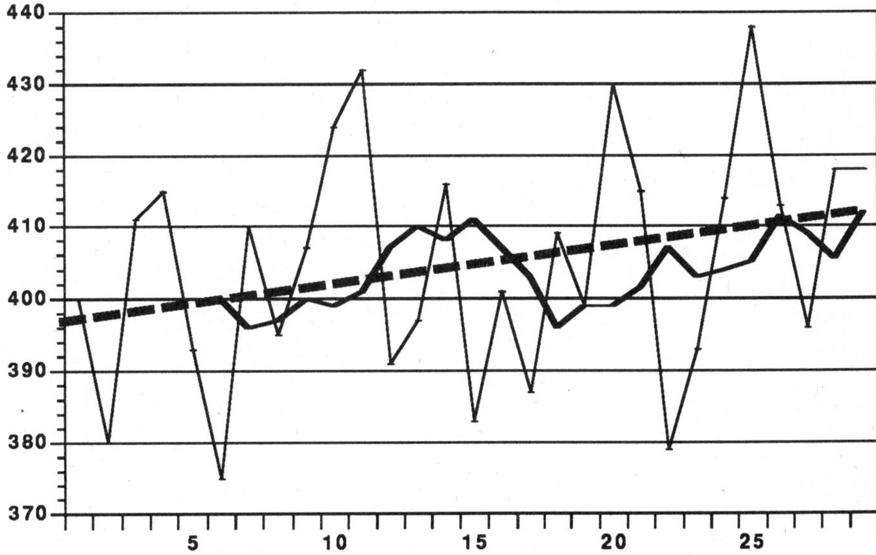

As *n* increases and/or the trend becomes more pronounced, this lagging effect becomes more exaggerated. All of the forecasting methods described in the "Estimating the Average" section share this flaw to some extent. Modifications to these simple techniques are recommended when a trend exists in the data.

Weighted Moving Average

If recent history is a better predictor of the future than is ancient history, then recent data ought to have more weight in calculating the forecast.

- Advantages
  - + recent data receives more weight
  - + more responsive to changes in level of demand
- Disadvantages
  - - will still lag behind a trend
  - - requires selection of weights to be applied to data

In this example, weights are arbitrarily assigned to conveniently sum to one.

> When the weights sum to equal one, I have found that several of my students can divide by the sum of the weights without the aid of a calculator.

$$A_t = \frac{0.50D_t + 0.30D_{t-1} + 0.20D_{t-2}}{\sum w}$$

$$F_{t+1} = A_t = \frac{0.50D_t + 0.30D_{t-1} + 0.20D_{t-2}}{1}$$

- The forecast for the next period is the weighted average of demand for the previous *n* periods.

Exponential Smoothing

This method is similar to the weighted moving average method in that more recent data receive more weight.

- Most frequently used
- Advantages
  - + simplicity
  - + minimal data storage requirements
- Disadvantages
  - - still lags behind a trend
- Larger α, more responsive
- Smaller α, more stable
- Getting started requires an initial estimate of the average
  - - either use the most recent demand, or
  - - use the average of several recent demands

"The effect of the initial estimate of the average on successive estimates of the average diminishes over time because, with exponential smoothing, the weights given to successive historical demands used to calculate the average decay exponentially." p. 473

Demand	Weight
D_t	$\alpha(1-\alpha)^0$
D_{t-1}	$\alpha(1-\alpha)^1$
D_{t-2}	$\alpha(1-\alpha)^2$
D_{t-3}	$\alpha(1-\alpha)^3$
D_{t-4}	$\alpha(1-\alpha)^4$
D_{t-5}	$\alpha(1-\alpha)^5$
…	…
D_{t-n}	$\alpha(1-\alpha)^n$

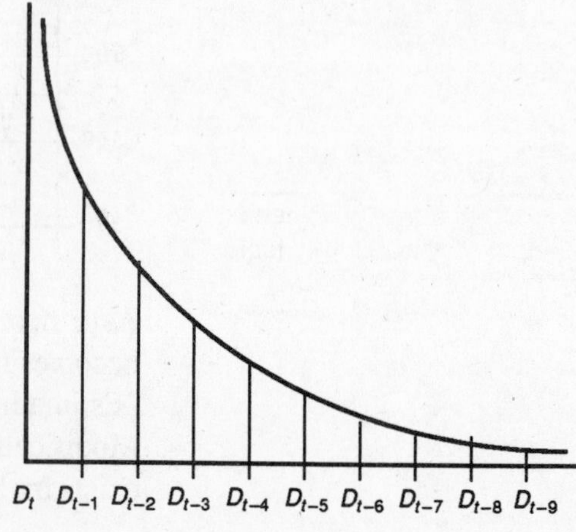

The simple exponential smoothing formula:

$$A_t = \alpha D_t + (1-\alpha) A_{t-1}$$

is equivalent to the expanded general formula:

$$A_t = \alpha D_t + \alpha(1-\alpha)^1 D_{t-1} + \alpha(1-\alpha)^2 D_{t-2} + \cdots + \alpha(1-\alpha)^n D_{t-n}$$

- The forecast for the next period equals the smoothed average for the current period.

  $$F_{t+1} = A_t$$

The selection of the smoothing parameter, α, is covered later. However, if a large smoothing parameter is required to keep up with fluctuations in demand, chances are a trend or seasonal influence exists in the data, which indicates a more sophisticated model is needed.

Including a Trend

$$x^* = \frac{\sum_i l_i x_i}{\sum_i l_i}$$

$$y^* = \frac{\sum_i l_i y_i}{\sum_i l_i}$$

All of the time-series forecasting methods presented so far share, to a varying degree, the problem of lagging behind trends. Figure 10.5, Study Guide page 195, shows the six-week moving average appearing just a bit too low. However, if we compare the center of gravity of the actual data to the center of gravity of the moving average (see center of gravity equations on Study Guide page 148), something interesting (if you're easily amused) becomes apparent. The moving average is not too low; it is too far to the right!

One solution to this unhappy state is simply to shift the moving average back to the left. In other words, plot the value for the moving average of the first six data points at the midpoint, $x = 3.5$ (instead of at $x = 7$). That does indeed solve the center of gravity problem, but it creates another one: Now there is no forecast! Before, the moving average of weeks 23 through 28 was plotted as the forecast for the twenty-ninth week. Shifting that point to the left 3 1/2 weeks places it back in history, halfway between weeks 25 and 26.

Many trend-adjusted forecasting methods are available, but they differ primarily in the way they calculate the "nudge" factor.

The solution is to keep the moving averages at their present position on the *x*-axis, then "nudge" them *upward* to account for the fact that we know they lag behind positive trends.

Trend-Adjusted Exponential Smoothing

- Getting started requires an initial estimate of the average and the trend.

  $$A_t = \alpha D_t + (1-\alpha)(A_{t-1} + T_{t-1})$$

  where

  $$T_t = \beta(A_t - A_{t-1}) + (1-\beta)T_{t-1}$$

- The forecast for the next period equals the smoothed average for the current period plus a trend adjustment for the current period.

  $$F_{t+1} = A_t + T_t$$

In trend-adjusted exponential smoothing, the "nudge" factor is T_t.

Seasonal Influences

- Many forecasting methods are available when seasonal influences are present in the data.
- The multiplicative seasonal method is the only one presented in the text book, but it is straightforward, intuitive, and appropriate for most seasonal situations.

Multiplicative Seasonal Method

- Seasonal factors are multiplied by an estimate of average demand to arrive at a seasonal forecast.

Three Steps for Calculating Seasonal Factors

1. Calculate the average demand per season for each year of past data.

Year	Quarter	Sales	Average
1	first	100	
	second	400	
	third	300	
	fourth	200	250
2	first	192	
	second	408	
	third	384	
	fourth	216	300

2. Divide the actual demand for each season by the average demand per season to get a seasonal factor for each season.

Year	Quarter	Sales	Average	Ratio
1	first	100	250	0.40
	second	400	250	1.60
	third	300	250	1.20
	fourth	200	250	0.80
2	first	192	300	0.64
	second	408	300	1.36
	third	384	300	1.28
	fourth	216	300	0.72

3. Calculate the average seasonal factor for each season.

Quarter	1	2	Average Ratio
first	0.40	0.64	0.52
second	1.60	1.36	1.48
third	1.20	1.28	1.24
fourth	0.80	0.72	0.76

Say the forecast for Year 3 is 1320. Breaking that total into seasons yields:

Year	Quarter	Average	Ratio	Forecast
3	first	330	0.52	172
	second	330	1.48	488
	third	330	1.24	409
	fourth	330	0.76	251
				1,320

Choosing a Time Series Method

Forecast Error

- Bias errors are the result of consistent mistakes. When biased techniques result in forecasts that are consistently too high, large inventories will accumulate. This increases investment, storage, and obsolescence costs. On the other hand, if the forecast is consistently too low, inventories are entirely consumed and lost sales occur. When forecasts are unbiased, an investment in safety stock will cover the errors until they cancel out over time.
- Random errors can be buffered by safety stock inventory or by investing in extra capacity. It is desirable to reduce the average size of errors, since large random errors require large investments in inventory or capacity.

Measures of Forecast Error

- Forecast error is the difference between the forecast and actual demand for a given period.

$$E_t = D_t - F_t$$

Cumulative forecast error (CFE) is used in measuring bias. CFE is the running sum of errors over the history of forecasts for the item.

$$CFE = \sum E_t$$

When the forecast is unbiased, negative errors and positive errors tend to cancel each other over time.

Mean squared error, (MSE).

Since the errors are squared, negative errors do not cancel positive errors. Squaring also gives much more weight to large errors than it does to small errors. Since forecasting is imprecise, we expect there will be small errors in forecasting. However, we do desire to avoid large errors. Therefore, it is desirable that forecasting techniques produce small MSE.

$$MSE = \frac{\sum E_t^2}{n}$$

When n is large, MSE is approximately equal to the variance of forecast error. Variance is equal to the square of standard deviation. MSE, variance, and standard deviation are alternative ways of measuring dispersion.

$$MSE \cong \sigma^2 \text{ or } \sigma \cong \sqrt{MSE}$$

Mean absolute deviation is simply the average (or mean) of the absolute values of the errors (or deviations). Since absolute values are used, negative errors do not cancel positive errors.

$$MAD = \frac{\sum |E_t|}{n}$$

MAD has the advantage of being intuitively meaningful. MAD is the average magnitude of errors. Is a MAD of 7 good or bad? If McDonald's forecasted hamburger demand with a MAD of 7, that would be very good indeed. If McDonnell-Douglas forecasted demand for space shuttles with a MAD of 7, that would be very bad. We need to put MAD in perspective.

Mean absolute percent error (MAPE) accomplishes that objective. It expresses the average error as a percentage of demand.

$$MAPE = \frac{\sum \left[|E_t|(100\%) \right] / D_t}{n}$$

Tracking signals compare bias (CFE) to the average magnitude of the errors (MAD).

$$\text{Tracking signal} = \frac{CFE}{MAD}$$

When a forecasting technique becomes inappropriate, a relatively large bias (CFE) relative to MAD develops over time. The tracking signal will increase, signaling that attention is needed. Assuming normally distributed errors, MAD is also related to the standard deviation of errors.

$$\sigma \approx 1.25 \times MAD$$

We can use this relationship to establish tracking signal limits with, say, 95% confidence intervals. This is similar to setting two-sigma upper and lower control limits in statistical process control.

$$\sigma \approx 1.25MAD$$
$$2\sigma \cong 2.5MAD$$

The tracking signal limits for 95% confidence is ± 2.5.
Tracking signal limits of ± 1.5 provides 77% confidence.

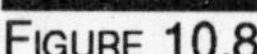

FIGURE 10.8

Tracking Signal

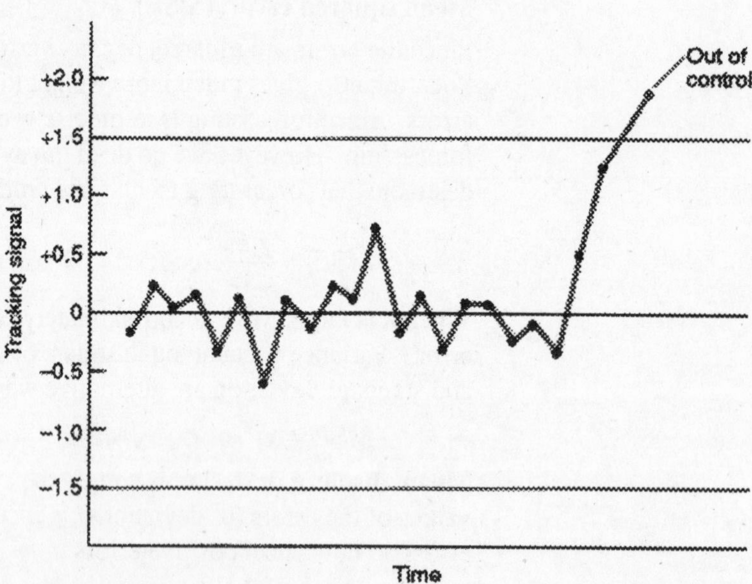

Forecast Error Ranges

- Single-number forecasts are rarely useful.
- More useful are forecasted value accompanied by an estimate of the error range, such as MAD, MSE, standard deviation, or 95% confidence interval.

What is involved in choosing the best time series forecasting method?

Criteria for Selecting Time Series Methods

1. Minimize bias — statistical criteria
2. Minimize *MAD* — statistical criteria
3. Meet managerial expectations — not rooted in the past

Using Statistical Criteria

- It is impossible to have zero bias and zero MAD. There is a trade-off.
- Large α in exponential smoothing or small n in moving average will respond to changes in the level of demand more quickly, reducing bias, but it also reduces stability and may increase MAD.

Recall that a large α or a small n also indicates that a more sophisticated forecasting technique may be required to adjust for trends or seasonal influences in the data.

Using Managerial Expectations

- Changes in demand level, rate of a trend, or the timing or magnitude of seasonal peaks can cause historical demand data to lose relevance.
- Managers should monitor forecast errors to detect the need to change forecasting parameters or techniques.

Is the most sophisticated forecasting system always the best one to use?

Using the Forecast Error Last Period

- Increased sophistication in forecasting technique reduces trust and understanding.
- Participation increases trust and understanding.

For each item, focus forecasting applies several simple techniques that are suggested by its users. The "best" technique is identified by comparing the resulting errors of each method. The method that resulted in the smallest error in the past month is used to produce the forecast for the next month. When a user proposes an alternative technique, it is tried along with the others. If it is better, it is used. If not, the user is expected to use whatever works best. This increases participation, understanding, trust, and *use* of the forecasting system.

Multiple-Choice Questions

1. Time series forecasts are appropriate for
   A. capacity planning decisions.
   B. facility location decisions.
   C. production planning decisions.
   D. inventory management.
2. Exponential smoothing is useful in forecasting which of the following components of a demand time series?
   A. Average
   B. Random
   C. Seasonal Influence
   D. Trend
3. The moving average is similar to exponential smoothing in which of the following ways?
   A. They are both used for long-range planning.
   B. They both lag trends.
   C. They both place more weight on more recent data.
   D. They both use leading indicators.
4. Which of the following demand forecasts is likely to be the most accurate?
   A. Forecasts of one item for the near future
   B. Forecasts of a product family for the near future
   C. Forecasts of one item for the distant future
   D. Forecasts of a product family for the distant future
5. Which of the following is most likely to use external leading indicators?
   A. Causal forecasts
   B. Qualitative forecasts
   C. Technological forecasts
   D. Time series forecasts
6. Which of the following methods of estimating the average level of demand requires the least amount of data to make the calculation?
   A. Average
   B. Exponential smoothing
   C. Moving average
   D. Weighted moving average
7. Which of the following is most useful in determining whether a forecast is biased?
   A. CFE, cumulative forecast error
   B. *r*, correlation coefficient
   C. MAD, mean absolute deviation
   D. MSE, mean squared error
8. An advantage of "focus forecasting" is
   A. focus on a single forecasting technique.
   B. increased sophistication of forecasting techniques.
   C. increased usage and trust in the forecasts.
   D. reduced forecasting computational requirements.
9. Which of the following represents the average magnitude of forecast errors?
   A. *CFE*
   B. *MAD*
   C. *MSE*
   D. Tracking signal
10. Which of the following is **most** useful in identifying when a forecasting technique is no longer appropriate?
    A. 95% confidence interval
    B. Coefficient of determination
    C. *MSE*
    D. Tracking signal
11. A strength of causal methods is
    A. ability to identify turning points.
    B. identifying relevant external factors for large numbers of short-term forecasts.
    C. minimal data requirements.
    D. simplicity.
12. Several forecasting techniques are tried on a set of time series data that contains a step function; in other words, the data abruptly shift from one level of sales to another, much higher level of sales. Which of the following techniques is likely to have the lowest bias?
    A. Average
    B. Exponential smoothing, $\alpha = 0.8$
    C. Exponential smoothing, $\alpha = 0.1$
    D. Moving average, n = a large number
13. Which of the judgement methods uses several rounds or iterations to arrive at a consensus regarding the rate of technological advancement?
    A. Delphi method
    B. Executive judgement
    C. Market research
    D. Sales force estimate

(Multiple-choice answers are on Study Guide page 205.)

Problems

1. The historical demand for a popular operations management course follows.

Year	Semester	Demand	Forecast	Deviation
1	fall	300		
	spring	400		
	summer	100		
2	fall	330	____	____
	spring	420	____	____
	summer	150	____	____
3	fall	345	____	____
	spring	???	____	

Moving average:

$$A_t = \frac{\text{Sum of last } n \text{ demands}}{n} = \frac{D_t + D_{t-1} + D_{t-2} + \ldots + D_{t-n+1}}{n}$$

a. Use the moving average, $n = 3$, to forecast demand for each semester from fall of Year 2 through spring of Year 3.

Weighted moving average:

$$A_t = \frac{0.6D_t + 0.3D_{t-1} + 0.1D_{t-2}}{\sum w} = \frac{0.6D_t + 0.3D_{t-1} + 0.1D_{t-2}}{0.6 + 0.3 + 0.1}$$

b. Repeat using the weighted moving average, $n = 3$, $W_1 = 0.6$, $W_2 = 0.3, W_3 = 0.1$.

Year	Semester	Demand	Forecast	Deviation
2	fall	330	____	____
	spring	420	____	____
	summer	150	____	____
3	fall	345	____	____
	spring	???	____	

c. Assume the demand for spring of Year 3 = 520 and for summer = 135. If the total forecast demand for Year 4 is 1,100, use the multiplicative seasonal method to forecast demand for each semester of the fourth school year.

Exponential Smoothing:

$$A_t = \alpha D_t + (1 - \alpha)A_{t-1}$$

2. Use exponential smoothing with $\alpha = 0.2$ and a starting average of 330 to forecast demand for each semester from spring of Year 3 through fall of Year 4.

Year	Semester	Demand	Forecast
3	fall	345	330
	spring	520	____
	summer	135	____
1993 - 94	fall	???	____

$$CFE = \sum E_t$$

$$MAD = \frac{\sum |E_t|}{n}$$

$$MSE = \frac{\sum E_t^2}{n}$$

3. Using the data from Problem 1, calculate CFE, MAD, and MSE for
   a. moving average

   b. weighted moving average

Linear regression:

$$Y = a + bX$$

where

$$a = \overline{Y} - b\overline{X}$$

$$b = \frac{\sum XY - n\overline{X}\overline{Y}}{\sum X^2 - n\overline{X}^2}$$

and where

$$\overline{X} = \frac{\sum X}{n}, \quad \overline{Y} = \frac{\sum Y}{n}$$

4. A professor is interested in determining whether average study hours per week is a good predictor of test scores. The results of her study are:

Hours	Score
3.0	90
2.1	95
5.8	65
3.8	80
4.2	95
3.2	60
5.3	85
4.6	70

A student says: "Professor, I would do *anything* to get a B on the next test." The professor asks, "On the average, how many hours do you spend studying for this course per week?" The student responds: "About 2 hours."

Use linear regression to forecast the student's test score.

5. Calculate the correlation coefficient and coefficient of determination for the data in Problem 4. Are hours per week spent studying correlated to test scores? How much of the variation in test scores is explained by variation in time spent studying?

Correlation coefficient:

$$r = \frac{n\sum XY - \sum X \sum Y}{\sqrt{\left[n\sum X - \left(\sum X^2\right)\right]\left[n\sum Y^2 - \left(\sum Y\right)^2\right]}}$$

Coefficient of determination:

$$r^2 = \frac{a\sum Y + b\sum XY - \sum X \sum Y}{\sum Y^2 - nY^2}$$

Solution

Moving average:

$$A_t = \frac{\text{Sum of last } n \text{ demands}}{n} = \frac{D_t + D_{t-1} + D_{t-2} + \ldots + D_{t-n+1}}{n}$$

1a. Use moving average $n = 3$ to forecast demand for each semester from fall of Year 1 through spring of Year 3.

Year	Semester	Demand	Forecast	Deviation
1	fall	300		
	spring	400		
	summer	100		
2	fall	330	266.7	63.3
	spring	420	276.7	143.3
	summer	150	283.3	−133.3
3	fall	345	300.0	45.0
	spring	???	305.0	

Weighted moving average:

$$A_t = \frac{0.6D_t + 0.3D_{t-1} + 0.1D_{t-2}}{\sum w} = \frac{0.6D_t + 0.3D_{t-1} + 0.1D_{t-2}}{0.6 + 0.3 + 0.1}$$

b. Repeat using weighted moving average, $n = 3$, $W_1 = 0.6$, $W_2 = 0.3, W_3 = 0.1$.

Year	Semester	Demand	Forecast	Deviation
2	fall	330	210.0	120.0
	spring	420	268.0	152.0
	summer	150	361.0	−211.0
3	fall	345	249.0	96.0
	spring	???	294.0	

c. Assume the demand for spring of Year 3 = 520 and summer = 135. If the total forecast demand for Year 4 is 1,100, use the multiplicative seasonal method to forecast demand for each semester of the fourth school year.

Average semester demand for Year 1 = 800 / 3 = **267**
Average semester demand for Year 2 = 900 / 3 = **300**
Average semester demand for Year 3 = 1,000 / 3 = **333**
Average semester demand for Year 4 = 1,100 / 3 = **367**

Seasonal factor for fall 1 = 300 / 267 = **1.12**
Seasonal factor for fall 2 = 330 / 300 = **1.10**
Seasonal factor for fall 3 = 345 / 333 = **1.04**

Avg. seasonal factor for fall = (1.12 + 1.10 + 1.04) / 3 = **1.09**
Avg. seasonal factor for spring = (1.50 + 1.40 + 1.56) / 3 = **1.49**
Avg. seasonal factor for summer = (0.37 + 0.50 + 0.40) / 3 = **0.42**

Forecast for fall of Year 4 = 367 * 1.09 = 400
Forecast for spring of Year 4 = 367 * 1.49 = 547
Forecast for summer of Year 4 = 367 * 0.42 = 154
1,101

	Average Demand				Seasonal Factor			
	Yr 1	Yr 2	Yr 3	Yr 4				
Semester	267	300	333	367	Y1	Y2	Y3	Y4
fall	300	330	345	**400**	1.12	1.10	1.04	**1.09**
spring	400	420	520	**547**	1.50	1.40	1.56	**1.49**
summer	100	150	135	**154**	0.37	0.50	0.40	**0.42**
				1,101				**3.00**

Multiple Choice Answers

1. D	8. C
2. A	9. B
3. B	10. D
4. B	11. A
5. A	12. B
6. B	13. A
7. A	

Exponential Smoothing:

$A_t = \alpha D_t + (1-\alpha)A_{t-1}$

2. Use exponential smoothing with a = 0.2 and a starting average of 330 to forecast demand for each semester from spring of Year 3 through fall of Year 4.

Forecast spring Year 3	= 0.2 (345) + 0.8 (330) =	333
Forecast summer Year 3	= 0.2 (520) + 0.8 (333) =	370
Forecast fall Year 4	= 0.2 (135) + 0.8 (370) =	323

Year	Semester	Demand	Forecast
3	fall	345	330
	spring	520	333
	summer	135	370
4	fall	???	323

$CFE = \sum E_t$

$MAD = \dfrac{\sum|E_t|}{n}$

$MSE = \dfrac{\sum E_t^2}{n}$

3. Using the data from Problem 1, calculate CFE, MAD, and MSE for
   a. moving average

CFE	= 63.3 + 143.3 – 133.3 + 45	= 118.3
MAD	= (63.3 + 143.3 + 133.3 + 45) / 4	= 96.2
MSE	= (4,007 + 20,535 + 17,769 + 2,025) / 4	= 11,084

   b. weighted moving average

CFE	= 120 + 152 – 211 + 96	= 157
MAD	= (120 + 152 + 211 + 96) / 4	= 145
MSE	= (14,400 + 23,104 + 44,521 + 9,216) / 4	= 22,810

Linear regression:

$Y = a + bX$

where

$a = \overline{Y} - b\overline{X}$

$b = \dfrac{\sum XY - n\overline{X}\overline{Y}}{\sum X^2 - n\overline{X}^2}$

and where

$\overline{X} = \dfrac{\sum X}{n}, \quad \overline{Y} = \dfrac{\sum Y}{n}$

4. A professor is interested in determining whether average study hours per week is a good predictor of test scores. The results of her study follow.

Hours(X)	Score(Y)	XY	X^2	Y^2
3.0	90	270.0	9.00	8,100
2.1	95	199.5	4.41	9,025
5.8	65	377.0	33.64	4,225
3.8	80	304.0	14.44	6,400
4.2	95	399.0	17.64	9,025
3.2	60	192.0	10.24	3,600
5.3	85	450.5	28.09	7,225
4.6	70	322.0	21.16	4,900
ΣX= 32.0	ΣY=640	ΣXY=2514.0	ΣX^2=138.62	ΣY^2= 52,500

$\overline{X} = 32/8 = 4, \quad \overline{Y} = 640/8 = 80$

$b = \dfrac{2514 - 8(4)(80)}{138.62 - 8(4)(4)} = \dfrac{-46}{10.62} = -4.331$

$a = 80 - (-4.331 \times 2) = 97.32$

$Y = 97.32 - 4.331X$

Use linear regression to forecast the student's test score when study hours, $X = 2$.

$Y = 97.32 - 4.331(2) = 88.66$ or about 89

5. Calculate the correlation coefficient and coefficient of determination for the data in Problem 4.

   Are hours per week spent studying correlated to test scores?

$$r = \frac{8(2514) - 32(640)}{\sqrt{[8(138.62) - 32(32)][8(52{,}500) - 640(640)]}} = \frac{-348}{\sqrt{84.96(10{,}400)}}$$

$$= \frac{-348}{940} = -0.39$$

   Based on the data, increased hours spent studying have very little relationship to test scores, if anything there is a detrimental effect. A ten-year study at Michigan University (see "Study Schmuddy," *Forbes*, October, 1985) showed that there is no correlation between *study hours* and grades. There is a correlation with attendance, which affects *study efficiency*. No amount of study hours can make up for cutting classes.

   How much of the variation in test scores is explained by variation in time spent studying?

   $r^2 = (-0.39)^2 = 0.1532$ or about 15%

Correlation coefficient:

$$r = \frac{n\sum XY - \sum X \sum Y}{\sqrt{\left[n\sum X - \left(\sum X^2\right)\right]\left[n\sum Y^2 - \left(\sum Y\right)^2\right]}}$$

Coefficient of determination:

$$r^2 = \frac{a\sum Y + b\sum XY - \sum X \sum Y}{\sum Y^2 - nY^2}$$

Chapter Eleven, Materials Management

Effective materials management is very important to most companies. Annual reports to stockholders typically reveal that the corporation spends more than half of income from sales on purchased materials and services. It is also common for firms to maintain an investment in inventory that exceeds the total of owner's equity. Although inventories appear on the "assets" side of the balance sheet, they are not productive assets. Considering the cost of storage, risk of obsolescence, interest, and other costs, the return on investment (ROI) in inventory is negative. A penny saved on materials is a penny earned. Because materials dominate investment and cash flow, a small improvement in materials management can have a dramatic effect on profits.

Importance of Materials Management

Materials Management Cycle

1. Acquisition
2. Storage
3. Conversion
4. Storage
5. Distribution

Central Role of Materials in the Economy

- A small percentage reduction in the cost of materials translates into large profit gains.

Impact of Inventory on Profitability

"Each dollar tied up in inventory is a dollar unavailable for investment in new products or services, technological improvement, or capacity increases." p. 508

- The pie chart at the left (Fig. 11.2) shows the proportion of inventory held by manufacturers, wholesalers, and retailers.

FIGURE 11.2

Where Inventories Are Held

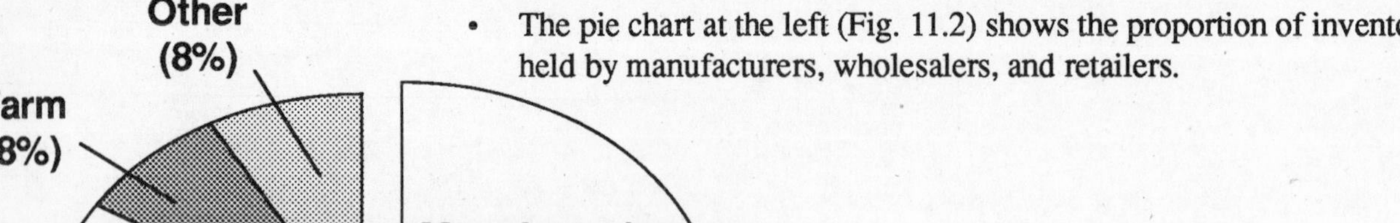

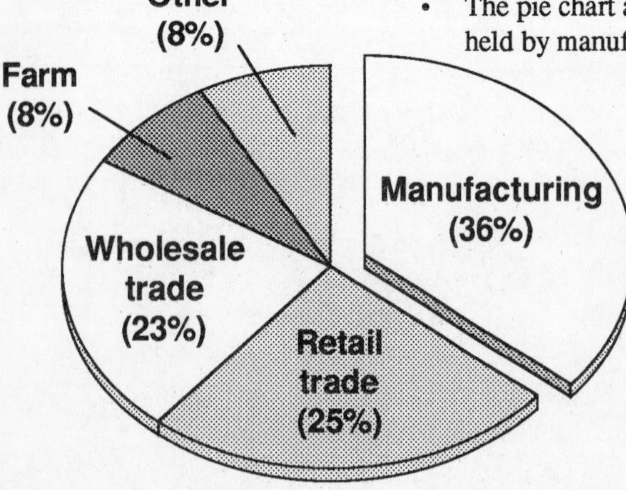

What organizational structure is best, and what activities require the most coordination with other functions?

Function of Materials Management

- Segmented (traditional) structure: purchasing, production control, and distribution report to different persons.
- Integrated structure: all tasks related to materials flow report to a materials management organization headed by a key executive.
- The trend is toward integrated or hybrid structures.
- In hybrid structures distribution usually reports to marketing.

Purchasing

- **Purchasing** is the management of the acquisition process, which includes
  - deciding which suppliers to use
  - negotiating contracts
  - deciding whether to buy locally or centrally

While working in the central office of a large electric utility, I overheard our end of a telephone conversation. The call was from the manager of one of our distant power plants, and his end of the conversation could nearly be heard without the aid of a telephone.

A supplier was in the manager's office, tools in hand, and ready to repossess a large garage door that had been installed at the unloading dock. The prospect of the Nebraska winter wind blowing through the plant did not do much for the manager's opinion of efficiency at the central purchasing department.

Although the company had billions in assets, it was very slow in paying bills. The local garage door supplier was not impressed by our balance sheet. *He* had not been paid, so he was taking his door back. Slow payment makes it very difficult to maintain good supplier relationships.

The Acquisition Process

1. Recognize a need.
   - receive a request to buy materials or services
   - review specifications
2. Select suppliers.
   - identify capable suppliers
   - group items supplied from the same supplier
   - request bids and proposals
   - evaluate bids
   - negotiate legal and technical exceptions
   - select a supplier
3. Place the order.
   - establish communication
4. Track the order.
   - anticipate late deliveries
   - delay is disruptive to production plans
5. Receive the order.
   - inspect for quality and quantity
   - send receipt notice to purchasing, requisitioning department, inventory control, and accounting
   - update supplier performance record
   - pay suppliers accurately and on time

- Electronic data interchange (EDI) streamlines the purchasing process by facilitating communication between computers by reducing data entry and checking procedures.

How should suppliers be selected, evaluated, and supported?

Supplier Selection

Competitive priorities are a starting point in developing the list of supplier performance criteria.

- Quality. The hidden costs of poor quality can be high.
- Delivery. Shorter lead times and on-time delivery help maintain acceptable customer service with less inventory.
- Price. Firms typically spend 60% of income on purchased items. Finding lower prices is key to profits.

Which purchased materials and services give a firm the greatest purchasing clout? How can the clout be used effectively?

Do arms-length negotiations assure the best possible price? Not always. Suppliers who are unsure of continued business may be reluctant to invest in the technological advancements neccesary to reduce costs. When they do reduce costs, there is little incentive to share benefits with their adversary (the customer).

In repetitive purchasing, short-term contracts become a bidding trap. Supplier's must bid high enough to cover fixed costs over the first contract period, because there is no assurance of repeat business. The first winner is thereafter in a position to underbid the "competition" in subsequent bids, because competitors haven't yet covered their fixed costs. Since the original supplier has an adversarial relationship with the customer, he will not reduce his bid to reflect the fact that his fixed costs have already been covered by previous business. Instead, he will bid just low enough to win. The customer is trapped. Repetitive bidding processes foster competition, but it is ineffective competition.

The customer is better served by forming a long-term partnership relationship with a single supplier.

Supplier Relations

- Of strategic importance is the type of relations maintained with suppliers.
- Competitive orientation is prevalent in North America.
  - negotiations are a zero-sum game
  - the upper hand is determined by clout
- The trend is toward cooperative orientation
  - \+ buyer and seller are partners, synergy, win-win
  - \+ fewer but closer long-term supplier relationships
  - \+ increased volume, dependence, investment in technology
  - \+ shared information
  - \+ increased trust, efficiency

The Buyer Has More Clout When

1. The buyer represents a significant share of the supplier's sales.
2. The purchased item is standardized, and substitutes are available.
3. The buyer could integrate backward.
4. The supplier cannot integrate forward.
5. Switching suppliers is not costly.

Contracting

- Contracting procedure depends on volume
- When contract value is high and volume is low; capital equipment
  - use competitive bidding
  - several suppliers submit formal quotations
  - lowest *and best* bidder receives contract
- When the contract value is low or time for negotiations is limited,
  - use sole-source contracting or supplier catalogs
  - the cost of negotiating with several suppliers exceeds any potential savings
  - negotiate contract with a single supplier
- When there is continuous high-volume demand
  - use preselected suppliers and long-term contracts
  - delays are avoided

"Most long-term contracts are either *blanket* or *open-ended* contracts. A blanket contract covers a variety of items, whereas an open-ended contract allows items to be added or the contract period extended." p. 515

- Blanket or open-ended contracts
  - reserve supplier capacity
  - volume discounts
  - remove uncertainty
  - consistent with the cooperative orientation to supplier relations

Should long-term contracts be used? Should buying be centralized?

Centralized Buying

- Advantages
  - \+ increased clout
  - \+ buyers develop specialized expertise
  - \+ consistent with globalization of production
  - \+ central control of specifications and consistent quality
  - \+ consistent with central computer information systems

- Disadvantages
  - Loss of local control
    - profit center responsibility requires local control of costs
  - Longer lead times
  - More difficult communication with requisitioning department

Value Analysis

- A systematic effort to reduce cost or improve performance
- On a team basis, involving purchasing, production, and engineering

Value Analysis Questions

1. What is the function of the item?
2. Is the function necessary?
3. Can a lower cost standard part that serves the purpose be identified?
4. Can the item be simplified or specifications relaxed to lower price?

Distribution

- Deals with outbound flows, from manufacturers to customers
- Broadens the marketplace, adding time and place value

Should distribution centers be added to position inventory closer to customers?

Placement of Finished Goods Inventory

- Forward placement is nearer the customer
  + fast delivery times
  + reduced transportation costs
- Backward placement
  - consistent with competitive priorities calling for customization
  - increased "pooling effect", decreased safety stock investment

Selection of Transportation Mode

Five Basic Modes of Transportation

1. Highway
   + flexibility, no rehandling
   + rates less than rail rates for small quantities, short hauls
2. Rail
   + low rates for large quantities
   - long and variable transit times
   - increased pipeline inventory requirements
   - shipping damage
3. Water
   + high capacity
   + low rates for large quantities
   - long and variable transit times
   - limited access to large portions of the continent
4. Pipeline
   + very low transportation costs
   - limited geographical flexibility
   - highly specialized
5. Air
   + fastest
   - most expensive
   - requires rehandling

Scheduling, Routing, and Carrier Selection

"The shipping schedule must mesh with purchasing and production control schedules. It also reflects the trade-off between transportation costs and customer response times. . . . The choices are complex. . . . rates and services vary markedly, depending on the specific mode and carrier chosen." p. 519

Inventory Concepts

"**Inventory** is a stock of anything held to meet future demand." p. 519

Accounting Categories

- Raw materials
- Work-in-process (WIP)
- Finished goods inventory (FGI)

Pressures for Low Inventories

Inventory holding (or carrying) cost

- Usually stated as a percentage of an item's value per period of time stored, such as 35% per unit per year.
- Interest or opportunity cost — time value of money
- Storage and handling — warehouse facilities and labor
- Taxes, insurance, utilities — usually proportional to inventory value
- Shrinkage — pilferage, obsolescence, and deterioration

Pressures for High Inventories

- Customer Service. For customers that have immediate or seasonal demands, finished goods inventory can speed up delivery and reduce stockouts, back orders, and lost sales.
- Ordering Costs. Costs associated with purchasing, follow-up, receiving, and paperwork are incurred each time an order is placed. By ordering in larger quantities, the resulting inventory provides a means of obtaining and handling materials in economic lot sizes.
- Setup Costs. Work orders have similar costs associated with each setup, and machines may be unproductive for several hours each time the product is switched.
- Labor and Equipment Utilization.
  - Throughput at bottleneck resources can be increased by placing larger production orders, reducing total setup time.
  - Inventories protect against supply errors, shortages, stockouts, and delivery uncertainties.
  - Inventories can be used to cover peaks in demand, level production activities, stabilize employment, and improve labor relations.
- Transportation Cost. Transportation costs can be reduced by building inventories and shipping full carloads. Similarly, per unit inbound material transportation costs can be reduced by ordering large lot sizes.
- Quantity Discounts. Ordering large quantities can provide a hedge against future price increases and provide a means to obtain quantity discounts.

Types of Inventory

Cycle Inventory

"Cycle inventory is the portion of total inventory that varies directly with lot size." p. 523

$$\text{Average cycle inventory} = \frac{Q}{2}$$

- Advantages of large cycle inventory:
  + better customer service
  + less frequent orders and setups
  + reduced transportation and purchasing costs

Safety Stock Inventory

Safety stock is a trade-off of the costs of carrying a buffer inventory against the costs associated with poor customer service. Note that if there is no uncertainty in demand, lead time, or supply, there is no need for safety stock.

"**Safety stock inventory** protects against uncertainties in demand, lead time, and supply." p. 523

Anticipation Inventory

"Inventory used to absorb uneven rates of demand or supply ...is referred to as **anticipation inventory.**" p. 523

- Changing output rates is costly.

Pipeline (Transit) Inventory

"Inventory moving from point to point in the materials flow system is called **pipeline inventory**." p. 524

- Suppliers to the plant
- One operation to the next
- A plant to a distribution center
- A distribution center to a retailer

- It is the sum of all scheduled receipts or open orders, which are orders that have been placed but not received.
- It is measured as the average demand during the lead time.

$$\text{Pipeline inventory} = \overline{D}_L = dL$$

- Lot size does not directly affect pipeline inventory.

How should inventory levels be measured and evaluated?

Inventory Management

Inventory Measures

"The **average aggregate inventory value** is the total value of all items held in inventory. It is an average because it usually represents the inventory investment over some period of time." p. 525

Many students mess up this simple calculation. Note that the average aggregate inventory value is found by adding the value of each inventory item. It is *not* then divided by the number of items. That calculation also results in an "average", but it is useless information.

- Total value summed over all items in inventory

$$\text{Average aggregate inventory value} = [\text{Quantity of Item A(Value per unit)}] + +[\text{Quantity of Item B(Value per unit)}] + \ldots + [\text{Quantity of Item } n\text{(Value per unit)}]$$

"**Weeks of supply** is an inventory measure obtained by dividing the average aggregate inventory value by the sales per week at cost.

$$\text{Weeks of supply} = \frac{\text{Average aggregate inventory value}}{\text{Weekly sales (at cost)}}$$

"**Inventory turnover** (or *turns*) is an inventory measure obtained by dividing annual sales at cost by the average aggregate inventory value maintained during the year." p. 525

$$\text{Inventory turnover} = \frac{\text{Annual sales (at cost)}}{\text{Average aggregate inventory value}}$$

Should most inventory be held at the raw material, WIP, or finished goods level? Which items should be standards?

Inventory Placement

- WIP inventory placement near the end-item reduces delivery time, but increases investment and reduces flexibility in final usage of the material.

What are the options for reducing inventory wisely?

Inventory Reduction

- Basic tactics for reducing inventory are called *levers.*
- Primary levers reduce inventory.
- Secondary levers decrease the cost of primary levers or reduce the need for having inventory.

Cycle Inventory

- Primary lever for reducing cycle inventory is the lot size, *Q*.

"However, making such reductions in *Q* without making any other changes can be devastating." p. 527

- Secondary levers
  - streamline methods for placing orders and making setups
  - increase repeatability, eliminate the need for changeovers

Safety Stock Inventory

- Primary lever for reducing safety stock is to place orders closer to the time when they must be received.

"However, this approach can lead to unacceptable customer service — unless demand, supply, and delivery uncertainties can be minimized." p. 527

A local manufacturer launched its JIT program by cutting lot sizes in half. However, they did not make corresponding changes to their cost accounting system. By halving the order quantity, the setup costs per unit doubled. In order to cover those costs, plus overhead and profit, catalog prices were increased by 30%.

Customer orders stopped almost immediately. The manufacturer had a mature product and was competing on cost. The 30% price increase made it uncompetitive. The firm quickly retreated to the larger lot sizes. It streamlined setup methods, and could *then* reduce lot sizes.

- Secondary levers
  - improve demand forecasts
  - reduce lead time
  - reduce supply uncertainties, communicate with suppliers, use preventive maintenance
  - capacity cushions and cross-trained workers

Anticipation Inventory

- Primary lever is to match demand rate with production rate.
- Secondary levers
  - add new products with different demand cycles
  - provide off-season promotional campaigns
  - offer seasonal pricing plans

Pipeline Inventory

- Primary lever is to reduce lead time.
- Secondary levers
  - find more responsive suppliers, improve materials handling
  - in cases where lead time varies with lot size, decrease *Q*

Which items demand the closest attention and control?

ABC Analysis

- Assign items to ABC classes according to annual dollar usage

Class	% of Items	% of Annual Dollar Usage
A	20%	80%
B	30%	15%
C	50%	5%

- Manage items according to class, with tightest control on the A items.

How can materials management be linked to other parts of operations strategy?

Links to Operations Strategy

"Managers must link their inventory and scheduling policies with operations strategy. Much depends on the positioning strategy chosen." p. 529

Process Focus	Product Focus
1. More need for cushions	1. Less tolerance for cushions
2. More pressure for an integrated organizational structure	2. Less pressure for an integrated organizational structure
3. Shorter planning horizons	3. Longer planning horizons
4. Less formalized supplier and customer relationships	4. More formalized supplier and customer relationships
5. Information systems oriented to specific customer orders	5. Information systems oriented to forecasts and inventory records

Cushions

- Extra equipment, personnel, and inventory

Integrated Organizational Structure

- Purchasing, production control, and distribution report to the same executive
- A high degree of cross-functional coordination

Planning Horizons

- Forward scheduling is feasible with a product focus
- Incentive to maximize utilization of capital intensive facilities encourages planning ahead

Supplier and Customer Relationships

- Repeat business justifies the time investment required to form long-term parterships

Information Systems

- Product focus requires information support for producing to forecasted demand for standard products which may be stored as finished goods inventory.
- Process focus requires information support for tracking customer orders, buying special materials, and detailed work order scheduling.

Multiple-Choice Questions

1. Switching to a more cooperative orientation to supplier relations is likely to
   A. discourage sole-source contracting.
   B. increase the importance of purchase price in making supplier selections.
   C. reduce the importance of quality in making supplier selections.
   D. reduce the number of suppliers.

2. In the prevalent orientation of supplier relationships in North America, which of the following is characteristic of the negotiations between buyers and sellers?
   A. Competitive advantages gained by sharing information
   B. Trust
   C. Long-term commitments prized over short-term advantages
   D. Viewed as a zero-sum game

3. Which of the following is an advantage of decentralized purchasing?
   A. Increased buyer expertise from specialization
   B. Profit centers responsible for controlling their own costs
   C. Increased purchasing "clout"
   D. Reduced costs due to obtaining more volume discounts

4. Which of the following describes a blanket purchase order?
   A. A contract for broad-ranging insurance "coverage"
   B. A contract governing the one-time purchase of a high-value item
   C. A long-term contract for repetitive purchases of a high volume item from one supplier
   D. A standard purchase agreement governing nearly all purchases from nearly all suppliers

5. Which of the following important variables has been viewed as most important in the competitive orientation to supplier relations?
   A. Delivery
   B. Price
   C. Quality
   D. Service/technical support

6. The type of inventory that is used to absorb uncertainty in supply or demand is called
   A. anticipation inventory.
   B. cycle inventory.
   C. pipeline inventory.
   D. safety stock inventory.

7. The buyer has more "clout" when
   A. switching suppliers is costly.
   B. the buyer represents a significant share of the supplier's sales.
   C. the purchased item is custom.
   D. the supplier can integrate forward.

8. Competitive bidding should be used
   A. for the purchase of capital equipment.
   B. when the contract value is low.
   C. when there is continuous high-volume demand.
   D. when time for negotiations is limited.

9. Holding costs include all of the following *except*
   A. interest.
   B. receiving.
   C shrinkage.
   D. taxes.

10. Which of the following types of inventory varies directly with order quantity?
    A. Anticipation inventory
    B. Cycle inventory
    C. Pipeline inventory
    D. Safety stock inventory

11. A product-focused firm tends to have
    A. more tolerance for "cushions."
    B. more pressure for an integrated organizational structure.
    C. shorter planning horizons.
    D. more formalized supplier and customer relationships.

12. An advantage of forward placement of inventory is
    A. consistency with competitive priorities calling for customized products.
    B. minimized reshipments from one distribution center to another.
    C. the pooling effect.
    D. reduced shipping costs.

(Multiple-choice answers are on Study Guide page 219.)

Problems

1. The Leonardo Company has the following items (among others) in inventory:

Item description	Price per Unit	Annual Usage	Cost * Volume
Chuks	$6.25	144	
Staffs	$4.50	50	
Stars	$3.50	400	
Swords	$1.10	1000	

   Leonardo uses ABC classification of its inventory. Which item is most likely to be an A item?

2. The Shreader Pizza Corporation would like to reduce its inventory. To this end, Donatello was asked to assess its inventory level. Given the following information from last year's financial statement, what was the inventory turnover ratio?

Raw Materials	Work-In-Process	Finished Goods	Cost of Goods Sold
$2,500,000	$1,000,000	$800,000	$15,000,000

3. A U.S. computer manufacturer receives disk drives from Japan. The manufacturer's assembly line works five days a week, 50 weeks per year, and consumes exactly 200 disk drives in its production of computers each workday. The lead time if the product is transported by ship, then truck, is six weeks.

   a. If each drive is worth $200, what is the investment in pipeline inventory?

   b. What is the investment in pipeline inventory if the product is transported by air and the lead time is reduced to one day?

4. An electric utility burns an average of 3000 tons of coal per day. Each rail car contains 100 tons of coal. Each unit train contains 100 rail cars. The lead time for a shipment of coal is four days. To protect against strikes, floods, and other events that may cut off supply, the utility keeps 270,000 tons of coal on site.

   a. What is the average pipeline inventory?

   b. How many weeks of supply is on site?

   c. What is the average cycle inventory?

Solutions

1. The Leonardo Company has the following items (among others) in inventory:

Item description	Price per Unit	Annual Usage	Cost * Volume
Chuks	$6.25	144	$900
Staffs	$4.50	50	$225
Stars	$3.50	400	$1400
Swords	$1.10	1000	$1100

Based on annual value of usage, the **stars** are most likely to be in the A category.

2. The Shreader Pizza Corporation would like to reduce its inventory. To this end, Donatello was asked to assess its inventory level. Given the following information from last year's financial statement, what was the inventory turnover ratio?

Raw Materials	Work-In-Process	Finished Goods	Cost of Goods Sold
$2,500,000	$1,000,000	$800,000	$15,000,000

$$\text{Inventory turnover ratio} = \frac{\$15,000,000}{\$4,300,000} = 3.49 \quad (\text{not } 1.16)$$

3. A U.S. computer manufacturer receives disk drives from Japan. The manufacturer's assembly line works five days a week, 50 weeks per year, and consumes exactly 200 disk drives in its production of computers each workday. The lead time if the product is transported by ship, then truck, is six weeks.

   a. If each drive is worth $200, what is the investment in pipeline inventory?

   Pipeline inventory:

$$\overline{D}_L = dL = 200 \,{}^{\text{drives}}\!/_{\text{day}} \left(5 \,{}^{\text{days}}\!/_{\text{week}}\right)(6 \text{ weeks})$$
$$= 6,000 \text{ disk drives}$$

   Pipeline value:

$$= 6,000 \text{ drives}\left({}^{\$200}\!/_{\text{drive}}\right) = \$1,200,000$$

   b. What is the investment in pipeline inventory if the product is transported by air and the lead time is reduced to one day?

   Pipeline inventory:

$$\overline{D}_L = dL = 200 \,{}^{\text{drives}}\!/_{\text{day}} (1 \text{ day})$$
$$= 200 \text{ disk drives}$$

   Pipeline value:

$$= 200 \text{ drives}\left({}^{\$200}\!/_{\text{drive}}\right) = \$40,000$$

4. An electric utility burns an average of 3000 tons of coal per day. Each rail car contains 100 tons of coal. Each unit train contains 100 rail cars. The lead time for a shipment of coal is four days. To protect against strikes, floods, and other events that may cut off supply, the utility keeps 270,000 tons of coal on site.

   a. What is the average pipeline inventory?

   Pipeline inventory:

   $$\overline{D}_L = dL = 3{,}000\,\text{tons}/_{\text{day}}(4\text{ days})$$

   $$= 12{,}000\text{ tons}$$

   Note that the train and car capacity are irrelevant.

   b. How many weeks of supply is on site?

   $$\frac{270{,}000\text{ tons}}{3{,}000\ \text{tons}/_{\text{day}}} = 90\text{ days, or about 12.9 weeks}$$

   c. What is the average cycle inventory?

   Cycle inventory:

   $$\frac{Q}{2} = \frac{100\ \text{tons}/_{\text{car}}\left(100\ \text{cars}/_{\text{train}}\right)}{2} = 5{,}000\text{ tons}$$

MULTIPLE CHOICE ANSWERS

1. D	6. D
2. D	7. B
3. B	8. A
4. C	9. B
5. B	10. B
	11. D
	12. D

Chapter Twelve, Independent Demand Inventory Systems

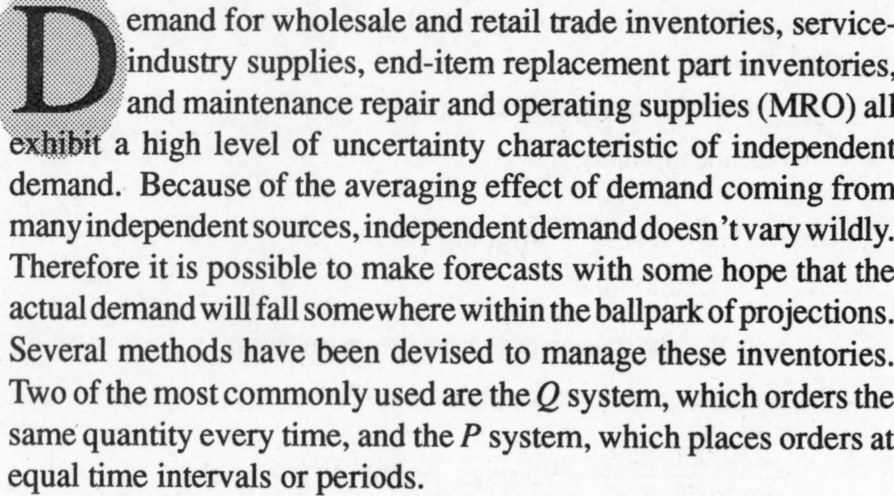

Demand for wholesale and retail trade inventories, service-industry supplies, end-item replacement part inventories, and maintenance repair and operating supplies (MRO) all exhibit a high level of uncertainty characteristic of independent demand. Because of the averaging effect of demand coming from many independent sources, independent demand doesn't vary wildly. Therefore it is possible to make forecasts with some hope that the actual demand will fall somewhere within the ballpark of projections. Several methods have been devised to manage these inventories. Two of the most commonly used are the *Q* system, which orders the same quantity every time, and the *P* system, which places orders at equal time intervals or periods.

Four Categories of Independent Demand Inventories

1. Wholesale and retail merchandise
2. Service industry inventory
3. Replacement part inventory
4. Maintenance, repair, and operating (MRO) supplies

Total demand

- The result of several customers making independent purchasing decisions
- Must be forecast
- Includes seasonal and some (but not a large) random variation
- Follows a fairly smooth pattern

FIGURE 12.1

Independent Demand

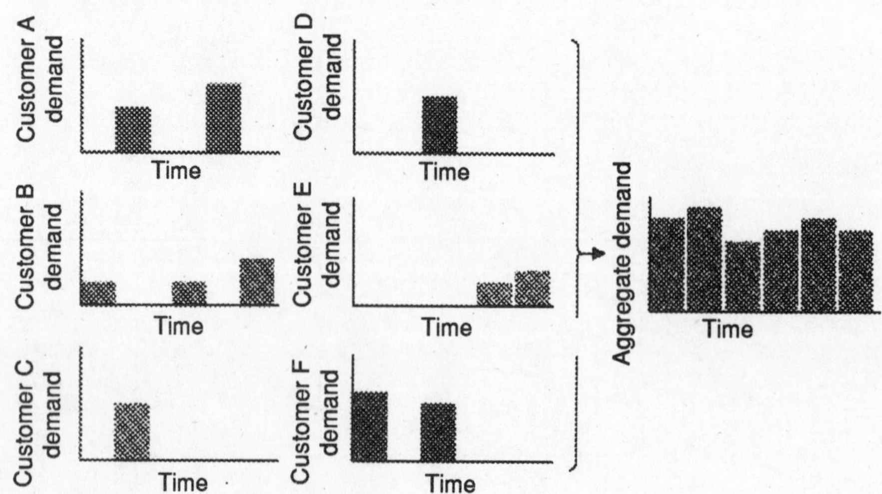

How much effort must be expended to maintain accurate inventory records?

A. Whatever it takes. How much time, energy and money will a bank expend to find a ten-cent error in an account? It is not the ten cents that is important, it is the flaw in the process that must be discovered.

The story about the battle being lost for want of a horse shoe nail is replayed every day in operations. Inventory is secured not so much as protection against theft as it is to communicate that keeping track of materials is important to the company. People tend to behave more responsibly when they enter a secured area, and are unlikely to go moving things around without keeping good records.

Should a manual or a computerized system be used?

Inventory Records

"A **scheduled receipt**, often called an **open order**, is an order that has been placed but not yet received." p. 541

With perpetual inventory records, accounts are maintained for on-hand inventory and open orders. Transactions such as issues, receipts, transfers and adjustments are posted to update these accounts so that the records accurately reflect the actual inventory position for every item.

- Some of the burden of data entry is eased with the use of bar codes and electronic data interchange

Tracking Methods

- Assign responsibility for reporting inventory transactions to specific employees
- Secure inventory in locked storage areas
- Use cycle counts to frequently check records against physical inventory
- Make logic checks to catch errors in inventory transactions

If inventory records prove to be accurate over several years time, the annual physical count can be avoided. The annual physical count is disruptive, costly, adds no value to the products, and often introduces as many errors into the records as it removes.

Computer Support

- Computers excel at massive data manipulation
- Several inventory system software packages are available

Five Common Uses of Computer Inventory Management Packages

1. Updating records
2. Providing management reports
3. Automating the reordering process
4. Generating exception reports
5. Recomputing decision parameters

How large should cycle inventories be?

Economic Order Quantity

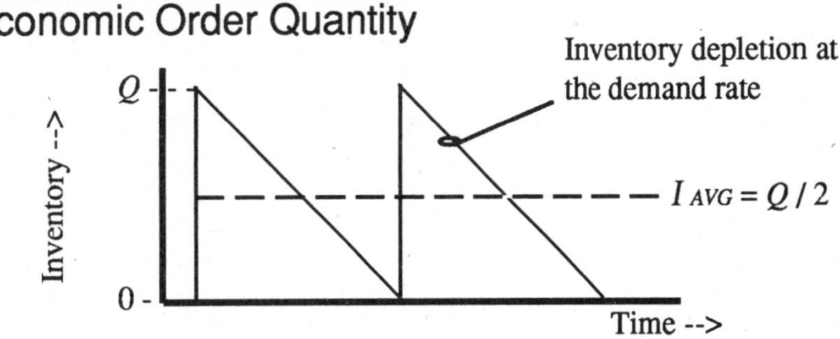

EOQ Assumptions

1. The demand rate is known and constant.
   - Therefore the depletion of inventory results in a straight line with slope equal to the negative of the demand rate.

> The *EOQ* model does not consider the competitive advantages of reduced rework, shorter manufacturing lead times, higher quality or other factors associated with small order quantities.
> Companies that do consider these other factors will favor a lot size quantity that is smaller than the EOQ. In JIT operations the philosophically ideal order quantity is one.

2. Replenishments arrive in a batch equal to the order quantity rather than piecemeal. There are no limitations on lot size.
   - The replenishment results in a *vertical* line on the graph, rather than a line with a positive finite slope.
3. Annual holding cost and annual ordering cost are the *only* costs which are relevant to the *order quantity* decision.
   - There are no quantity discounts, so per-unit price is irrelevant.
4. Replenishment decisions for one item (say doughnuts) are made independently from replenishment decisions for other items, (say coffee).
   - Model enhancements are required to consider situations where several items are purchased from the same supplier, or several items belong to a product family that can share the same setup.
5. There is no uncertainty in demand, lead time, or supply.
   - Therefore, replenishment orders can be timed so that no stockouts occur. Since none occur, stockout costs are irrelevant to the decision.
   - The minimum inventory equals zero, the maximum inventory equals the *EOQ*, and the average cycle inventory equals *EOQ*/2.

- The five assumptions describe an unrealistic situation.
- *EOQ* is a reasonable first approximation when the actual situation is only somewhat similar to the one stated by the assumptions.

Calculating the EOQ

The Annual Holding Cost increases as a direct linear function of order quantity, Q.

$$\text{Annual holding cost} = \frac{Q}{2}(H)$$

where

$Q/2$ = average inventory in cycle stock, and

H = cost of holding one unit in inventory for a year.

H = iP (if expressed as a proportion of the item's value)

With Q in the denominator, the annual ordering cost varies inversely with Q.

$$\text{Annual ordering cost} = \frac{D}{Q}(S)$$

where

D = *annual* demand

D/Q = number of (purchase/work) orders placed in one year

S = average cost of placing one (purchase/work) order (In manufacturing, this cost is called *setup*.)

Since these are the only relevant costs, the *annual* total of the relevant costs:

$$C = \frac{Q}{2}(H) + \frac{D}{Q}(S)$$

FIGURE 12.4

Total Inventory Cost Function

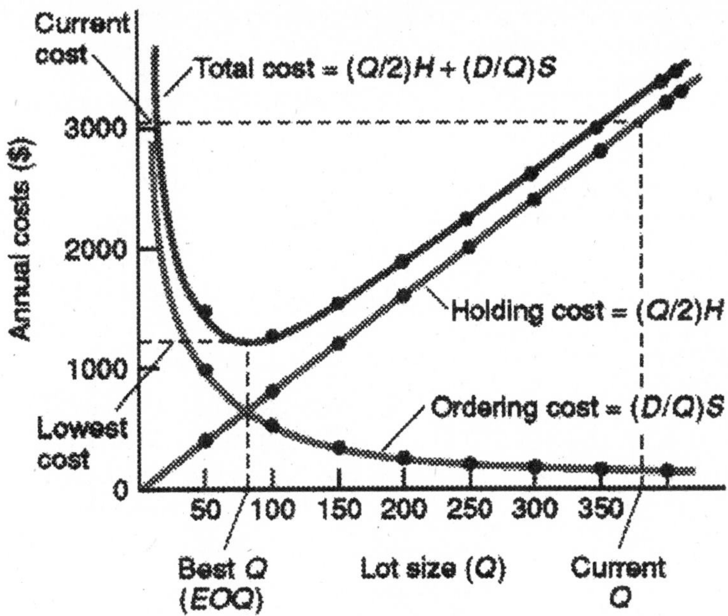

Note: See Fig. 12.4. The holding costs are linearly proportional to Q with a positive slope of H/2. The ordering costs vary inversely with Q. The sum of these two costs generates something of a "U" shaped total cost curve. Also note the minimum of the total cost curve occurs directly above the intersection of the line representing annual holding costs and the curve representing annual ordering costs. This is not a coincidence; this happens every time. At the *EOQ* these costs are equal.

Deriving the Economic Order Quantity:

The EOQ derives an order quantity decision that balances the costs of ordering with the costs of holding inventory to achieve the minimum *total* of these two costs.

Observe that the slope of a line drawn tangent to the minimum point on the total cost curve is equal to zero. In order to find that point, we take the derivative of the total cost function with respect to Q, set the result equal to zero, and solve for Q:

$$\frac{dC}{dQ} = \frac{H}{2} - \frac{DS}{Q^2} = 0$$

My goodness! There was a good reason for taking calculus after all. Now you can take it from here using algebra. Solve for Q and you will eventually arrive at the following equation. I know you can do it.

$$Q = \sqrt{\frac{2DS}{H}}$$

We call this special order quantity Q, the *economic* order quantity *EOQ*, because it results in the minimum of the total annual relevant costs. The average time between orders, *TBO*:

$$TBO = \frac{Q}{D}$$

This equation yields the time between orders in the same units of time used to express the demand rate D. For example, if D represents annual demand, this equation will express *TBO* in years.

How often should demand estimates, cost estimates, and lot sizes be updated?

$$Q=\sqrt{\frac{2DS}{H}}$$

Understanding the Effect of Changes

A Change in the Demand Rate

Q. What happens to cycle inventory if the demand rate increases?

A. D is in the numerator of the *EOQ* equation. *EOQ* varies directly as the square root of D. If D quadruples, *EOQ* doubles.

A Change in the Setup Costs

Q. What happens to lot sizes if setup costs decrease?

A. S is in the numerator of the *EOQ* equation. *EOQ* varies directly as the square root of S. If S decreases by a factor of 4, *EOQ* is halved.

A Change in the Holding Costs

Q. What happens if interest rates drop?

A. Interest charged on inventory investment is a component of holding cost. H is in the denominator of the *EOQ* equation. If the interest rate drops, *EOQ* increases.

Errors in Estimating D, H, and S.

Q. How critical are errors in estimating D, H, and S?

A. Errors such as overestimating ordering cost may be offset by other errors such as overestimating holding cost. The square root also reduces the effect of errors. If one misses a cost or demand estimate by 10%, the effect on total annual cost is often undetectable. Differences between EOQ assumptions and real-world situations in combination with normal year-to-year variations will usually completely mask any effect from common estimation errors.

Inventory Control Systems

Continuous Review System (Q System)

In a continuous review system, the inventory position of the item is known at all times (continuously).

> "The **inventory position (*IP*)** measures the item's ability to satisfy future demand. It includes scheduled receipts (SR) plus on-hand inventory (OH) minus backorders (BO)..." p. 550

Rule for the Continuous Review System:

Place an order for Q units whenever a withdrawal brings the inventory position to the reorder point R.

Selecting the Reorder Point When Demand and Lead Time Are Certain

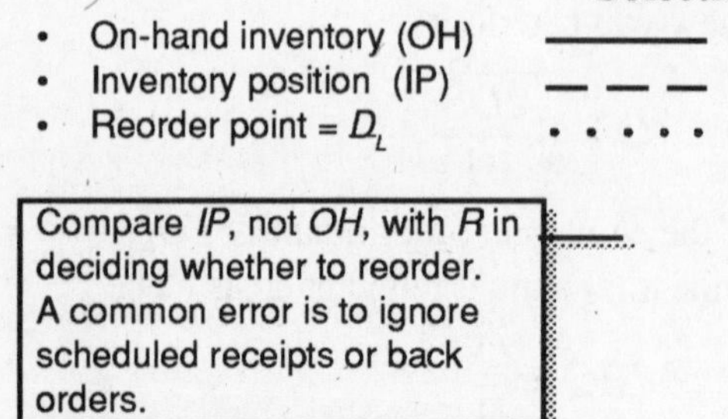

Compare *IP*, not *OH*, with *R* in deciding whether to reorder. A common error is to ignore scheduled receipts or back orders.

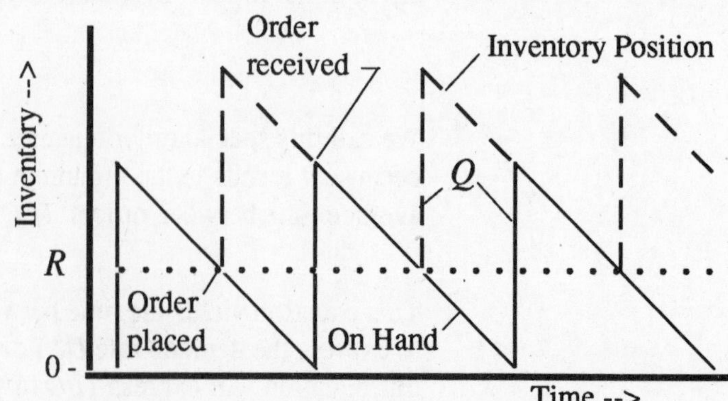

Selecting the Reorder Point When Demand and Lead Time Are Uncertain

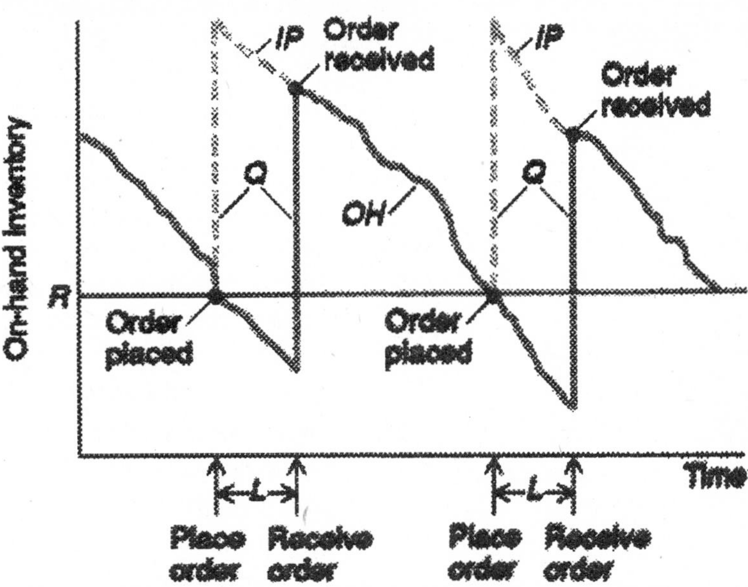

How large should safety stocks be?

Recall that safety stock inventory is inventory used to protect against uncertainties in demand, lead time, and supply.

- Reorder point equals pipeline inventory plus safety stock inventory.
  $$R = \bar{D}_L + \text{Safety stock}$$
- When there are no uncertainties in demand, lead time, or supply, safety stock is zero and $R = \bar{D}_L$.
- The average demand during the lead time is determined by customers. As a management issue, the reorder point decision is really a matter of selecting the safety stock quantity.
- Safety stock depends on two factors
  1. service level policy
  2. amount of uncertainty in demand, lead time, or supply

Choosing an Appropriate Service Level Policy

- Weigh benefits of holding safety stock against the cost of holding it.
- Cycle-service level — the probability of not running out of stock during any one inventory cycle.

Finding the Safety Stock by Using the Normal Probability Distribution

FIGURE 12.7

Safety Stock with a Normal Distributed Demand During the Lead Time

Cycle-service level

Probability of stockout

$z\sigma_L$

$\bar{D}_L$

R

"When selecting the safety stock, the inventory planner often assumes that the actual demand during lead time L, is normally distributed, as shown in Fig. 12.7." p. 553

The figure on the previous page shows that actual demand during the lead time is usually near the average demand $\bar{D}_L$. When demand during the lead time is less than or equal to R, all demand is satisfied. The shaded area in the right tail of the distribution shows the probability of demand during the lead time being greater than R, therefore incurring a stockout. As R increases, the area in the right tail decreases, which improves cycle-service level.

Given $R = \overline{D}_L$ + Safety stock, then Safety stock $= R - \overline{D}_L$. The figure shows that the safety stock is the distance between R and $\overline{D}_L$, and that distance is:

$$\text{Safety stock} = z\sigma_L$$

Notice that as stated before, safety stock depends on two factors, service level (which is related to z), and uncertainty (which is related to σ_L). Notice that safety stock *does not* depend on the magnitude of demand during the lead time. The magnitude of demand during the lead time is accounted for by the pipeline inventory $\overline{D}_L$.

- Demand rate data are usually collected for a time period t, which is different than the lead time L.
- It is a simple matter to calculate standard deviation of that data, σ_t.
- However, we need σ_L, (which is not the same as σ_t).

A conversion from standard deviation of demand during some other time period t to standard deviation of demand during the lead time L can be made if we assume independence between the demands occurring in each time period t. Making that assumption, variances σ_t^2 can be added.

$$\sigma_L{}^2 = \sum_{i=1}^{L} \sigma_t{}^2 \cong L\left(\sigma_t{}^2\right)$$

$$\sigma_L = \sigma_t\sqrt{L}$$

Finding the Safety Stock by Using a Discrete Probability Distribution

- Data history, judgement or simulation are used to estimate the joint probability distribution (variations of lead time and demand)
- List each possible discrete demand level, along with its probability.
- Select R from the list of possible demand levels so the cumulative probability is greater than or equal to the desired cycle-service level.
- Safety stock is the difference between R and the expected average demand during the lead time.

How can inventory be controlled if the time between replenishment orders should be fixed?

Periodic Review System (P System)

- Inventory position is reviewed periodically rather than continuously.
- There is greater uncertainty, because inventory position is not known at all times.
- Since safety stock is proportional to uncertainty, safety stock requirements are higher in P systems than in Q systems.
- P systems facilitate combining orders placed on a common supplier.
- Time between orders is constant, but order quantity varies.

Rule for the Periodic Review System

Review the item's inventory position IP every P time periods. Place an order for $(T - IP)$ units, where T is the target inventory position.

Selecting the Time Between Reviews

The order interval P is determined by substituting EOQ for Q in the formula for average time between orders:

$$P = \frac{EOQ}{D}$$

This result will have the units of "years" and may easily be converted to months, weeks, or days by the usual conversion factors.

Selecting the Target Inventory Level

The target T must be set high enough to cover average demand during the next review period P plus the average demand during the lead time L. It must also provide a safety stock to cover the uncertainties for the longer period $(P + L)$.

$$T = \overline{D}_{P+L} + z\sigma_{P+L}$$

$$\sigma_{P+L} = \sigma_t \sqrt{P + L}$$

What type of system—a *Q* system, a *P* system, or some hybrid—should be used to control inventories?

Comparative Advantages of the *Q* and *P* Systems

P-System Advantages

1. Replenishments can be made at fixed time intervals.
   - better for planning activities
   - better for scheduled transportation systems
2. Orders for multiple items can be combined.
   - potential price discounts for combined orders
   - reduced paperwork, ordering, and follow-up costs
3. Inventory position does not have to be known continuously.

Q-System Advantages

1. Review frequency of each item can be individualized.
2. Fixed lots sizes are sometimes desirable.
3. Safety stocks are lower.

What other types of systems are possible?

Hybrid Systems

Optional Replenishment System, S system

The **optional replenishment system** reviews the inventory position at fixed time intervals and, if the position has dropped to (or below) a predetermined level, places a variable-sized order to cover expected needs.

- This ensures that a reasonably large order is placed.

Base-stock system

- A replenishment order is issued each time a withdrawal is made.
- Order quantities vary to keep the inventory position at R at all times.
- Minimizes cycle inventory, but increases ordering costs.

Visual systems

- Inventory position records are not kept.
- Used with low value items that have steady demand.
- Overstocking is common, but these are "C" items in the ABC classification. Little money is tied up by overstocking.

Single-bin system

- Essentially a *P* system
- Target inventory T and current inventory position IP are established visually

Two-bin system

- Essentially a *Q* system
- When the first bin is empty, it triggers the replenishment order.
- The second bin contains an amount equal to $\overline{D}_L$ + Safety stock

Multiple-Choice Questions

1. Which of the following is not consistent with the five assumptions used in deriving *EOQ*?
   A. Decisions for one item are made independently of decisions made for other items.
   B. The per unit price decreases when the order quantity is greater than or equal to the discount quantity. There are quantity discounts.
   C. The quantity received is equal to the quantity ordered. There is no uncertainty in the quantity that will be received.
   D. The demand and the lead time are known and constant.

2. The safety stock should vary depending on
   A. Service level policy
   B. Uncertainty of demand during the lead time
   C. Magnitude of demand during the lead time
   D. Service level policy and uncertainty of demand during the lead time

3. In a continuous review system, which of the following is true when the interest rates rise?
   A. Cycle inventory decreases.
   B. Order quantity increases.
   C. Pipeline inventory increases.
   D. Safety stock increases.

4. In a reorder point system, what happens if the demand rate doubles, holding costs increase by 60%, and setup costs decrease by 20%?
   A. Cycle inventory decreases.
   B. Order quantity increases.
   C. Nothing.
   D. Safety stock increases.

5. Which of the following is an advantage of periodic review systems?
   A. Inventory records are more accurate.
   B. Safety stock requirements are lower.
   C. Order quantities are constant.
   D. Orders for multiple items can be combined.

6. Which of these hybrid systems is most like a continuous review system?
   A. *S*-system
   B. Base-stock system
   C. Visual system
   D. Two-bin system

7. Which is false (based on the five assumptions used to derive the *EOQ*)?
   A. At the *EOQ*, annual ordering costs equal annual holding costs.
   B. At the *EOQ*, the sum of annual order costs and annual holding costs is at its minimum.
   C. At the *EOQ*, annual order costs and annual carrying costs are each at their minimums.
   D. No stockout costs are ever incurred.

8. In a continuous review system, when deciding when to order
   A. compare *IP* to *OH*.
   B. compare *IP* to *R*.
   C. compare *OH* to *R*.
   D. compare *R* to the sum of $\overline{D}_L$ plus Safety stock.

9. Average demand during the lead time is analogous to
   A. anticipation inventory.
   B. buffer inventory.
   C. cycle inventory.
   D. pipeline inventory.

10. When the demand during a two-week lead time is normally distributed and safety stock is zero
    A. cycle service level is zero.
    B. the standard deviation of demand during the lead time equals two times the standard deviation of demand during one week.
    C. *R* equals $\overline{D}_L$.
    D. *Q* equals *R*.

11. Which system has the advantage of minimum cycle inventory?
    A. *P*-system
    B. *Q*-system
    C. *S*-system
    D. Base-stock system

12. If the demand is 90 per year, the order quantity is 15 per order and the service level is 83.3%, how many order cycles per year are expected to incur a stockout?
    A. one
    B. 2 1/2
    C. five
    D. fifteen

(Multiple-choice answers are on Study Guide page 232.)

Problems

1. Ish Kabibble nibbles coconut quiche in Kenosha. Kabibble canoes to Cocamo to acquire the best coconut quiche. That is costly commuting, so Kabibble cannot canoe from Kenosha to Cocamo for coconut quiche continuously. Given:
   - The price for a case of coconut quiche is $60. $P =$
   - It costs Kabibble $100 for each commute to Cocamo. $S =$
   - The cost to carry a case of coconut quiche for a year is 40% of the price. $i =$
   - Therefore the holding cost, $H = iP$. $H =$
   - Kabibble's consumption of coconut quiche is 12.25 cases *per month.* $d =$

Economic order quantity:

$$EOQ = \sqrt{\frac{2DS}{H}}$$

a. How many cases of coconut quiche should Ish Kabibble order?

Total relevant costs:

$$C = \frac{Q}{2}H + \frac{D}{Q}S$$

b. What is the total of the annual relevant costs?

Reorder interval:

$$P = \frac{EOQ}{D}$$

c. If Kabbible converts from continuous review to periodic review, what would the reorder interval be?

2. The average demand rate during a four-week lead time is 100 units per week and is normally distributed. The standard deviation of the weekly demand is ten units. If the company uses a continuous review system, desires a service level of 96%, has 260 on hand, 200 on order and 15 allocated (backordered)

Safety stock:

$$= z\sigma_L$$

a. What is value for z?

b. What is the safety stock?

Standard deviation of demand during the lead time L:

$$\sigma_L = \sigma_t\sqrt{L}$$

c. What is the reorder point R?

Reorder point:

$$R = \overline{D}_L + \text{Safety Stock}$$

d. What is the inventory position?

Inventory position:

$$IP = OH + SR - BO$$

e. A new customer order just arrived for 7 units. Should the firm place an order?

3. George Herman operates Honest Babe's Experienced Cars. George sells program cars he purchases in his mother's name at auctions. "This one here is my mother's personal car". And of course "Mom" lives in Pasadena just across the street from her church, and so forth. The lead time varies because both the time between auctions and the time required for title paperwork vary. The sales history reveals the following distribution of program car sales during the lead time:

Sales	Probability
0	0.05
1	0.10
2	0.20
3	0.18
4	0.15
5	0.12
6	0.10
7	0.06
8	0.02
9	0.02

Safety stock:
$= R - \overline{D}_L$

Calculate the reorder point and the safety stock required for a 95% service level.

Standard deviation of demand during the replenishment interval $P + L$:

$$\sigma_{P+L} = \sigma_t \sqrt{P+L}$$

4. A sales executive runs (on the average) nine pairs of hose per month, with a standard deviation of monthly demand equal to three pairs. The executive is too busy to maintain continuous inventory records of personal items. While packing for travel to the quarterly sales meeting held in the big city, the executive routinely checks the inventory of hose. While in town for the meeting, the executive will place an order to bring the inventory position up to the target. The retailer then arranges to ship the hose directly to the executive's home, with a lead time of two months. The executive places a high value on having an inventory of hose, so the cycle service level policy is 99%. What is the target inventory position?

Solutions

1. Ish Kabibble nibbles coconut quiche in Kenosha. Given:
   - The price for a case of coconut quiche is $60. $P = \$60$
   - It costs Kabibble $100 for each commute to Cocamo. $S = \$100$
   - The cost to carry a case of coconut quiche for a year is 40% of the price. $i = 40\%$
   - Therefore the holding cost, $H = iP$. $H = \$24$
   - Kabibble's consumption of coconut quiche is 12.25 cases *per month.* d = 12.25 cases/month, D = 147 cases/year

   a. How many cases of coconut quiche should Ish Kabibble order?

   $$EOQ = \sqrt{\frac{2DS}{H}} = \sqrt{\frac{2 \times 147 \times 100}{24}} = 35 \text{ cases}$$

Economic order quantity:

$$EOQ = \sqrt{\frac{2DS}{H}}$$

   b. What is the total of the annual relevant costs?

Total relevant costs:

$$C = \frac{Q}{2}H + \frac{D}{Q}S$$

   $$C = \frac{Q}{2}H + \frac{D}{Q}S = \frac{35}{2}(\$24) + \frac{147}{35}(\$100)$$
   $$= \$420 + \$420 = \$840$$

   Note: It is not a coincidence that the annual holding cost equals the annual ordering cost.

   c. If Kabbible converts from continuous review to periodic review, what would the reorder interval be?

Reorder interval:

$$P = \frac{EOQ}{D}$$

   $$P = \frac{EOQ}{D} = \frac{35}{147} = 0.2381 \text{ years, or } 2.86 \text{ months}$$

2. The average demand rate during a four-week lead time is 100 units per week and is normally distributed. The standard deviation of the weekly demand is ten units. If the company uses a continuous review system, desires a service level of 96%, has 260 on hand, 200 on order and 15 allocated (backordered)

   a. What is value for z? From the normal distribution table, $z \approx 1.75$

   b. What is the safety stock?

   Safety stock $z\sigma_L = 1.75(\sigma_t\sqrt{L}) = 1.75(10\sqrt{4}) = 35$

Safety stock:

$= z\sigma_L$

Standard deviation of demand during the lead time L:

$\sigma_L = \sigma_t\sqrt{L}$

   c. What is the reorder point R?

   $$R = \overline{D}_L + \text{ Safety Stock}$$
   $$= (100 \times 4) + 35 = 435$$

Reorder point:

$R = \overline{D}_L + \text{ Safety Stock}$

   d. What is the inventory position?

   $$IP = OH + SR - BO$$
   $$= 260 + 200 - 15 = 445$$

Inventory position:

$IP = OH + SR - BO$

   e. A new customer order just arrived for 7 units. Should the firm place an order? IP = (445 – 7) = 338 > 335. Therefore, do not place an order.

3. Honest Babe's Experienced Cars.

Sales	Probability	Cumulative Probability
0	0.05	0.05
1	0.10	0.15
2	0.20	0.35
3	0.18	0.53
4	0.15	0.68
5	0.12	0.80
6	0.10	0.90
7	0.06	0.96
8	0.02	0.98
9	0.02	1.00

Calculate the reorder point and the safety stock required for a 95% service level.

The cumulative probability must be greater than or equal to the desired service level. When the reorder point, *R* is 6, the cumulative probability that demand during the lead time will be served is only 90%. The correct reorder point, ***R* is 7 automobiles.** At 96%, it is the lowest quantity with a cumulative probability greater than or equal to the service level.

The expected demand is:

(0 x 0.05) + (1 x 0.10) + (2 x 0.20) + (3 x 0.18) + (4 x 0.15) + (5 x 0.12) + (6 x 0.10) + (7 x 0.06) + (8 x 0.02) + (9 x 0.02) = 3.6

Safety stock:
$= R - \overline{D}_L$

Safety stock $= R - \overline{D}_L = 7 - 3.6 = 3.4$ automobiles

4. A sales executive. What is the target inventory position?

$d = 9$, $\sigma_t = 3$, $P = 3$, $L = 2$, Service level = 99%.

$P + L = 5$ months

Standard deviation of demand during the replenishment interval $P + L$:

$\sigma_{P+L} = \sigma_t \sqrt{P+L}$

$\overline{D}_{P+L} = dL = 9(5) = 45$ pairs

$z = 2.33$

$\sigma_{P+L} = \sigma_t \sqrt{P+L} = 3\sqrt{3+2} = 6.71$ pairs

Safety stock $= z\sigma_L = 2.33(6.71) = 15.63$ or 16 pairs

Target inventory $= \overline{D}_{P+L} + z\sigma_{P+L} = 45 + 16 = 61$ pairs

MULTIPLE CHOICE ANSWERS

1. B	7. D
2. D	8. B
3. A	9. D
4. C	10. C
5. D	11. D
6. D	12. A

Supplement H, Special Inventory Models

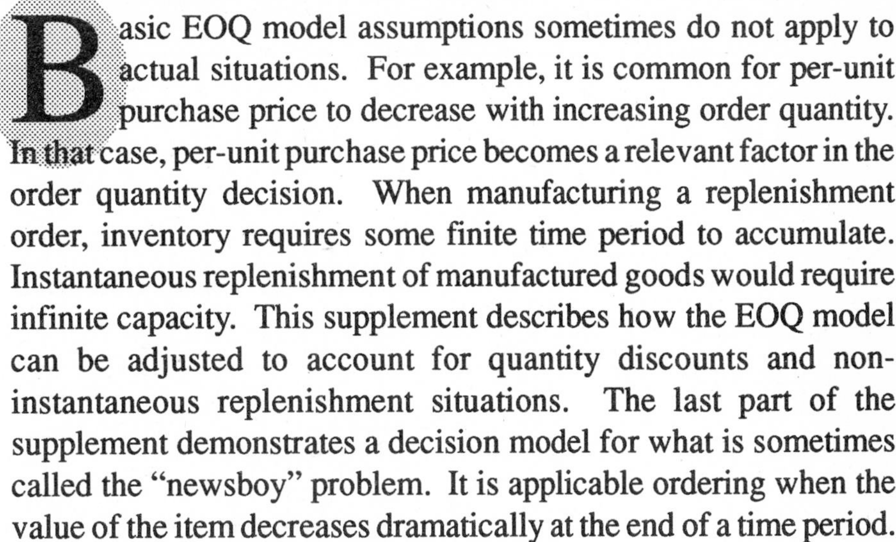

Basic EOQ model assumptions sometimes do not apply to actual situations. For example, it is common for per-unit purchase price to decrease with increasing order quantity. In that case, per-unit purchase price becomes a relevant factor in the order quantity decision. When manufacturing a replenishment order, inventory requires some finite time period to accumulate. Instantaneous replenishment of manufactured goods would require infinite capacity. This supplement describes how the EOQ model can be adjusted to account for quantity discounts and non-instantaneous replenishment situations. The last part of the supplement demonstrates a decision model for what is sometimes called the "newsboy" problem. It is applicable ordering when the value of the item decreases dramatically at the end of a time period.

Non-instantaneous Replenishment

- Production of an order quantity Q occurs at some finite rate p.
- The production period is Q/p in length.
- The product may be consumed at the demand rate d at the same time a replenishment order is being manufactured.
- Inventory accumulates during the production run at the rate $(p - d)$.
- Inventory declines while the item is not in production at the rate $-d$.
- The maximum amount of cycle stock, I_{max} is equal to the accumulation rate $(p - d)$ times the production period Q/p.

$$I_{max} = \frac{Q}{p}(p-d)$$

- The average amount of cycle stock I_{avg} is $I_{max}/2$.

$$I_{avg} = \frac{Q}{2}\left(\frac{p-d}{p}\right) = \frac{Q}{2}\left(1-\frac{d}{p}\right)$$

- Total cost = Annual holding costs + Annual ordering costs (as before)

$$C = \frac{Q}{2}\left(\frac{p-d}{p}\right)H + \frac{D}{Q}S$$

- The minimum cost occurs when the slope of the total cost curve with respect to $Q = 0$.

$$\frac{dC}{dQ} = \left(\frac{p-d}{2p}\right)H - \frac{DS}{Q^2} = 0$$

$$\left(\frac{p-d}{p}\right)\frac{H}{2} = \frac{DS}{Q^2}$$

$$Q^2 = \frac{2DS}{H}\left(\frac{p-d}{p}\right)$$

$$Q = \sqrt{\frac{2DS}{H}}\sqrt{\frac{p}{p-d}}$$

We call this quantity the Economic Lot Size (*ELS*) because the total of annual holding and annual ordering costs are minimized.

$$ELS = \sqrt{\frac{2DS}{H}}\sqrt{\frac{p}{p-d}} = EOQ\sqrt{\frac{p}{p-d}}$$

By inspection we can see that the *ELS* is equal to the *EOQ* increased by a factor to account for the effect of inventory accumulation at a finite rate.

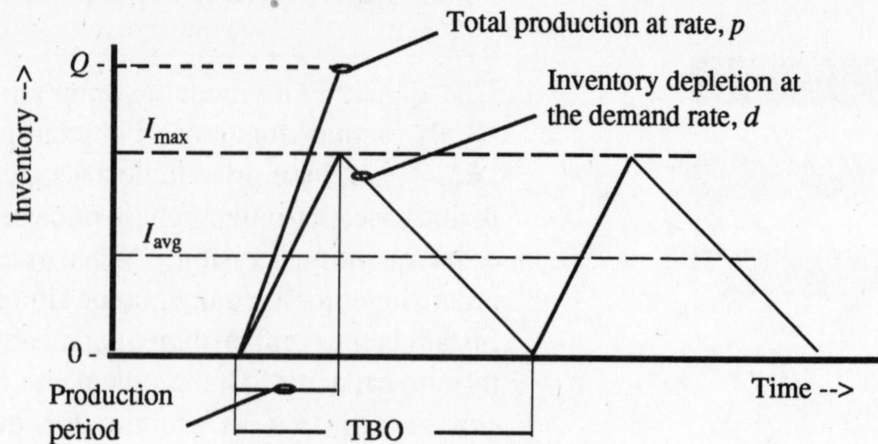

Economic Lot Size Exercise

A domestic automobile manufacturer schedules 12 two-person teams to assemble 4.6 liter DOHC V-8 engines per work day. Each team can assemble 5 engines per day. The automobile final assembly line creates an annual demand for the DOHC engine at 10,080 units per year. The engine and automobile assembly plants operate 6 days per week, 48 weeks per year. The engine assembly line also produces SOHC V-8 engines. The cost to switch the production line from one type of engine to the other is $100,000. It costs $2000 to store one DOHC V-8 for one year.

a. What is the economic lot size?

$$ELS = \sqrt{\frac{2DS}{H}}\sqrt{\frac{p}{p-d}} = \sqrt{\frac{2(10{,}080)(100{,}000)}{2{,}000}}\sqrt{\frac{60}{60-35}}$$

$$= 1004\sqrt{2.4} = 1{,}555.378 \text{ or about } 1{,}555 \text{ engines}$$

b. How long is the production run?

$$\frac{Q}{p} = \frac{1{,}555}{60} = 25.91 \text{ or about 26 production days}$$

c. What is the average quantity in inventory?

$$I_{avg} = \frac{I_{max}}{2} = \frac{Q}{2}\left(\frac{p-d}{p}\right) = \frac{1{,}555}{2}\frac{(60-35)}{60} = 324 \text{ engines}$$

d. What is the total of the annual relevant costs?

$$C = \frac{Q}{2}\left(\frac{p-d}{p}\right)H + \frac{D}{Q}S$$

$$= \frac{1{,}555}{2}\left(\frac{60-35}{60}\right)\$2{,}000 + \frac{10{,}080}{1{,}555}(\$100{,}000)$$

$$= \$647{,}916.67 + \$648{,}231.51$$

$$= \$1{,}296{,}148.18$$

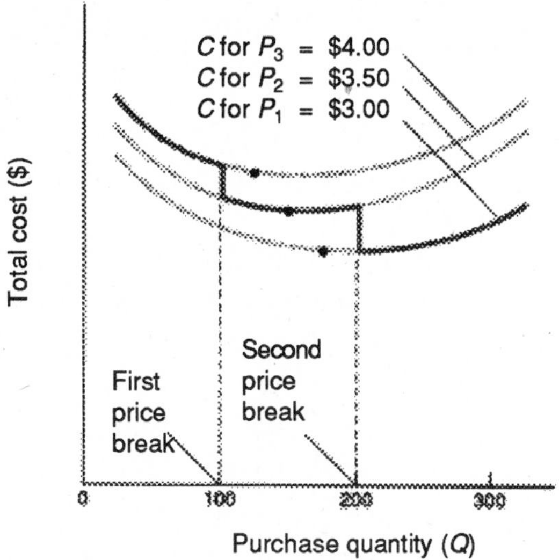

Quantity Discounts

The *EOQ* model assumes that there are no quantity discounts, so per-unit price is not relevant. If discounts are offered, then price becomes a factor in choosing the order quantity. For example, if doughnuts cost $0.30 each or $2.98 per dozen (even with sprinkles!), then one would never order ten doughnuts. It would be cheaper to buy twelve and throw two away.

We assume an "all units" discount. In other words, when the order quantity is from one to eleven doughnuts, the price is $0.30 each. When the order quantity is twelve or more, all units, including the first eleven, cost just under $0.25 each. This introduces a "discontinuity" in the total cost curve. A discontinuity is a sharp change occurring at a point. Now it will probably break your heart to read this, but we cannot use calculus to find the slope of discontinuous functions. Therefore we cannot derive a single formula (as with the *EOQ* and *ELS*) to provide the optimum answer. Instead, we must investigate each of several possible optimums to determine which really results in the lowest total cost. This is most reliably accomplished by following a process involving several steps.

It is convenient to explain this process by using an example:

Order Quantity	Price per Doughnut	
0 - 11	P_1	$0.300
12 - 143	P_2	$0.248
144 - •	P_3	$0.237

Ordering Cost, S = $1.00

Demand = 32 doughnuts *per month*

Holding Cost, H = 40% of price

Step 1. Beginning with the *lowest* price, calculate *EOQ*s for each price level.

$EOQ_{\$0.237}$ = 90 doughnuts. This is not feasible, because if we buy 90 doughnuts, the price is not $0.237 each.

$EOQ_{\$0.248}$ = 88 doughnuts. This is feasible.

Step 2. If the *EOQ* for the *lowest* price is feasible, stop. Order the *EOQ*.

Alas, this is not the case in our example. We must continue to the next step.

Step 3. Calculate the total cost for each price level. Use the *EOQ* when feasible. Order the quantity with the lowest total cost.

$$C = \frac{Q}{2}(H) + \frac{D}{Q}(S) + PD$$
$$= \frac{Q}{2}(iP) + \frac{D}{Q}(S) + PD$$

$$C_{88} = \frac{88}{2}(0.4 \times \$0.248) + \frac{(32 \times 12)}{88}(\$1.00) + \$0.248(32 \times 12)$$
$$= \$4.365 + \$4.364 + \$95.232$$
$$= \$103.961$$

$$C_{144} = \frac{144}{2}(0.4 \times \$0.237) + \frac{(32 \times 12)}{144}(\$1.00) + \$0.237(32 \times 12)$$
$$= \$6.826 + \$2.667 + \$91.008$$
$$= \$100.501$$

The firm should order doughnuts by the gross. Beware that it is not always best to order the quantity required to get a price break. If the discount is small or the order quantity required to get the discount is large, increased holding costs will more than offset the savings in price and ordering costs. It is also likely that we have vastly underestimated the costs of pilferage and obsolescence for the doughnuts.

One-Period Decisions

- Used when the inventory has a limited shelf life, after which its value drastically declines.
- Solution method finds an order quantity *Q* that results in the maximum expected payoff.
- The calculation process bears some resemblance to the one used for finding safety stocks with a discrete distribution of demand during the lead time.

One-Period Decision Exercise:

The buyer for a Los Angles sports apparel shop is placing an order for jerseys bearing local professional football team logos. The jerseys cost $20 each. At the begining of the season, the jerseys sell for $45. At the end of the season, the buyer believes that the market for LA professional football team apparel will all but disappear. Leftover jerseys could be sold in a distress sale for $3 each.

Demand	Probability
10,000	0.05
20,000	0.15
30,000	0.30
40,000	0.20
50,000	0.15
60,000	0.10
70,000	0.05

Probability	0.05	0.15	0.30	0.20	0.15	0.10	0.05	
Quantity, D/Q	**10,000**	**20,000**	**30,000**	**40,000**	**50,000**	**60,000**	**70,000**	**Expected Profit**
10,000	$25,000	$25,000	$25,000	$25,000	$25,000	$25,000	$25,000	$25,000
20,000	$8,000	$50,000	$50,000	$50,000	$50,000	$50,000	$50,000	$47,900
30,000	($9,000)	$33,000	$75,000	$75,000	$75,000	$75,000	$75,000	$64,500
40,000	($18,000)	$26,000	$58,000	$100,000	$100,000	$100,000	$100,000	**$70,400**
50,000	($35,000)	$9,000	$41,000	$83,000	$125,000	$125,000	$125,000	$66,000
60,000	($52,000)	($8,000)	$24,000	$66,000	$108,000	$150,000	$150,000	$55,300
70,000	($69,000)	($25,000)	$9,000	$49,000	$91,000	$133,000	$175,000	$41,000

The maximum expected profit occurs when the buyer orders 40,000 jerseys.

Problems

Economic Lot Size:

$$ELS = \sqrt{\frac{2DS}{H}}\sqrt{\frac{p}{p-d}}$$

Average Inventory:

$$I_{avg} = \frac{Q}{2}\left(\frac{p-d}{p}\right)$$

Total Relevant Costs:

$$C = \frac{Q}{2}\left(\frac{p-d}{p}\right)H + \frac{D}{Q}(S)$$

Economic Order Quantity:

$$EOQ = \sqrt{\frac{2DS}{H}}$$

Total Annual Relevant Costs:

$$C = \frac{Q}{2}(H) + \frac{D}{Q}(S) + PD$$

1. A manufacturer has a hot new product...a computer mouse that resists the ordinary build up of crud on the rollers. The product design requires production to close tolerances, so only 250 mice can be produced per day, five days per week, 48 weeks per year. The demand rate is 12,000 mice per year (50 per day of operations). Setup costs are $200. The cost to store one mouse per year is $32.

   a. What is the Economic Lot Size?

   b. What is the average quantity of mice in cycle stock inventory? (Assume these mice don't multiply.)

   c. What is the total of the annual relevant costs?

2. A purchasing manager acquires external hard disk drives for use with the firm's work-station computers. The demand for disks is 25 per month. Ordering costs are $225 per order. There is a high risk of obsolescence, so the holding cost per disk per year is 40% of the price.

Order Quantity	Price per Unit
1 - 34	$254.25
35 - 349	$250.00
350 - ∞	$244.50

   How many should be ordered at a time?

3. The concession manager for the college football stadium must decide how many hot dogs to order for the next game. Each hot dog sold makes a profit of $0.75. Hot dogs left over after this game are sold to the student cafeteria at a loss of $0.30 each. Based on previous games the probability of demand is as shown:

Demand, *D*	Probability
1,000	0.30
2,000	0.40
3,000	0.20
4,000	0.10

   Complete the payoff matrix to determine how many hot dogs to order.

Probability	0.30	0.40	0.20	0.10	Expected
Demand/Buy	1000	2000	3000	4000	Payoff
1000					
2000					
3000					
4000					

Solutions

Economic Lot Size:

$$ELS = \sqrt{\frac{2DS}{H}}\sqrt{\frac{p}{p-d}}$$

Average Inventory:

$$I_{avg} = \frac{Q}{2}\left(\frac{p-d}{p}\right)$$

Total Relevant Costs:

$$C = \frac{Q}{2}\left(\frac{p-d}{p}\right)H + \frac{D}{Q}(S)$$

Economic Order Quantity:

$$EOQ = \sqrt{\frac{2DS}{H}}$$

Total Annual Relevant Costs:

$$C = \frac{Q}{2}(H) + \frac{D}{Q}(S) + PD$$

1. Clean Mice.
   $d = 50, p = 250, D = 12{,}000, S = \$200, H = \$32$

   a. What is the Economic Lot Size?

$$ELS = \sqrt{\frac{2DS}{H}}\sqrt{\frac{p}{p-d}}$$
$$= \sqrt{\frac{2(12{,}000)(200)}{32}}\sqrt{\frac{250}{250-50}} = 433 \text{ mice}$$

   b. What is the average quantity of mice in cycle stock inventory?

$$I_{avg} = \frac{Q}{2}\left(\frac{p-d}{p}\right) = \frac{433}{2}\left(\frac{250-50}{250}\right)$$
$$= 173.2 \text{ or about } 173 \text{ mice}$$

   c. What is the total of the annual relevant costs?

$$C = \frac{Q}{2}\left(\frac{p-d}{p}\right)H + \frac{D}{Q}(S) = \frac{433}{2}\left(\frac{250-50}{250}\right)(\$32) + \frac{12{,}000}{433}(\$200)$$
$$= \$11{,}085.13$$

2. Disk drives.

Order Quantity	Price per Unit
1 - 34	$254.25
35 - 349	$250.00
350 - ∞	$244.50

   How many should be ordered at a time?

$$EOQ_{\$254.25} = \sqrt{\frac{2DS}{H}} = \sqrt{\frac{2(25\times12)(225)}{(0.4\times254.25)}}$$
$$= 36.43 \text{ or about } 36 \text{ units (not feasible)}$$

$$EOQ_{\$250.00} = \sqrt{\frac{2DS}{H}} = \sqrt{\frac{2(25\times12)(225)}{(0.4\times250.00)}}$$
$$= 36.74 \text{ or about } 37 \text{ units (feasible)}$$

$$C_{37} = \frac{Q}{2}(H) + \frac{D}{Q}(S) = PD = \frac{37}{2}(0.4\times\$250) + \frac{300}{37}(\$225) + \$250(300)$$
$$= \$1{,}850.00 + \$1{,}824.32 + \$75{,}000$$
$$= \$78{,}674.32$$

$$C_{350} = \frac{Q}{2}(H) + \frac{D}{Q}(S) + PD = \frac{350}{2}(0.4\times\$244.50) + \frac{300}{350}(\$225) + \$244.50(300)$$
$$= \$17{,}115.00 + \$192.86 + \$73{,}350$$
$$= \$90{,}657.86$$

In this problem it would be better to order the EOQ of 37 than to take advantage of the price discount at 350 units.

3. The concession manager for the college football stadium must decide how many hot dogs to order for the next game. Each hot dog sold makes a profit of $0.75. Hot dogs left over after this game are sold to the student cafeteria at a loss of $0.30 each. Based on previous games the probability of demand is as shown:

Demand, *D*	Probability
1,000	0.30
2,000	0.40
3,000	0.20
4,000	0.10

Complete the payoff matrix to determine how many hot dogs to order.

Probability	0.30	0.40	0.20	0.10	Expected
Demand/Buy	**1000**	**2000**	**3000**	**4000**	Payoff
1000	$750	$750	$750	$750	$750
2000	$450	$1500	$1500	$1500	$1185
3000	$150	$1200	$2250	$2250	**$1200**
4000	($150)	$900	$1950	$3000	$1005

Chapter Thirteen, Aggregate Planning

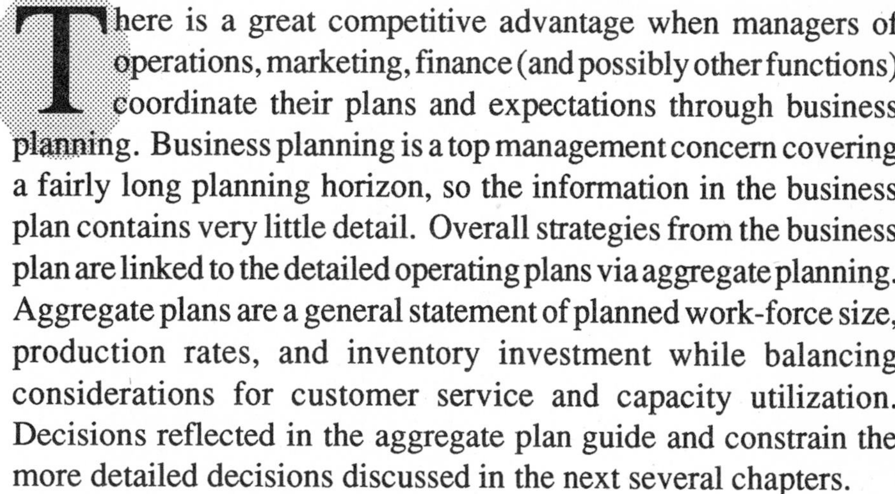

There is a great competitive advantage when managers of operations, marketing, finance (and possibly other functions) coordinate their plans and expectations through business planning. Business planning is a top management concern covering a fairly long planning horizon, so the information in the business plan contains very little detail. Overall strategies from the business plan are linked to the detailed operating plans via aggregate planning. Aggregate plans are a general statement of planned work-force size, production rates, and inventory investment while balancing considerations for customer service and capacity utilization. Decisions reflected in the aggregate plan guide and constrain the more detailed decisions discussed in the next several chapters.

"...the plan must balance conflicting objectives involving customer service, work-force stability, cost, and profit." p. 589

What items should be aggregated?

The Purpose of Aggregate Plans

Aggregation

- Useful because it is general
- Based on aggregate quantities for similar products and services

Product Families

- Have similar markets and manufacturing processes
- Share in common relevant units of measurement
  - units, barrels, tons, etc.
  - dollars
  - standard hours

Labor

- Aggregation depends on degree of work-force flexibility
- May be considered a single aggregate group if
  - work force is flexible and
  - entire work force produces every product family
- Aggregated on a product family basis if
  - different parts of the work force are used in the production of different product families or
  - different product families are produced in different plants at scattered locations

Time

"A **planning horizon** is the length of time covered by an aggregate plan. Typically, the planning horizon is one year, although it can differ in various situations." p. 592

- Updated monthly or quarterly
- Planning periods are months or quarters, not weeks or days

How should an aggregate plan fit with other plans?

Relationship to Other Plans

"A **business plan** is a projected statement of income, costs, and profits." p. 592

- Accompanied by
  - budgets
  - projected balance sheet
  - projected cash flow
- Brings together operations, finance, and marketing plans
- The business plan is analogous to the annual plan for nonprofit services.

<u>Business plan</u>

- Provides the overall framework of
  - demand projections
  - functional area inputs and
  - capital budget
- Guides and constrains the aggregate plan

<u>Production plan</u>

- Specifies corresponding product family
  - production rates
  - inventory levels
  - work-force levels
- Guides and constrains master production schedule

<u>Master production schedule</u>

- Specifies timing and size of production quantities for each product in the product family

"Thus the aggregate plan plays a key role in translating the strategies of the business plan into an operational plan for the manufacturing process." p. 592

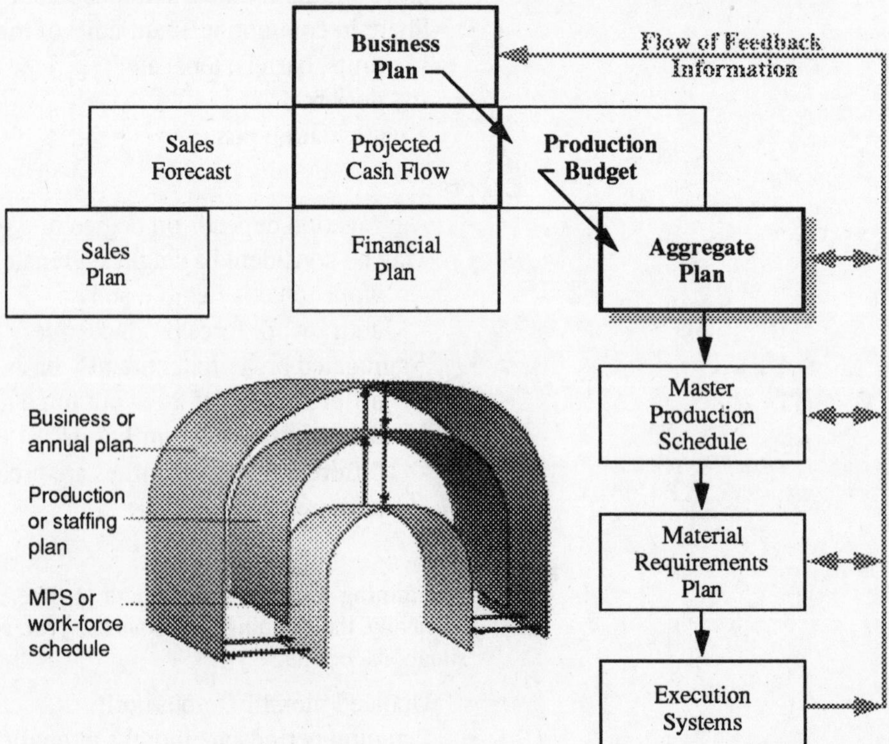

In the service sector:

Annual plan or business plan

- Sets the organization's direction and objectives
- Provides the framework for the staffing plan and the work-force schedule

Staffing plan

- Presents the number and types of employees required to meet objectives stated in the annual or business plan

Work-force schedule

- Details specific work schedule for each employee category.

Managerial Importance of Aggregate Plans

What kind of cross-functional coordination is needed?

Managerial Inputs

- Create a committee of functional-area representatives
- Committee chaired by a general manager having overall responsibility
- Each representative furnishes information essential to development of the aggregate plan.

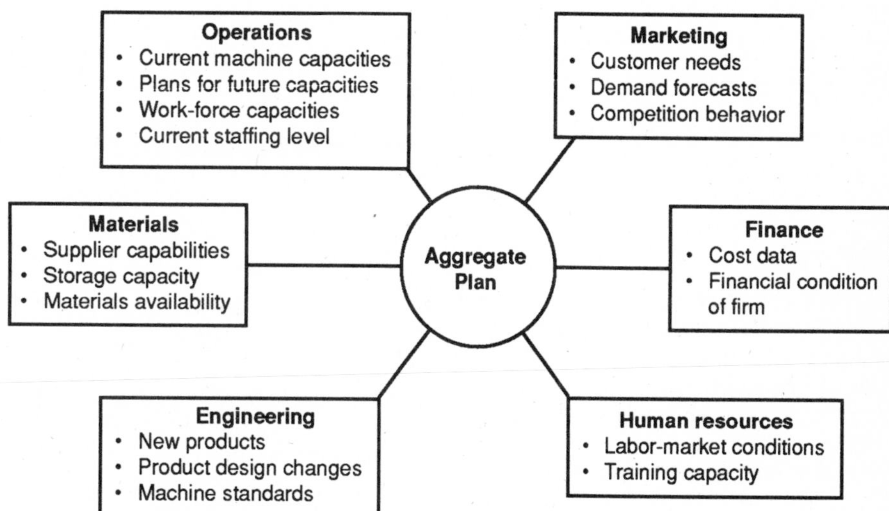

Typical Objectives

"The many functional areas in an organization that give input to the aggregate plan typically have conflicting objectives for the use of the organization's resources." p. 594

- Involves cost trade-offs and consideration of qualitative factors.

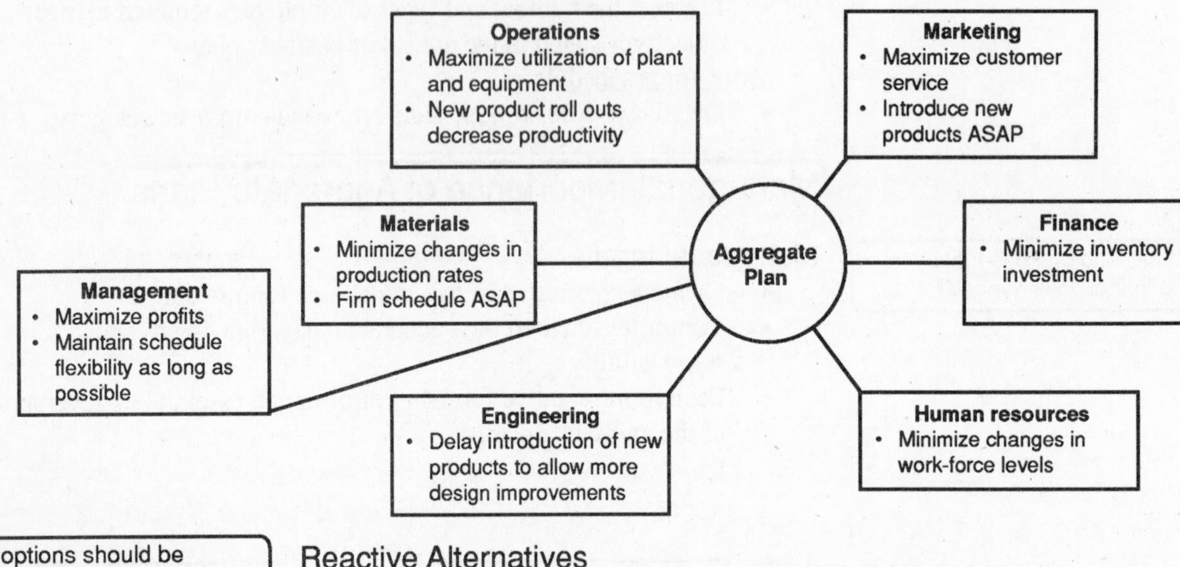

What options should be considered in responding to uneven demand?

Reactive Alternatives

"**Reactive alternatives** are actions that can be taken to cope with demand requirements." p. 595

- Accept demand forecast as a given
- React to fluctuations in demand

Work-force adjustment

- Hiring and firing
- Varies by industry, training requirements, labor pool

Overtime and undertime

- Excessive overtime leads to declining quality and productivity.
- To retain skilled employees in a slack busines period, undertime is preferable to layoffs.

Vacation schedules

- Schedule vacations to decrease output when inventories are high, or when replacement labor is available.

Anticipation inventory

- Build inventory in slack periods to be used in peak demand periods and level demand on operations.
- This option is generally not available to services because services can not be stored.

During a class held at a local manufacturing facility, my lecture was interrupted by a "good-news, bad-news" announcement over the public address system. The good news was that everyone would get an extra week off during the end-of-the-year holidays. The bad news was that no one would be paid for that time.

Sales were down, and it was important to reduce inventory. Although the firm used undertime, they never had a layoff. Many employees continued to work full time even during those periods of reduced pay. Before one says that they would never do that, consider which employees the company would keep if a layoff did become necessary.

Subcontractors

- A common approach in aerospace and auto industries.
- Subcontractors provide extra capacity, but scheduling, quality, and labor relations issues are more difficult to control.

Backlogs, back orders, and stockouts

- Backlog — an accumulation of customer orders promised for a future date. Backlogs are used when customers expect to wait some defined time period for delivery as a normal course of business.
- A backorder is an *order* that not ready when promised, delivery is delayed. This may lead to customer dissatisfaction.
- A stockout is an inability to satisfy demand for a *stock* item at the time it occurs. This may lead to lost sales.

How can demand be leveled to reduce operating costs?

Aggressive Alternatives

"**Aggressive alternatives** are actions that attempt to modify demand and, consequently, resource requirements." p. 597

- Adjust the demand pattern to achieve efficiency and reduce costs.
- These actions are typically specified in the marketing (sales) plan.

Complementary products

- Peak demand occurs at different times, leveling demand on production facilities

Creative pricing

- Gives customers an incentive to shift demand from peak times.

All of these alternatives have costs and adverse factors associated with them. The challenge is to find a combination of alternatives that mitigates adverse factors while minimizing cost. It is a difficult challenge, but hey, if it was easy, anybody could do it.

Planning Strategies

"A **chase strategy** adjusts output rates or work-force levels to match demand over the planning horizon without using anticipation inventory and/or undertime." p. 598

- Anticipation inventory or undertime is not used.
- Advantages
  + low inventory investment and backlogs
- Disadvantages
  - expense of adjusting output rates and/or work force
  - alienation of the work force
  - loss of productivity
  - lower quality

"A **level strategy** maintains a constant output rate or work-force level over the planning horizon by using anticipation inventory and/or undertime." p. 598

- Anticipation inventory or undertime is used.
- Advantages
  + level output rates
  + stable work force
- Disadvantages
  - increased inventory investment
  - increased undertime and overtime expense
  - increased backlogs

There is a continuum or infinite number of mixed strategies that lie between these two "pure" strategies. Chances are, a mixed strategy will produce an aggregate plan that reduces costs and mitigates adverse factors. In addition, the plan must be consistent with corporate policy and objectives regarding the controllable variables: hiring/firing, overtime/undertime, subcontracting, anticipation inventories, backlogs, and so forth. For example, if a corporate policy is to have a stable work force, the aggregate plan cannot call for hiring or firing.

> "The aggregate plan not only is a product of managerial inputs from the various functional areas, but it also has an impact on their activities." p. 598

The short-term salary savings of "Reductions in force" (RIF), "restructuring", "alternative career opportunities", "right-sizing" and other euphemisms for firing large numbers of employees are often viewed positively by myopic investors. However, the inevitable write-off to restructuring is typically in the lower six figures per employee fired!

And that does not include costs that are difficult to measure. These unmeasured costs may be more significant than the reported costs. They include loss of morale and loyalty, time spent in worry and commiseration, hurdles to attracting skilled employees in the future, and time to redefine jobs, retrain, and reorganize departments.

Lost revenue opportunities are also ignored. Publicity about large layoffs may give customers reason to seek a more stable supplier. The employees most likely to take RIF buy outs are the ones with the most marketable skills. They will soon be serving former customers while working for competitors.

Layoffs are a sign that the firm's managers can not make productive use of available resources. However, boards often base executive bonuses upon a reduction in *measured* costs. This practice rewards ruthless short-term cost cutting to the detriment of long-term resource planning.

The Planning Process

Determining Demand Requirements

- Future requirements for finished goods are derived from backlogs or forecasts for product families.

Identify Alternatives, Relationships, Constraints, and Costs

Physical and Policy Constraints

- Training may limit rate of new hiring.
- Machine capacity may limit output.
- Storage space, investment costs, and customer service may limit inventory.
- Customer service may limit back orders.
- Quality, delivery uncertainty, or cost may limit subcontracting.
- Cost or diminishing return may limit overtime.
- Union contracts may limit undertime.

Many plans can satisfy a specific set of constraints. Costs are important to the choice among alternative plans.

Types of Costs

- Regular-time costs
  - wages
  - benefits
  - social security
  - vacations

Benefit packages add about 35% to the employer's costs for wages. Workmen's compensation insurance for dangerous work such as installing drywall can by itself add 50% to labor costs.

- Overtime costs — typically 150 – 200% of regular-time rate
  - significant amounts of overtime cannot be sustained without incurring diminishing returns

There also are costs associated with undertime, or unused regular-time. Benefits must still be paid. Labor contracts may require payment for a certain number of hours, whether they are worked or not.

- Hiring and layoff costs
  - severance
  - loss of productivity and morale
  - retraining

- Inventory holding costs
  - interest or opportunity costs of capital
  - storage, utilities
  - pilferage and obsolescence
  - insurance and taxes
- Backorder and stockout costs
  - expediting
  - potential cost of lost sales
  - potential loss of goodwill

Preparing an Acceptable Plan

An Iterative Process

1. Develop a prospective plan — specify monthly or quarterly
   - production rates
   - inventory and backlog accumulations
   - subcontracted production
   - work-force levels
   - overtime and undertime
2. Check prospective plan against constraints and cost objectives. If not acceptable, return to step 1; otherwise proceed to step 3.
3. Insist the top managers of finance, marketing, and operations and the planning committee general manager sign (authorize) the plan.
4. Implementation can begin.

Implementing and Updating the Plan

- Requires the commitment of top management (refer to step 3 in the iterative process above).
- Commitment begins with creation of a planning committee.
  - commitment expands with input from its members
  - recommend changes to better balance conflicting objectives
- Signing the plan is taken as a commitment to work toward achieving the plan, whether the manager totally agrees with it or not.
- Attempting to implement the plan without first obtaining this written commitment is inviting failure.

Should a level work-force strategy or some variable work-force strategy be used in providing services?

Aggregate Planning for Services

Level Strategy for Services

- Work-force level doesn't change

Chase Strategy for Services

- Adjusts work-force levels without using overtime, undertime, or subcontractors

Cost Calculations and Mixed Strategies

- Look at the higher cost elements in the plan for clues to selecting an improved mixed strategy.
- Spreadsheet programs, some with solver routines, easily handle the calculations required to quickly analyze many alternatives.

Should subcontracting be used to achieve short-term capacity increases or should some combination of inventory accumulation and overtime be used?

Mathematical Methods for Aggregate Planning

The same trial-and-error approach used in the services examples can be used in the manufacturing environment. However, with the addition of inventory and subcontracting alternatives, the problem quickly becomes complex. Finding a good solution requires planner ingenuity.

An electronic spreadsheet can release the planner from the drudgery of calculating the effects of decisions. However the planner must still make good choices regarding the controllable variables (amount of anticipation inventory to produce, the amount of overtime to use, the number of units to subcontract, etc.). Random choices of controllable variables will never zero in on the relatively small subset of good compromises that exist in an infinite population of bad compromises.

Tableau Method of Production Planning

For a *given* demand forecast and a *given* capacity plan (no hires or layoffs) with constraints on regular time, overtime, and subcontractor production for each period of the planning horizon, and *assuming* production costs, holding costs, and backorder costs are linear, *and assuming* there are no costs for unused capacity, *then* the tableau method will identify the minimum cost production plan that satisfies demand.

- Each row represents an alternative source of production output and the associated time period. The constraint on each production source is the last number in each row.
- Each column represents a demand and the timing of that demand. The total demand for each period appears at the bottom of its column.
- The numbers in the small boxes are the *total of all* costs associated with producing one unit using the source represented by that row to satisfy a demand represented by that column.
- Demand may be satisfied from existing inventory, or regular time, overtime, or subcontracted production.
- Production might not occur during the same time period as demand. If produced before demand, a holding cost is added. If backorders are allowed and occur, a backorder cost is added.

Additional Capacity Plans

- Tableau method finds the optimal solution <u>for a given capacity plan</u>.
- Adjusting the work-force level by hires and layoffs changes the capacity plan, resulting in better or worse solutions.

Incorporating Backorders

If appropriate penalty costs for backorders can be determined, they are placed in the boxes in the lower left area of the tableau. In that region, production occurs *after* demand … a backorder situation. The same solution method applies, but now alternatives involving back orders are also considered in finding the optimal solution.

Computer Solution

"In practice, we recommend using computers for complex problems, trial-and-error analysis of the capacity plan or demand forecasts, and problems involving back orders." p. 612

Linear Programming for Production Planning

- Tableau method is a specialized form of linear programming.
- Linear programming models can determine optimal
  - inventory levels
  - back orders
  - subcontractor quantities
  - production quantities
  - overtime
  - hires and layoffs
- Major drawbacks
  - all variables must be linear
  - optimal values may be fractional (for example, the optimal solution may require firing part of a person)

Managerial Considerations

- Mathematical techniques are useful aids to the planning process.
- Planning process is dynamic and complicated by conflicting objectives.
- Managers — not techniques — make the decisions.

Multiple-Choice Questions

1. "Thus the ________________ plays a key role in translating the strategies of the business plan into an operational plan for the manufacturing process."
   A. aggregate plan
   B. annual plan
   C. master production schedule
   D. staffing plan

2. In the *nonprofit service* sector, top management sets the organization's direction and objectives in the
   A. annual plan.
   B. business plan.
   C. production plan.
   D. staffing plan.

3. Chaired by the ______________, the aggregate planning committee has the overall responsibility to see that company policies are followed, conflicts are resolved, and a final plan is approved.
   A. finance manager
   B. general manager
   C. marketing manager
   D. operations manager

4. Which functional area provides inputs to the aggregate planning activity concerning competitors?
   A. Finance
   B. Marketing
   C. Materials (Purchasing)
   D. Operations

5. Which functional area provides inputs to the aggregate planning activity concerning current work-force capacity?
   A. Engineering
   B. General management
   C. Human resources
   D. Operations

6. Which of the following is *most* likely to use undertime in its aggregate plan?
   A. A firm that has no work-force union
   B. A manufacturer with a process focus
   C. A manufacturer with a product focus
   D. A seasonal service such as tourism

(Multiple-choice answers are on Study Guide page 253.)

7. Which of the following is an *aggressive* aggregate planning alternative?
   A. Build anticipation inventory
   B. Deliberately accumulate backlogs
   C. Fire workers
   D. Introduce complementary products

8. Anticipation inventory or undertime is *not* used
   A. in a chase strategy.
   B. in a level strategy.
   C. in a mixed strategy.
   D. in reactive alternatives.

9. Which of the following is an advantage of a level strategy?
   A. Improved customer service
   B. Minimum total costs
   C. Reduced inventory investment
   D. Stable work force

10. The tableau method finds the optimal production plan assuming that which one of the following is *not* a variable?
    A. Backorders
    B. Overtime
    C. Subcontracted production
    D. Work-force size

11. Which of the following is usually considered to be a good thing?
    A. Backlogs
    B. Backorders
    C. Stockouts
    D. Loss of goodwill

12. Aggressive alternatives are typically specified
    A. in chase strategies.
    B. by financial plans.
    C. by marketing plans.
    D. by production plans.

13. The *first* step in the planning process is to
    A. authorize the plan.
    B. determine the demand requirements.
    C. identify the alternatives and basic relationships.
    D. prepare a prospective plan.

14. Which of the following is not a relevant cost when aggregate planning for services?
    A. hiring and firing costs
    B. inventory costs
    C. overtime costs
    D. subcontracting costs

Problems

1. A tutoring service experiences highly variable demand for help with operations management homework. The service hires tutors on a part-time basis to work 40 hours per month. Hiring and training cost is $500 per tutor. Firing cost is $200 per tutor. Scheduled work time, whether used or not, is paid at $10.00 per hour. Revenue from tutoring is $26 per hour. The semester begins with 6 part-time tutors already on the staff and must end with 6 tutors on the staff.

Month	Demand	Month	Demand
Sept	120 hr	Nov	200 hr
Oct	320 hr	Dec	400 hr

a. What is the gross profit associated with a *chase* strategy?

Month	Demand	Begin W-F	Hire (Fire)	H/F Cost	Work Force	Labor Cost
Sept	120 hr	6	(_)	$____	___	$1200
Oct	320 hr	___	___	$____	___	$____
Nov	200 hr	___	___	$____	___	$____
Dec	400 hr	___	___	$____	___	$____
End of semester		___	(_)	$____	___	

Demand Served @ $26/hr = $ ______
Total Costs = $ ______
Gross Profit = $ ______

b. What are the costs associated with a strategy of hiring to serve all demand, but not firing until the end of the semester? At the end of the semester the service must return to the original work-force size of 6 tutors.

Month	Demand	Begin W-F	Hire (Fire)	H/F Cost	Work Force	Labor Cost
Sept	120 hr	6	0	$0	6	$2400
Oct	320 hr	6	2	$____	___	$____
Nov	200 hr	__	__	$____	___	$____
Dec	400 hr	__	__	$____	___	$____
End of semester		__	(_)	$____	___	

Demand Served @ $26/hr = $ ______
Total Costs = $ ______
Gross Profit = $ ______

c. Evaluate a strategy of *never* hiring or firing, and not serving demand exceeding the existing capacity.

Month	Demand	Work Force	Labor Cost	Demand Served
Sept	120 hr	6	$____	_____ hr
Oct	320 hr	__	$____	_____ hr
Nov	200 hr	__	$____	_____ hr
Dec	400 hr	__	$____	_____ hr
End of semester		6		

Demand Served @ $26/hr = $ ______
Total Costs = $ ______
Gross profit = $ ______

2. A manufacturer's policy prohibits the use of subcontractors or backorders in its production plans. Its initial inventory is 20 units. The fourth quarter demand is actually 300 units but has been increased to 360 units to provide the desired ending inventory of 60 units. There is no cost for unused regular-time or unused overtime capacity.

   a. Use the tableau method to create an aggregate plan to fulfill all of the projected demand.

		Capacity, units		Costs, per unit		
Quarter	Demand	Regular time	Over time	Holding cost/qtr	Reg. time cost	Overtime cost
1	130	200	50	$18	$100	$150
2	320	210	50			
3	200	240	60			
4	360	240	40			

		Quarter				Capacity	
Q	Sources	First	Second	Third	Fourth	Unused	Total
1	Beginning Inventory	$0	$18	$36	$54		20
	Regular Time	$100	$118	$136	$154		210
	Overtime	$150	$168	$186	$204		50
2	Regular Time		$100	$118	$136		200
	Overtime		$150	$168	$186		50
3	Regular Time			$100	$118		240
	Overtime			$150	$168		30
4	Regular Time				$100		240
	Overtime				$150		40
	Demand	130	320	200	360	70	1080

   b. What are the regular time, overtime, and holding costs associated with this production plan?

Solutions

MULTIPLE CHOICE ANSWERS

1. A	7. D
2. A	8. A
3. B	9. D
4. B	10. D
5. D	11. A
6. B	12. C
	13. B
	14. B

1. A tutoring service experiences highly variable demand for help with operations management homework. The service hires tutors on a part-time basis to work 40 hours per month. Hiring and training cost is $500 per tutor. Firing cost is $200 per tutor. Scheduled work time, whether used or not, is paid at $10.00 per hour. Revenue from tutoring is $26 per hour. The semester begins with 6 part-time tutors already on the staff and must end with 6 tutors on the staff.

Month	Demand	Month	Demand
Sept	120 hr	Nov	200 hr
Oct	320 hr	Dec	400 hr

a. What is the gross profit associated with a *chase* strategy?

Month	Demand	Begin W-F	Hire (Fire)	H/F Cost	Work Force	Labor Cost
Sept	120 hr	6	(3)	$ 600	3	$1200
Oct	320 hr	3	5	$2500	8	$3200
Nov	200 hr	8	(3)	$ 600	5	$2000
Dec	400 hr	5	5	$2500	10	$4000
End of semester		10	(4)	$ 800	6	

Demand Served @ $26/hr	=	$ 27,040
Total Costs	=	$ 17,400
Gross profit	=	$ 9,640

Although the plan in part b of the tutor staffing problem is slightly ($240) more profitable, it requires hiring and firing four tutors. Most operations managers would rather make up the $240 out of their own pockets than have to hire and fire four people.

b. What are the costs associated with a strategy of hiring to serve all demand, but not firing until the end of the semester? At the end of the semester the service must return to the original work-force size of 6 tutors.

Month	Demand	Begin W-F	Hire (Fire)	H/F Cost	Work Force	Labor Cost
Sept	120 hr	6	0	$ 0	6	$2400
Oct	320 hr	6	2	$1000	8	$3200
Nov	200 hr	8	0	$ 0	8	$3200
Dec	400 hr	8	2	$1000	10	$4000
End of semester		10	(4)	$ 800	6	

Demand Served @ $26/hr	=	$ 27,040
Total Costs	=	$ 15,600
Gross profit	=	$ 11,440

c. Evaluate a strategy of *never* hiring or firing, and not serving demand exceeding the existing capacity.

Month	Demand	Work Force	Labor Cost	Demand Served
Sept	120 hr	6	$2400	120 hr
Oct	320 hr	__	$2400	240 hr
Nov	200 hr	__	$2400	200 hr
Dec	400 hr	__	$2400	240 hr
End of semester		6		

Demand Served @ $26/hr	=	$ 20,800
Total Costs	=	$ 9,600
Gross profit	=	$ 11,200

2. A manufacturer's policy prohibits the use of subcontractors or backorders in its production plans.

   a. Use the tableau method to create an aggregate plan to fulfill all of the projected demand.

Q	Sources	Quarter: First	Quarter: Second	Quarter: Third	Quarter: Fourth	Capacity: Unused	Capacity: Total
1	Beginning Inventory	$0 20	$18	$36	$54		20
	Regular Time	$100 110	$118 100	$136	$154		210
	Overtime	$150	$168	$186	$204	50	50
2	Regular Time		$100 200	$118	$136		200
	Overtime		$150 20	$168	$186 10	20	50
3	Regular Time			$100 200	$118 40		240
	Overtime			$150	$168 30		30
4	Regular Time				$100 240		240
	Overtime				$150 40		40
	Demand	130	320	200	360	70	1080

   b. What are the regular time, overtime, and holding costs associated with this production plan?

The beginning inventory is consumed in the first period. In the first quarter, 210 units are produced during regular time. 110 are consumed by demand in the first quarter. The remaining 100 are held until the second quarter at an additional carrying cost of $18 each. In the second quarter 200 units are produced during regular time and 30 units during overtime. 10 units of second quarter production are carried to the fourth quarter. The third quarter is the most complicated. 240 units are produced during regular time to serve immediate demand. 40 of these are carried in inventory to the fourth quarter. Also during the third quarter, 30 units are produced during overtime. Those units are also held until the fourth quarter ... a total of 80 units held at the beginning of the 4th quarter. That inventory, along with the full regular time and overtime capacity are required to satisfy demand and leave the required 60 units in inventory as required to begin the next year.

Quarter	Regular Time		Overtime		Holding Cost	Total
1	210 * $100	+	$ 0	+	100 * $ 18	$ 22,800
2	200 * $100	+	30 * 150	+	10 * $ 36	24,860
3	240 * $100	+	30 * 150	+	70 * $ 18	29,760
4	240 * $100	+	40 * 150	+	$ 0	30,000
	$ 89,000	+	$ 15,000	+	$ 3,420	= **$107,420**

Supplement I, Linear Programming

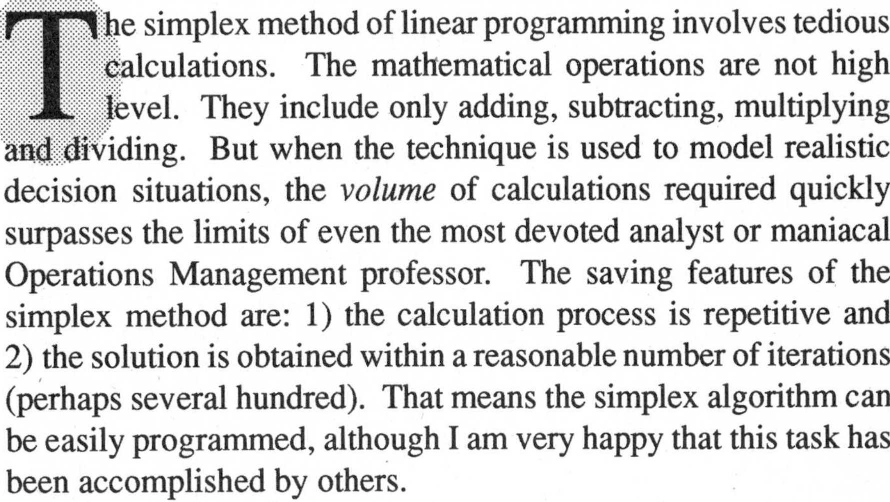

The simplex method of linear programming involves tedious calculations. The mathematical operations are not high level. They include only adding, subtracting, multiplying and dividing. But when the technique is used to model realistic decision situations, the *volume* of calculations required quickly surpasses the limits of even the most devoted analyst or maniacal Operations Management professor. The saving features of the simplex method are: 1) the calculation process is repetitive and 2) the solution is obtained within a reasonable number of iterations (perhaps several hundred). That means the simplex algorithm can be easily programmed, although I am very happy that this task has been accomplished by others.

The idea of several hundred iterations may seem overwhelming, but it is better than the alternative. The alternative is to evaluate every possible combination of decision variables. As the number of decision variables increases beyond the realm of trivial decisions, the number of possible combinations quickly takes on astronomical proportions. To solve a practical linear programming problem by enumeration would require the total of the world's computing power until well after our sun burns out! So it was a big deal in the Operations Research community when George Dantzig developed the simplex method shortly after World War II. Problems that had been hopelessly impossible to solve became only extremely difficult to solve.

All this occurred before my time as a student. But it wasn't until after my time as a student that the technique was widely applied. When Dantzig developed the technique, computers were not available to take on the mathematical drudgery. Until about 1970, few college graduates had ever heard of linear programming.

Since then, the techinque has been widely applied in military logistics, owing to its roots in Operations Research, and in process industries such as oil refining, brewing, and agricultural feed and grain. The technique can also be applied to human nutrition, but the most cost effective nutrition usually turns out to be a steady diet of pizza.

It is possible to spend an entire semester teaching the simplex solution method, proving the method's validity, and interpreting useful information contained in the final solution tableau. That is beyond our scope here. This supplement makes creative use of graphic analogies to communicate the concepts of what is happening in the simplex solution method and to provide an intuitive interpretion of information contained in the final tableau. This overview is usually lost when one gets involved in the details of simplex calculations (dividing 3/64ths by –6/23rds is a typical example).

The graphic approach uses the *x* and *y* axes to model situations with two, and only two, decision variables. Although this approach is useless for practical problems, it is a very powerful instructional technique for those willing to invest the required time and concentrated effort.

Basic Concepts

Characteristics and Assumptions of All Linear Programming Models

1. Objective function — a goal to maximize or to minimize.
2. Continuous decision variables — alternative choices within analyst's control which may take on noninteger values. The objective might be optimized by producing two and 3/64ths cue balls.
3. Constraints — limits on decision variables due to the availability of resources.
4. Feasible region — all of the combinations of decisions to use resources in ways that are possible within the constraints. This region contains the optimal solution, if it exists at all, and usually also contains many inferior solutions.
5. Parameters — a coefficient or constant beyond the analyst's control. For example the time between impact of a dropped Operation Management text and the time when pain is felt in one's foot.
6. Linearity — the decision situation can be modeled by equations where all of the exponents of decision variables are equal to one. No higher math is required, and no localized optimums exist to deceive the solution process.
7. Nonnegativity — this assumption rarely causes any difficulty since all resources are either zero or positive. One can not use negative time to complete past due homework.

Linear Programming Exercise

Georgia White's clay mine can produce 45 tons of clay per week. The clay is the primary ingredient in two products; 1) high gloss (magazine cover) paper, and 2) a diarrhea remedy. Besides the limited availability of clay, there are two other constraints on operations. One is a limited amount of production time on pill-making machines and another is a limited amount of labor.

Formulating a Problem

Step 1. Define the decision variables.

In our example, Georgia must decide whether to make paper, diarrhea remedy, or some combination of the two.

$X1$ = tons of high gloss paper

$X2$ = tons of diarrhea remedy

Step 2. Write out the objective function.

Georgia's objective is to maximize profits. Let's say that Georgia's profits are \$100 per ton of diarrhea pills and \$40 per ton of paper.

$$\text{Max } z = \$40\,X1 + \$100\,X2$$

Step 3. Write out the constraints.

Say that 60% (by weight) of high gloss paper and 90% of diarrhea remedy is made of clay. None of the other materials used for balance of the products (fiber and water) are in short supply. The pill machinery operates two thirty-two-hour shifts per week, and it takes 1.6 hours per ton to process pills. 180 hours of labor are available per week. It takes 3 labor hours to process one ton of paper, and 2 labor hours to process one ton of diarrhea remedy.

(1)	$0.60\,X1 + 0.90\,X2 \leq 45$	raw material
(2)	$1.60\,X2 \leq 64$	equipment
(3)	$3.00\,X1 + 2.00\,X2 \leq 180$	labor

Graphic Analysis

Plot the Constraints

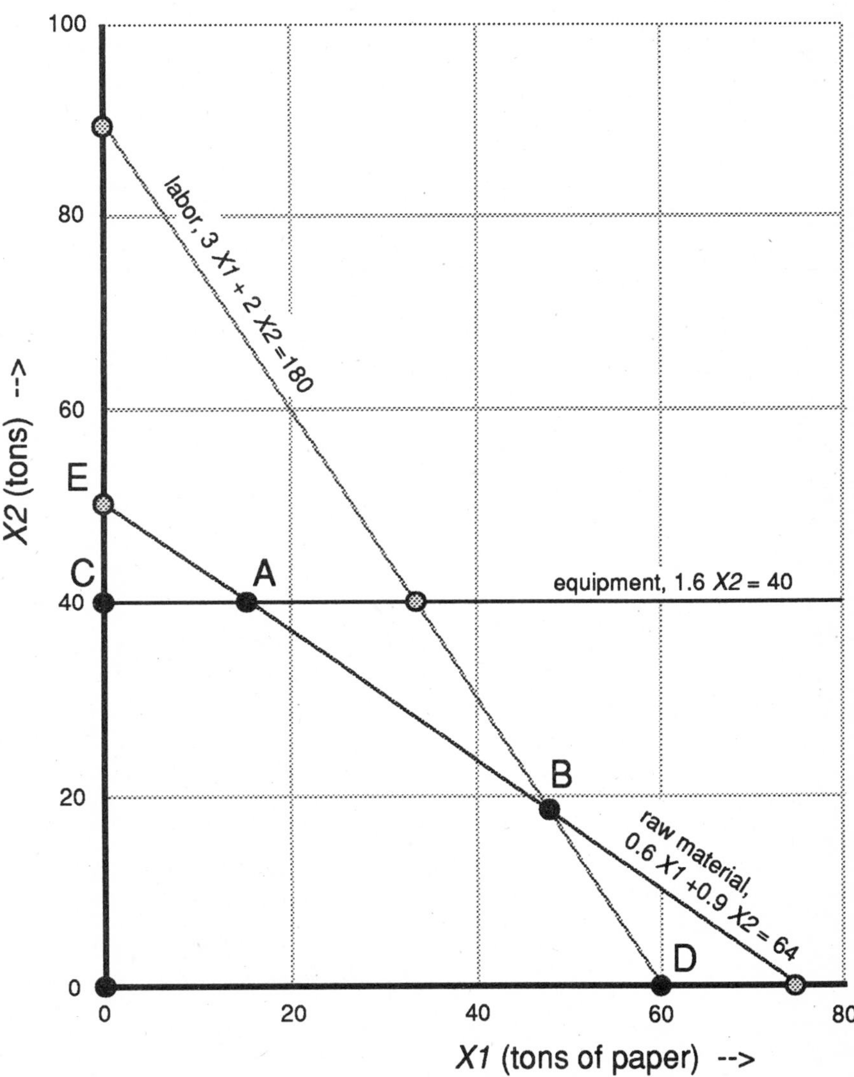

Identify the Feasible Region

The gray area shown in the graph satisfys all constraints.

Plot an Objective Function Line

$z = \$40\,X1 + \$100\,X2$

All points on the thin dashed line result in a profit of $2000. However, the points that are not in the feasible region do not represent viable alternatives.

$2000 = \$40\,X1 + \$100\,X2$

Find the Visual Solution

Move the objective function in the optimizing direction (in this case, away from the origin) until only one point on the line remains in the feasible region. That last feasible point represents the optimal solution. Note which of the constraints intersect at that point. As we move the objective function it is very important to keep it precisely parallel to the first one.

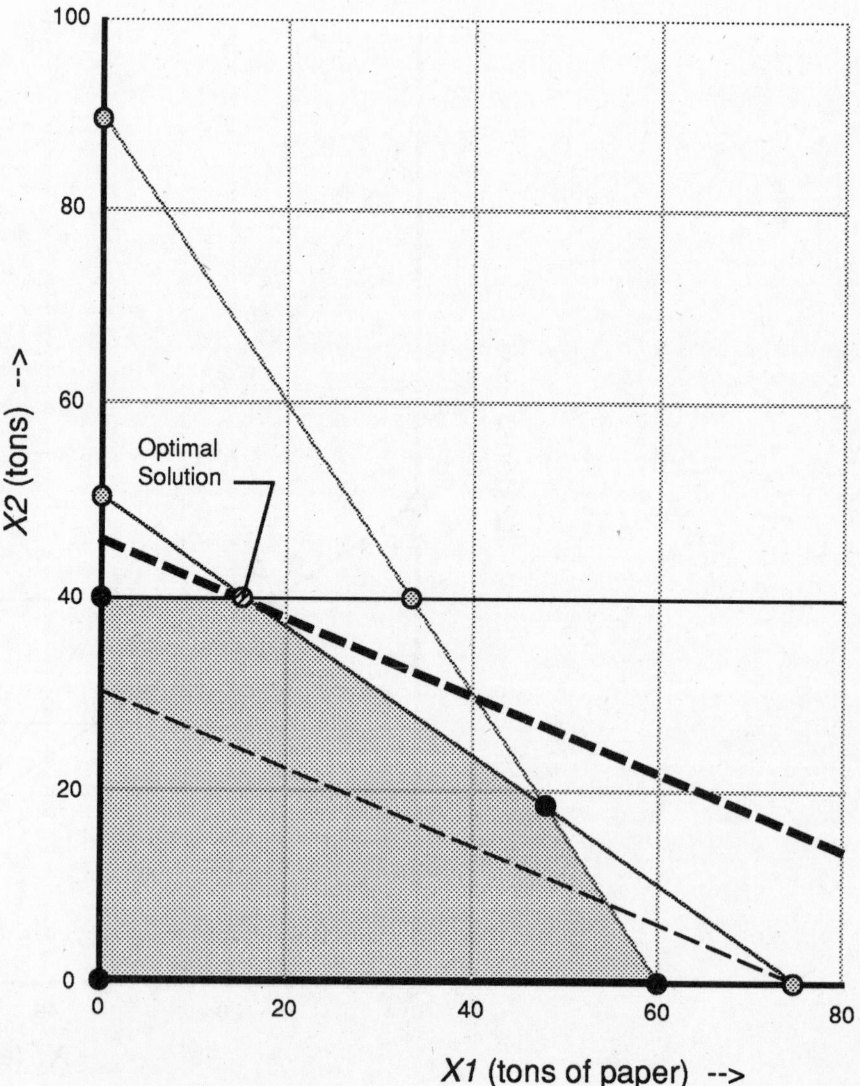

Find the Algebraic Solution

By inspecting the graph we see the optimal solution occurs at the intersection of the equipment and the raw material constraints. The labor constraint lies above that intersection. We have more available labor than is needed.

Usually the next step is to solve the two constraints simultaneously, (see examples in the text) but in this example we already know from the equipment constraint, that $X2 = 40$.

Substituting $\mathbf{X2 = 40}$ into the raw material constraint:

(2) $0.60\,X1 + 0.90\,X2 = 45$

$0.60\,X1 + 0.90\,(40) = 45$

$\mathbf{X1 = 15}$

The optimal solution is to produce 15 tons of paper and 40 tons of diarrhea remedy per week. The maximum possible profit per week is:

$$\text{Max } z = \$40\,X1 + \$100\,X2$$
$$= \$40(15) + \$100(40)$$
$$= \$4{,}600 \text{ per week}$$ <--- "The Answer."

Operations managers usually don't care much about this "answer". The maximum is going to be the maximum. In order to formulate complex models we sometimes creatively manipulate the objective function. The objective might be expressed in some bizarre units of measure. No matter. As operations managers we are evaluated on whether we can make the best use of available production resources. We need answers to *operations* questions such as: Which production schedule is optimal? What resources will be used; and just as important, what resources are not needed? If additional resources become available, what would they be worth to us? What quantity of an additional resource has value to us? Would the product mix change if the market for paper becomes more profitable? All this information and more is available from the linear programming model, but it doesn't appear in "The Answer".

Slack and Surplus Variables

The optimal solution occurs at the intersection of:

(1) $0.60\,X1 + 0.90\,X2 = 45$ raw material (clay)

(2) $1.60\,X2 = 64$ equipment

Those two resources are entirely consumed when:

$X1 = 15$ and $X2 = 40$

For example, when we substitute these values into the first constraint:

(1) $0.60\,X1 + 0.90\,X2 = 45$ raw material

$0.6\,(15) + 0.9\,(40) = 45$

If we were to define a new variable, $S1$, as "tons of unused clay," and add it to the left side of the equation:

(1) $0.60\,X1 + 0.90\,X2 + S1 = 45$ raw material

The only way we can maintain the equality is if $S1 = 0$. In other words, there is no slack in the first constraint.

But the third resource, labor, has some slack. We will add the slack variable, *S3*, "unused labor hours" to the left side of the equation to absorb the slack and create an equality.

(3)	$3.00\, X1 + 2.00\, X2$	≤ 180	labor
(3)	$3\,(X1) + 2\,(X2) + S3$	$= 180$	labor
(3)	$3\,(15) + 2\,(40) + S3$	$= 180$	labor
	$S3$	$=$ 55 hours	

The optimal solution leaves 55 hours of labor per week unused. Some of our labor might be offered "an alternative career opportunity".

Georgia White's clay mine is a maximization problem, and includes the typical "less-than-or-equal-to" constraints. It is also possible to have "equal-to" constraints, but if many of these exist, there probably won't be any feasible solution. "Greater than-or-equal-to" constraints usually appear in minimization problems. It is possible to have all three in the same problem.

For example, minimize the cost of food while providing greater-than-or-equal-to 2000 calories per day and protein equal-to 80 grams per day and sodium less-than-or-equal-to 2400 mg per day. An employee of Ben and Jerry's could minimize costs within these three constraints by eating 20 servings (5 small cartons) of ice cream per day, but there would be a *surplus* variable in the calories constraint.

$260\, X1 \geq 2000$

$260\, X1 - Surplus = 2000$

$260\,(20) - Surplus = 2000$

$Surplus = 3200$

Don't try this diet. 3200 surplus calories is equal to one pound of fat.

Sensitivity Analysis

> "Rarely are the parameters in the objective function and constraints known with certainty." p. 638

Fortunately, a small change probably won't change the optimal solution. In Georgia White's clay, *what if* the profitability of making paper increases?

Objective Function Coefficients

$$40X_1 + 100X_2 = Z$$

$$100X_2 = -40X_1 + Z$$

$$X_2 = -0.4X_1 + 0.01Z$$

In our example *X2* is represented by the *y* axis, and *X1* is represented by the *x* axis. Therefore, the objective function has the form of $y = mx + b$. No matter the value of Z, the slope of the objective function will always be equal to –0.4. The coefficient of *X1* is *c1*. The coefficient of *X2* is *c2*. The slope of the objective function is the ratio: $-c1/c2$. The text explains (p. 639) how the changing *c1* and *c2* (one at a time) affects the slope of the objective function and causes the optimal solution point to shift. Note that this point does not shift gradually. It stays put until the objective function slope changes enough to match one of the binding constraints, then the optimal solution jumps to a new location. We will try to show this effect graphically.

In the graphical solution below, we have removed the constraint lines and other clutter to show that the dashed line optimal objective function is connected to the feasible region only at one point (the optimal point A). As we change the slope of the objective function (by fiddling with *c1* and *c2*) the dashed line will pivot about the optimal point A like a teeter totter.

If the dashed line pivots clockwise far enough, so that it aligns with the raw material constraint, the solution will jump from point A to point B. A counterclockwise change to the horizontal (equipment constraint) will likewise cause a change from point A to point C.

Now it is just a matter of figuring out the range values for the objective function slope ($-c1/c2$) that will retain the optimal solution at point A. This is called the range of optimality

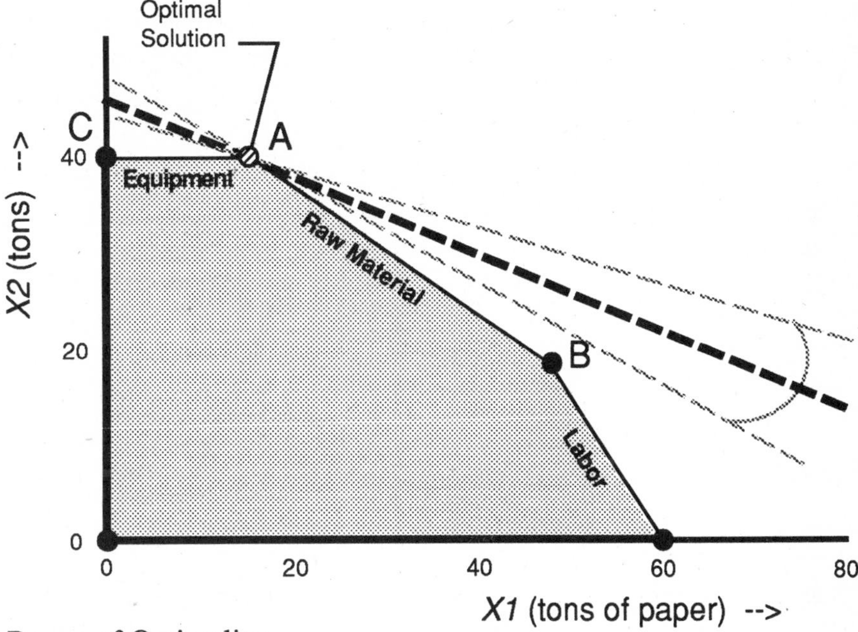

Range of Optimality.

The slope of the equipment constraint is zero.
The slope of the raw material constraint is –2/3.
As long as the slope of the objective function stays within that range, the solution will remain at its present location (point A).

$$-\frac{2}{3} \le -\frac{c_1}{c_2} \le 0$$

If we hold the profitability of diarrhea remedy constant at $100 per ton,

$$-\frac{2}{3} \le -\frac{c_1}{100} \le 0$$

$$\frac{200}{3} \ge c_1 \ge 0$$

the profit per ton of paper can vary anywhere between 0 and $66.66 and the optimal solution will remain at point A. If the paper begins to take a loss, we would shift to point C and stop paper production. If paper profitability increases to $66.67, we would shift to point B and make more paper and less diarrhea remedy.

Coefficient Sensitivity

- Coefficient sensitivity shows how much a decision variable coefficient must improve in order to bring the decision variable into the solution.

The optimal solution to the Georgia White's clay problem called for a positive quantity of both *X1* and *X2* to be produced. In order to demonstrate coefficient sensitivity let's change the problem so the profitability of diarrhea remedy is only $20 per ton, while paper profits remains at $40 per ton. If so, the objective function and the optimal solution would shift to point D as shown below. Now the company would make only *X1* (paper). *X2* is zero, and no longer "in the solution." Okay, how much would profitability of diarrhea remedy have to improve in order to bring it back into the solution?

Step 1. The objective function would have to rotate *counter-clockwise* in order to shift the solution from point D to B.

Step 2. The objective function would then be parallel to the *labor* constraint. The slope of the labor constraint is – 3/2. When *c1* is held at $40, the value of *c2* that would make the objective function slope equal to the labor constraint is $26.67.

Step 3. The coefficient sensitivity is the improvement difference ($26.67 – $20) = $6.67.

If the profitability of diarrhea remedy improves by $6.67 per ton (from $20 per ton to $26.67 per ton), the solution will change from making no diarrhea remedy at all to point B, which calls for the production of 18 tons of *X2*.

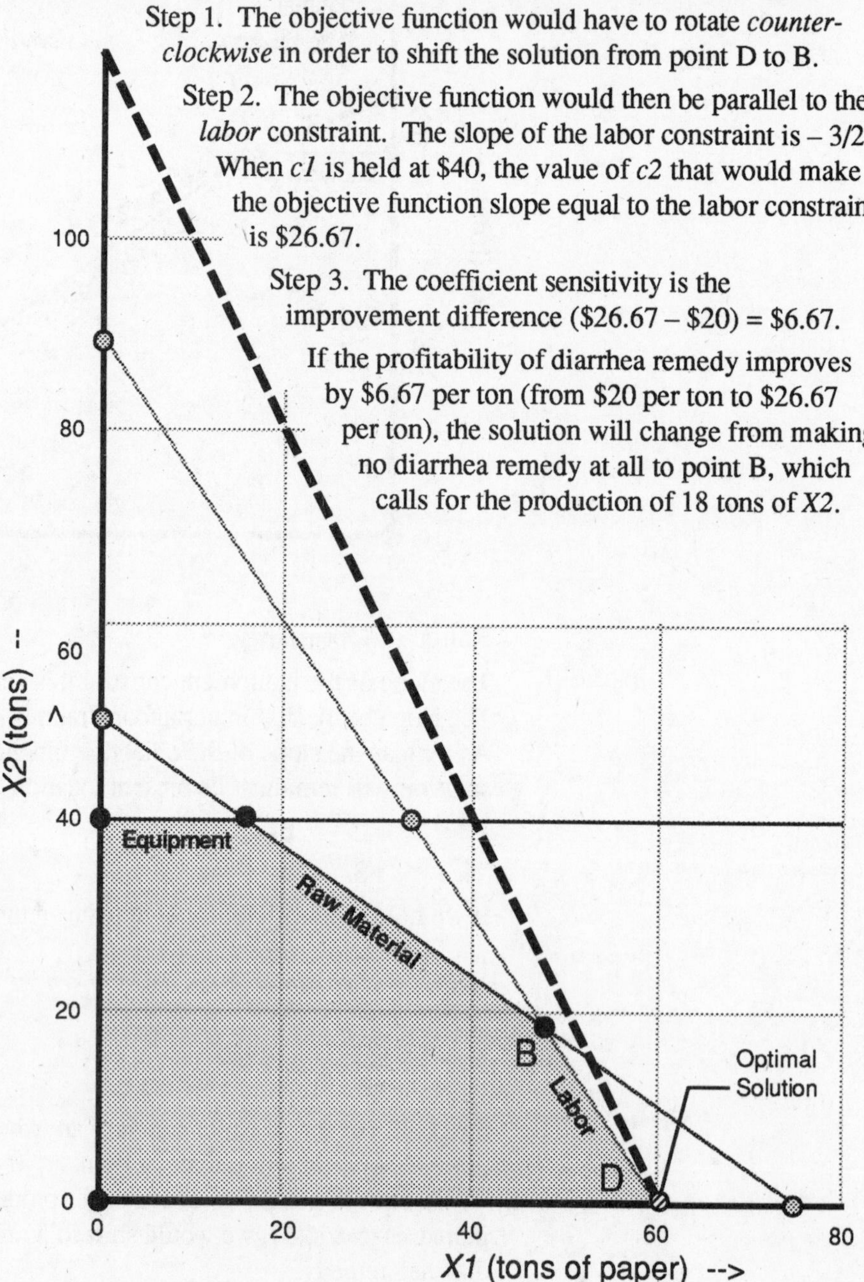

Right-Hand-Side Parameters

Let's go back to the original version of the Georgia White's clay problem.

$c1 = \$40$
$c2 = \$100$

Shadow Prices

Q. Could we make more profit if we had additional labor resources?

A. No. Labor is a nonbinding constraint. We are not using all of the labor we already have available. More labor resources would increase the slack variable *S3*, but not make any improvement in the objective.

Q. What about the resources currently binding the solution? Would more of those resources have any value?

A. Yes. The shadow price is the marginal improvement in *Z* caused by relaxing a binding constraint by one unit.

Let's use the equipment constraint for an example. We presently have 64 equipment hours available per week. Each ton of diarrhea remedy requires 1.6 hours, so this constraint limits production of remedy to 64/1.6 = 40 tons per week. It is difficult to show the effect of just one additional hour of equipment resources on the graph. Instead, we show the effect of 8 more hours. Note the equipment constraint stays horizontal, but moves upward by 5 units. 72/1.6 = 45 tons per week.

The old solution was *X1* = 15 @ \$40 ea., *X2* = 40 @ \$100 ea. = \$4,600.

The new solution is *X1* = 7.5 @ \$40 ea., *X2* = 45 @ \$100 ea. = \$4,800.

Eight hours improved the solution \$200, one hour is worth \$200/8 = \$25.

A similar analysis would show that one ton of clay is worth \$66.67.

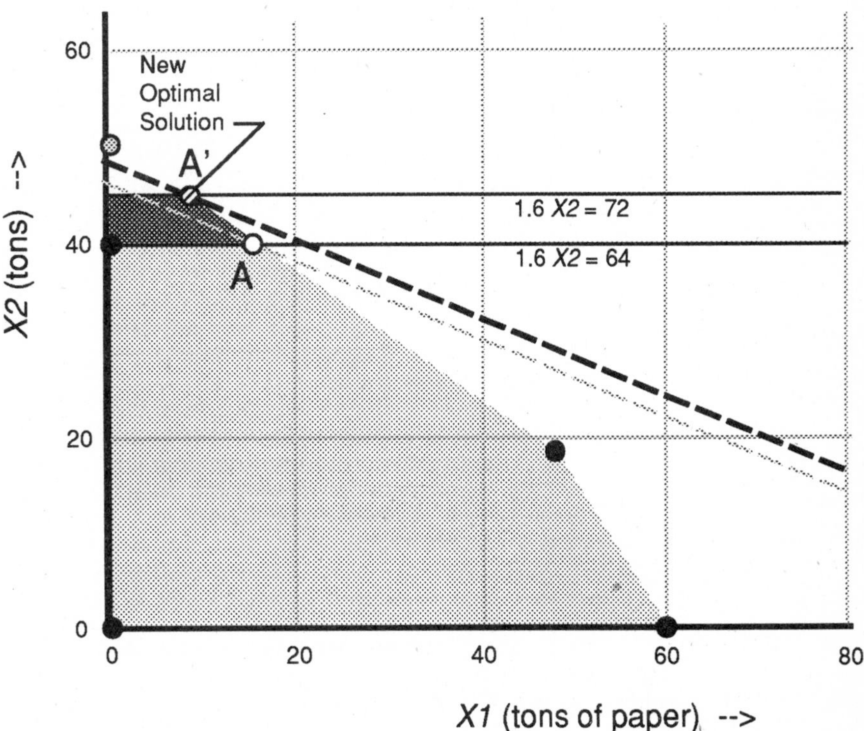

Range of Feasibility

Q. If one additional equipment hour is worth $25 per week, then would 1000 hours be worth $25,000 per week?

A. No. These answers hold true over a limited range. Note that if the total equipment hours is equal to 88, the solution moves to point E. The solution is bound by only the raw material constraint. The equipment constraint 1.6 *X2* = 88 now floats above the feasible region. We can not make good use of all 88 hours.

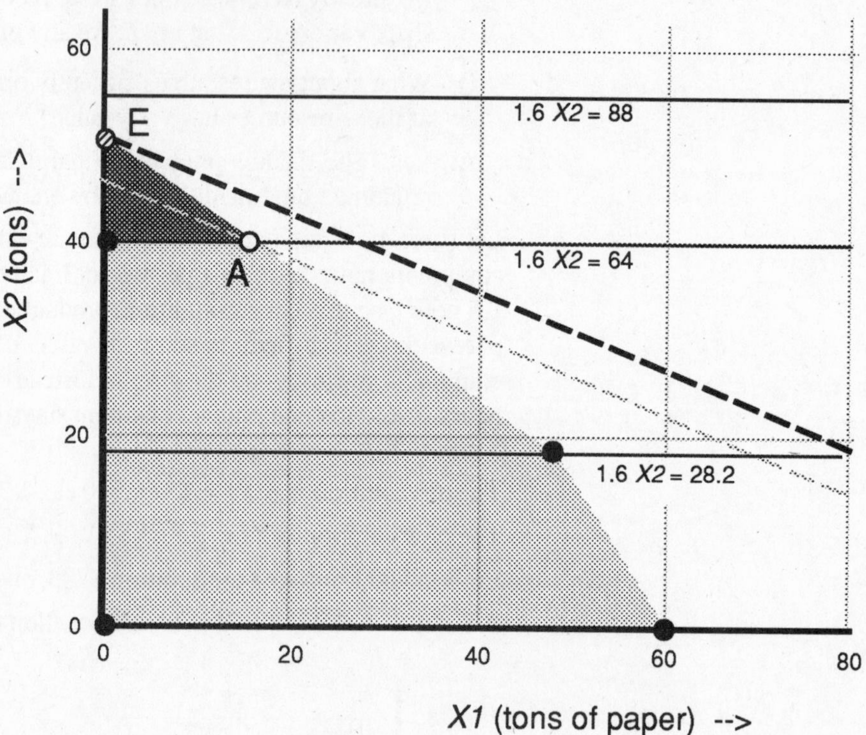

The range of feasibility may have both an upper limit and a lower limit. In this problem, the number of hours of equipment time can increase from the original 64 hours to an upper limit of 80 hours, and the shadow price of $25 per hour will hold true. However, the 81st hour of equipment time has no value because it will not result in any improvement of the objective. The lower limit of validity for this shadow price is 28.8 hours. Below that point, the value of equipment hours changes from $25 to some other value.

What is happening here? The optimal solution occurs at the intersection of the equipment and raw material constraints. We are simply sliding the equipment constraint up or down until we hit another constraint. The shadow price is valid up to the point where we hit some constraint other than the raw material constraint.

Computer Solution

Simplex Method

- Most real-world linear programming problems are solved on a computer.
- The simplex method is an iterative algebraic procedure.
- Graphic analysis gives insight into the logic of the simplex method.
- The initial feasible solution of the simplex method usually starts out at the origin (do nothing) solution.
- Each subsequent iteration results in an improved intermediate solution which we have represented graphically by the intersection of linear constraints.
- When no further improvement is possible, the optimal solutions has been found and the algorithm stops.

Computer Output

- Contained within the final (optimal) tableau are the shadow price, feasibility range, coefficient sensitivity and other information useful to the decision analyst.
- An analysis of the final tableau is provided as part of the output.

Other Applications

- Aggregate planning
- Distribution
- Inventory
- Location
- Process management
- Scheduling

Chapter Fourteen, Material Requirements Planning

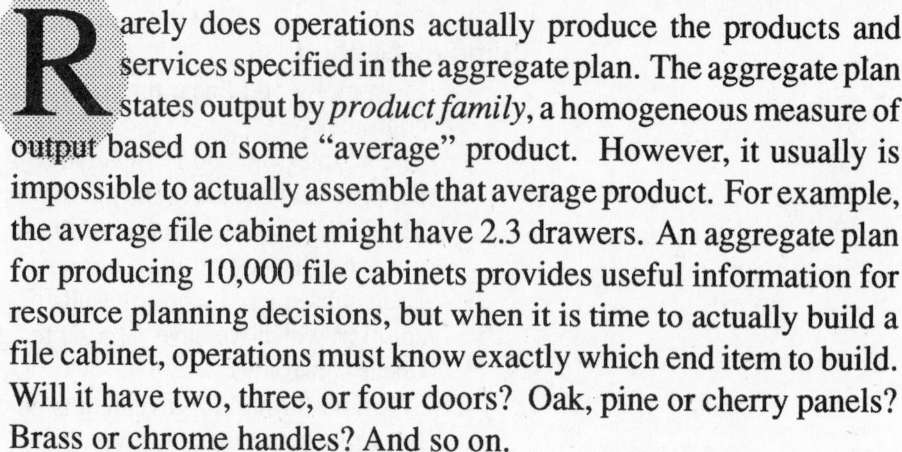

Rarely does operations actually produce the products and services specified in the aggregate plan. The aggregate plan states output by *product family*, a homogeneous measure of output based on some "average" product. However, it usually is impossible to actually assemble that average product. For example, the average file cabinet might have 2.3 drawers. An aggregate plan for producing 10,000 file cabinets provides useful information for resource planning decisions, but when it is time to actually build a file cabinet, operations must know exactly which end item to build. Will it have two, three, or four doors? Oak, pine or cherry panels? Brass or chrome handles? And so on.

The master production schedule (MPS) provides the necessary detail missing from the aggregate plan. It states how many of each *end item* will be produced within specified periods of time. The bill of materials (BOM) lists exactly how much of each raw material and component is required to assemble one unit of that item. Material requirements planning (MRP) multiplies the MPS quantity for each period by the BOM to determine the gross requirements for all raw materials and components. MRP then subtracts the raw materials and components already on hand and on order from the gross requirements. A final adjustment is made to account for the replenishment lead time. The result is a set of time-phased net requirements for every raw material and component, and a *plan* for acquiring the *required materials*. (Hence the term: material requirements planning)

As part of a computerized management information system, MRP calculations *must* be completely logical. Unlike the human brain, computers cannot cope with nebulous decision rules. Therefore the key to understanding this topic lies in understanding the logic. When a system behaves logically, that is, when user actions result in predictable outcomes, we say the system is transparent. Although dependent demand relationships between parent and component items can cause complexity in managing inventory of those items, MRP systems are designed to handle prodigious clerical detail in a manner that is transparent to the user. For large corporations, the calculations may take 6 to 24 hours to compute on a large mainframe computer! But all that calculation is based on just a few logical principles.

Material requirements planning (MRP) is logical. Unfortunately your personal information parallel processor (your brain) is not particularly well designed for processing serial logic. Be assured there are no unsolvable mysteries here. If you take the time to think this through, you will uncover the fundamental reasoning, and from then on it is crystal clear. The experience is a lot like waiting for the image to materialize in those "magic eye" posters.

Dependent Demand

Independent demand

- Influenced by market conditions
- Not related to production decisions for any other item
- Must be forecast
- End items have independent demand
- Component items may have independent demand as spare-part replacements

Dependent demand

- Derived from the production decisions for its parent(s)
- Demand can be calculated, forecast is not necessary
- Complexity comes from interdependencies between items.
- Production cannot complete an order for a parent if even one of its components is missing.

Benefits of Material Requirements Planning

- MRP was developed specifically to aid in managing dependent demand inventory and in scheduling replenishment orders.
- Reduced inventory levels
- Increased customer service
- Improved utilization of resources

Three advantages of MRP

1. Lumpy demand varies wildly. Statistical approaches to forecasting lumpy demand are ineffective. Variances from ineffective forecasts can not be buffered efficiently or effectively by safety stock. MRP calculates the quantity and timing of dependent demand material requirements based upon a stated production schedule and upon defined parent-component relationships. Uncertainty is reduced.
2. Production schedules and material plans can be translated into capacity and financial requirements.
3. MRP systems automatically realign and coordinate material acquistion plans for all components when production schedules of parent items change.

Inputs to Material Requirements Planning

Three Key Inputs to MRP

1. Master production schedule
2. Bills of materials
3. Inventory records

First, the master production schedule (MPS) is the input that "drives" MRP. The MPS states how many of each end item will be produced. Second, the bill of materials (BOM), sometimes called product structure diagram, states how many of each component, subassembly, or raw material is required to produce one of each master scheduled item.

If the company has no inventories, the material requirements could be determined by multiplying (extending or "exploding") the MPS by the quantities shown on the BOM. But it isn't quite that simple. Inventories of components and subassemblies are likely to exist. We must subtract (net) those inventories from the gross requirements.

The inventory record contains information including gross requirements, scheduled receipts, projected on-hand inventory, planned order receipts, planned order releases, and the planning factors: lead time, lot-sizing rules, and safety stock size. It may also include supplier and buyer identification, standard costs, storage locations, pegging records (described later), and more. Inaccurate inventory records are a common cause of failure of MRP systems.

Bill of Materials

"A **bill of materials (BOM)** is a record of all the components of an item, the parent—component relationships, and usage quantities derived from engineering and process designs." p. 666

Terminology in this text is consistent with the *Official Dictionary of Production and Inventory Management Terminology and Phrases* published by the American Production and Inventory Control Society (APICS). The figure at the right includes examples of these key terms.

If ten of the end item A are *completely* disassembled how many of each of the items B, C, D, and E would remain? See the solutions section at the end of this chapter for the answers.

Key Terminology

- bill of materials
- parent
- component
- usage quantity
- end item
- intermediate item
- subassembly
- purchased item
- part commonality

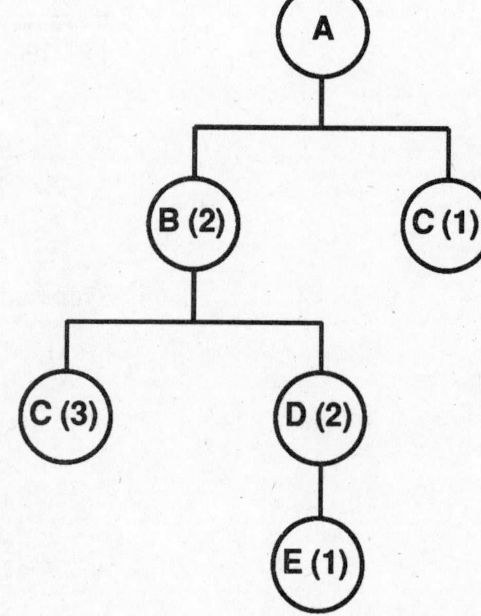

Master Production Schedule

- Disaggregates the production plan into schedules for specific items.
- Time buckets are planning periods usually of one-week duration.

MPS Constraints

1. MPS quantities must sum to equal the aggregate plan.
2. Consider setup costs, inventory costs, utilization, and customer service when allocating planned production to time buckets.
3. Timing and size of MPS quantities are subject to resource (equipment capacity, labor, materials, capital, space) limits.

The Master Production Scheduling Process and Strategies.

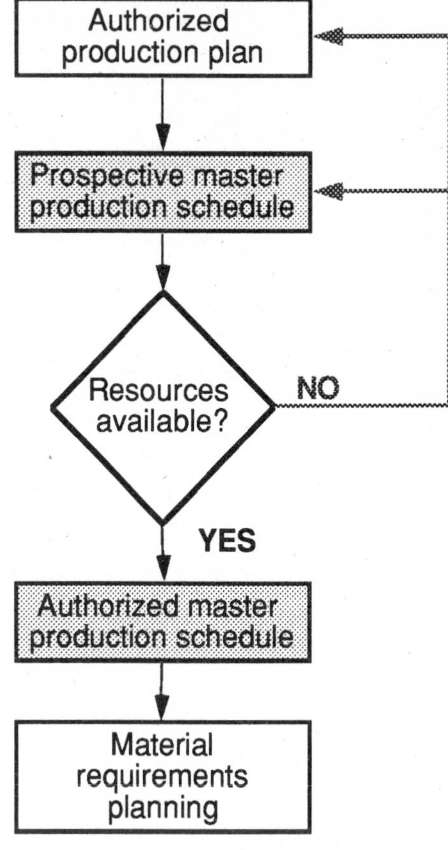

The authorized production plan guides and constrains the master scheduling activity.

The prospective MPS is a disaggregation of the production plan. It is a trial statement of how many end items will be produced in specified time periods.

The rough-cut capacity plan is a feasibility check. If the resources required to produce the end items in the prospective MPS do not exist, the master schedule is not feasible. Develop and evaluate alternative schedules which may be consistent with the production plan.

If a feasible schedule is found, it is authorized. The authorized MPS then drives material requirements planning, which acquires materials necessary to produce the end items.

If no MPS that is both feasible and consistent with the production plan can be found, then either the production plan must be revised downward or additional resources must be added to the production budget.

> "Three basic MPS strategies enable a firm to manage inventories in support of its competitive priorities. The strategy chosen will determine the manager's approach to master production scheduling." p. 669

1. Make-to-Stock Strategy
   - Inventory is placed forward to finished goods.
   - Example — McDonald's hamburgers.
   - Advantage — customer delivery times are minimized.
2. Assemble-to-Order Strategy
   - Produces end items with many options from a relatively small number of major subassemblies *after* customer orders are received.
   - Inventory is held at major subassembly level.
   - Example — Wendy's hamburgers.
   - Advantage — product flexibility and fast delivery time.
3. Make-to-Order Strategy
   - Produces end items to customer's specifications.
   - Inventory is staged at raw material level or acquired after receiving the customer order.
   - Example — home-cooked hamburgers.
   - Advantage — high degree of product flexibility

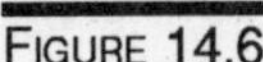

FIGURE 14.6

Relationship of the Master Production Schedule to Competitive Priorities

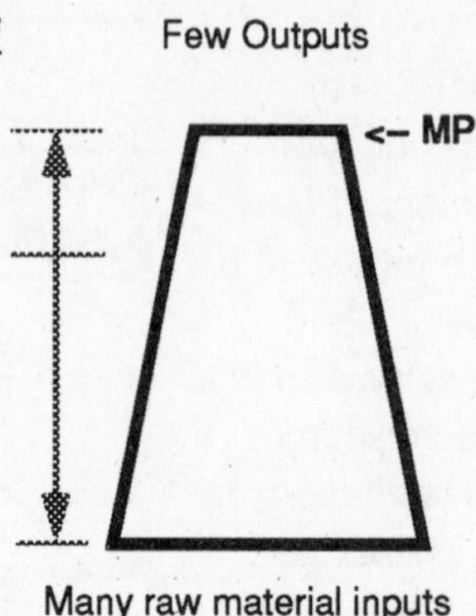

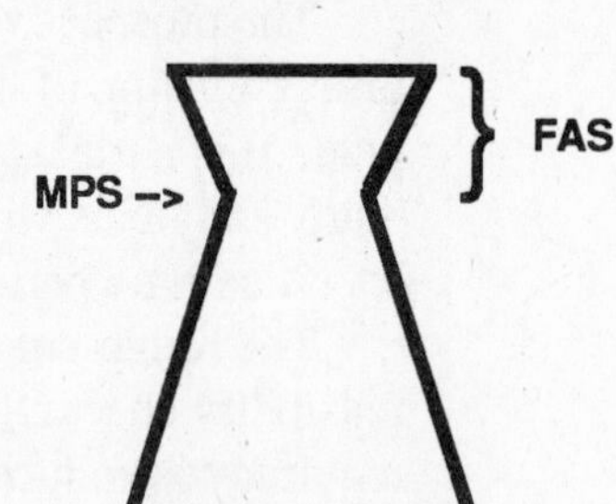

- In some make to order businesses such as aerospace, the number of possible end-items is almost infinite, but the actual number of end items is very small (a space shuttle, a stealth bomber). This type of master schedule is done at the end-item level because the customer expects to wait several years for the entire design, development, material acquistion, manufacturing and delivery processes to occur *after* placing the order. The principle still holds true:

  Principle: Master schedule at the level that minimizes the number of different items stated in the schedule.

Functional Interfaces

- Finance uses the MPS to estimate budgets and cash flows.
- Marketing uses it to project the impact of product mix changes on the firm's ability to satisfy customer demand and manage delivery schedules.
- Manufacturing can estimate the effects of MPS changes on loads at critical work stations.
- Many software packages perform these types of calculations.
- The techniques project *what if* analyses of prospective MPS's devised by the master scheduler.

Developing a Prospective Master Production Schedule

Step#1. Calculate projected on-hand inventories

$$\begin{pmatrix}\text{Projected on-hand}\\ \text{inventory at end of}\\ \text{this period}\end{pmatrix} = \begin{pmatrix}\text{On-hand}\\ \text{inventory}\\ \text{last period}\end{pmatrix} + \begin{pmatrix}\text{MPS quantity}\\ \text{due this}\\ \text{period}\end{pmatrix} - \begin{pmatrix}\text{Projected}\\ \text{requirements}\\ \text{this period}\end{pmatrix}$$

$$I_t = I_{t-1} + \text{MPS}_t - \max(F_t \text{ or } CO_t)$$

In the last term, the projected requirements for this period is the *larger* of the *forecasted demand* for the current period or the *actual customer orders* for the current period. MPS_t indicates a quantity that management expects to be completed and ready to ship in week t.

Use this equation to determine when the projected on-hand inventory will drop below zero for item X.

Item: X	January				February				March				
Quantity on hand: 65	**1**	**2**	**3**	**4**	**5**	**6**	**7**	**8**	**9**	**10**	**11**	**12**	**13**
Forecast	20	20	20	20	25	25	40	40	60	90	100	60	20
Customer orders (booked)	18	25	23	10	16	28	0	2	0	15	0	0	0
Projected on-hand inventory													

Answer: It occurs in the *third* week, not the fourth. Be sure you always subtract the *larger* of the forecast or booked orders from the previous inventory. If you did this correctly, the projected on-hand inventory at the end of the third week is: 65 – 20 – 25 – 23 = – 3.

Step 2. Determining the timing and size of MPS quantities.

- The goal is to schedule enough production to prevent the projected on-hand inventory from becoming negative.
- In this case where we have no safety stock, zero inventory is okay, but any negative balance should trigger an MPS quantity to be completed and ready to ship in that period.
- For the purposes of this example, let us assume the order quantity is fixed (perhaps the result of an *EOQ* calculation) and is equal to 80.

We have already determined that the inventory balance will drop below zero in the third period. Therefore, in the MPS quantity row of the table below, schedule 80 to be completed and ready to ship in the *third* period, *not* the second period. The projected on-hand inventory at the end of the third period is 20 from the second period plus 80 from the MPS quantity completed in the third period minus the 23 booked sales during the third period (because it is larger than the forecast) and the result is 77. Place 77 in the third column of the projected on-hand inventory row. Use step 1 to determine when the next MPS should occur and continue this calculation process to complete the prospective master production schedule for item X. The solution appears on the next page.

Item: X	January				February				March				
Quantity on hand: 65	**1**	**2**	**3**	**4**	**5**	**6**	**7**	**8**	**9**	**10**	**11**	**12**	**13**
Forecast	20	20	20	20	25	25	40	40	60	90	100	60	20
Customer orders (booked)	18	25	23	10	16	28	0	2	0	15	0	0	0
Projected on-hand inventory	45	20											
Master production schedule quantity			80										

Item: X	January				February				March				
Quantity on hand: 65	1	2	3	4	5	6	7	8	9	10	11	12	13
Forecast	20	20	20	20	25	25	40	40	60	90	100	60	20
Customer orders (booked)	18	25	23	10	16	28	0	2	0	15	0	0	0
Projected on-hand inventory	45	20	77	57	32	4	44	4	24	14	74	14	74
Master production schedule quantity			80				80		80	80	160		80

Not seven!

Depending on policy, either 86 or two batches of 80 each would be ordered here.

This prospective master schedule has some severe drawbacks. This product has a dramatic seasonal peak in demand which is forecast to occur in March. This MPS does not build any anticipation inventory, so the demands on the factory get out of hand in mid March. The double lot in week 11 may cause great difficulty in the shop. The master scheduler may respond to this situation in a number of ways. An aggressive choice would be to shift, say, ten units of demand from the 11th to the 12th week. Then one of the two production lots could be shifted to the 12th week. Keep in mind that this compromise may reduce customer service.

Item: X	January				February				March				
Quantity on hand: 65	1	2	3	4	5	6	7	8	9	10	11	12	13
Forecast	20	20	20	20	25	25	40	40	60	90	90	70	20
Customer orders (booked)	18	25	23	10	16	28	0	2	0	15	0	0	0
Projected on-hand inventory	45	20	77	57	32	4	44	4	24	14	4	14	74
Master production schedule quantity			80				80		80	80	80	80	80

Another alternative would be to order 80 during even-numbered weeks. That would level the work load on the factory but greatly increase the average inventory investment in February and risk a small stockout in March.

Item: X	January				February				March				
Quantity on hand: 65	1	2	3	4	5	6	7	8	9	10	11	12	13
Forecast	20	20	20	20	25	25	40	40	60	90	100	60	20
Customer orders (booked)	18	25	23	10	16	28	0	2	0	15	0	0	0
Projected on-hand inventory	45	100	77	137	112	164	124	164	104	94	–6	14	–6
Master production schedule quantity		80		80		80		80		80		80	

These changes smooth demand on the factory so manufacturing should be happy. However they also reduce customer service and increase inventory investment. The master scheduler should be prepared to explain the need for these schedule changes to sales and finance camps, who will surely object.

> The "available-to-promise concept seems to cause students some difficulty. The calculation process can be confusing because the first week's calculation differs slightly from all subsequent ones. But the intent is simple ... we just want to know how many units are for sale.
> Out of each production batch, some may have already been allocated or "promised" to cover an actual customer order. Those which have not been sold remain for sale. They are available-to-promise.

Step 3: Calculating available-to-promise quantities.

For the purposes of continuing our example, let us assume the second version of master schedule shown on the previous page is approved.

- For the first time bucket:

  $ATP_1 = I_t + MPS_t$ – (cumulative total of booked orders up to but not including the week in which the next MPS quantity arrives)
- This states that if you promise to ship an item before any more are produced, you have to sell it from your existing inventory.
- Note that the forecast is *never* used in this calculation, even when the forecast is larger than the booked orders.

In our example, the 18 units sold in the first week plus the 25 units sold in the second week must come from our existing inventory of 65 units. No more will arrive until the MPS quantity in the third week. Therefore,

$ATP_1 = 65 + 0 - (18+25) = 22$

The available to promise in the second week is also 22, but that number is generally not entered for fear that someone will interpret that we have 22 for sale in the first week *and* 22 for sale in the second week. 22 must cover the total demand occurring at any time until the next MPS quantity arrives.

- All subsequent time buckets.

  Make the calculation only for periods that include an MPS quantity.

  $ATP_t = MPS_t$ – (cumulative total of booked orders up to but not including the week in which the next MPS quantity arrives)
- Note the formula is different because we have already included the existing inventory I_t as available in the first week.

In our example, the 23, 10, 16, and 28 units promised for shipment in weeks 3 through 6 must all come from the batch of 80 to be completed in week 3. That leaves 3 for sale from that batch. Of course the previous 22 are still for sale but they are not added to the ATP record for the 3rd week because if we do, someone will sell 22 *and* 25. Our jail populations include several people who sold the same thing twice.

> For several reasons it is important to take control over near-term scheduling away from the computer. First, the computer can make schedule changes much more rapidly than the shop floor can respond to them. Attempting to hit such a moving target only results in chaos.
> Second, we do not want the computer to automatically launch production orders when they mature. It is a bad idea to let computers spend money, because they can do so at the speed of light.
> Finally, computer-suggested master schedules are greatly influenced by computer-generated forecasts which in turn are greatly influenced by marketing. If we don't at some point intercede with a neutral party (the master scheduler), then in effect, scheduling of the factory is abdicated to marketing. Now there's a really scary thought.

Freezing the MPS

- Near-term changes to the MPS disrupt production, are costly to attempt, and are usually impossible to accomplish.
- Stability is achieved by preventing unimportant changes to the MPS within the time fence(s).
- The demand time fence is placed at a number of periods into the future usually equal to the final assembly lead time. Within that near term period, no changes can be made to the MPS without special authorization from management. As a practical matter, they would be impossible to accomplish in any event.
- The planning time fence (sometimes called firm-planned time fence) is a point further into the future than the demand time fence. It is usually equal to the cumulative lead time and marks the point at which control over MPS quantities is taken away from the computer.
- MPS quantities within the planning time fence are considered to be "firm-planned orders."
- The length of time fences should be reviewed periodically.

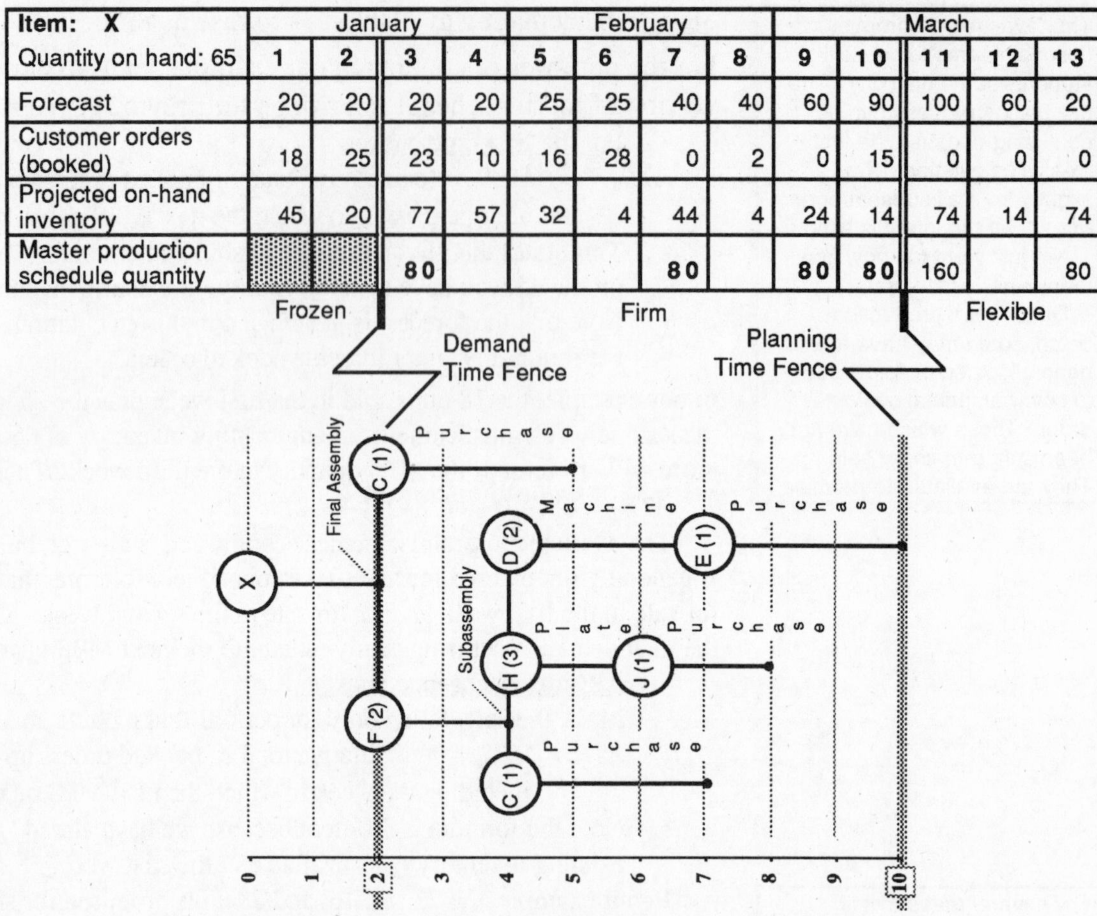

Item: X	January				February				March				
Quantity on hand: 65	1	2	3	4	5	6	7	8	9	10	11	12	13
Forecast	20	20	20	20	25	25	40	40	60	90	100	60	20
Customer orders (booked)	18	25	23	10	16	28	0	2	0	15	0	0	0
Projected on-hand inventory	45	20	77	57	32	4	44	4	24	14	74	14	74
Master production schedule quantity			80				80		80	80	160		80

The bill of materials for item X has been redrawn to show the lead times in the horizontal direction. For example, the final assembly of X from two F's and one C has a lead time of two weeks.

The demand time fence is placed at two weeks. At that time, all materials have been purchased and the final assembly process for X has begun. It would be very costly or impossible to make changes in the production schedule within two weeks of shipment.

The planning time fence is placed at ten weeks. That is the cumulative lead time for this product. In other words, at a point ten weeks in advance of shipment, we have begun to contract for raw material E. Any changes within ten weeks require contract renegotiation and production rescheduling. Computers are not particularly good at either of these activities, so these orders become firm when they roll inside of the ten- week planning horizon.

Rough-Cut Capacity Planning

Several Approaches Are in Use

1. Capacity bills
   - analogous to bills of material
   - more accurately represents the effects of changing product mix
2. Resource profiles
   - uses capacity bills and lead time estimates to more accurately determine when the workload will occur at the work centers
3. Capacity planning using overall factors
   - uses time standards to estimate the total number of direct labor hours required. Based on historical data, the load is apportioned to critical work stations.

Method of Overall Factors

1. Identify the critical work stations.
   - Critical (bottleneck) work station operations limit output.

   Example:

Work Centers	Critical?
Final assembly	No
Subassembly	Yes
Machining	Yes
Plating	No
Purchasing	No

2. Estimate direct labor factors for each item.
   - Critical hours determine the feasibility of a prospective MPS.
   - Time lost at bottleneck work stations can never be recovered.
   - Time saved at nonbottleneck work stations is irrelevant.

   Example:

Item	Critical Hours
A	4.4 hours
X	5.4 hours

3. Develop load factors for each critical work station.

   Example:

Work Centers	Load Factor
Subassembly	35%
Machining	65%

4. Multiply each MPS quantity by its direct labor factor (such as direct labor hours per unit) for work performed at critical work centers.

Item: A	January				February				March				
Quantity on hand: 40	1	2	3	4	5	6	7	8	9	10	11	12	13
Master production schedule quantity			50		50			50					
MPS Qty * 4.4 hours			220		220			220					

Item: X	January				February				March				
Quantity on hand: 65	1	2	3	4	5	6	7	8	9	10	11	12	13
Master production schedule quantity			80				80		80	80	160		80
MPS Qty * 5.4 hours			432				432		432	432	864		432

5. Then the total direct labor hours for all critical work centers in a period is multiplied by each critical work center's load factor to arrive at an estimate of total hours for that work center.

	January				February				March				
	1	2	3	4	5	6	7	8	9	10	11	12	13
Total Critical Hours			652		220		432	220	432	432	864		432
Subassembly load factor 35%			228.2		77		151.2	77	151.2	151.2	302.4		151.2
Machining load factor 65%			423.8		143		280.8	143	280.8	280.8	561.6		280.8

6. Finally, the resulting load profiles for each critical work center can be compared to its capacity. Management can decide to keep the proposed schedule or modify it.
   Example: If the subassembly capacity is 200 hours per week and the machining capacity is 400 hours per week, the first ten weeks of this schedule look pretty good. There is a small overload that appears will occur in the third week, but it is within the ballpark. This overload might be handled in a variety of ways, perhaps using overtime or shifting the timing of the work slightly.
   There is a significant overload in the eleventh week. The master scheduler may decide to shift one batch of product X back to the twelfth week.

Evaluating the Method of Overall Factors

- One of the simplest methods available
- Labor requirements are proportioned to each work station solely on the basis of historical labor requirements.
- If product mix changes, the capacity bills approach provides more accurate results.
- The timing of the workloads in the load profile is not accurate. For example, the heavy amount of work projected for the eleventh week in the example will actually hit the subassembly area four weeks earlier, in the seventh week. The peak load will hit the machining work center in the fourth week, not the eleventh week. There is a seven-week lead time offset between the beginning of machining and the shipment of X.

Inventory Record

- Resembles an MPS record
- Divides future into *time buckets*
- Has no standard format
  - Planned receipts row (shown in the text) is sometimes not displayed.
  - A net requirements row (not shown in the text) is sometimes displayed.

Item: A	January				February				March				
Quantity on hand: 40	1	2	3	4	5	6	7	8	9	10	11	12	13
Master production schedule quantity			(50)		50			50					
MPS start date, Production releases	(50)		50			50							

Item: X	January				February				March				
Quantity on hand: 65	1	2	3	4	5	6	7	8	9	10	11	12	13
Master production schedule quantity			(80)				80		80	80	160		80
MPS start date, Production releases	(80)				80		80	80	160		80		

The final assembly of end-items A and X requires two weeks of lead time. Most of that time is spent in preparing paperwork and waiting in queues. Nevertheless, the time between *releasing* the production order authorizing final assembly and the time the product is inspected and ready to ship is two weeks. The MPS states when the production lots are completed and ready to ship. Therefore, the work order releases to final assembly must occur two weeks before the MPS dates. Component items needed for final assembly (such as component C) will be committed from inventory at the time the production orders are *released.* For the example end items A and X shown at the bottom of this page, one C is consumed during final assembly of either end item A or end item X. In total, the gross requirements for component C will be 130 in the first week, 50 in the third, 80 in the fifth, and so on.

Item: C Description: Widget	Lot Size: 400				Lead Time: 3				Safety Stock: 0				
	January				February				March				
	1	2	3	4	5	6	7	8	9	10	11	12	13
Gross requirements	(130)		50		80	50	80	80	160		80		
Scheduled receipts													

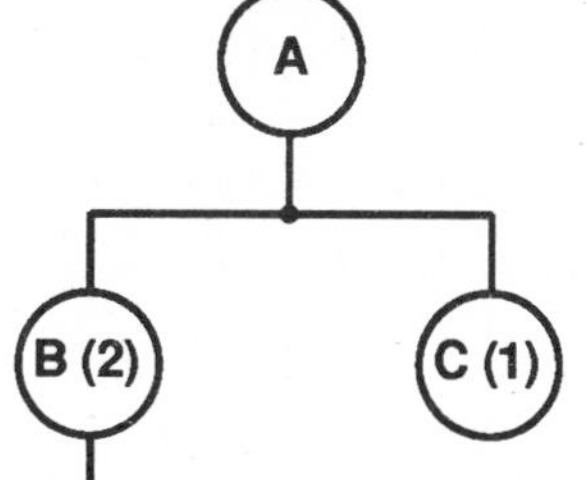

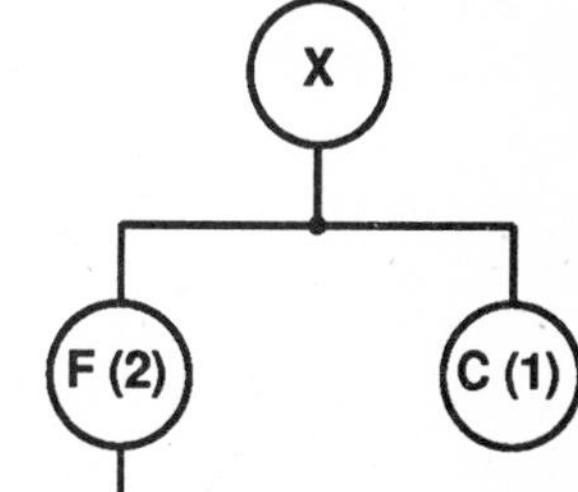

Gross Requirements

> "The **gross requirements** are the total demand derived from *all* parent production plans. They also include demand not otherwise accounted for, such as replacement parts for units already sold." p. 680

The preceding example shows that the planned usage of component C comes from its parents A and X, and when they occur during the same period of time, those requirements are added together. Those of you who are way ahead of me may have noticed that C also has other parents. Therefore, we have not really derived the total demand for component C from *all* parents. This minor complication will be addressed later, when we discuss level-by-level processing. To keep this first example as simple as possible, pretend that A and X are C's only parents.

When materials are released to the work center for final assembly, a transaction is processed to erase the gross requirement and to reduce the on-hand inventory to reflect the fact that storeroom inventory has decreased.

Scheduled Receipts

- Sometimes called open orders
- Orders that have been placed but not yet completed and received.
- When scheduled receipts arrive, a transaction is processed to increase the on-hand inventory by the number of good units received, and the scheduled receipt record is erased.

In our example, 400 units of purchased widget C are expected to arrive at the beginning of week 3. Since the lead time is three weeks, this order must have been released at the beginning of the last week in December.

Item: C Description: Widget	Lot Size: 400				Lead Time: 3				Safety Stock: 0				
	January				February				March				
	1	**2**	**3**	**4**	**5**	**6**	**7**	**8**	**9**	**10**	**11**	**12**	**13**
Gross requirements	130		50		80	50	80	80	160		80		
Scheduled receipts			400										

Projected On-Hand Inventory

- Similar to the MPS projected on-hand inventory calculation

$$I_t = I_{t-1} + SR_t + PR_t - GR_t$$

$$\begin{pmatrix}\text{Projected on-hand}\\ \text{inventory balance}\\ \text{at end of week } t\end{pmatrix} = \begin{pmatrix}\text{Inventory on}\\ \text{hand at end of}\\ \text{week } t-1\end{pmatrix} + \begin{pmatrix}\text{Scheduled}\\ \text{receipts due}\\ \text{in week } t\end{pmatrix} - \begin{pmatrix}\text{Gross}\\ \text{requirements}\\ \text{in week } t\end{pmatrix}$$

$$\begin{aligned}
I_1 &= 200 + 0 + 0 - 130 = 70\\
I_2 &= 70 + 0 + 0 - 0 = 70\\
I_3 &= 70 + 400 + 0 - 50 = 420\\
I_4 &= 420 + 0 + 0 - 0 = 420\\
I_5 &= 420 + 0 + 0 - 80 = 340\\
I_6 &= 340 + 0 + 0 - 50 = 290\\
I_7 &= 290 + 0 + 0 - 80 = 210\\
I_8 &= 210 + 0 + 0 - 80 = 130\\
I_9 &= 130 + 0 + 0 - 160 = -30
\end{aligned}$$

Item: C Description: Widget		Lot Size: 400				Lead Time: 3				Safety Stock: 0				
		January				February				March				
		1	2	3	4	5	6	7	8	9	10	11	12	13
Gross requirements		130		50		80	50	80	80	160		80		
Scheduled receipts				400										
Projected on-hand inventory	200	70	70	420	420	340	290	210	130	–30				
Planned receipts										X				

Planned Receipts

> "A **planned receipt** is a new order not yet released to the shop or the supplier. Planning for receipt of these new orders will keep the projected on-hand balance from dropping below the desired safety stock level." p. 682

In this example, the projected on-hand inventory drops below the desired safety stock (zero) in the ninth week. Using the convention that receipts occur before withdrawals, we plan a receipt to occur during the ninth week, *not the eighth week!* The *midpoint convention* we use here is consistent with that used by APICS and most educational references. If scheduled receipts tend to occur later in the week than do the withdrawals, then the system would be programmed to move the planned order release back one more time bucket to the eighth week. We won't get involved with that detail here.

$$
\begin{aligned}
I_t &= I_{t-1} + SR_t + PR_t - GR_t \\
I_9 &= 130 + 0 + 0 - 160 = -30 \\
I_9 &= 130 + 0 + 400 - 160 = 370 \\
I_{10} &= 370 + 0 + 0 - 0 = 370 \\
I_{11} &= 370 + 0 + 0 - 80 = 290
\end{aligned}
$$

The result of all this calculation is that we have a planned receipt for 400 units of component item C to occur in week 9. Now we need a valid plan for acquiring those 400 Cs.

Planned Order Releases

> "A **planned order release** indicates when an order for a specified quantity of an item is to be issued. The release date is found by subtracting the lead time from the receipt date; ..." p. 683

Therefore, with a lead time of three weeks, planned order releases for component item C of 400 units should occur in week 6. The completed inventory record is shown on the next page. The planned order releases row is truly "the bottom line" to the material planner. It states the time-phased plan for covering net requirements for every part. The computer can be programmed to send a message to the appropriate material planner when a planned order release matures. A planned order release is mature when it rolls into the first (lower left) bucket, sometimes called the "action" bucket.

- If a shortage can be eliminated by expediting a scheduled receipt, there is no need to release a new order.

Item: C Description: Widget		Lot Size: 400				Lead Time: 3				Safety Stock: 0				
		January				February				March				
		1	2	3	4	5	6	7	8	9	10	11	12	13
Gross requirements		130		50		80	50	80	80	160		80		
Scheduled receipts				400										
Projected on-hand inventory	200	70	70	420	420	340	290	210	130	370	370	290	290	290
Planned receipts										400				
Planned order releases							400							

Planning Factors

Lead Time

- The amount of time allowed to get the item into stock once the order is issued, including
  - setup time
  - process time
  - materials handling time between operations
  - waiting time
    - .. process focus; a large proportion of planning lead time
    - .. product focus; less significant proportion of lead time

Lot-Sizing Rules

- Determine the timing and size of order quantities
- Rule is preassigned to each item

Fixed Order Quantity

- Maintain the same order quantity
- Fixed order quantity (FOQ)
  - equal to *EOQ* or
  - equal to discount quantity
- When gross requirements in a period exceed the fixed order quantity
  - increase order quantity above FOQ to bring the projected on-hand inventory up to the desired safety stock level or
  - order an integer multiple of the FOQ
- In the example, component item C uses a fixed order quantity

Periodic order quantity (POQ)

- Order quantity equals the total required to cover *P* weeks of requirements and restore the safety stock
- In the following example, raw materials E and J use periodic order quantity lot sizes.

Lot-for-lot (L4L)

- Special case of POQ, where $P = 1$.
- In the following example, components D and H and subassemblies B and F use lot-for-lot order quantities.

Comparison of Lot-Sizing Rules

1. FOQ — used at the top of the bill of materials
   - Generates remnants, increasing average inventory level
   - Reduces ordering costs
   - Greater stability — remnants buffer changes in an item's requirements, preventing small changes from cascading through to component item requirements
2. POQ — used at the bottom of the bill of materials
   - Eliminates remnants, reducing average inventory level
   - Combines orders, reduces ordering costs
   - If used in the middle or top of the bill of material, it tends to magnify changes — sometimes causes wild and illogical changes in the gross requirements for the item's components.
3. L4L — used at the middle levels of the bill of materials
   - Used at all levels of a custom product to make a specific quantity of an end item, for example, aerospace production of one Magellan spacecraft; or 20 Titan rockets.
   - Minimizes inventory holding costs
   - Maximizes ordering costs

Safety Stock

- Safety stock of a component is of little value unless we also have matching safety stocks of the other components required to make an assembly.
- Safety stock should be carried only where there is uncertainty
  - at the master schedule level, to cover independent demand forecast errors
  - as a temporary measure at the component item level to cover uncertainty in delivery or yield

Outputs from Material Requirements Planning

Material Requirements Planning Explosion

The Explosion Process

Level-by-Level Processing

- Gross requirements are accumulated from three sources:
  1. the MPS for immediate parents that are end items
  2. the planned order releases for parents below the MPS level
  3. any other requirements not originating in the MPS
- The computer starts with the MPS and works downward through the bills of materials, calculating the planned releases of items as it goes.

Refer to the product structure diagrams in the middle of the next page. The order in which these items would be computed is:

level 0 A and X

level 1 B, **C (source is MPS parents A and X)**, and F

level 2 **C (source is subassembly parents B and F**), D, and H

level 3 E and J

However, if we follow that sequence, we will process the record for item C twice (on level 1 and on level 2), needlessly complicating the process. This problem can be avoided by delaying processing the C record until *all* of C's parents' planned order releases have been determined. When the planned order releases of A, X, B, and F have all been calculated, then we can process the record for component C all in one "swell foop". This is accomplished by assigning C a *level code* = 2. Now the computer will delay the calculations for C until the level-by-level processing reaches level 2. At that point, all of C's parent planned order releases have been determined.

Item: A	January				February				March				
	1	2	3	4	5	6	7	8	9	10	11	12	13
Master production schedule quantity			50		50			50					
MPS start date, Production releases	50		50			50							

Item: X	January				February				March				
	1	2	3	4	5	6	7	8	9	10	11	12	13
Master production schedule quantity			80				80		80	80	160		80
MPS start date, Production releases	80				80		80	80	160		80		

Item: B Description: Subassembly		Lot Size: L4L				Lead Time: 3				Safety Stock: 0				
		January				February				March				
		1	2	3	4	5	6	7	8	9	10	11	12	13
Gross requirements		100		100			100							
Scheduled receipts				80										
Projected on-hand inventory	120	20	20											
Planned receipts														
Planned order releases														

Item: F Description: Subassembly		Lot Size: L4L				Lead Time: 2				Safety Stock: 10				
		January				February				March				
		1	2	3	4	5	6	7	8	9	10	11	12	13
Gross requirements		160												
Scheduled receipts		100												
Projected on-hand inventory	110													
Planned receipts														
Planned order releases														

Since it requires two Bs to make one A, the master schedule quantities for A (50) are multiplied by the usage quantity (2) to obtain the gross requirements for B. Similarly, the master schedule quantities for X (80 and 160) are multiplied by the usage quantity (2) to obtain the gross requirements for F. Complete the inventory records below. Solutions appear on page 285.

The first gross requirement for component C is derived by adding the material requirements associated with MPS start orders for 50 A and 80 X. [(50*1) + (80*1)] = 130 The gross requirement for the third week is derived from MPS start order for 50 A, plus MRP planned order releases for 100 of subassembly B and 120 of subassembly F. [(50*1)+(100*3)+(120*1)] = 470 Very carefully continue this process to complete the gross requirements row for component C, then complete the rest of the inventory record.

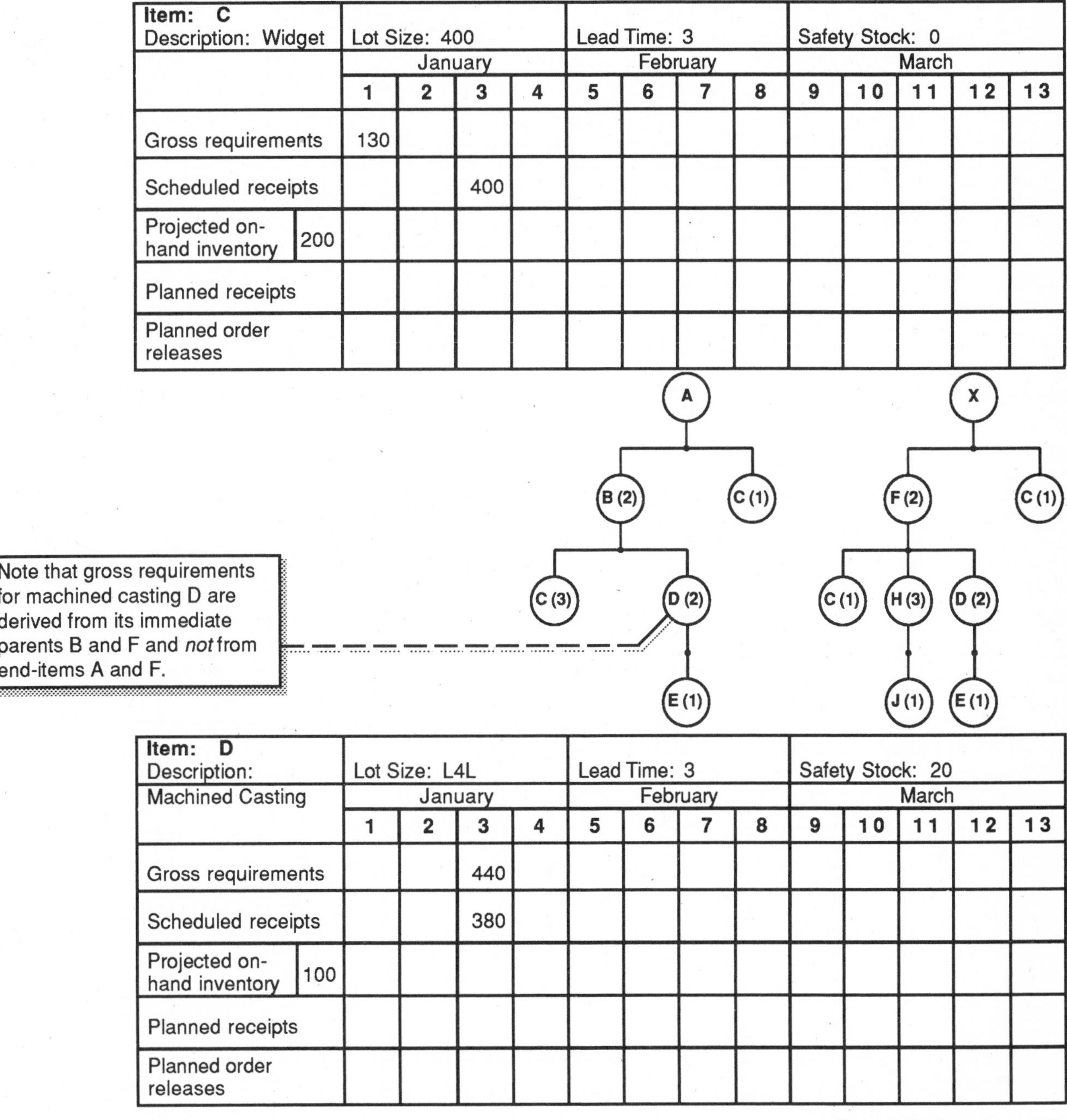

Item: C Description: Widget		Lot Size: 400				Lead Time: 3				Safety Stock: 0				
		January				February				March				
		1	2	3	4	5	6	7	8	9	10	11	12	13
Gross requirements		130												
Scheduled receipts				400										
Projected on-hand inventory	200													
Planned receipts														
Planned order releases														

Item: D Description: Machined Casting		Lot Size: L4L				Lead Time: 3				Safety Stock: 20				
		January				February				March				
		1	2	3	4	5	6	7	8	9	10	11	12	13
Gross requirements				440										
Scheduled receipts				380										
Projected on-hand inventory	100													
Planned receipts														
Planned order releases														

Item: H Description:	Lot Size: L4L				Lead Time: 2				Safety Stock: 0				
Plated component	January				February				March				
	1	2	3	4	5	6	7	8	9	10	11	12	13
Gross requirements													
Scheduled receipts													
Projected on-hand inventory 0													
Planned receipts													
Planned order releases													

Item: E Description:	Lot Size: POQ=3				Lead Time: 3				Safety Stock: 0				
Purchased casting	January				February				March				
	1	2	3	4	5	6	7	8	9	10	11	12	13
Gross requirements													
Scheduled receipts		600											
Projected on-hand inventory 20													
Planned receipts													
Planned order releases													

Item: J Description:	Lot Size: POQ=3				Lead Time: 2				Safety Stock: 0				
Purchased	January				February				March				
component	1	2	3	4	5	6	7	8	9	10	11	12	13
Gross requirements													
Scheduled receipts													
Projected on-hand inventory 840													
Planned receipts													
Planned order releases													

Item: B		Lot Size: L4L				Lead Time: 3				Safety Stock: 0				
Description: Subassembly		1	2	3	4	5	6	7	8	9	10	11	12	13
Gross requirements		100		100			100							
Scheduled receipts				80										
Projected on-hand inventory	120	20	20	0	0	0	0	0	0	0	0	0	0	0
Planned receipts							100							
Planned order releases				100										

Item: C		Lot Size: 400				Lead Time: 3				Safety Stock: 0				
Description: Widget		1	2	3	4	5	6	7	8	9	10	11	12	13
Gross requirements		130		470		240	210	400	80	320		80		
Scheduled receipts				400										
Projected on-hand inventory	200	70	70	0	0	160	350	350	270	350	350	270	270	270
Planned receipts						400	400	400		400				
Planned order releases			400	400	400		400							

Item: D		Lot Size: L4L				Lead Time: 3				Safety Stock: 20				
Description: Machined casting		1	2	3	4	5	6	7	8	9	10	11	12	13
Gross requirements				440		320	320	640		320				
Scheduled receipts				380										
Projected on-hand inventory	100	100	100	40	40	20	20	20	20	20	20	20	20	20
Planned receipts						300	320	640		320				
Planned order releases			300	320	640		320							

Item: E		Lot Size: POQ=3				Lead Time: 3				Safety Stock: 0				
Description: Purchased casting		1	2	3	4	5	6	7	8	9	10	11	12	13
Gross requirements			300	320	640		320							
Scheduled receipts			600											
Projected on-hand inventory	20	20	320	0	320	320	0	0	0	0	0	0	0	0
Planned receipts					960									
Planned order releases		960												

Item: F		Lot Size: L4L				Lead Time: 2				Safety Stock: 10				
Description: Subassembly		1	2	3	4	5	6	7	8	9	10	11	12	13
Gross requirements		160				160		160	160	320		160		
Scheduled receipts		100												
Projected on-hand inventory	110	50	50	50	50	10	10	10	10	10	10	10	10	10
Planned receipts						120		160	160	320		160		
Planned order releases				120		160	160	320		160				

Item: H		Lot Size: L4L				Lead Time: 2				Safety Stock: 0				
Description: Plated component		1	2	3	4	5	6	7	8	9	10	11	12	13
Gross requirements				360		480	480	960		480				
Scheduled receipts														
Projected on-hand inventory	0	0	0	0	0	0	0	0	0	0	0	0	0	0
Planned receipts				360		480	480	960		480				
Planned order releases		360		480	480	960		480						

Item: J		Lot Size: POQ=3				Lead Time: 2				Safety Stock: 0				
Description: Purch. component		1	2	3	4	5	6	7	8	9	10	11	12	13
Gross requirements		360		480	480	960		480						
Scheduled receipts														
Projected on-hand inventory	840	480	480	0	960	0	0	0	0	0	0	0	0	0
Planned receipts				1440				480						
Planned order releases		1440				480								

Types of MRP Systems

"A **regenerative MRP system** periodically performs the explosion process, typically on a weekly basis, and completely recomputes all inventory records."

"A **net change MRP system** recomputes records as needed. With each change in the MPS and with each transaction, the system executes a partial explosion to update the affected records." p. 690

When the system is installed in a large corporation, the inputs from many users cause the data base to be in a continuous state of change. Action notices generated as a result of one transaction may be cancelled out by another transaction. A balance is required between the interest in having the most current information and the problems of trying to hit a moving target.

- Many companies update the data base on line, but print action notices overnight. Each planner receives only one daily "to do" list.

Action Notices

Actions the MRP System Identifies

1. Initiating (or canceling) production orders
2. Increasing (or decreasing) order quantities
3. Expediting (or de-expediting) the timing of orders

During a typical week, many items may require no action at all. By using this management by exception approach, one planner can be responsible for a large number of items. Since the action notices are generated by item, the system can be programmed to direct all action notices for a class of items, such as fasteners or electronic components, to one planner. The planner can develop expertise in one area of buying or in one area of the shop floor. As priorities change in a dynamic manufacturing environment, the system generates action notices prompting the planner to initiate or change orders as required to coordinate the flow of materials and support the new priorities. Without this system, changes were too difficult to implement and coordinate, resulting in acquiring the wrong quantity of the wrong items at the wrong time, and poor customer service.

Action Notices

"An **action notice** is a computer-generated memo indicating the need to release an order or adjust the due date of a scheduled receipt." p. 662

Releasing New Orders

- Nonzero quantity in the action bucket triggers action notice to order that quantity.
- Having completed the calculations for end items A and X and for all their components, only five actions are required to be accomplished this week:

1. Initiate a work order for the final assembly of 50 A.
2. Initiate a work order for the final assembly of 80 X.
3. Initiate a purchase order for 960 E.
4. Initiate a work order to plate 360 J to create 360 H.
5. Initiate a purchase order for 1440 J.

An analogy for valid priorities is to look at homework assignments as work orders. Say a professor delays the due date of an impending homework assignment. The date of need has changed. If we are unaware of the change (Did we cut that class?), we might spend time working on that assignment. If so, we would not be working to valid priorities. The due date has diverged from the need date.

Instead, we should have been spending that time on some other task, such as doing other homework which now has a higher priority than the delayed assignment. High grades result from having the right (valid) priorities, in other words, doing first things first.

Adjusting Due Dates of Scheduled Receipts

- The *due dates* of orders are shown by placing the order quantities in the scheduled receipt row.
- Planned usage of the item is shown on the gross requirements row. Quantities are placed in the gross requirements row according to the *need dates*.
- The system's response to changed priorities results in changes in the gross requirements row. New priorities create new need dates.
- In order to minimize inventory and maximize customer service, we must work to valid priorities.
- Priorities are valid when due dates match need dates. When priorities change, we must realign the scheduled receipt due dates with the new need dates. Otherwise, the materials requirements plan becomes obsolete, and we will be working on the wrong orders with the wrong quantity of the wrong items at the wrong time.
- Scheduled receipts are open orders. In other words, a contractual commitment for a specified item, quantity, delivery, and price has already been made.
- Computers can not unilaterally change contracts.
- Expediting or de-expediting open orders requires negotiation between human agents to reach a new agreement or change order.
- MRP systems indicate the need for realigning the due dates with dates of need, but it does not *assume* those realignments will be implemented.

Only competent humans having reached the age of majority are allowed to contract. Computers have not yet reached that status in our society.

Making Decisions

- Decisions such as converting a planned receipt to a scheduled receipt by releasing the associated planned order are made by the inventory planner, not the computer.

Capacity Reports

- MRP doesn't recognize capacity limits.
- "What if..." model. What materials are required to build the items in the MPS? MRP does not by itself check to see whether the MPS is an attainable goal.

Capacity Requirements Planning

"**Capacity requirements planning (CRP)** is a technique for projecting time-phased capacity requirements for work stations in order to match the material requirements plan with the plant's production capacity." p. 692

- Goal of CRP is to match the MPS with production capacity.
- *Planned* hours represent labor at a work center associated with *planned* receipts.
- *Actual* hours represent labor at a work center associated with *scheduled* receipts (open orders).

MRP uses backward scheduling. In other words, starting with a due date (scheduled receipt date) it uses lead time to move backward in time to schedule each event to occur as late as possible (without delaying the completion). Backward scheduling minimizes inventory. In our example, we will load the work associated with open and planned orders into the same time bucket as the due date, as though the work would be accomplished at the last minute. It is possible to calculate the work load by spreading the work even over the three-week lead time, but that needlessly complicates the example. We will look only at the subassembly work center, which has the following actual and planned orders:

Status	Due Date	Item	Quantity	Time, in Hours: Setup	Run	Total
Actual	Week # 1	F	100	1.0	0.5	51
Actual	Week # 3	B	80	2.0	0.4	34
Planned	Week # 5	F	120	1.0	0.5	61
Planned	Week # 6	B	100	2.0	0.4	42
Planned	Week # 7	F	160	1.0	0.5	81
Planned	Week # 8	F	160	1.0	0.5	81
Planned	Week # 9	F	320	1.0	0.5	161
Planned	Week #11	F	160	1.0	0.5	81

Subassembly	January				February				March				
Capacity: 80 hr/wk	1	2	3	4	5	6	7	8	9	10	11	12	13
Actual hours	51		34										
Planned hours					61	42	81	81	161		81		
Total hours	51		34		61	42	81	81	161		81		

There is a significant overload for the subassembly work center in the ninth week. We might solve this problem by splitting the order for 160 F into two orders of 80 each, one order to be completed in the ninth week and the other in the tenth week. If we decide to do that, we should also change the material plans for components, C, D, E, H, and J. Otherwise, some of those materials will arrive too soon, and increase inventory. If we do not make those changes, sources of supply for C, D, E, H, and J will waste time working toward invalid priorities. They may consume capacity and materials making unneeded components of F when they should have been making items now having a higher priority.

The point is, if this process wasn't automated would you really have gone back and made those coordinating changes? No, not if you're dealing with tens of thousands of items. Instead, we would let those folks go on working to an obsolete plan, wasting time, materials, and capacity. The value of MRP lies not so much in its ability to make plans as it is in its ability to automatically replan when priorities change.

Input — Output Control

- Compares planned input from prior CRP reports with actual input
- Compares planned output with actual output

Two Reasons Actual Outputs Can Fall Behind Planned Outputs

1. Insufficient inputs
   - problems at an upstream operation
   - purchased material shortage
2. Insufficient capacity
   - absenteeism
   - equipment failure
   - inadequate staffing
   - low productivity

MRP II: A Comphrehensive Information System

- Ties MRP system to the financial system
- "What-if" scenarios
- Performance reports that project dollar value of shipments, product costs, overhead allocations, inventories, backlogs, and profits
- Cash flow projections broken down by product families

Implementation Issues

> Many companies use software packages to integrate material planning, sales, purchasing, inventory, shop floor and distribution operations with financial reporting, and accounting. These packages are quite complex and prices easily run into six figures. And that amount is very small in comparison to education costs.
>
> Custom classes for small groups of user employees typically cost about $300 per employee per day. To become functionally knowledgeable on several system modules will cost around $30,000 per employee. One very large corporation spent one hundred million dollars on MRPII system implementation and education, but operational savings quickly repaid that amount. Yes, education is expensive, until you consider the alternative.

- MRP II systems sometimes fail because of
  - poor implementation
  - unfavorable manufacturing environment

Prerequisites

1. Management support
2. Computer support
3. Accurate and realistic input
4. User knowledge and acceptance

Favorable Environments for Material Requirements Planning

1. Number of BOM levels is high (about six or more)
2. Magnitude of lot sizes is high (not like JIT small lots)
3. Volatility is low (low scrap rates, excess capacity, few rush orders, reliable suppliers)
4. Manufacturing's positioning strategy (intermediate)

Distribution Requirements Planning

- Provides centralized control of distribution inventories
- Inventory record is maintained for each item *at each location*
- Requires forecast of demand for end items *by location*
- Calculation is similar to MRP calculation
- Planned shipments are analogous to planned order releases
- Requires an integrated information system to collect independent-demand data as they occur at the location
- Reduced uncertainty
- Centralized control
  - reduces safety stock requirements
  - allows transportation planning, combine orders, full truck loads
  - allows rational allocation of items that are in short supply

Multiple-choice Questions

1. Lumpy demand for component items is the result of
   A. end-of-period activity to meet monthly shipping budgets.
   B. inadequate stirring of inventory.
   C. lumpy demand for end items.
   D. production lot size decisions for parent items.

2. Which of the following is true of master schedules?
   A. Master scheduling work loads that exceed existing capacity limits is an effective method of increasing production output.
   B. If the production plan states output in terms of total labor hours, the MPS should state output in terms of total labor hours.
   C. The length of the time periods used in the MPS should be the same as those used in the production plan.
   D. The sum of the quantities in the MPS must equal those in the production plan.

3. Which of the following types of information is a result of, or an output from, the master production scheduling calculations?
   A. Authorized production plan
   B. Available to promise
   C. Customer (booked) orders
   D. Product family forecast

4. Which of the following is true of master schedules?
   A. Interactions with nonmanufacturing functional areas end with the inputs they provide.
   B. A master schedule that maintains a stable work force is in the best interests of the marketing function.
   C. A master schedule that maintains a large finished goods inventory is in the best interests of the finance function.
   D. Trade-offs involve high customer service, low inventory level, and stable work-force size.

5. Which of the following is a purpose of the master production schedule?
   A. Achieve production plan's objectives
   B. Maximize customer service
   C. Minimize inventory investment
   D. Order required component materials

6. An assemble-to-order business should master schedule
   A. finished goods, shippable items.
   B. major subassemblies.
   C. raw materials, components.
   D. customer booked orders.

7. "Freezing" the MPS
   A. means that no changes are allowed anywhere within the planning horizon.
   B. means that no changes are allowed within the time fence.
   C. means that management approval is required for changes within the time fence.
   D. means that the master schedule records have been entered in a large computer storage device called "the icebox".

8. The MPS projected on-hand inventory for week 9 shows a negative amount.
   A. The firm has sold more units than will exist at that point in time.
   B. The firm should increase the booked orders to compensate for this error.
   C. The firm should release a master schedule quantity in week 9.
   D. The firm should master schedule a production lot to be completed in week 9.

9. "Rough-cut" capacity planning can best be described as
   A. a capacity planning activity which preceeds the "precision-cut."
   B. analyzing the production plan for feasibility before beginning the MPS process.
   C. checking the feasibility of the prospective MPS before authorizing it.
   D. determining the best plan for machine locations on the shop floor.

10. Which of the following capacity planning methods is the simplest but provides the least accurate load profiles?
    A. capacity bills
    B. capacity requirements planning
    C. overall factors
    D. resource profiles

(Multiple-choice answers are on Study Guide page 299.)

11. The gross requirements schedule for a component used in making a parent-item subassembly are based on
    A. forecasts of usage for the component item.
    B. gross requirements of the parent item.
    C. planned order releases of the parent item.
    D. production release schedule of the end item.

12. Which row of the MRP inventory record contains quantity and timing information about open orders for a component?
    A. Gross requirements
    B. Scheduled receipts
    C. Planned receipts
    D. Planned order releases

13. What is the main difference between a scheduled receipt and a planned receipt?
    A. It is the amount of lead time offset.
    B. Planned receipts refer to a future receipt, scheduled receipts do not.
    C. Scheduled receipts are associated with open orders, planned receipts are not.
    D. Scheduled receipts are associated with closed orders, planned receipts are not.

14. Which row of the MRP inventory record is the equivalent of the MPS row for an end item?
    A. Gross requirements
    B. Projected on-hand inventory
    C. Planned receipts
    D. Planned order releases

15. Which of the following is a lot-sizing rule that generates a higher level of average inventory because it creates inventory remnants?
    A. Fixed order quantity
    B. Lot-for-lot
    C. Periodic order quantity
    D. Wall-to-wall inventory

16. Which one of the following is a lot-sizing rule that tends to minimize average inventory?
    A. Economic order quantity (*EOQ*)
    B. Fixed order quantity (FOQ)
    C. Lot-for-lot (L4L)
    D. Periodic order quantity (POQ)

17. Which of the following is the input that details how many end items will be produced within specified periods of time?
    A. Bill of materials
    B. Capacity requirements plan
    C. Master production schedule
    D. Item master/inventory records

18. Safety stock in an MRP system
    A. is effective protection against variations in manufacturing lead time for component items.
    B. is intended to buffer variations in lumpy demand.
    C. serves as temporary protection against unreliable suppliers of components
    D. should be stored at the intermediate item level.

19. In the product structure diagram shown below, which of these items would have a level code of 2?
    A. A
    B. B
    C. C
    D. D

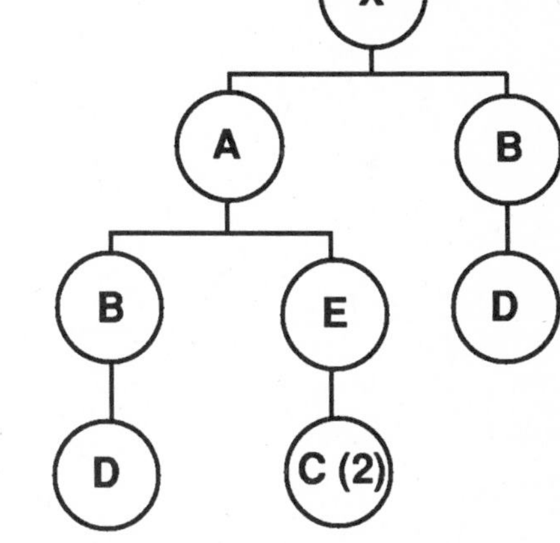

20. Order priorities are said to be valid
    A. if they are ranked in the order in which they are released.
    B. if their due dates match their need dates.
    C. if they are ranked in the order of customer importance.
    D. if there are no horizontal dependencies.

21. The type of MRP system that periodically processes all inventory records
    A. a batch system
    B. a net change system
    C. a periodic review system
    D. a regenerative system

22. Which of the following is not a valid action notice?
    A. Close an existing open order
    B. De-expedite an existing open order
    C. Expedite an existing open order
    D. Initiate, (open) a new order

23. When priorities change, due dates and need dates
    A. tend to become invalid.
    B. tend to converge.
    C. tend to diverge.
    D. tend to remain equidistant.

Problems

1. Complete the following master production schedule for item A.

Item: A	Quantity on hand: 40				Order quantity: 50				Safety stock: 0				
	January				February				March				
	1	2	3	4	5	6	7	8	9	10	11	12	13
Forecast	20	20	20	20	15	15	15	15	10	10	10	5	5
Customer orders (booked)	18	15	23	10	6	8	2	0	0	5	0	0	0
Projected on-hand inventory													
MPS quantity													

2. The demand and planning time fences are at weeks 5 and 11, respectively. Customer service receives three calls for the following orders. In determining whether the orders can be accepted, *do not* change any production lots currently inside the time fences.

   a. 20 units to ship in week 5. Should you accept the order?

Item: A	Quantity on hand: 40				Order quantity: 50				Safety stock: 0				
	January				February				March				
	1	2	3	4	5	6	7	8	9	10	11	12	13
Forecast	20	20	20	20	15	15	15	15	10	10	10	5	5
Customer orders (booked)	18	15	23	10	26	8	2	0	0	5	0	0	0
Projected on-hand inventory													
MPS quantity													

   b. 20 units to ship in week 3. Should you accept the order?

Item: A	Quantity on hand: 40				Order quantity: 50				Safety stock: 0				
	January				February				March				
	1	2	3	4	5	6	7	8	9	10	11	12	13
Forecast	20	20	20	20	15	15	15	15	10	10	10	5	5
Customer orders (booked)	18	15	43	10	26	8	2	0	0	5	0	0	0
Projected on-hand inventory													
MPS quantity													

   c. 10 units to ship in week 4. Should you accept the order?

Item: A	Quantity on hand: 40				Order quantity: 50				Safety stock: 0				
	January				February				March				
	1	2	3	4	5	6	7	8	9	10	11	12	13
Forecast	20	20	20	20	15	15	15	15	10	10	10	5	5
Customer orders (booked)	18	15	43	20	26	8	2	0	0	5	0	0	0
Projected on-hand inventory													
MPS quantity													

3. Complete the following master production schedule for item Z.

Item: Z	Quantity on hand: 42				Order quantity: 144					Safety stock: 0			
	April				May					June			
	14	15	16	17	18	19	20	21	22	23	24	25	26
Forecast	40	80	60	40	45	199	100	40	40	50	50	50	50
Customer orders (booked)	45	83	38	24	4	0	82	6	0	15	0	0	0
Projected on-hand inventory													
MPS quantity													

4. Complete the following master production schedule for item Y.

Item: Y	Quantity on hand: 90				Order quantity: 100					Safety stock: 0			
	April				May					June			
	14	15	16	17	18	19	20	21	22	23	24	25	26
Forecast	40	40	40	40	50	50	50	50	50	40	40	40	40
Customer orders (booked)	45	23	8	4	0	0	62	6	0	15	0	0	0
Projected on-hand inventory													
MPS quantity													

5. Use the overall factors method to determine the load profile resulting from the MPS of problems 3 and 4. The direct labor factors by item for critical drilling and milling work centers are shown below.

Item	Critical hours
Z	2.0
Y	3.2

The load factors for each critical work station are:

Work Centers	Load Factor
Drilling	30%
Milling	70%

Item: Z	April				May					June			
Quantity on hand: 42	14	15	16	17	18	19	20	21	22	23	24	25	26
MPS Quantity													
MPS Qty * 2.0 hours													

Item: Y	April				May					June			
Quantity on hand: 90	14	15	16	17	18	19	20	21	22	23	24	25	26
MPS Quantity													
MPS Qty * 3.2 hours													

	April				May					June			
	1	2	3	4	5	6	7	8	9	10	11	12	13
Total Critical Hours													
Drilling load factor 30%													
Milling load factor 70%													

6. Complete the following material requirements plan for subassembly R.

Item: R Description:		Lot Size: 144				Lead Time: 2				Safety Stock: 12				
Subassembly		**1**	**2**	**3**	**4**	**5**	**6**	**7**	**8**	**9**	**10**	**11**	**12**	**13**
Gross requirements		108	24	60		60	84	120	60	48	12		60	60
Scheduled receipts			144											
Projected on-hand inventory	144													
Planned receipts														
Planned order releases														

Would there be any action notices?

7. Complete the following material requirements plan for purchased component S, first with a lot size rule of L4L, then with a lot size rule of POQ = 3.

Item: S Description:		Lot Size: L4L				Lead Time: 1				Safety Stock: 20				
Purchased gizmo		**1**	**2**	**3**	**4**	**5**	**6**	**7**	**8**	**9**	**10**	**11**	**12**	**13**
Gross requirements		70	20	60		60		120	40	40	10		60	80
Scheduled receipts														
Projected on-hand inventory	160													
Planned receipts														
Planned order releases														

Item: S Description:		Lot Size: POQ = 3				Lead Time: 1				Safety Stock: 20				
Purchased gizmo		**1**	**2**	**3**	**4**	**5**	**6**	**7**	**8**	**9**	**10**	**11**	**12**	**13**
Gross requirements		70	20	60		60		120	40	40	10		60	80
Scheduled receipts														
Projected on-hand inventory	160													
Planned receipts														
Planned order releases														

8. Oh my goodness! Oh my goodness! Our supplier of purchased gizmo S, which we ordered with a lot size rule of POQ = 3 in Problem 2, has called to inform us they've had a flood of orders in their factory. The lead time for gizmos is now *four* weeks instead of one week! Oh my goodness! That means that even if we immediately place the order we planned to place in week 2, it will not arrive until the beginning of week 5. What should we do? Should we expedite a new order for gizmos? Should we delay production of assemblies that use gizmos? Should we expedite those parent assemblies so they take less time in our shop? Complete the following record, however this time ignore the safety stock requirement in the periods marked with the circles. What action is required?

Item: S Description: Purchased gizmo		Lot Size: POQ = 3				Lead Time: 1				Safety Stock: 20				
		1	2	3	4	5	6	7	8	9	10	11	12	13
Gross requirements		70	20	60		60		120	40	40	10		60	80
Scheduled receipts														
Projected on-hand inventory	160			◯	◯									
Planned receipts														
Planned order releases														

9. January has gone by in the example company that makes As and Xs. Miraculously, things have gone pretty much according to plan. The master scheduler did split the large lot of 160 Xs and push back the release of 80 units of end-item X from week 9 to week 10, and we now have a master schedule for April. Complete the MRP plan for the components of A and X.

Item: A	February				March					April			
	5	6	7	8	9	10	11	12	13	14	15	16	17
Master production schedule quantity	50			50							50		50
MPS start date, Production releases		50							50		50		

Item: X	February				March					April			
	5	6	7	8	9	10	11	12	13	14	15	16	17
Master production schedule quantity			80		80	80	80	80	80		80		80
MPS start date, Production releases	80		80	80	80	80	80		80		80		

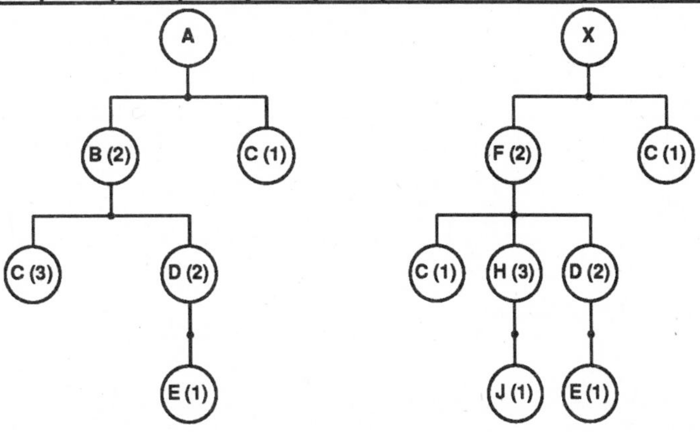

Item: B Description: Subassembly		Lot Size: L4L				Lead Time: 3					Safety Stock: 0			
		5	**6**	**7**	**8**	**9**	**10**	**11**	**12**	**13**	**14**	**15**	**16**	**17**
Gross requirements			100											
Scheduled receipts			100											
Projected on-hand inventory	0													
Planned receipts														
Planned order releases														

Item: F Description: Subassembly		Lot Size: L4L				Lead Time: 2					Safety Stock: 10			
		5	**6**	**7**	**8**	**9**	**10**	**11**	**12**	**13**	**14**	**15**	**16**	**17**
Gross requirements		160												
Scheduled receipts		120												
Projected on-hand inventory	50													
Planned receipts														
Planned order releases														

Item: C Description: Widget		Lot Size: 400				Lead Time: 3					Safety Stock: 0			
		5	**6**	**7**	**8**	**9**	**10**	**11**	**12**	**13**	**14**	**15**	**16**	**17**
Gross requirements		240	210											
Scheduled receipts		400	400											
Projected on-hand inventory	0	160												
Planned receipts														
Planned order releases														

Item: D Description: Subassembly		Lot Size: L4L				Lead Time: 3					Safety Stock: 20			
		5	**6**	**7**	**8**	**9**	**10**	**11**	**12**	**13**	**14**	**15**	**16**	**17**
Gross requirements		320	320	320										
Scheduled receipts		300	320	640										
Projected on-hand inventory	40													
Planned receipts														
Planned order releases														

Item: H Description: Plated component	Lot Size: L4L				Lead Time: 2					Safety Stock: 0			
	5	6	7	8	9	10	11	12	13	14	15	16	17
Gross requirements	480	480											
Scheduled receipts	480	480											
Projected on-hand inventory 0													
Planned receipts													
Planned order releases													

Item: E Description: Purchased casting	Lot Size: POQ = 3				Lead Time: 3					Safety Stock: 0			
	5	6	7	8	9	10	11	12	13	14	15	16	17
Gross requirements													
Scheduled receipts			720										
Projected on-hand inventory 320													
Planned receipts													
Planned order releases													

Item: J Description: Purchased raw mat'l	Lot Size: POQ = 3				Lead Time: 2					Safety Stock: 0			
	5	6	7	8	9	10	11	12	13	14	15	16	17
Gross requirements	480												
Scheduled receipts													
Projected on-hand inventory 960													
Planned receipts													
Planned order releases													

Solutions

1. Complete the following master production schedule for item A.

Item: A	Quantity on hand: 40				Order quantity: 50				Safety stock: 0				
	January				February				March				
	1	2	3	4	5	6	7	8	9	10	11	12	13
Forecast	20	20	20	20	15	15	15	15	10	10	10	5	5
Customer orders (booked)	18	15	23	10	6	8	2	0	0	5	0	0	0
Projected on-hand inventory	20	0	27	7	42	27	12	47	37	27	17	12	7
MPS quantity			50		50			50					

2. a. 20 units to ship in week 5. Should you accept the order? **Yes,**

Item: A	Quantity on hand: 40				Order quantity: 50				Safety stock: 0				
	January				February				March				
	1	2	3	4	5	6	7	8	9	10	11	12	13
Forecast	20	20	20	20	15	15	15	15	10	10	10	5	5
Customer orders (booked)	18	15	23	10	26	8	2	0	0	5	0	0	0
Projected on-hand inventory	20	0	27	7	31	16	1	36	26	16	6	1	46
MPS quantity			50		50			50					50

b. 20 units to ship in week 3. Should you accept the order?

Item: A	Quantity on hand: 40				Order quantity: 50				Safety stock: 0				
	January				February				March				
	1	2	3	4	5	6	7	8	9	10	11	12	13
Forecast	20	20	20	20	15	15	15	15	10	10	10	5	5
Customer orders (booked)	18	15	43	10	26	8	2	0	0	5	0	0	0
Projected on-hand inventory	20	0	7	-13	11	-4	-19	16	6	-4	-14	31	26
MPS quantity			50		50			50				50	

This one is difficult, but the answer is: "Yes". Although the projected on-hand goes negative, available to promise remains positive. Before accepting this order, of the original on-hand inventory, 7 are available: 40 – (18 + 15) = 7 For the first MPS quantity 50 – (23 + 10) = 17 are available. This customer wants 20 units to ship in the third week, and as of that time we will have 7 + 17 = 24 available to promise. We accept this order and only 4 will remain available to promise. Other concerns: actual sales are running ahead of forecast, and the time fence prevents expediting 50 units into the 10th week.

c. 10 units to ship in week 4. Should you accept the order? No, even though the projected on hand is exactly the same as in part b. Only 4 units are available to promise up until the second MPS quantity arrives in week 5.

Item: A	Quantity on hand: 40				Order quantity: 50				Safety stock: 0				
	January				February				March				
	1	2	3	4	5	6	7	8	9	10	11	12	13
Forecast	20	20	20	20	15	15	15	15	10	10	10	5	5
Customer orders (booked)	18	15	43	20	26	8	2	0	0	5	0	0	0
Projected on-hand inventory	20	0	7	-13	11	-4	-19	16	6	-4	-14	31	26
MPS quantity			50		50			50				50	

3. Complete the following master production schedule for item Z.

Item: Z	Quantity on hand: 42				Order quantity: 144					Safety stock: 0			
	April				May					June			
	14	**15**	**16**	**17**	**18**	**19**	**20**	**21**	**22**	**23**	**24**	**25**	**26**
Forecast	40	80	60	40	45	199	100	40	40	50	50	50	50
Customer orders (booked)	45	83	38	24	4	0	82	6	0	15	0	0	0
Projected on-hand inventory	141	58	142	102	57	2	46	6	110	60	10	104	54
MPS quantity	144		144			144	144		144			144	

4. Complete the following master production schedule for item Y.

Item: Y	Quantity on hand: 90				Order quantity: 100					Safety stock: 0			
	April				May					June			
	14	**15**	**16**	**17**	**18**	**19**	**20**	**21**	**22**	**23**	**24**	**25**	**26**
Forecast	40	40	40	40	50	50	50	50	50	40	40	40	40
Customer orders (booked)	45	23	8	4	0	0	62	6	0	15	0	0	0
Projected on-hand inventory	45	5	65	25	75	25	63	13	63	23	83	43	3
MPS quantity			100		100		100		100		100		

MULTIPLE CHOICE ANSWERS

1. D	6. B	11. C	18. C
2. D	7. C	12. B	19. B
3. B	8. D	13. C	20. B
4. D	9. C	14. C	21. D
5. A	10. C	15. A	22. A
		16. C	23. C
		17. C	

5. Use the overall factors method to determine the load profile resulting from the MPS of problems 3 and 4. The direct labor factors by item for critical drilling and milling work centers are shown below.

Item	Critical hours
Z	2.0
Y	3.2

The load factors for each critical work station are:

Work Centers	Load Factor
Drilling	30%
Milling	70%

Item: Z	April				May					June			
Quantity on hand: 42	**14**	**15**	**16**	**17**	**18**	**19**	**20**	**21**	**22**	**23**	**24**	**25**	**26**
MPS Quantity	144		144			144	144		144			144	
MPS Qty * 2.0 hours	288		288			288	288		288			288	

Item: Y	April				May					June			
Quantity on hand: 90	**14**	**15**	**16**	**17**	**18**	**19**	**20**	**21**	**22**	**23**	**24**	**25**	**26**
MPS Quantity			100		100		100		100		100		
MPS Qty * 3.2 hours			320		320		320		320		320		

	April				May					June			
	14	**15**	**16**	**17**	**18**	**19**	**20**	**21**	**22**	**23**	**24**	**25**	**26**
Total Critical Hours	288		608		320	288	608		608		320	288	
Drilling load factor 30%	86.4		182.4		96.0	86.4	182.4		182.4		96.0	86.4	
Milling load factor 70%	201.6		425.6		224.0	201.6	425.6		425.6		224.0	201.6	

6. Complete the following material requirements plan for subassembly R.

Item: R Description: Subassembly		Lot Size: 144				Lead Time: 2				Safety Stock: 12				
		1	**2**	**3**	**4**	**5**	**6**	**7**	**8**	**9**	**10**	**11**	**12**	**13**
Gross requirements		108	24	60		60	84	120	60	48	12		60	60
Scheduled receipts			144											
Projected on-hand inventory	144	36	156	96	96	36	96	120	60	12	144	144	84	24
Planned receipts							144	144			144			
Planned order releases					144	144			144					

Would there be any action notices? Yes. The scheduled receipt due date preceeds the date of need. The action notice would suggest the open order be de-expedited to arrive in the third week.

7. Complete the following material requirements plan for purchased component S, first with a lot size rule of L4L, then with a lot size rule of POQ = 3.

Item: S Description: Purchased gizmo		Lot Size: L4L				Lead Time: 1				Safety Stock: 20				
		1	**2**	**3**	**4**	**5**	**6**	**7**	**8**	**9**	**10**	**11**	**12**	**13**
Gross requirements		70	20	60		60		120	40	40	10		60	80
Scheduled receipts														
Projected on-hand inventory	160	90	70	20	20	20	20	20	20	20	20	20	20	20
Planned receipts				10		60		120	40	40	10		60	80
Planned order releases			10		60		120	40	40	10		60	80	

Item: S Description: Purchased gizmo		Lot Size: POQ = 3				Lead Time: 1				Safety Stock: 20				
		1	**2**	**3**	**4**	**5**	**6**	**7**	**8**	**9**	**10**	**11**	**12**	**13**
Gross requirements		70	20	60		60		120	40	40	10		60	80
Scheduled receipts														
Projected on-hand inventory	160	90	70	80	80	20	20	100	60	20	80	80	20	20
Planned receipts				70				200			70			
Planned order releases			70				200			70				

8. Oh my goodness! What action is required? By allowing the safety stock to buffer this problem. No action is required.

Item: S Description:		Lot Size: POQ = 3				Lead Time: 1				Safety Stock: 20				
Purchased gizmo		1	2	3	4	5	6	7	8	9	10	11	12	13
Gross requirements		70	20	60		60		120	40	40	10		60	80
Scheduled receipts														
Projected on-hand inventory	160	90	70	10	10	140	140	20	70	30	20	20	100	20
Planned receipts						190			90				140	
Planned order releases					190			90				140		

9. January has gone by in the example company that makes As and Xs. Miraculously, things have gone pretty much according to plan. The master scheduler did split the large lot of 160 Xs and push back the release of 80 units of end-item X from week 9 to week 10, and we now have a master schedule for April. Complete the MRP plan for the components of A and X.

Item: A	February				March					April			
	5	6	7	8	9	10	11	12	13	14	15	16	17
Master production schedule quantity	50			50							50		50
MPS start date, Production releases		50							50		50		

Item: X	February				March					April			
	5	6	7	8	9	10	11	12	13	14	15	16	17
Master production schedule quantity			80		80	80	80	80	80		80		80
MPS start date, Production releases	80		80	80	80	80	80		80		80		

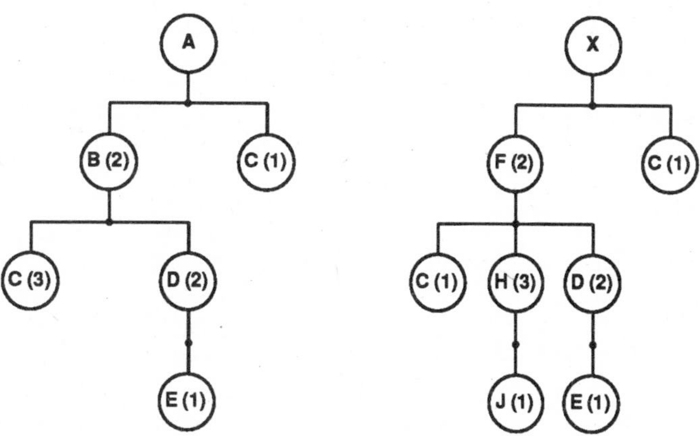

Item: B Description: Subassembly		Lot Size: L4L				Lead Time: 3					Safety Stock: 0			
		5	**6**	**7**	**8**	**9**	**10**	**11**	**12**	**13**	**14**	**15**	**16**	**17**
Gross requirements			100							100		100		
Scheduled receipts			100											
Projected on-hand inventory	0	0	0	0	0	0	0	0	0	0	0	0	0	0
Planned receipts										100		100		
Planned order releases							100		100					

Item: F Description: Subassembly		Lot Size: L4L				Lead Time: 2					Safety Stock: 10			
		5	**6**	**7**	**8**	**9**	**10**	**11**	**12**	**13**	**14**	**15**	**16**	**17**
Gross requirements		160		160	160	160	160	160		160		160		
Scheduled receipts		120												
Projected on-hand inventory	50	10	10	10	10	10	10	10	10	10	10	10	10	10
Planned receipts				160	160	160	160	160		160		160		
Planned order releases		160	160	160	160	160		160		160				

Item: C Description: Widget		Lot Size: 400				Lead Time: 3					Safety Stock: 0			
		5	**6**	**7**	**8**	**9**	**10**	**11**	**12**	**13**	**14**	**15**	**16**	**17**
Gross requirements		240	210	240	240	240	380	240	300	290		130		
Scheduled receipts		400	400											
Projected on-hand inventory	0	160	350	110	270	30	50	210	310	20	20	290	290	290
Planned receipts					400		400	400	400			400		
Planned order releases		400		400	400	400			400					

Item: D Description: Subassembly		Lot Size: L4L				Lead Time: 3					Safety Stock: 20			
		5	**6**	**7**	**8**	**9**	**10**	**11**	**12**	**13**	**14**	**15**	**16**	**17**
Gross requirements		320	320	320	320	320	200	320	200	320				
Scheduled receipts		300	320	640										
Projected on-hand inventory	40	220	20	340	20	20	20	20	20	20	20	20	20	20
Planned receipts						320	200	320	200	320				
Planned order releases			320	200	320	200	320							

Item: H Description: Plated component		Lot Size: L4L				Lead Time: 2					Safety Stock: 0			
		5	**6**	**7**	**8**	**9**	**10**	**11**	**12**	**13**	**14**	**15**	**16**	**17**
Gross requirements		480	480	480	480	480		480		480				
Scheduled receipts		480	480											
Projected on-hand inventory	0	0	0	0	0	0	0	0	0	0	0	0	0	0
Planned receipts				480	480	480		480		480				
Planned order releases		480	480	480		480		480						

Item: E Description: Purchased casting		Lot Size: POQ = 3				Lead Time: 3					Safety Stock: 0			
		5	**6**	**7**	**8**	**9**	**10**	**11**	**12**	**13**	**14**	**15**	**16**	**17**
Gross requirements			320	200	320	200	320							
Scheduled receipts				720										
Projected on-hand inventory	320	320	0	520	200	0	0	0	0	0	0	0	0	0
Planned receipts							320							
Planned order releases				320										

Item: J Description: Purchased raw mat'l		Lot Size: POQ = 3				Lead Time: 2					Safety Stock: 0			
		5	**6**	**7**	**8**	**9**	**10**	**11**	**12**	**13**	**14**	**15**	**16**	**17**
Gross requirements		480	480	480		480		480						
Scheduled receipts														
Projected on-hand inventory	960	480	0	480	480	0	0	0	0	0	0	0	0	0
Planned receipts				960				480						
Planned order releases		960			480									

Chapter Fifteen, Just-In-Time Systems

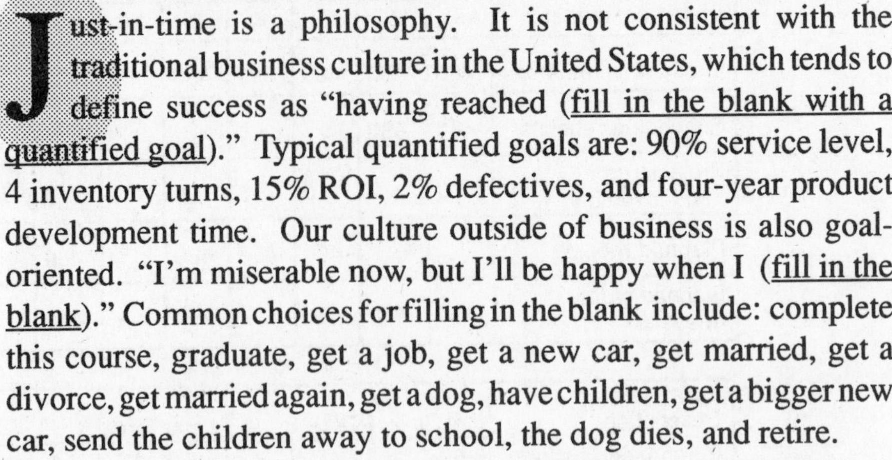

Just-in-time is a philosophy. It is not consistent with the traditional business culture in the United States, which tends to define success as "having reached (fill in the blank with a quantified goal)." Typical quantified goals are: 90% service level, 4 inventory turns, 15% ROI, 2% defectives, and four-year product development time. Our culture outside of business is also goal-oriented. "I'm miserable now, but I'll be happy when I (fill in the blank)." Common choices for filling in the blank include: complete this course, graduate, get a job, get a new car, get married, get a divorce, get married again, get a dog, have children, get a bigger new car, send the children away to school, the dog dies, and retire.

The problem of course, is that when we reach those goals, we find that we are not happy for very long. The JIT philosophy recognizes that enjoyment comes from the struggle, not the victory. Accordingly, many of the goals are unreachable, for example: zero inventory, zero defects. Success is measured in terms of being happy and fulfilled *while progressing* toward a goal. JIT performance measures are based on continuous improvement.

Reachable goals get in the way of continuous improvement. When we reach a goal, it is almost impossible to overcome the urge to stop. For example: "When I graduate, then I can stop learning." Of course, the world quickly passes us by, and we must begin again. Plus we will have to overcome the inertia of having stopped learning. The same cycle occurs in business: crisis, set goals for change, overcome inertia and resistance to change, reach goals, stop improvement, crisis.

In JIT, inventory reduction is primarily a process to stimulate continuous improvement. The cost of the effort involved to reduce inventory rarely pays for itself with reduced inventory investment. Such trade-off thinking is a natural part of our culture, but it ignores the real payoffs of reduced inventory: more compact operations, better visibility of problems, better communication, shorter manufacturing lead time, and faster response to market changes.

Characteristics of Just-in-Time Systems

- Pull method of material flow — kanban communication system
- Consistent high quality — total quality control
- Small lot size, short setup times — inventory reduction
- Uniform workstation loads — stable master schedules
- Standardized components, product focus — supplier partners
- Flexible work force — employee involvement
- Automated production — continuous improvement
- Preventive maintenance — eliminate sources of variation

Pull Method of Material Flow

The push method

- Associated with MRP
- Low volumes with low repeatability
- Variable material flow
- Schedule the receipt of raw materials
- Management authorizes production lots in advance of need

The pull method

- Associated with JIT
- Highly repetitive manufacturing processes
- Assemble-to-order with well-defined material flow
- Schedules the production to replace what was taken
- Authorization to produce comes from demand
- Closer control between inventory needs and production

Consistently High Quality

- Scrap and rework disrupt material flow in JIT systems.
- TQM and quality at the source are required by JIT systems.
- Workers are encouraged to expose quality problems and stop the line rather than pass on defects to others.

One cannot assume all workers are prepared to accept responsibility for quality. Management must *never* punish workers for stopping the line, even if they were wrong in stopping it. Such punishment will guarantee that the line will never stop again, no matter how poor the quality.

Small Lot Sizes

- Continuously reduce lot size. Goal is lot size = 1.

Reasons Small Lots Sizes Are Important

1. Reduce cycle inventory.
   - reduced investment, obsolescence
   - reduced floor space
   - improved communication
   - increased setup frequency makes it easier to improve setup times
   - reduced rework
2. Cut lead times.
   - faster response to market changes
   - better customer service
3. Achieve uniform workload.
   - accommodate mixed-model production
   - utilize capacities more efficiently
   - allow suppliers to produce using JIT

Short Setup Times

- Reduce setup time to less than ten minutes (single-digit setup)
- Required to realize the benefits of small lot sizes
- Close cooperation among engineering, management, and labor
- Worker involvement
- Long setups reduce productive time and throughput at bottleneck work centers.

Manufacturing efficiency is an obsolete performance measure. Since JIT workers must stop work upon reaching the quota (the material supply has been consumed), it is therefore impossible to improve manufacturing efficiency. The output is the same every day.

Fortunately, it is recognized that manufacturing efficiency has little to do with making money. Producing the wrong products with a very high manufacturing efficiency merely hastens bankruptcy.

Uniform Workstation Loads

- Produce the same type and number of units every day for an extended time period (typically a month).
- Creates a uniform daily demand at all work stations.
- Assembly lines are balanced to produce that quantity in less than the available time, leaving a capacity cushion.
- Must stop production upon reaching daily quota (operations runs out of materials at that point)
- Use the remaining time productively in terms of cross-training, organizing the work area, quality circles, but *never* send the workers home early (wastes resources).

Lot Size Options for a JIT Master Production Schedule

Option			Comment
Big-Lot Production			Setups = 3 per shift
Sedans	=	200	Do once per shift;
Coupes	=	150	high cycle inventories;
Wagons	=	100	lumpy requirements on feeder work stations
Mixed-model Assembly			Setups = 150 per shift
Sedans	=	4	Do 50 cycles per shift;
Coupes	=	3	low cycle inventories;
Wagons	=	2	smoother requirements on feeder work stations
Single-Unit Lot Sizes			Setups = 450 per shift
S-W-S-C-S-C-S-W-C			Do 50 cycles per shift;
			very low cycle inventories;
			most uniform flow on feeder work stations

The cycle repeats every nine cars. In each cycle there are 4 sedans (S), 3 coupes (c), and 2 wagons (W).

Standardization of Components and Work Methods

- Reduces the number of parts
- Increases repeatability
  - increased volume of fewer parts reduces cost per unit
- Reduces inventory/service part inventory
- Reduces number of parts purchased
  - reduces number of suppliers
  - builds stronger relationships with fewer suppliers
- Increases design reliability
  - fewer parts reduces the probability of failure
- Reduces design time
  - reuses library of approved standard designs

Close Supplier Ties

- JIT systems are dependent on good supplier performance
- Use suppliers that are geographically closer
- Improve relations with suppliers
- Reduce the number of suppliers
- Philosophy is to reduce inventory throughout the supplier chain, not just store it at another location.

Flexible Work Force

- Workers can perform more than one job.
- Workers can be shifted to relieve bottlenecks.
- Job rotation relieves boredom.

Product Focus

- High volume may justify dedication of an assembly line to one product, eliminating setup.
- Group technology can be used to identify a product family.
  - total volume sufficient to dedicate equipment
  - reduced changeover time because the products are similar

Automated Production

- Automation should be planned carefully

Preventive Maintenance

- Unplanned machine downtime can be very disruptive because successive operations are not buffered with work-in-process inventory.
- Preventive maintenance reduces the frequency and duration of machine downtime.
- Working two shifts instead of three allows time between shifts for preventive maintenance.
- Workers (instead of specialists) are responsible for routine maintenance of their own equipment.
  - more immediate attention to problems
  - better care of the equipment

Continuous Improvement

- Clear sailing implies the possibility of too much inventory and waste
- Reducing inventory is a process of exposing problems that must be solved in order to continuously improve.

The Kanban System

- A visible signal is the authorization to produce what has been consumed.

> Those of you who are old enough to remember when dairies delivered milk door to door, how did the "milkman" know how much milk to leave? He looked in the milk box. If there were three empty bottles in there, he left three full bottles. He returned the empties to the dairy, and they were washed and refilled. The billing record took the form of three hash marks on a card, and the customers were billed monthly for the total. It wasn't rocket science, but it worked. Today we would call this a kanban system.
>
> Notice that trust is a required part of this system. There is no six-part purchase order form to create a paper trail for every transaction.
>
> JIT's frequent deliveries require paperwork reduction. To issue purchase orders, match shipping documents and invoices and write a check for each delivery several times a day for each of hundreds of suppliers, well that would be chaos.

General Operating Rules

- Simple operating rules are designed to
  - facilitate the flow of materials
  - maintain control of inventory levels
- Discipline is required in following the rules, since the system will collapse if they are not followed.

Determining the Number of Containers (Kanban Card Sets)

"The number of authorized containers in a JIT system determines the amount of authorized inventory." p. 734

- Management must determine
  1. the size of the containers — lot size
  2. the number of containers

"The key to determining the number of containers required is to estimate accurately the average lead time needed to produce a container of parts." p. 734

- Lead time is a function of
  - w, waiting time at the production process plus waiting time for materials handling
  - p, processing time per container at the supplier station
- Amount of pipeline inventory equals the average demand during the lead time $\bar{D}_L = \bar{d}L$ where $\bar{d}$ = daily demand rate and L = lead time in days $= (\bar{w} + \bar{p})$
- Adjusting changes the amount of safety stock.
- The stocking level is $\bar{d}(\bar{w} + \bar{p})(1 + \alpha)$
- c = quantity in a container

The number of kanban card sets is:

$$k = \frac{d(\bar{w} + \bar{p})(1 + \alpha)}{c}$$

Other Kanban Signals

Container System

- An empty container signals the need to fill it.

Containerless Systems

- An empty storage area or painted space on the floor or work bench is the signal to produce what was taken.

JIT II

- An in-plant representative is employed by the supplier, but works in the customer's purchasing office.
- The in-plant representative is empowered to issue the customer's purchase orders to the supplier.

Benefits to Customer

1. Purchasing staff can work on other priorities
2. Improved communication with suppliers
3. Supplier's expertise is brought into early stages of product design
4. Reduced transaction costs

Benefits to Supplier

1. Eliminates sales effort
2. Improved communication with customers and customers engineers
3. Increased volume of business
4. Reduced transaction costs

JIT Systems in Services

- Repetitive, high-volume operations dealing with tangible items — food, mail, bills, insurance or loan applications

Instead of reducing inventory as a process for continuous improvement, reduce the number of employees doing a particular task. It is important that management find something productive for those removed from tasks to do. They must never fire these workers, or all cooperation required for productivity improvement will stop.

Strategic Implications of Just-In-Time Systems

Competitive Priorities

- Low cost
- Consistent quality
- Ability to provide customization depends on flexibility designed into the production system

Positioning Strategy

- Product focus

Operational Benefits

Operational Benefits of Just-in-Time Systems

- Reduce space requirements.
- Reduce inventory investment in purchased parts, raw materials, work in process, and finished goods.
- Reduce manufacturing lead times.
- Increase the productivity of direct labor employees, indirect support employees, and clerical staff.
- Increase equipment utilization.
- Reduce paperwork and require only simple planning systems.
- Set valid priorities for production scheduling.
- Encourage participation by the work force.
- Increase product quality.

- Goal is lot size of one
- Simplicity, flexibility
- Worker participation
- Improved quality

Implementation Issues

Organizational Considerations

Human Costs of JIT Systems

- Requires a high degree of regimentation
- Stress may build
- Lost sense of autonomy

Cooperation and Trust

"In a JIT system workers and first-line supervisors must take on responsibilities formerly assigned to middle managers and support staff." p. 742

- Organizational relationships must be reoriented to build cooperation and trust between the work force and management.

Reward Systems and Labor Classifications

- Performance measures and reward systems must be changed.
- Labor contracts must call for fewer labor classifications and greater worker flexibility.

Process Considerations

- Move work stations closer together
- Loading docks must handle more traffic, smaller shipments

Inventory and Scheduling

MPS Stability

- Work stations execute the same work schedule each day.
- Production rates are adjusted once per month.

Setups

- Must achieve significant reductions in setup times

Purchasing and Logistics

- Arrange frequent, small shipments
- Reduce the number of suppliers

Production and Inventory Management System Choice

Reorder Point Versus Material Requirements Planning Systems

- MRP outperforms ROP in discrete-item manufacturing environments producing to stock.
- Advantages increase as number of levels and lots sizes increase.

Material Requirements Planning Vs Just-in-Time Systems

- These methods are not mutually exclusive
- MRP II systems are good at
  - overall materials planning
  - data management
  - support information needs of other functions
- JIT systems
  - are more effective way to control material flow
  - maintain low levels of inventory
  - can be used to adjust production rates over time
  - work well for line flows
- Hybrid systems
  - MRP used for order release and coordinating with suppliers on long lead time items
  - JIT used for actual material flow on the shop floor

"The nature of the production process determines the appropriate system." p. 744

The Manufacturing Environment

- Reduced lot size and setup time will decrease investment and improve customer service in any system.

"A focus on continuous improvement is a key to shaping a manufacturing environment." p. 745

Multiple-Choice Questions

1. Just-in-time systems are also known as all of the following *except*:
   A. Just-in-case systems
   B. Stockless production
   C. Synchronous manufacturing
   D. Zero inventory
2. The material flow discipline used in JIT is called
   A. the push method.
   B. the pull method.
   C. the push, pull, or tow method.
   D. the work order method.
3. Firms that use JIT tend to have
   A. a competitive orientation with suppliers
   B. a process focus
   C. repetitive processes
   D. variable material flows
4. Advantages of small lot sizes include all of the following *except*
   A. reduced inventory investment.
   B. reduced lead times.
   C. reduced rework.
   D. reduced setup frequency.
5. A prerequisite for mixed-model production and small lot sizes is
   A. a two-card kanban system.
   B. fast setup and changeover.
   C. the use of quality circles.
   D. statistical process control.
6. A *single-digit setup* refers to
   A. a visible communication signal between labor and management.
   B. the lot size quantity.
   C. the number of setups that occur during a shift.
   D. the time required for changeover from one production lot to another.
7. In a JIT environment, when the production goes smoothly and the quota for the day is produced before the end of the work shift, all of the following should happen *except*
   A. continue production.
   B. cross-train workers.
   C. hold quality circle meetings.
   D. improve setup procedures.

(Multiple-choice answers are on Study Guide page 313.)

8. Mixed-model assembly is associated with
   A. big-lot production.
   B. small-lot production.
   C. single-unit lot sizes.
   D. long setup times.
9. Consistent, high quality is obtained in a JIT system by
   A. controlling quality at the source.
   B. increasing lot sizes.
   C. increasing line supervision.
   D. increasing the number of inspectors.
10. Which of the following is associated with JIT's close supplier ties?
    A. Increased inspection of incoming materials
    B. Reduced number of suppliers
    C. Short-term purchasing contracts
    D. Suppliers holding inventories
11. The most important reason for inventory reduction in JIT is
    A. it is a process for continuous improvement.
    B. it increases throughput capacity.
    C. it reduces inventory investment and holding costs.
    D. it reduces vulnerability to variable supplier lead times.
12. Which of the following is *not* a JIT implementation issue for managers?
    A. Cooperation and trust must replace adversarial management-labor relations.
    B. Decrease the number of labor classifications.
    C. Performance measures based on trade-offs establish when to stop improvement efforts.
    D. Workers will be trained to perform responsibilities formerly done by management and administrative staff.
13. Kanban refers to
    A. a visible signal to control the flow of material
    B. honest, open communications with suppliers
    C. reuse and recycling metal containers
    D. stopping lines to prevent production of defects
14. The key to shaping a manufacturing environment is
    A. a focus on continuous improvement.
    B. reduced lot sizes and setup times.
    C. reduced yield losses.
    D. the choice of production and inventory management system.

Problems

1. The Hama motorcycle company produces dirt bikes, street bikes, and touring bikes with the model names Llama, Yoka, and Mama, respectively. This month's master production schedule calls for the production of 54 Mama, 42 Yoga, and 30 Llama Hamas per seven-hour shift.

   a. What is the cycle time for the assembly line?

$$c = \frac{1}{r}$$

   b. If Hama uses mixed-model production, what is the batch size of each model?

2. The Hama company works two seven-hour shifts per day. It ships the motorcycles in very large expanded styrofoam packing crates which are produced JIT by a local supplier. The supplier's truck can carry eighteen of these crates at a time. The average lead time ($\overline{w} + \overline{p}$) is 1/2 day. The safety stock policy variable, α, is 14%. How many trucks (containers) are needed in this system?

Solutions

1. The Hama motorcycle company produces dirt bikes, street bikes, and touring bikes with model names Llama, Yoka, and Mama, respectively. This month's master production schedule calls for the production of 54 Mama, 42 Yoga, and 30 Llama Hamas per seven-hour shift.

   a. What is the cycle time for the assembly line?

   $$c = \frac{1}{r} = \frac{7 \text{ hours}}{126 \text{ motorcycles}} = 0.0555 \text{ hour/motorcycle}$$

   $$= 3.33 \text{ minutes/motorcycle}$$

   b. If Hama uses mixed-model production, what is the batch size of each model?

   Dirt bike, Llama Hama = 9
   Street bike, Yoka Hama = 7
   Touring bike, Mama Hama = 5

   Repeat the sequence six times per shift.

2. The Hama company works two seven-hour shifts per day. It ships the motorcycles in very large expanded styrofoam packing crates which are produced JIT by a local supplier. The supplier's truck can carry 18 of these crates at a time. The average lead time ($\overline{w} + \overline{p}$) is 1/2 day. The safety stock policy variable, α, is 14%. How many trucks (containers) are needed in this system?

   $$k = \frac{d(\overline{w} + \overline{p})(1 + \alpha)}{c} = \frac{252(0.5)(1.14)}{18} = 7.98 \text{ or } 8 \text{ trucks}$$

Multiple Choice Answers

1. A	8. B
2. B	9. A
3. C	10. B
4. D	11. A
5. B	12. C
6. D	13. A
7. A	14. A

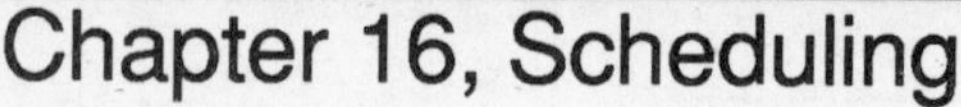

Chapter 16, Scheduling

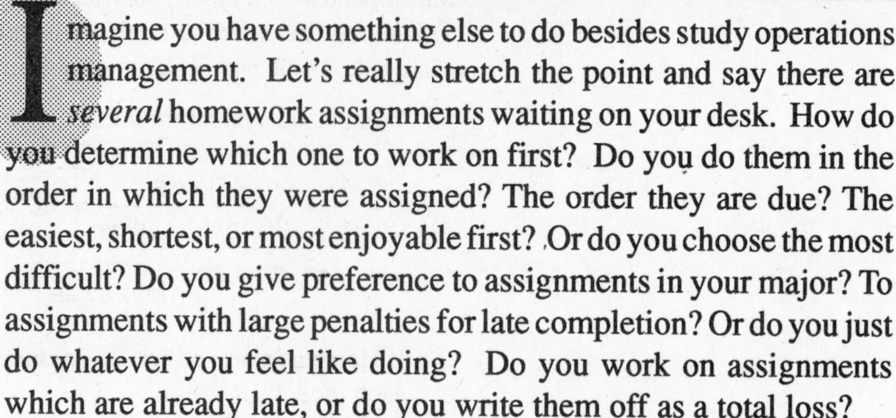

Imagine you have something else to do besides study operations management. Let's really stretch the point and say there are *several* homework assignments waiting on your desk. How do you determine which one to work on first? Do you do them in the order in which they were assigned? The order they are due? The easiest, shortest, or most enjoyable first? Or do you choose the most difficult? Do you give preference to assignments in your major? To assignments with large penalties for late completion? Or do you just do whatever you feel like doing? Do you work on assignments which are already late, or do you write them off as a total loss?

It does not matter in which order the work is accomplished, the total effort will be the same. However, the grades earned will differ. If you do the work in the wrong order, some assignments will be done early, and others will be very late. There is a direct analogy with scheduling operations in manufacturing. A large job shop may have a backlog of 12,000 orders of which 6,000 are late. Which job has top priority?

How did your college decide to schedule this course at this particular time? How did you determine your class schedule this semester? Did you have difficulty coordinating your class schedule with work, family, or play? These are scheduling decisions typical of service operations.

Two basic types of scheduling:

- Work-force scheduling — determines when human resources are available for work
- Operations scheduling — assigns workers to tasks or jobs to machine work centers

Scheduling in Manufacturing

"Operations schedules are short-term plans designed to implement the master production schedule." p. 753

Gantt Charts

- An activity progress chart graphically displays the current status of each job relative to its due date.
- A machine chart depicts the sequence of work for each machine and can be used to monitor progress.

Performance Measures

"In general, for n jobs, each requiring m machines, there are $(n!)^m$ possible schedules." p. 754

> Let's estimate the number of possible schedules for 12,000 jobs requiring an average of 20 operations each.
>
> $(12{,}000!)^{20}$ = *ERROR*!
>
> There are too many combinations to enunumerate. Optimization is impossible.

Commonly Used Performance Measures of Operations Schedules

1. Job flow time — the time a job spends in the shop
2. Makespan — for a group of jobs, the time between the start of the first job and the finish of the last job
3. Past due
   - the amount of time late, average job lateness
   - the percentage of jobs completed late
4. Work-in-process or pipeline inventory expressed in units, number of jobs, dollar value, or weeks of supply
5. Total inventory — the sum of scheduled receipts and on-hand inventory
6. Utilization — the percentage of paid time spent productively

Job Shop Dispatching

Priority Sequencing Rules

Which customers or jobs should have top priority?

1. Critical ratio (CR) — the ratio of the time remaining until a job is needed (need date – current date) divided by the total work time for all of the remaining operations, including setup, processing, move, and *planned* queuing times.

   $$CR = \frac{\text{Dute date} - \text{Today's date}}{\text{Total shop time remaining}}$$

   The *smallest* critical ratio has the highest priority. Note that if a job is behind schedule, it has high priority and will spend *less* than the *planned* amount of time in the queue. It will catch up. If it is ahead of schedule, the critical ratio will be large. Other jobs will be done first. The job will spend more than the planned time in the queue. Critical ratio adjusts priorities to match the due date with the date of need.

Job-shops often use EDD. They typically have large work-in-process inventory and low utilization rates. Job shops compete on the basis of product flexibility. Often the work is make-to-order, so customers are concerned with on-time completion.
Chances are you use EDD to prioritize your homework.

2. Earliest due date (EDD) — The job with the earliest due date has highest priority. This is a natural for use with MRP systems, which match due dates with dates of need.
   EDD performs well with respect to:
   - minimizing percentage of jobs past due
   - minimizing the maximum amount of time a job is late.

   EDD does not do well with respect to:
   - job flow time
   - work-in-process inventory
   - utilization.
3. First come, first served (FCFS) — The job that arrives first has the highest priority. This is the most common queue discipline in nonessential services. It is perceived as being fair because it tends to even out the waiting time. In other words, customers will all have to wait about the same amount of time for service. It does not consider job urgency, so FCFS would not be the basis for getting help in an inner-city hospital emergency room when the moon is full. Because it does not consider job priority, FCFS is rarely used in manufacturing operations. FCFS performs poorly with respect to all performance measures.

SPT is useful in "clearing the deck" ... quickly completing lots of small tasks and getting them out of the way so you can work on the big tasks. Problems arise when you're so swamped with details, you can't get around to the big tasks. The advantages of this rule diminish as the load increases.

4. Shortest processing time (SPT) — The job requiring the shortest processing time has the highest priority.
   SPT performs well with respect to:
   - average job flow time
   - work-in-process inventory
   - minimizing percentage of jobs past due
   - utilization

   SPT does not do well with respect to:
   - minimizing the maximum amount of time a job is late
   - minimizing total inventory (it pushes work to finished goods before it is needed)
   - adjusting schedules when due date changes (due date is not used in the calculation of priority).
5. Slack per remaining operations (S/RO) — The job with the *least* slack per remaining operation has highest priority. The effect is similar to EDD with added advantages of a global (more than one work center) view and accounting for the duration of the jobs.

Sequencing Operations for One Machine

Single-Dimension Rules

- FCFS, EDD, SPT
- Determines priority for only those jobs that are physically present at a single work station.

Exercise:

A machine shop has three machines, a Sandirooski, a Donnaramma and the Laurelmeister. Use earliest due date, and shortest processing time priority rules to determine priorities for the following work at the Sandirooski:

Job	Operation Time at Sandirooski in Days	Time Remaining to Due Date in Days
A	3.6	15
B	2.1	20
C	6.3	17
D	3.8	8
E	4.0	14
F	3.2	34

(Solution is on Study Guide page 318.)

How important is the choice of priority dispatching rules to the effectiveness of the operating system?

- SPT pushes more jobs through the system quickly
  - This is an advantage only if jobs can be delivered and revenue collected earlier than the due date.
  - Some lengthy jobs will be very late.
- EDD performs well with respect to the percentage of jobs past due and the variance of hours past due.

Multiple-Dimension Rules

- CR, S/RO
- Considers information about succeeding operations before setting the priority

Exercise:

A machine shop has three machines, a Sandirooski, a Donnaramma and the Laurelmeister. Use critical ratio and least slack per remaining operation priority rules to determine priorities for the work at the Sandirooski:

Job	Operation Time at Sandirooski in Days	Time Remaining to Due Date in Days	# of Operations Remaining Incl. Sandirooski	Shop Time Remaining Incl. Sandirooski
A	3.6	15	6	8.4
B	2.1	20	5	12.6
C	6.3	17	3	11.5
D	3.8	8	2	8.0
E	4.0	14	7	5.0
F	3.2	34	4	7.4

(Solution is on Study Guide page 318.)

Multiple-Workstation Scheduling

- Each operation is scheduled independently.
- When a job is completed, the scheduling rule is applied to a changing queue of jobs to determine which of the jobs will be processed next.

Sequencing Operations for a Two-Station Flow Shop

With a single work station, the makespan is the same regardless of the job sequence, but with two work stations, makespan will vary.

- Special case with
  - two work stations, say, sanding and painting
  - routing for all jobs is the same, (always sand then paint, never paint then sand)
  - performance criteria is to minimize makespan

Johnson's Rule

1. Find the shortest process time among the jobs not yet scheduled.
2. If the shortest process time is on the first work station, schedule the job as early as possible in the sequence. If the shortest process time is on the second work station, schedule the job as late as possible in the sequence.
3. That job has been scheduled, so eliminate it from further consideration. If jobs remain to schedule, go to step 1; if not, stop.

Solutions to Exercises on Study Guide pages 316 and 317.

Note that if SPT is used, Job D will certainly be late. It is due in 8 days, but will not even be through the first work center in 12.7 days. SPT reduces WIP inventory, but does not consider due dates in setting priorities.

Earliest Due Date

Job	Due Date	Priority
A	15	3
B	20	5
C	17	4
D	8	1
E	14	2
F	34	6

Shortest Processing Time

Job	Processing Time	Priority
A	3.6	3
B	2.1	1
C	6.3	6
D	3.8	4
E	4.0	5
F	3.2	2

Critical Ratio

Job	Priority Index	Priority
A	1.79	4
B	1.59	3
C	1.48	2
D	1.00	1
E	2.80	5
F	4.59	6

Slack/Remaining Operation

Job	Priority Index	Priority
A	1.10	2
B	1.48	4
C	1.83	5
D	0.00	1
E	1.29	3
F	6.65	6

Exercise

Buffy and Chip are Denver DINKs (double income, no kids) and have several items around the apartment that need to be sanded and painted. The only time to do the work is Sunday morning. The DINKs like to sleep in as late as possible on Sunday, but they do not want to miss the Broncos versus the Browns football game. It is an away game and has an 11:30 a.m. kickoff. The pair have learned they do not work well together on such projects, so they will specialize. Buffy will sand and Chip will paint. When is the latest time Buffy can get started sanding so that Chip will not miss the kickoff?

Item	Sand	Paint
Anvil	15 min.	10 min.
BMW	30 min.	20 min.
Chair	20 min.	25 min.
Desk	30 min.	30 min.
Exercise Bike	40 min.	15 min.
Futon	5 min.	15 min.

(Solution is on Study Guide page 320.)

Labor-Limited Environments

- Resource constraint is the amount of labor available
- Must determine job sequence (as with machine-limited environment)
- Added dimension — must assign workers to work stations

Labor Assignment Rules

1. Assign labor to the workstation having the most senior job
2. Assign labor to the workstation having the most jobs
3. Assign labor to the workstation having the most standard hours
4. Assign labor to the workstation having the earliest due date job

What scheduling methods can be used to manage the capacity of a service system?

Scheduling in Services

- Services can not buffer demand uncertainties with inventory.
- Demand for services is difficult to predict.
- Scheduling systems can facilitate the capacity management of service providers.

Scheduling Customer Demand

Appointments

- Assigns customers to specific times for service.
- Advantages
  + timely customer service
  + high utilizations of servers
- Disadvantages
  – customers expect adherance to the schedule
  – vulnerable to late arrivals of no-shows

Reservations

- Similar to appointment systems
- Customer occupies or uses facilities associated with the service. Examples include hotel rooms, airline seats, and classroom seats.
- Downpayments reduce no-shows

Backlogs

- Less precise than appointments or reservations
- Usual rule is first-come, first-served

Scheduling the Work Force

- Translate the staffing plan into work schedules for each employee.
- Work-force capacity available each day must meet or exceed daily work-force requirements
- Work-force schedule reallocates employees as requirements change

Constraints

- Technical constraints
  - resources provided by the staffing plan
  - requirements placed on the operating system
- Other constraints
  - legal
    . requirements for licensed or certified persons
    . examples include hospitals and nuclear reactors
  - behavioral considerations
    . rotating schedule
    . fixed schedule

Rotating schedules have the advantage of sharing the misery. Consider a three-shift example, such as a hospital or capital-intensive manufacturer. With a fixed schedule, senior and experienced personnel will tend to be grouped together on the first shift. The third shift may be made up entirely of new hires, with no one who really knows how to do the work. Third shift output and quality will suffer.

With a rotating schedule, there is no particular advantage in being on the first shift, because soon it will rotate to the second, then third. Expertise can be spread throughout the shifts. Periodically, all workers will work the first shift with management, so face-to-face communication is possible.

There are disadvantages associated with rotating shifts. It causes difficulty in planning family events. Perhaps most significant is the time required to become accustomed to a new shift. It is not easy to change eating and sleeping patterns. Workers turn into zombies for a while after changing shifts. That is neither productive nor safe.

Solution to exercise on Study Guide Page 318.

The shortest processing time is sanding the futon, 5 minutes. Sanding is the *first* of the two-operation process, so place the futon as early as possible in the job sequence:

Futon					

The next shortest task is painting the anvil, 10 minutes. That occurs on the *second* work center so the anvil is scheduled *last* in the job sequence.

Futon					Anvil

The next shortest task is painting the exercise bike, 15 minutes. This will take the same amount of time as sanding the anvil and painting the futon, but since those jobs have already been scheduled, they have been eliminated from further consideration. There is really no tie here. Painting is the second work center, so the exercise bike is placed as late in the sequence as possible, which is the fifth position.

Futon				Exercise Bike	Anvil

There are two tasks which tie as the next shortest tasks. Painting the BMW and sanding the chair each take 20 minutes. This tie is easily resolved. Simply place the chair as early as possible and the BMW as late as possible in the sequence.

Futon	Chair		BMW	Exercise Bike	Anvil

A point that is often missed is that once the work sequence is established, it governs the priority of the jobs at *both* of the work centers.

Finally, there is a tie as the next shortest task at 30 minutes. They are sanding and painting the desk. Since there is only one position in the sequence remaining, it doesn't really matter. The desk is third in the sequence.

Futon	Chair	Desk	BMW	Exercise Bike	Anvil

Make a Gantt chart for the work, starting at time zero:

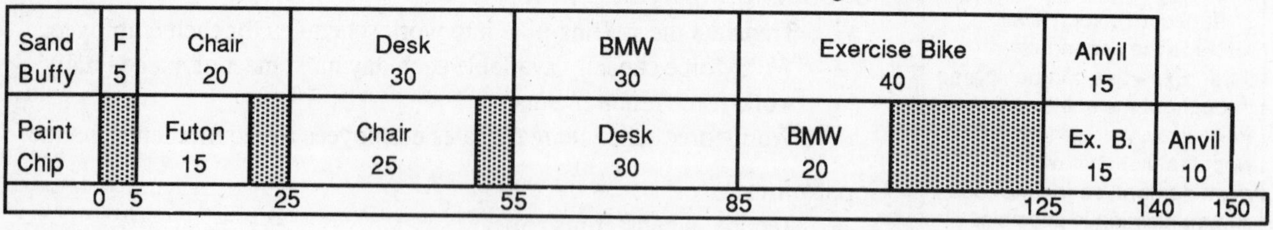

Sand Buffy	F 5	Chair 20	Desk 30	BMW 30	Exercise Bike 40	Anvil 15

Paint Chip	(idle)	Futon 15	(idle)	Chair 25	(idle)	Desk 30	BMW 20	(idle)	Ex. B. 15	Anvil 10

Time: 0 5 25 55 85 125 140 150

If the kickoff is at 11:30 a.m., Buffy must start 150 minutes before that, which is at 9:00 a.m. If Buffy does the work in the opposite sequence, A-E-B-D-C-F, her work will still take 140 minutes, but she will have to get started at 8:35 a.m. because the makespan will increase to 175 minutes.

Developing a Work-Force Schedule

The method presented has the objective of creating a work schedule so that all of the employees will have two consecutive days off per week. They won't all have the *same* two days off, but when they do have time off, they'll take two days in a row. We want to accomplish this without incurring great amounts of slack capacity. That means we don't want to have lots of folks standing around just so they can work five days in a row.

The key to understanding this method lies in recognizing there are *two* examples shown in the text. Example 16.4 on page 768 is consistent with the Final Schedule Table 16.3 on page 770. Make sure you have these open in front of you before you proceed. Got it? Okay, on Table 16.3 for Wednesday, see there are ten Xs, indicating that everybody is scheduled to work. The table shows the capacity of workers is ten. However, we really only need eight workers. See the second to the bottom row labeled "Requirements (*R*)."

Now compare that "Requirements" row on Table 16.3 with the first row of numbers in Example 16.4. See? They are the same:

M	T	W	Th	F	S	Su
6	4	(8)	9	10	3	2

Now look at the requirements that are used when we go through the first step of the method on page 768:

M	T	W	Th	F	S	Su
8	9	(2)	12	7	4	2

Different ... right? Okay, now we have established that we are looking at two altogether different schedules. Example 16.4 shows the solution to the Amalgamated Parcel Service, so there is no point in my using space to repeat it here. Besides, I'd probably type a wrong number and mess up everybody. Instead, lets spend a little time and space with the example on page 768.

<u>Step 1</u> of the method identifies the day(s) of the week when the requirements are lowest. In this example, that is Wednesday *and* Sunday. We need hardly anyone on those days, so someone should take time off. But Wednesday and Sunday are not consecutive days. Let's look at the consecutive pairs of days that involve Wednesday and Sunday.

T and W require 9 and 2 workers; a total of 11 workers.

W and Th require 2 and 12 workers; a total of 14 workers.

S and Su require 4 and 2 workers; a total of **6** workers.

Su and M require 2 and 8 workers; a total of 10 workers.

<u>Step 2</u> ...there is no tie. S and Su are the lowest *pair* of days.

<u>Step 3</u> ...give someone, say Alyson, S and Su off. That means Alyson will work on M T W Th F.

The original requirements were:

M	T	W	Th	F	S	Su
8	9	2	12	7	[4	2]

but now that Alyson is working M T W Th F the unfilled requirements are:

M	T	W	Th	F	S	Su
7	8	1	11	6	[4	2]

S and Su are still the pair of days with the lowest unfilled requirements, so Alissa will work M T W Th F. The unfilled requirements are:

M	T	W	Th	F	S	Su
6	7	0	10	5	4	2

S and Su are *still* the pair of days with the lowest unfilled requirements. Alice will work M T W Th F. The unfilled requirements are:

M	T	W	Th	F	S	Su
5	6	0	9	4	4	2

S and Su are now tied with T and W for the lowest unfilled requirements (6), but S and Su are preferred in the tie breaker, so let's give Allen those days off. Allen will work M T W Th F. The unfilled requirements are:

M	T	W	Th	F	S	Su
4	5	0	8	3	4	2

Now T and W are the pair of days with the lowest unfilled requirements. Nile will work M Th F S Su. Bad luck, Nile. The unfilled requirements are:

M	T	W	Th	F	S	Su
3	5	0	7	2	3	1

S and Su are now tied with Su and M for the lowest unfilled requirements (4), but S and Su are preferred in the tie breaker, so let's give those days off to Alona. Alona will work M T W Th F. The unfilled requirements are:

M	T	W	Th	F	S	Su
2	4	0	6	1	3	1

Now Su and M are the pair of days with the lowest unfilled requirements (3). Alynn will work T W Th F S. The unfilled requirements are:

M	T	W	Th	F	S	Su
2	3	0	5	0	2	1

F and S are the pair of days with the lowest unfilled requirements (2). Alvin will work M T W Th Su. The unfilled requirements are:

M	T	W	Th	F	S	Su
1	2	0	4	0	2	0

Su and M are the pair of days with the lowest unfilled requirements (1). Albert will work T W Th F S. The unfilled requirements are:

M	T	W	Th	F	S	Su
1	1	0	3	0	1	0

S and Su are the pair of days with the lowest unfilled requirements (1). Alma will work M T W Th F. The unfilled requirements are:

M	T	W	Th	F	S	Su
0	0	0	2	0	1	0

Su and M are the pair of days with the lowest unfilled requirements (0). Alicia will work T W Th F S. The unfilled requirements are:

M	T	W	Th	F	S	Su
0	0	0	1	0	0	0

S and Su are the pair of days with the lowest unfilled requirements (0). Alex will work M T W Th F. There are no unfilled requirements.

	M	T	W	Th	F	S	Su
Alyson	X	X	X	X	X	O	O
Alissa	X	X	X	X	X	O	O
Alice	X	X	X	X	X	O	O
Allen	X	X	X	X	X	O	O
Nile	X	O	O	X	X	X	X
Alona	X	X	X	X	X	O	O
Alynn	O	X	X	X	X	X	O
Alvin	X	X	X	X	O	O	X
Albert	O	X	X	X	X	X	O
Alma	X	X	X	X	X	O	O
Alicia	O	X	X	X	X	X	O
Alex	X	X	X	X	X	O	O
Total	9	11	11	12	11	4	2
Req'd	8	9	2	12	7	4	2

We will have lots of idle time on Wednesdays!

Multiple-Choice Questions

1. Assigning jobs to machines or workers to jobs is
   A. backlogging.
   B. operations scheduling.
   C. utilization.
   D. work-force scheduling.

2. The ________________ graphically displays the current status of each *job* relative to its due date and its scheduled completion date.
   A. dispatch list
   B. machine chart
   C. program evaluation and review technique
   D. progress chart

3. The percentage of work time productively spent by a machine or worker is called
   A. efficiency.
   B. job flow time.
   C. makespan.
   D. utilization.

4. Which of the following is a multiple-dimension priority sequencing rule?
   A. Critical ratio
   B. Earliest due date
   C. First come, first served
   D. Shortest processing time

5. Which of the following priority sequencing rules tends to reduce work-in-process inventory, but not total inventory?
   A. Critical ratio
   B. Earliest due date
   C. First come, first served
   D. Shortest processing time

6. Which of the following priority sequencing rules will not change the priority of a job when its due date changes?
   A. Critical ratio
   B. Earliest due date
   C. Least slack per remaining operation
   D. Shortest processing time

7. A college student who wishes to minimize the percentage of homework assignments that are completed late should
   A. use earliest due date job priority rule.
   B. use first come, first served job priority rule.
   C. use Johnson's job priority rule.
   D. use shortest processing time rule.

8. Which of the following priority sequencing rules is rarely used in manufacturing operations because it performs poorly with respect to all performance measures?
   A. Earliest due date
   B. First come, first served
   C. Least slack per remaining operation
   D. Shortest processing time

9. The job sequencing rule developed by Johnson for two-work station flow shops optimizes which of the following performance measures?
   A. Inventory
   B. Makespan
   C. Past due
   D. Utilization of the first work station

10. Which of the following statements is true with respect to scheduling labor-limited or machine-limited environments?
    A. Choice of labor assignment rules in labor-limited environments has little effect on performance.
    B. Labor-limited environments are simpler to schedule because of the relative flexibility of humans.
    C. Scheduling in labor-limited environments assumes that the worker will stay at a work station for the duration of a work shift.
    D. Scheduling in machine-limited environments assumes that a job never has to wait for lack of a worker.

11. Which of the following methods is commonly used for scheduling customer demand for college classes?
    A. Appointments
    B. Backlogs
    C. Critical ratio
    D. Reservations

12. Which of the following is a *technical* constraint of work-force schedules?
    A. Legal requirements for the presence of licensed personnel
    B. Resources provided by the staffing plan
    C. Rotating schedules
    D. Union contract requirements for consecutive days off

(Multiple-choice answers are on Study Guide page 327.)

Problems

1a. Use Johnson's rule to determine the job sequence that will minimize makespan for a two-work station flow shop.

Job	Work Sta. #1	Work Sta. #2
A	25 min.	10 min.
B	10 min.	20 min.
C	20 min.	5 min.
D	15 min.	20 min.
E	20 min.	25 min.
F	30 min.	25 min.

b. What is the makespan?

2. Law student Perot Bono does research for the law firm of Dewey, Cheetham and Howe for free. The partners have asked him to complete the following six research jobs by the given court dates. Perot labeled the jobs in the order the assignments were received, A, B, C, and so forth.

Job	Research Time, Days	Days Until Court Date
A	5	12
B	8	27
C	2	30
D	7	18
E	3	25
F	4	6

a. Use earliest due date to determine the job sequence.

b. Use shortest processing time to determine the job sequence.

3a. Which priority sequencing rule, FCFS, EDD, or SPT results in the lowest percentage of late jobs?

b. Which priority sequencing rule results in the lowest average job lateness?

FCFS	Job	Due	Comp.	Late
	A	12	5	0
	B			
	C			
	D			
	E			
	F			

EDD	Job	Due	Comp.	Late
	F	6	4	0
	___			
	___			
	___			
	___			
	___			

SPT	Job	Due	Comp.	Late
	C	30	2	0
	___			
	___			
	___			
	___			
	___			

4. Use critical ratio and least slack per remaining operation to determine the job sequence for this work station.

Job	Operation Time at Work Station in Days	Time Remaining to Due Date, Days	# of Operations Remaining Incl. This Work Station	Shop Time Remaining Incl. This Work Station
A	2.6	8	3	8.4
B	1.8	20	5	8.6
C	4.3	12	3	13.5
D	3.8	18	2	8.0
E	2.0	14	7	9.0
F	3.2	17	4	7.4

Critical Ratio

Job	Priority Index	Priority
A		
B		
C		
D		
E		
F		

Slack/Remaining Operation

Job	Priority Index	Priority
A		
B		
C		
D		
E		
F		

5. Develop a work-force schedule for Alyson, Buffy, Chip, Dale, Eva, Fred, and George so that they each can take two consecutive days off. The required capacities of workers each day are:

M	T	W	Th	F	S	Su
6	4	5	3	6	3	2

S and Su are the pair of days with the lowest unfilled requirements, so let's give Alyson those days off. Alyson will work M T W Th F. The unfilled requirements are:

M	T	W	Th	F	S	Su
5	3	4	2	5	3	2

__ and __ are the pair of days with the lowest unfilled requirements, so lets give Buffy those days off. Buffy will work______________. The unfilled requirements are:

M	T	W	Th	F	S	Su
__	__	__	__	__	__	__

__ and __ are the pair of days with the lowest unfilled requirements, so lets give Chip those days off. Chip will work ______________. The unfilled requirements are:

M	T	W	Th	F	S	Su
__	__	__	__	__	__	__

__ and __ are the pair of days with the lowest unfilled requirements, so let's give Dale those days off. Dale will work ______________. The unfilled requirements are:

M	T	W	Th	F	S	Su
__	__	__	__	__	__	__

M and T, T and W, W and Th, and Th and F are *all* now tied for the lowest unfilled requirements (2). The S, Su tie breaker doesn't help us, so let's arbitrarily give Eva W and Th off. Eva will work M T F S Su. The unfilled requirements are:

M	T	W	Th	F	S	Su
__	__	__	__	__	__	__

Now M and T, Th and F, S and Su, and Su and M are all tied, but S and Su win the tie breaker, so let's give Fred those days off. Fred will work ______________. The unfilled requirements are:

M	T	W	Th	F	S	Su
__	__	__	__	__	__	__

There are a large number of ties now, but only two work schedules will span __ and __ within 5 days. They are ________ or________.

Solutions

Multiple Choice Answers	
1. B	8. B
2. D	9. B
3. D	10. D
4. A	11. D
5. D	12. B
6. D	
7. A	

1a. Use Johnson's rule to determine the job sequence that will minimize makespan for a two-work station flow shop.

Job	Work Sta. #1	Work Sta. #2
A	25 min.	10 min.
B	10 min.	20 min.
C	20 min.	5 min.
D	15 min.	20 min.
E	20 min.	25 min.
F	30 min.	25 min.

B	D	E	F	A	C

b. What is the makespan?

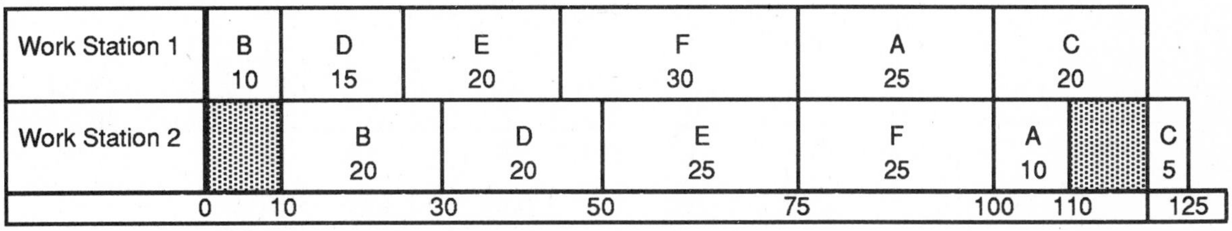

Work Station 1	B 10	D 15	E 20	F 30	A 25	C 20	
Work Station 2	(idle)	B 20	D 20	E 25	F 25	A 10	(idle) C 5
	0	10	30	50	75	100	110 125

2. Law student Perot Bono does research for the law firm of Dewey, Cheetham and Howe for free. The partners have asked him to complete the following six research jobs by the given court dates. Perot labeled the jobs in the order the assignments were received, A, B, C, and so forth.

Job	Research Time, Days	Days Until Court Date
A	5	12
B	8	27
C	2	30
D	7	18
E	3	25
F	4	6

a. Use earliest due date to determine the job sequence.

F	A	D	E	B	C

b. Use shortest processing time to determine the job sequence.

C	E	F	A	D	B

3a. In Problem 2, which priority sequencing rule results in the lowest percentage of late jobs?

b. Which priority sequencing rule results in the lowest average job lateness?

FCFS	Job	Due	Comp.	Late	
	A	12	5	0	
	B	27	13	0	a. 2 of 6 jobs late = **33.3%**
	C	30	15	0	
	D	18	22	4	b. 27 days late/6 jobs =
	E	25	25	0	average of **4.5 days** late
	F	6	29	23	

EDD	Job	Due	Comp.	Late	
	F	6	4	0	
	A	12	9	0	a. 0 of 6 jobs late = **0.0%**
	D	18	16	0	
	E	25	19	0	b. 0 days late/6 jobs =
	B	27	27	0	average of **0.0 days** late
	C	30	29	0	

SPT	Job	Due	Comp.	Late	
	C	30	2	0	
	E	25	5	0	a. 4 of 6 jobs late = **66.7%**
	F	6	9	3	
	A	12	14	2	b. 10 days late/6 jobs =
	D	18	21	3	average of **1.67 days** late
	B	27	29	2	

4. Use critical ratio and least slack per remaining operation to determine the job sequence for this work station.

Job	Operation Time at Work Station in Days	Time Remaining to Due Date, Days	# of Operations Remaining Incl. This Work Station	Shop Time Remaining Incl. This Work Station
A	2.6	8	3	8.4
B	1.8	20	5	8.6
C	4.3	12	3	13.5
D	3.8	18	2	8.0
E	2.0	14	7	9.0
F	3.2	17	4	7.4

Critical Ratio

Job	Priority Index	Priority
A	0.95	2
B	2.33	6
C	0.89	1
D	2.25	4
E	1.56	3
F	2.30	5

Slack/Remaining Operation

Job	Priority Index	Priority
A	– 0.13	2
B	2.28	4
C	– 0.50	1
D	5.00	6
E	0.71	3
F	2.40	5

5. Develop a work-force schedule for Alyson, Buffy, Chip, Dale, Eva, Fred, and George so that they each can take two consecutive days off. The required capacity of workers each day are:

M	T	W	Th	F	S	Su
6	4	5	3	6	3	2

S and Su are the pair of days with the lowest unfilled requirements, so let's give Alyson those days off. Alyson will work M T W Th F. The unfilled requirements are:

M	T	W	Th	F	S	Su
5	3	4	2	5	3	2

S and Su are the pair of days with the lowest unfilled requirements, so let's give Buffy those days off. Buffy will work M T W Th F. The unfilled requirements are:

M	T	W	Th	F	S	Su
4	2	3	1	4	3	2

W and Th are the pair of days with the lowest unfilled requirements, so let's give Chip those days off. Chip will work M T F S Su. The unfilled requirements are:

M	T	W	Th	F	S	Su
3	1	3	1	3	2	1

S and Su are the pair of days with the lowest unfilled requirements, so let's give Dale those days off. Dale will work M T W Th F. The unfilled requirements are:

M	T	W	Th	F	S	Su
2	0	2	0	2	2	1

M and T, T and W, W and Th, and Th and F are *all* now tied for the lowest unfilled requirements (2). The S, Su tie breaker doesn't help us, so let's arbitrarily give Eva W and Th off. Eva will work M T F S Su. The unfilled requirements are:

M	T	W	Th	F	S	Su
1	0	2	0	1	1	0

Now M and T, Th and F, S and Su, and Su and M are all tied, but S and Su win the tie breaker, so let's give Fred those days off. Fred will work M T W Th F. The unfilled requirements are:

M	T	W	Th	F	S	Su
0	0	1	0	0	1	0

There are a large number of ties now, but only two work schedules will span W and S within 5 days. They are T W Th F S or W Th F S Su. Since it doesn't matter to us, let's ask George which he prefers.

Chapter Seventeen, Managing Complex Projects

Everyone works on projects. Planning major construction activities, marketing new products, preparing annual reports and budgets, fund raising, designing training programs, research and development, elections, getting married, moving, planning parties or sporting events, even writing study guides can be viewed as projects. Perhaps the most pervasive type of project is the implementation of change. The commitment to continuous improvement requires implementation of many changes. Chances of success increase when the change is carefully planned, scheduled and controlled using project management techniques.

What tools are available to schedule and control projects?

Managing Projects

"We define **a project** as an interrelated set of activities that has a definite starting and ending point and that results in a unique product or service." p. 787

This aspect (disbanding upon completion) of project work can be unnerving. Unless career paths are determined in advance, participation in a project can be the kiss-of-death to your career. During a project, the regular duties of an employee are taken over by others. When the project is completed, there often is no job to return to.

Projects also get a bad name because in many firms, when it is desired to ease someone out, they are assigned to a special project. These special projects don't really have any duties associated with them. They are just a means of providing the employee some time and company resources to conduct a job search.

The career-ending nature of projects is well known among experienced workers. So if you ask a veteran employee to work on a special JIT implementation project, don't be surprised to see them run screaming into the streets.

- Goal oriented. The project team disbands upon completion.
- Usually, the activities to be performed are unique.
- Many team members will not be associated with the project for its full duration.
- Rewards
  - excitement of dynamic work
  - satisfaction of solving challenging problems
  - status of membership on an elite team
  - opportunity to work with and learn from skilled professionals
- For large projects, Gantt charts are difficult to work with.
- Gantt charts don't directly recognize precedence relationships.
- Gantt charts don't identify critical activities.
- PERT and CPM visually display a network diagram consisting of nodes and arcs that depict the activities and their precedence relationships.
- PERT was developed to handle uncertain project activity durations.
- CPM uses a single time estimate for project activities.
- Differences between PERT and CPM are minor, so this text refers to them collectively as PERT/CPM.

Network Methods

Describing the Project

- Include a clear statement of the project's end point.
- Project description reflects only the level of detail needed to make scheduling and resource allocation decisions.

"An **activity** is the smallest unit of work effort consuming both time and resources that the project manager can schedule and control. A **precedence relationship** determines a sequence for undertaking activities..." p. 789

Diagramming the Network

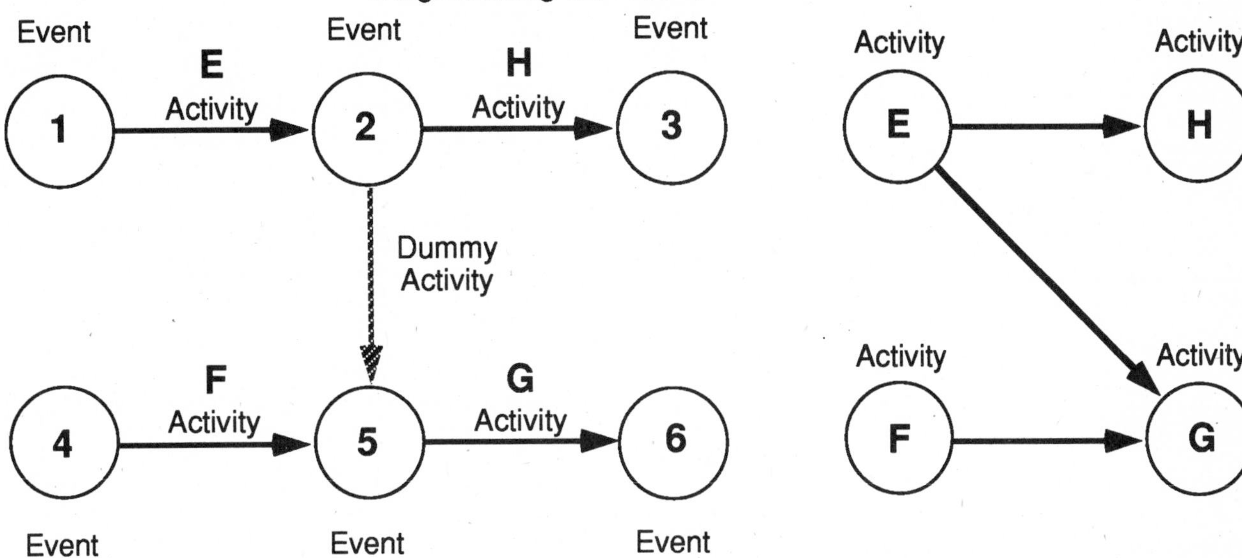

(a) AOA approach: Activity H cannot take place until activity E is completed. Activity G cannot take place until E, F, and dummy are completed.

(b) AON approach: Activity H cannot take place until activity E is completed. Activity G cannot take place until both E and F are completed.

In the AOA approach, dummy activities have no duration and serve only to indicate precedence relationships. Note that if we were to eliminate the dummy and merge events 2 and 5 into one event, that would not accurately represent the situation. If we drew it that way, it would be interpreted that activity H cannot take place until *both* E and F are competed. We desire to show that H can begin when *only* E is completed.

In the AON approach, dummy activities are never required. The AON approach is easier to draw. *Any* project made up of activities with definite beginning and ending points can be modeled by either of these approaches.

Which activities determine the duration of an entire project?

Estimating Time of Completion

- Decide whether to use probabilistic or deterministic time estimates for activities.
- Deterministic (single) time estimates are used here.
- Probabilistic (considering uncertainty) time estimates are addressed later in the chapter.

For our example project, these are the deterministic estimates of duration times for each activity:

Activity	A	B	C	D	E	F	G	H	J	K	L	M
Time	2	6	1	1	3	4	3	4	9	2	8	4

The most common mistake students make here is to attempt to complete all of the numbers in the node all at once. The solution process has *two* distinct steps. First, the forward pass determines the project duration while completing the top two numbers (*ES* & *EF*) *only*. Second, the backward pass completes the lower two numbers so that slack can be calculated and the critical activities identified.

Earliest Start and Earliest Finish Times

Since activity A has a duration of 2 (days, weeks, or months) and no immediate predecessors, the earliest we can start is right now (at time = 0) and the earliest we can finish is time = 2. This is not rocket science.

C and G can start as soon as A is completed, which is at time = 2. C is done at time = 3, G is finished at time = 5, and F is complete at time = 7. When can we begin L? Not until *both* F and G are done, which occurs at time = 7. The earliest possible finish time for L = 15.

For practice, complete the rest of the network. Start with B. The earliest start time is time = 0. The duration is 6. So the earliest finish for B is 6.

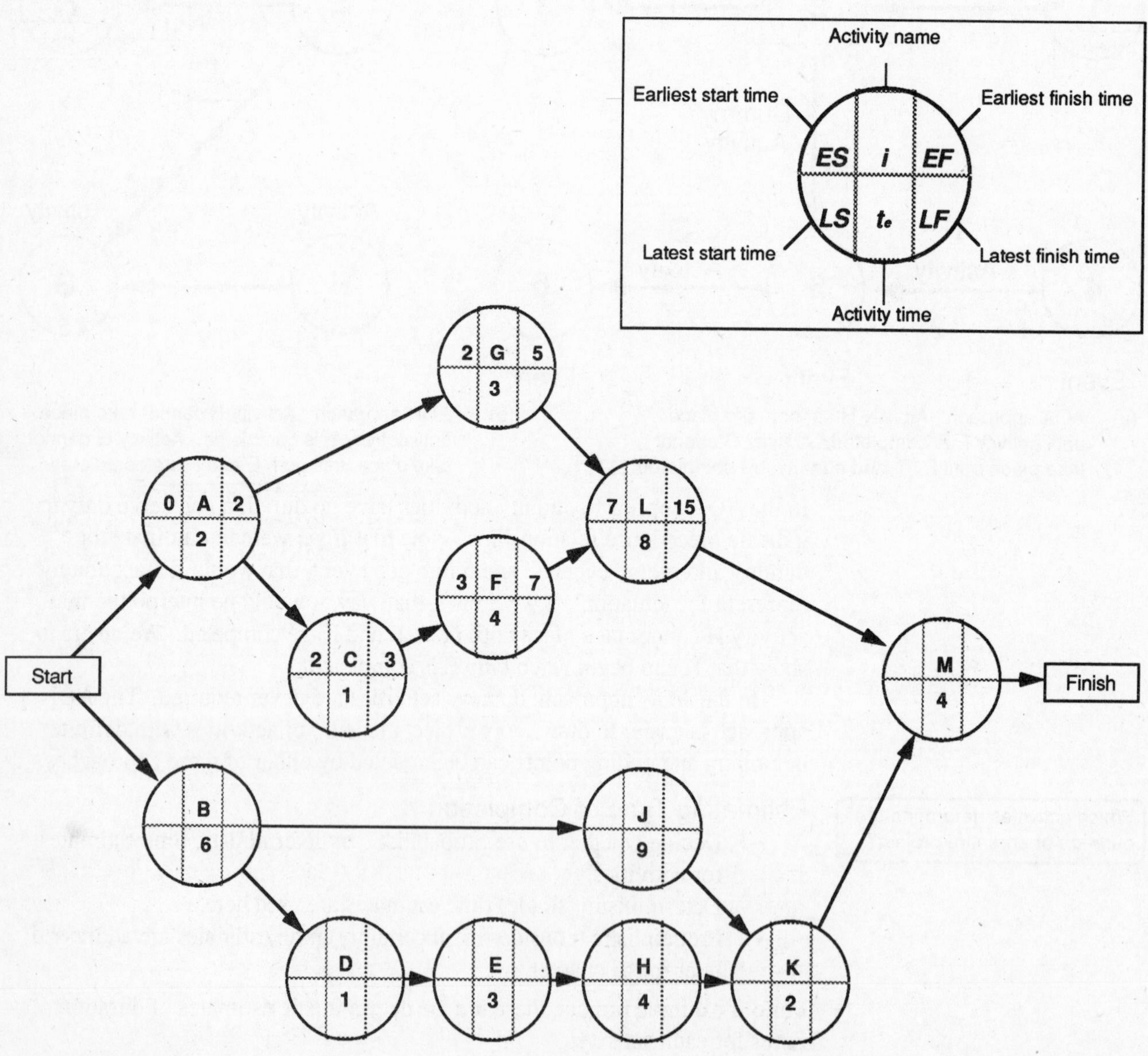

Okay, if you completed the forward pass correctly, it should look like this. We have determined that the project will take 21 days, weeks, or months to complete.

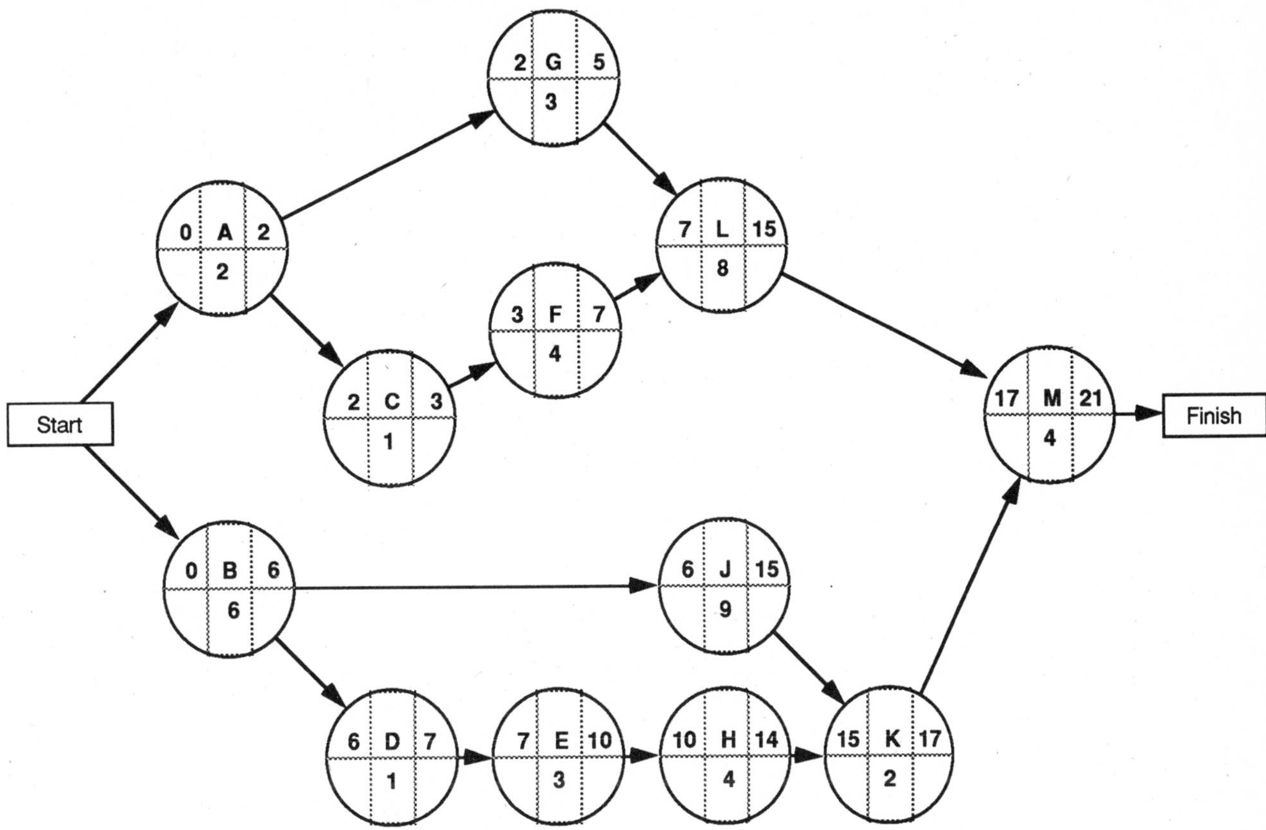

Latest Start and Latest Finish Times

Now let's try the backward pass. We start at the finish and, oddly enough, work backward. The backward pass is similar to the backward scheduling that occurs in material requirements planning (MRP). In MRP we order all material as late as possible while still meeting the need date. In the backward pass of PERT/CPM we schedule all activities to occur as late as possible while still meeting the completion date. If we take the PERT/CPM network diagram and rotate it 90° counter-clockwise, you see something that looks a lot like the bill of materials diagram in MRP.

Anyway, place a "21" in the lower right quadrant for activity M. That is, saying the latest finish time for M is equal to the earliest finish time for M. Now if M has a duration of 4, the latest we can get started with it is at (let's see now, 21 – 4 = 17). That's it, 17. If we start M any later than time = 17, the project will not be completed at time 21. Place a "17" in the lower left quadrant for M.

Activities L and K must *both* be done by time 17 at the latest, or we will not be able to start M at time = 17. Therefore, the latest finish time for L and K is 17. Place a "17" in the lower right for L and K. Subtract their durations, and place a "9" and "15" at the lower left for L and K, respectively. Got it? Okay, keep going. Things will probably go smoothly until you get back to activities A or B.

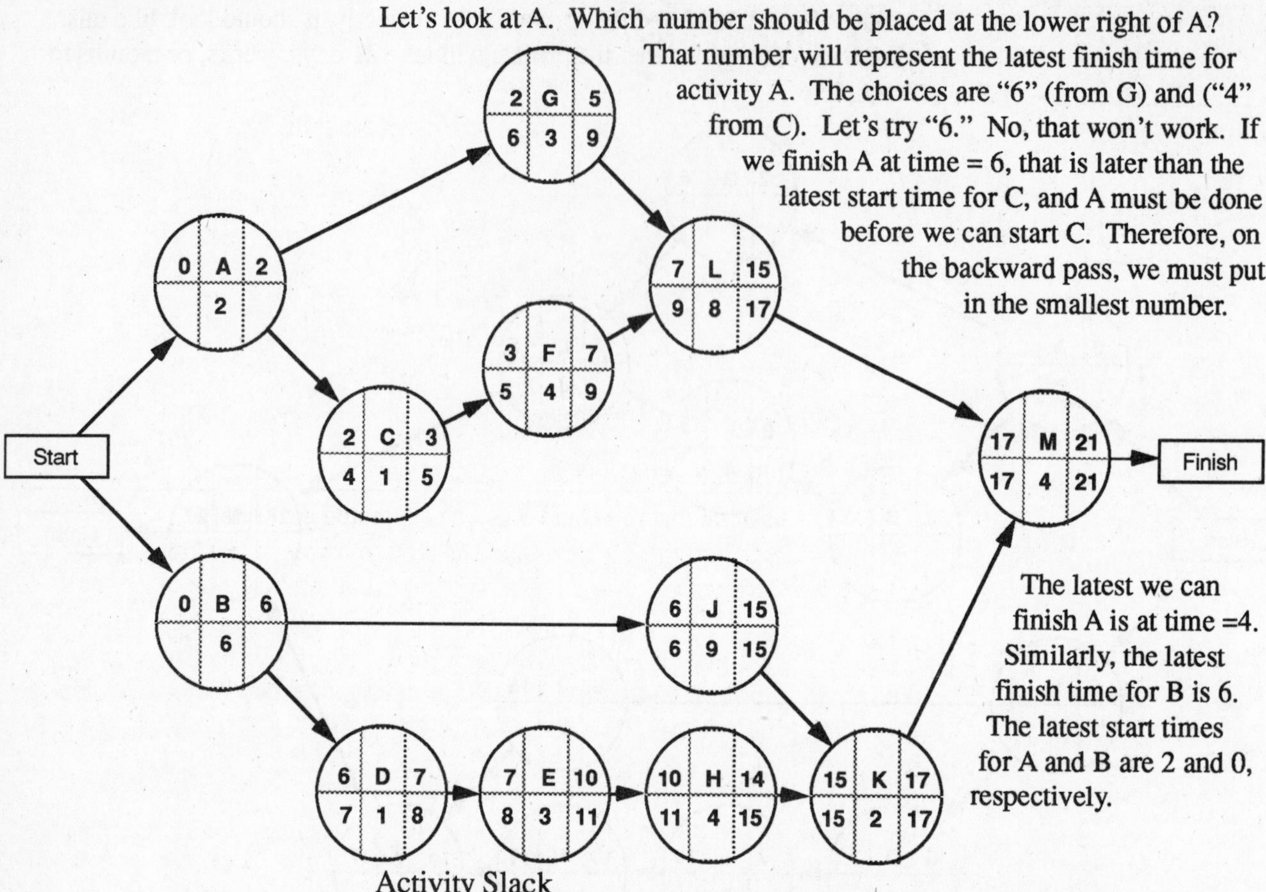

Let's look at A. Which number should be placed at the lower right of A? That number will represent the latest finish time for activity A. The choices are "6" (from G) and ("4" from C). Let's try "6." No, that won't work. If we finish A at time = 6, that is later than the latest start time for C, and A must be done before we can start C. Therefore, on the backward pass, we must put in the smallest number.

The latest we can finish A is at time =4. Similarly, the latest finish time for B is 6. The latest start times for A and B are 2 and 0, respectively.

Activity Slack

- Helps make decisions regarding reallocation of resources
- Resources diverted from activities with slack may be used to speed activities which are behind schedule.

The calculation is done by simply subtracting the early start or early finish numbers from the number directly below it. For example, the slack in activity D is 8 – 7 = 1 or 7 – 6 = 1. Note that activities E and H also have one unit of slack. Actually, they don't *each* have one unit of slack. The one unit of slack must be *shared* among D, E, and H. If D consumes the slack by finishing at time = 8, there is no slack remaining for E or H.

- The critical path is the *longest* path.
- Activities with no slack are critical.
- There will always be at least one path of critical activities that connect the start to the finish. That is the critical path.
- The critical path for the example = B-J-K-M.

Monitor Project Progress

- Monitor projects so that delays can be identified.
- Slack-sorted report lists the activities in ascending order of slack.
- Activities at the top of the report are more critical. They may have negative slack.
- Negative slack occurs when the start date of an activity is delayed past its latest start date.
- The critical path may shift if formerly noncritical activities are delayed to make project duration dependent upon their completion.

How can uncertainty in time estimates be incorporated into project planning?

Probabilistic Time Estimates

Three Time Estimates

1. Most optimistic time (a). The one chance in a hundred that all goes exceptionally well.
2. Most likely time (m). The best guess.
3. Most pessimistic time (b). The one chance in a hundred that everything that could go wrong, does go wrong.

$$t_e = \frac{a + 4m + b}{6}$$

The expected activity time is a weighted average of these three time estimates

Calculating Time Statistics

Key Statistical Assumptions

1. Assume that a, m, and b can be estimated accurately.
2. Each activity time is treated as though it were a random variable derived from a beta probability distribution.
   a. The standard deviation of the activity time is one-sixth of the range ($b - a$).
   b. The durations of the activities are independent of each other, so that the variances of the critical activities can be added to obtain the variance of the critical path.

$$\sigma^2 = \left(\frac{b-a}{6}\right)^2$$

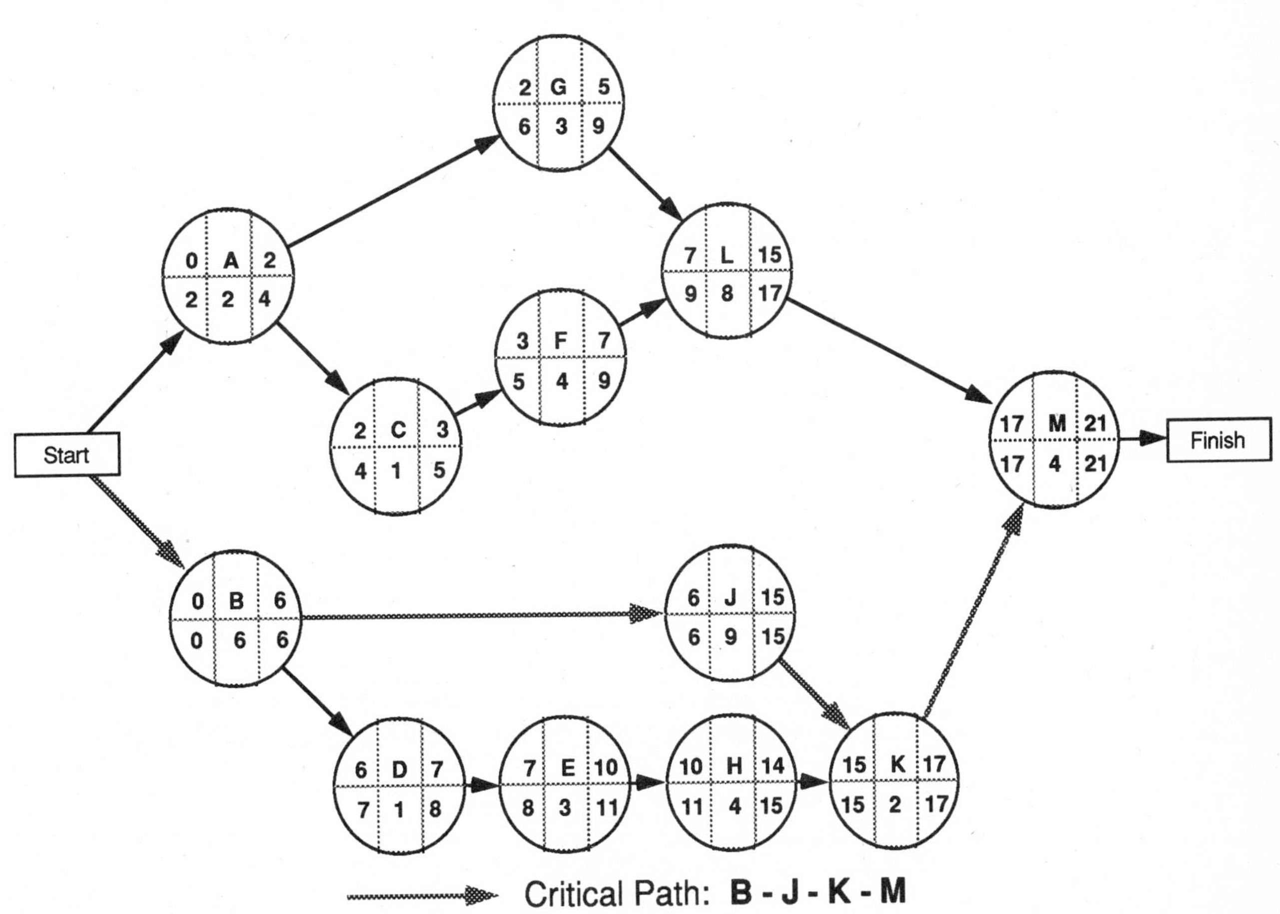

Analyzing Probabilities

- Assume that the duration times of activities along the critical path will determine the completion time of the project. There are no near critical paths that are likely to become critical.
- Because activity durations are independent random variables, by the central limit theorem, the duration of the project will vary around the sum of the critical path activities according to the normal probability distribution.

Normal distribution:

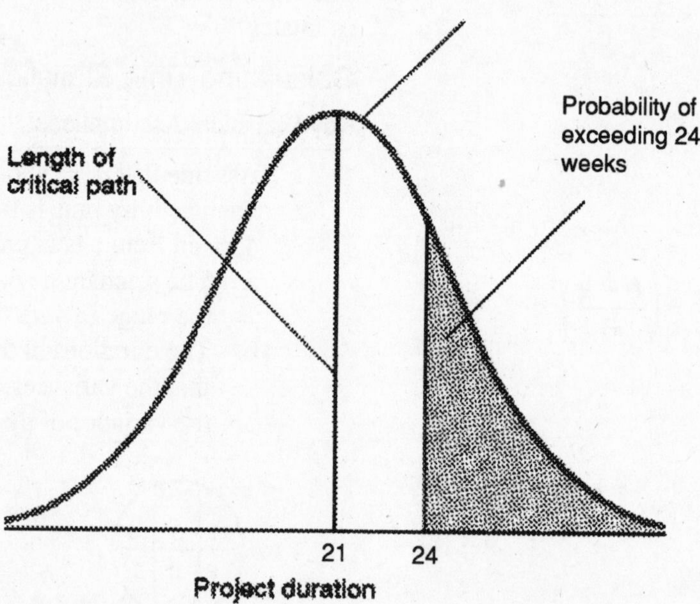

Time Estimates (weeks)				Activity Statistics		
Most Optimistic (*a*)	Most Likely (*m*)	Most Pessimistic (*b*)	Expected Time (t_e)	Variance (σ^2)	**Critical Path?**	**Activity**
B	2	5	14	6	2.000	Yes
J	3	10	11	9	1.778	Yes
K	1	2	3	2	0.111	Yes
M	3	4	5	4	0.111	Yes
			TE = 21		**4.000**	

What is the probability of completing this project in 24 or less time periods?

$$z = \frac{X - \mu}{\sqrt{\sigma_{cp}^{2}}} = \frac{24 - 21}{2} = 1.5$$

From the normal distribution, $z = 1.5$, probability $= 93.32\%$. This is optimistic because there are near critical paths that may become critical.

How do project planning methods increase the potential to control costs and provide better customer service?

Cost Considerations

Analyzing Costs

- There are always cost-time trade-offs.
- The shorter the duration of the project, the lower the indirect costs.
- The best schedule may require *crashing* some activities to reduce overall project completion time.

Direct Costs and Times

1. Normal time (*NT*) — analogous to the expected time, *t*
2. Normal cost (*NC*) — cost associated with the normal time
3. Crash time (*CT*) — shortest possible time to complete an activity
4. Crash cost (*CC*) — cost associated with the crash time

Cost Assumptions

- Assume costs increase linearly as activity duration decreases

$$\text{Cost to crash per week} = \frac{CC - NC}{NT - CT}$$

EQUATION 19.5
Project costs

$$\text{Crash cost per week} = \frac{CC - NC}{NT - CT}$$

Indirect and Penalty Costs

- Penalty costs incurred if project takes longer than specified duration.
- Determine target project completion time that minimizes total costs.

Activity	Normal Time (NT)	Normal Cost (NC)	Crash Time (CT)	Crash Cost (CC)	Maximum Time Reduction (wk)	Cost to Crash per Week
A	2	$10,000	1	$13,000	1	$ 3,000
B	6	20,000	4	34,000	2	7,000
C	1	5,000	1	5,000	---	---
D	1	8,000	1	8,000	---	---
E	3	24,000	2	27,100	1	3,100
F	4	10,000	2	14,000	2	2,000
G	3	7,000	1	10,000	2	1,500
H	4	37,000	1	40,900	3	1,300
J	9	58,000	5	62,000	4	1,000
K	2	12,000	1	18,000	1	6,000
L	8	54,000	3	79,000	5	5,000
M	4	15,000	1	42,000	3	9,000
Total		$ 260,000		$ 353,000		

To demonstrate normal and minimum-time schedules we will assume:

- Time periods shown are in weeks
- Indirect costs are $5,000 per week.
- Penalty costs are $4,000 per week, beginning the 19th week.

Normal schedule costs are:

Total direct cost is	$260,000	
Indirect costs are	$105,000	($5,000 * 21 weeks)
Penalty costs are	$ 12,000	($4,000 * 3 weeks)
Total, 21 week project	$377,000	

Crash schedule costs:

Total direct cost is	$353,000	
Indirect costs are	$ 55,000	($5,000 * 11 weeks)
Penalty costs are	$ 0	
	$408,000	

1. Determine the project's critical path(s). In this case, the critical path is B-J-K-M, with a duration equal to 21 time periods.
2. Finding the cheapest activity on the critical path that is the *least* expensive to crash.
   - That would be activity J, which will be crashed one week at a cost of $1,000 per week.
3. Reduce the time for this activity until (a) it cannot be further reduced, (b) another path becomes critical, or (c) the increase in direct costs exceeds the savings that result from shortening the project. If more than one path is critical, the time for an activity on each path may have to be reduced simultaneously.

Duration = 20.

Crash Activity J by one week.

Penalty costs:	$4,000
Indirect costs:	$5,000
Crash costs:	– $1,000
Net Savings:	$8,000

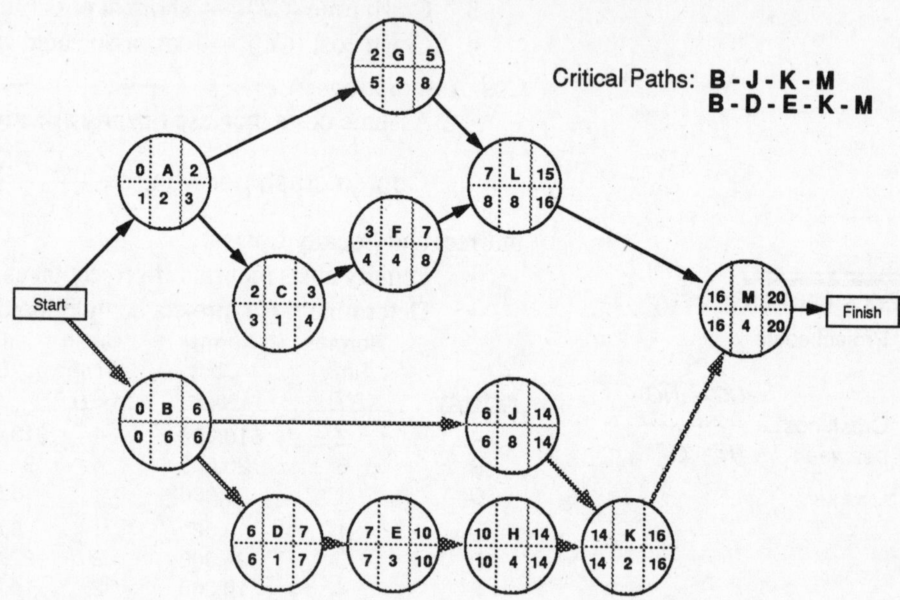

Duration = 19.

Crash Activity J by one week.
$1,000
Crash activity H by one week.
$1,300

Penalty costs:	$4,000
Indirect costs:	$5,000
Crash costs:	– $2,300
Net Savings:	$8,000

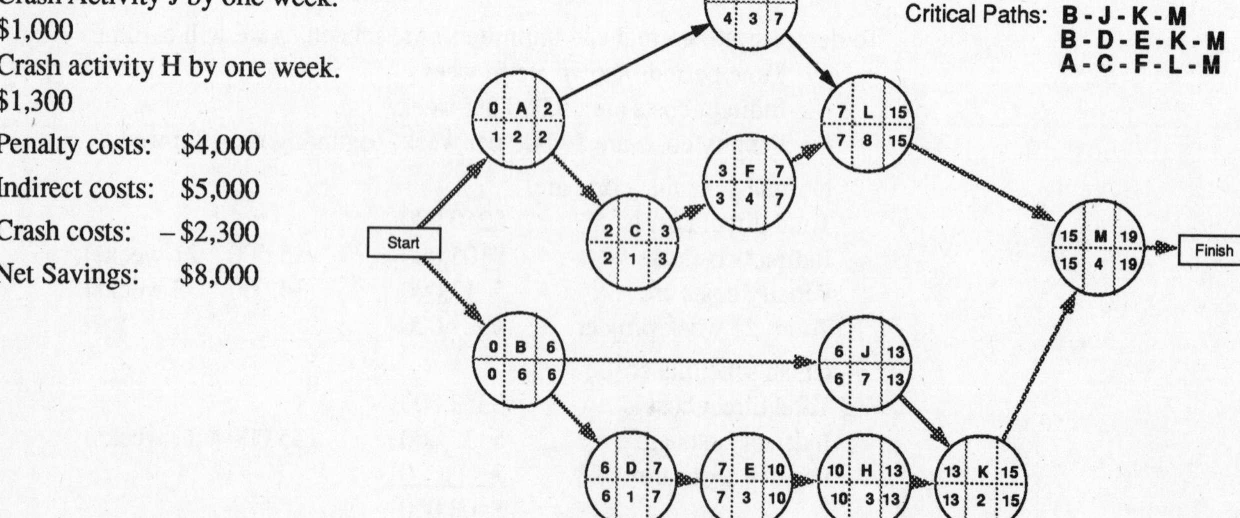

Duration = 18.

Crash Activity J by one week. $1,000

Crash activity H by one week. $1,300

Crash activity F by one week. $2,000

Penalty costs: $0,000

Indirect costs: $5,000

Crash costs: – $4,300

Net Savings: $ 700

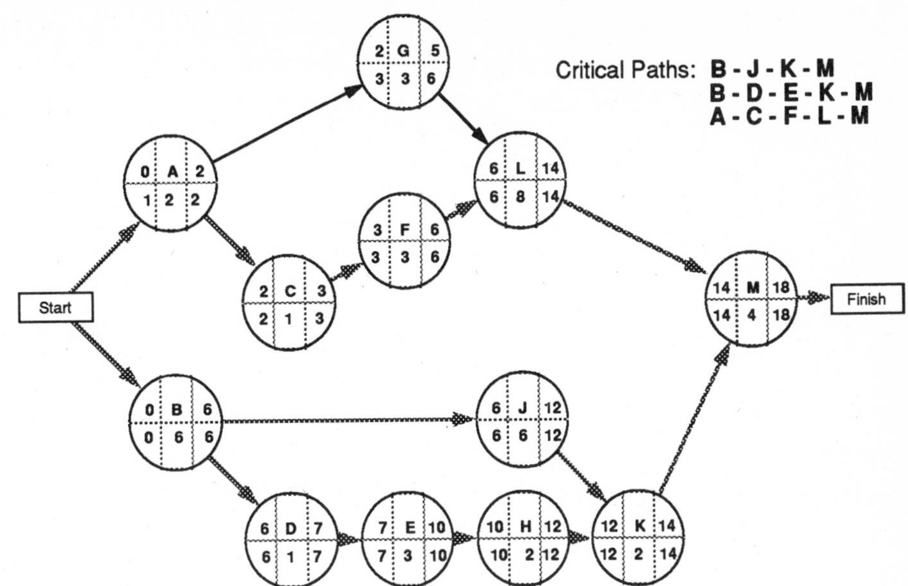

Duration = 17.

Crash Activity J by one week. $1,000

Crash activity H by one week. $1,300

Crash activity F by one week. $2,000

Penalty costs: $0,000

Indirect costs: $5,000

Crash costs: – $4,300

Net Savings: $ 700

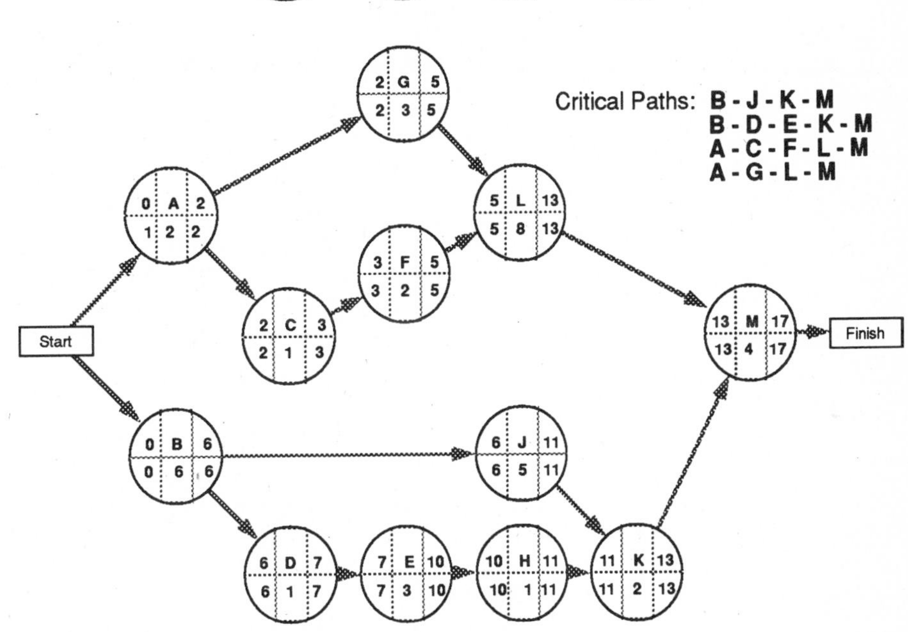

The minimum cost schedule is 17 days (shown above).

Duration = 16.

Activities F, H, and J have been fully crashed. The least costly way to reduce the project duration to 16 days is:

Crash Activity M by one week. $9,000

Penalty costs: $0,000

Indirect costs: $5,000

Crash costs: – $9,000

Net Savings: – $4,000

What is the effect of limited resources on project duration?

Resource Limitations

- Developing schedules without considering the load placed on resources can result in
  - inefficient resource use
  - project delays
- Gantt charts are more useful for showing implications of resource requirements for a schedule of activities.

Steps to Generate a Schedule that Recognizes Resource Constraints

1. Start with the first day of the project and schedule as many activities as possible.
2. When several activities compete for the same resources, give preference to the activities with the least slack.
3. Reschedule noncritical activities, to free resources for critical activities.

Benefits and Limitations of PERT/CPM Systems

Benefits

1. Requires managers to organize, determine activity interrelationships
2. Graphic displays, progress reports
3. Estimate of project duration
4. Critical activities are highlighted
5. Indicates resources that can be reallocated
6. Analyze cost-time trade-offs

Network Diagrams

- Project activities may not have clear beginning and ending points.
- Activity sequence relationships may not be identifiable at the beginning of the project.
- Project content can change.

Control

- Near-critical paths may become critical, causing delays in project completion.

Time Estimates

- The choice of the beta distribution was arbitrary.
- Formulas used to calculate mean and variance are only approximate
- Arriving at one to three accurate time estimates for project activities is very difficult.
- Pessimistic time estimates inflate expected times and become an excuse for failure.

Resource Limitations

- Assumes sufficient resources will be available

"Although PERT/CPM has shortcomings, its skillful application to project management can significantly aid project managers in their work." p. 815

Computerized Project Scheduling and Control

"Computerized network planning models are used extensively for projects in government, construction, aerospace, entertainment, pharmaceuticals, utilities, manufacturing, and architectural engineering." p. 815

- Computers are needed when
  - project has many activities
  - there are frequent updates
  - management needs to track resource usage
  - management desires actual-versus-planned comparisons

Multiple-Choice Questions

1. The smallest unit of work effort consuming both time and resources that the project manager can schedule and control is
   A. a node.
   B. a precedence relationship.
   C. an activity.
   D. an arc.

2. Which of the following is true of PERT/CPM networks?
   A. An event consumes neither time nor resources.
   B. AOA networks are easier to construct than AON networks.
   C. AOA networks use arcs to represent events.
   D. AON networks use nodes to represent events.

3. A "critical" activity is so named because it
   A. has a deterministic time estimate.
   B. has no activity slack.
   C. has the longest expected duration.
   D. is on the shortest path through the network.

4. The critical path is the path that
   A. has the least activities.
   B. has the most activities.
   C. takes the longest time to complete.
   D. takes the shortest time to complete.

5. Slack is determined by the difference between
   A. earliest start and earliest finish times
   B. earliest start and latest start times
   C. earliest start and latest finish times
   D. latest start and earliest finish times

6. An activity always has negative slack when
   A. it is completed ahead of schedule.
   B. its duration is longer than planned.
   C. current date is greater than earliest start date.
   D. current date is greater than latest start date.

7. Which of the following tends to encourage the use of probabilistic (rather than deterministic) time estimates for PERT/CPM activities?
   A. It is difficult to obtain time estimates.
   B. Inflation of expected times automatically builds in slack.
   C. Management realizes that the project will not be quite like others they have managed.
   D. Probabilistic times are more useful for projects that have been done many times before.

8. Which of the following is characteristic of the beta distribution?
   A. It is symmetrical.
   B. The expected time does not occur to the left of the most likely time.
   C. The standard deviation is one-sixth the range.
   D. The standard deviation is the square root of the mean.

9. Analyzing probabilities in PERT/CPM networks relies on
   A. deterministic activity time estimates.
   B. several near-critical paths for good estimates of project duration.
   C. the independence of the activities.
   D. the Poisson probability distribution.

10. When analyzing costs, we assume
    A. direct costs increase linearly with increased activity duration.
    B. indirect costs increase linearly with increased activity duration.
    C. penalty costs decrease linearly with increased activity duration.
    D. total costs increase linearly with increased activity duration.

11. Which of the following is *least* likely to cause difficulty in the use of computerized PERT/CPM systems to analyze project networks?
    A. A large number of activities (say 200)
    B. Near critical paths
    C. Errors in time estimates
    D. Actual precedence relationships which cannot be specified beforehand

12. Which of the following is most useful in showing the implications of resource limitations for a schedule of activities?
    A. CPM charts
    B. Gantt charts
    C. PERT charts
    D. Zodiac charts

13. Network planning models are useful in all of the following except:
    A. contract negotiations
    B. highlighting critical activities
    C. identifying resources to be reallocated
    D. scheduling overlapping activities

(Multiple-choice answers are on Study Guide page 346.)

Problems

1. Use the first two columns of data to label the nodes and draw the AON network. All data are in weeks.

Activity	Immediate Predecessor	Optimistic Duration	Most Likely Time	Pessimistic Time	Expected Duration	Activity Variance
A	---	3	4	11		
B	A	3	6	9		
C	A	1	8	9		
D	A	3	5	7		
E	C,D	2	3	10		
F	B	4	7	16		
G	B	4	4	4		
H	E,F	6	7	14		
J	F	5	5	11		
K	H,J,L	2	4	6		
L	G	3	9	9		

2. Then complete the last two columns of data. Use it to:

   a. Estimate the project duration.

$$t_e = \frac{a + 4m + b}{6}$$

   b. Find the critical path.

   c. Compute the slack in activities B, D, G, J, and L.

   d. Which of those activities must share their slack with each other?

$$\sigma^2 = \left(\frac{b - a}{6}\right)^2$$

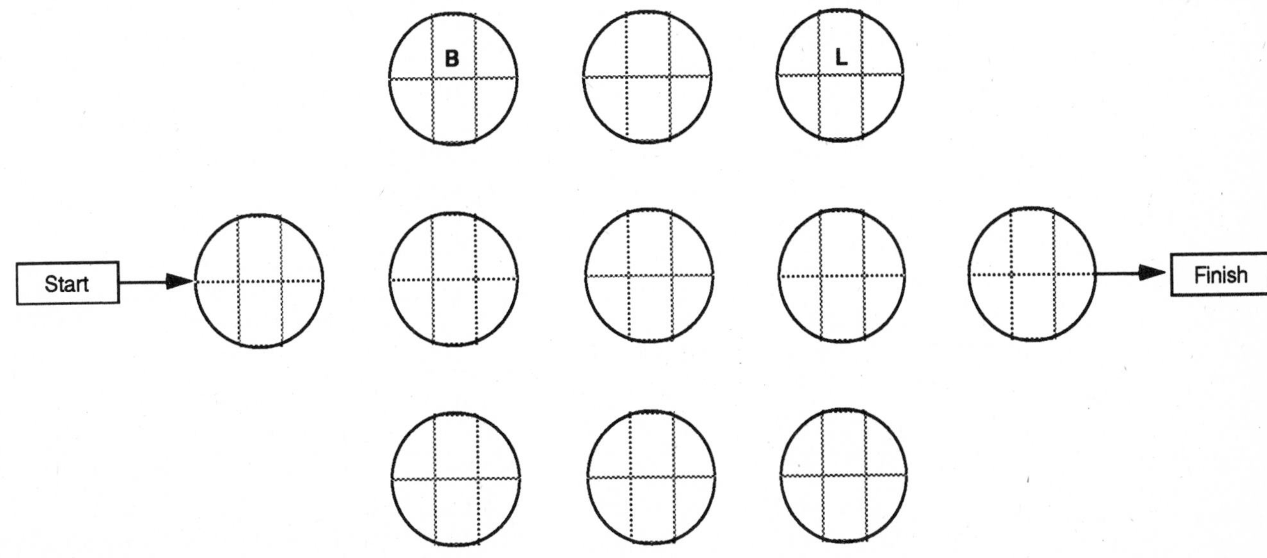

3. What are the chances of completing this project in 34 weeks or less?

   a. First find the variance of the critical path.

$$\sigma^2 = \left(\frac{b-a}{6}\right)^2$$

   b. Find z.

$$z = \frac{T_E - \mu}{\sigma}$$

   c. From the normal distribution table, find the probability of the project duration being 34 weeks or less.

4. Given the following information, find the minimum-cost schedule:
   - Indirect costs are $6,000 per week.
   - Penalty costs are $4,000 per week beginning the 30th week.

Activity	Normal Time (NT)	Normal Cost (NC)	Crash Time (CT)	Crash Cost (CC)	Maximum Time Reduction (wk)	Cost to Crash per Week
A	5	$10,000	3	$16,000	2	$ 3,000
B	6	20,000	4	34,000	2	7,000
C	7	5,000	5	8,000	2	1,500
D	5	8,000	3	15,000	2	3,500
E	4	24,000	2	27,600	2	3,300
F	8	10,000	5	26,500	3	5,500
G	4	7,000	4	7,000	---	---
H	8	37,000	6	49,600	2	6,300
J	6	58,000	5	62,000	1	4,000
K	4	12,000	2	21,000	2	4,500
L	8	54,000	3	79,000	5	5,000
Total		$245,000		$345,700		

Solutions

1. Use the first two columns of data to label the nodes and draw the AON network. All data are in weeks.

Activity	Immediate Predecessor	Optimistic Duration	Most Likely Time	Pessimistic Time	Expected Duration	Activity Variance
A	- - -	3	4	11	5	1.778
B	A	3	6	9	6	1.000
C	A	1	8	9	7	1.778
D	A	3	5	7	5	0.444
E	C,D	2	3	10	10	1.778
F	B	4	7	16	8	4.000
G	B	4	4	4	4	0.000
H	E,F	6	7	14	8	1.778
J	F	5	5	11	6	1.000
K	H,J,L	2	4	6	4	0.444
L	G	3	9	9	8	1.000

2. Then complete the last two columns of data. Use it to:

   a. Estimate the project duration.

   31 weeks

   b. Find the critical path.

   A - B - F - H - K

   c. Compute the slack in activities B, D, G, J, and L.

   B = 0, D = 5, G = 4, J = 2, L = 4

   d. Which of those activities must share their slack with each other?

   G and L are on the same loop of the network, so they must share their 4 weeks of slack.

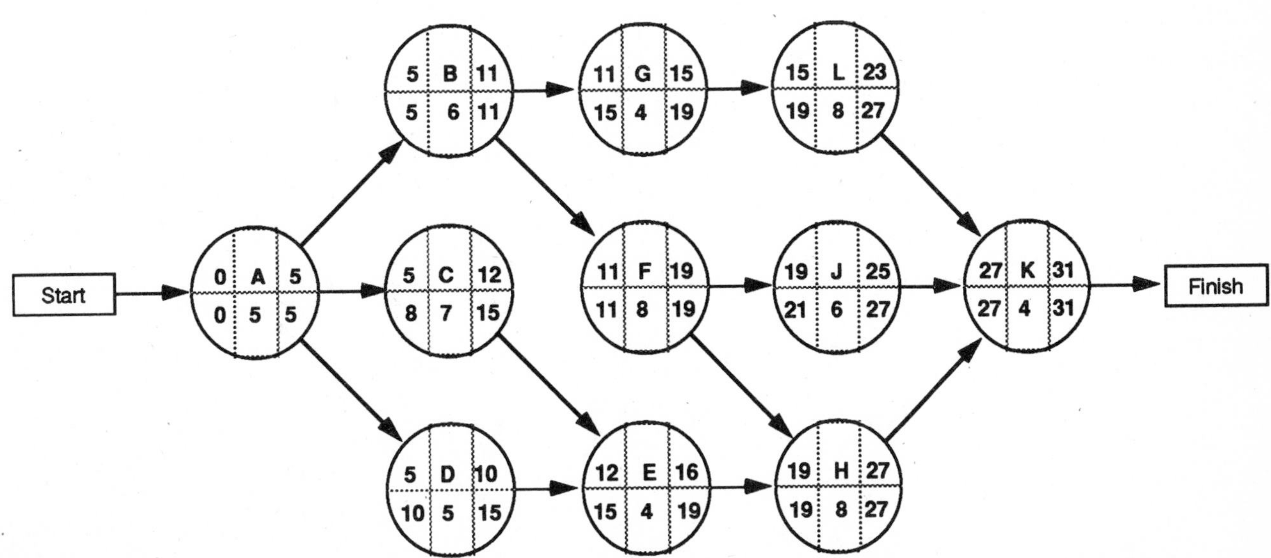

MULTIPLE CHOICE

ANSWERS

1. C	8. C
2. A	9. C
3. B	10. B
4. C	11. A
5. B	12. B
6. D	13. D
7. C	

3. What are the chances of completing this project in 34 weeks or less?

   a. First find the variance of the critical path.

$$\sigma^2 = \Sigma\left(\frac{b-a}{6}\right)^2 = 1.778 + 1.000 + 4.000 + 1.778 + 0.444 = 9$$

   b. Find z.

$$z = \frac{X-\mu}{\sqrt{\sigma_{cp}{}^2}} = \frac{34-31}{3} = 1.0$$

   c. From the normal distribution table, find the probability of the project duration being 34 weeks or less.

   When $z = 1$, probability = 84.13%.

4. Given the following information, find the minimum-cost schedule:
   - Indirect costs are $6,000 per week.
   - Penalty costs are $4,000 per week beginning the 30th week.

Activity	Normal Time (NT)	Normal Cost (NC)	Crash Time (CT)	Crash Cost (CC)	Maximum Time Reduction (wk)	Cost to Crash per Week
A	5	$10,000	3	$16,000	2	$ 3,000
B	6	20,000	4	34,000	2	7,000
C	7	5,000	5	8,000	2	1,500
D	5	8,000	3	15,000	2	3,500
E	4	24,000	2	27,600	2	3,300
F	8	10,000	5	26,500	3	5,500
G	4	7,000	4	7,000	---	---
H	8	37,000	6	49,600	2	6,300
J	6	58,000	5	62,000	1	4,000
K	4	12,000	2	21,000	2	4,500
L	8	54,000	3	79,000	5	5,000
Total		$245,000		$345,700		

Duration = 29.

Crash Activity A by two weeks @ $3,000.

Penalty costs:	$ 8,000
Indirect costs:	$12,000
Crash costs:	– $ 6,000
Net Savings:	$14,000

Start
0 A 3 / 0 3 3
3 B 9 / 3 6 9
3 C 10 / 8 7 15
3 D 8 / 10 5 15
9 G 13 / 13 4 17
9 F 17 / 9 8 17
10 E 14 / 15 4 17
13 L 21 / 17 8 25
17 J 23 / 19 6 25
17 H 25 / 17 8 25
25 K 29 / 25 4 29
Finish

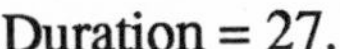

Duration = 27.

Crash Activity K by two weeks @ $4,500.

Penalty costs: $ 0,000

Indirect costs: $12,000

Crash costs: – $ 9,000

Net Savings: $ 3,000

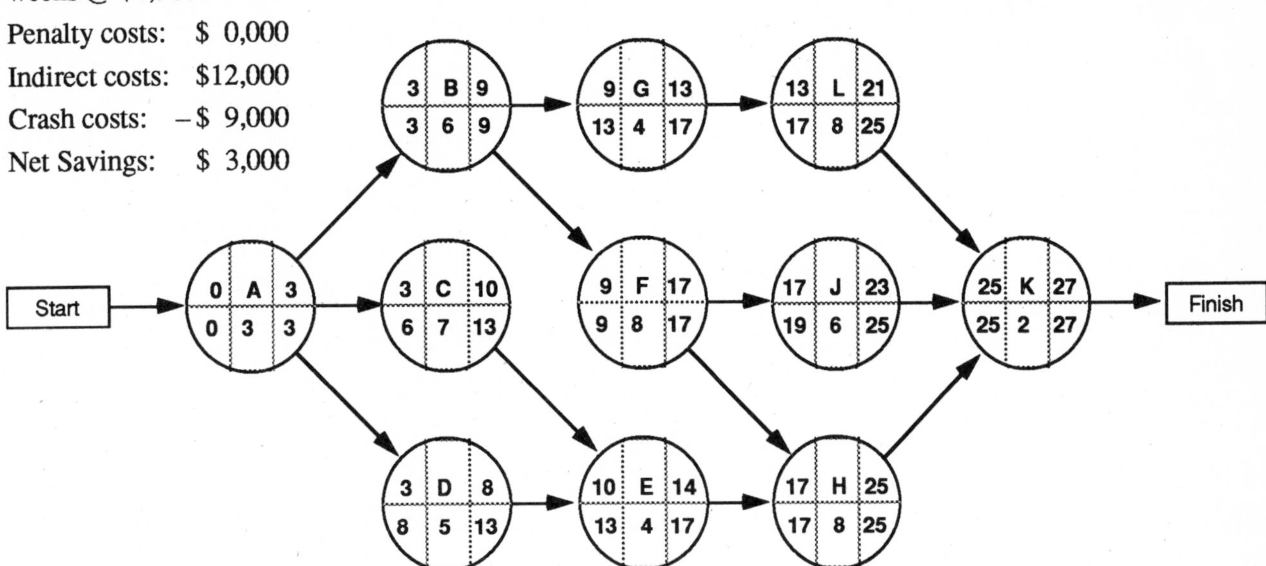

Duration = 24.

Crash Activity F by three weeks @ $5,500.

Penalty costs: $ 0,000

Indirect costs: $18,000

Crash costs: – $16,500

Net Savings: $ 1500

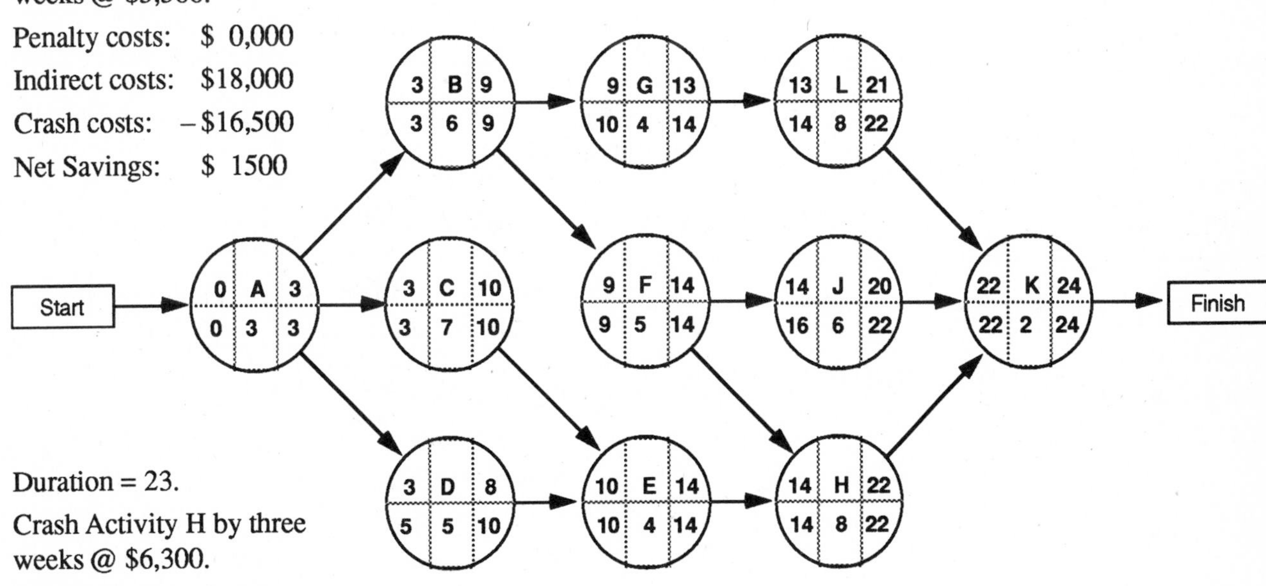

Duration = 23.

Crash Activity H by three weeks @ $6,300.

Penalty costs: $0,000

Indirect costs: $6,000

Crash costs: – $6,300

Net Savings: –$ 300

The minimum cost schedule is 24 weeks.

Formula Summary

Chapter One — Operations

$$\text{Productivity} = \frac{\text{Output}}{\text{Input}}$$

Supplement A — Decisions

Break-even volume

$$Q = \frac{F}{p - c}$$

Make-or-buy indifference quantity

$$Q = \frac{F_m - F_b}{c_b - c_m}$$

Expected value

$$EV = \sum PX$$

Chapter Four — TQM

Product reliability

$$r_s = (r_1)(r_2)\ldots(r_n)$$

Chapter Five —SPC

Mean

$$\bar{x} = \sum_{i=1}^{n} \frac{x_i}{n}$$

Standard deviation of a sample

$$\sigma_{\bar{x}} = \sqrt{\frac{\sum (x_i - \bar{x})^2}{n-1}}$$

$$= \sqrt{\frac{\sum x^2 - \frac{(\sum x_i)^2}{n}}{n-1}}$$

Control limits for variable process control charts

R-chart, range of sample

$$UCL_R = D_4 \bar{R}$$

$$LCL_R = D_3 \bar{R}$$

$\bar{x}$-chart, sample mean

$$UCL_{\bar{x}} = \bar{\bar{x}} + A_2 \bar{R}$$

$$LCL_{\bar{x}} = \bar{\bar{x}} - A_2 \bar{R}$$

or when the standard deviation of the process distribution, σ, is known:

$$UCL_{\bar{x}} = \bar{\bar{x}} + z\sigma_{\bar{x}}$$

$$LCL_{\bar{x}} = \bar{\bar{x}} - z\sigma_{\bar{x}}$$

where $\sigma_{\bar{x}} = \frac{\sigma}{\sqrt{n}}$

Chapter Five, continued

Control limits for attribute process control charts

p-chart, proportion defective

$$UCL_{\bar{p}} = \bar{p} + z\sigma_p$$

$$LCL_{\bar{p}} = \bar{p} - z\sigma_p$$

where $\sigma_p = \sqrt{\bar{p}(1-\bar{p})/n}$

c-chart, number of defects

$$UCL_{\bar{c}} = \bar{c} + z\sqrt{\bar{c}}$$

$$LCL_{\bar{c}} = \bar{c} - z\sqrt{\bar{c}}$$

where $\sigma_c = \sqrt{\bar{c}}$

Process capability ratio

$$C_p = \frac{\text{Upper spec} - \text{Lower spec}}{6\sigma}$$

Process capability index

$$C_{pk} = \text{minimum of}$$

$$= \frac{x - \text{Lower specification}}{3\sigma}, \text{ or}$$

$$= \frac{\text{Upper specification} - x}{3\sigma}$$

Supplement C — Acceptance Sampling

Average outgoing quality:

$$AQL = \frac{p(P_a)(N-n)}{N}$$

Chapter Six — Work Force Management

Required sample size in a time study

$$n = \left[\left(\frac{z}{p}\right)\left(\frac{s}{\bar{t}}\right)\right]^2$$

Normal time for a work element

$$NT = \bar{t}(F)(RF)$$

Normal time for the cycle

$$NTC = \sum NT$$

Standard time:

$$ST = NTC(1 + A)$$

Required sample size in a work sampling study

$$n = (z/e)^2 \hat{p}(1-\hat{p}) = \frac{z^2 \hat{p}(1-\hat{p})}{e^2}$$

where $e = z\sqrt{\frac{\hat{p}(1-\hat{p})}{n}}$

Supplement D — Learning Curves

Learning curve

$$k_n = k_1 n^b$$

where $b = \log r / \log 2$

Supplement E — Waiting Lines

Customer arrival Possion distribution

$$P_n = \frac{(\lambda T)^n}{n!} e^{-\lambda T}$$

Service-time exponential distribution

$$P(t \le T) = 1 - e^{-\mu T}$$

Single-Server Model	Multiple-Server Model	Finite Source Model
$\rho = \frac{\lambda}{\mu}$	$\rho = \frac{\lambda}{s\mu}$	$\rho = 1 - P_0$
	$P_0 = \left[\sum_{n=0}^{s-1} \frac{(\lambda/\mu)^n}{n!} + \frac{(\lambda/\mu)^s}{s!}\left(\frac{1}{1-\rho}\right)\right]^{-1}$	$P_0 = \left[\sum_{n=0}^{N} \frac{N!}{(N-n)!}\left(\frac{\lambda}{\mu}\right)^n\right]^{-1}$
$P_n = (1-\rho)\rho^n$	$P_n = \begin{cases} \frac{(\lambda/\mu)^n}{n!} P_0 & 0 < n < s \\ \frac{(\lambda/\mu)^n}{s!s^{n-s}} P_0 & n \ge s \end{cases}$	
$L_q = \rho L$	$L_q = \frac{P_0(\lambda/\mu)^s \rho}{s!(1-\rho)^2}$	$L_q = N - \frac{\lambda + \mu}{\lambda}(1 - P_0)$
$W_q = \rho W$	$W_q = \frac{L_q}{\lambda}$	$W_q = L_q[(N-L)\lambda]^{-1}$
$W = \frac{1}{\mu - \lambda}$	$W = W_q + \frac{1}{\mu}$	$W = L[(N-L)\lambda]^{-1}$
$L = \frac{\lambda}{\mu - \lambda}$	$L = \lambda W$	$L = N - \frac{\mu}{\lambda}(1 - P_0)$

Chapter Seven — Capacity Planning

Utilization percent, U

$$U = \frac{\text{Average output rate}}{\text{Maximum Capacity}} \times 100\%$$

Capacity cushion percent, C

$$C = 100\% - U$$

Capacity requirements for one product

$$M = \frac{Dp + \left(\frac{D}{Q}\right)s}{N\left(1 - \frac{C}{100}\right)}$$

Capcity requirements for multiple products

$$M = \frac{[D_p + (D/Q)s]_{\text{product }1} + [D_p + (D/Q)s]_{\text{product }2} + \ldots + [D_p + (D/Q)s]_{\text{product }n}}{N[1 - (C/100)]}$$

Chapter Eight — Location

Euclidean distance

$$d_{AB}=\sqrt{(x_A-x_B)^2+(y_A-y_B)^2}$$

Rectilinear distance

$$d_{AB}=|x_A-x_B|+|y_A-y_B|$$

Load-distance score

$$ld=\sum_i l_i d_i$$

Center of gravity

$$x^*=\frac{\sum_i l_i x_i}{\sum_i l_i} \quad \text{and} \quad y^*=\frac{\sum_i l_i y_i}{\sum_i l_i}$$

Chapter Nine — Layout

Cycle time (in seconds)

$$c=\left(\frac{1}{r}\right)(3600 \text{ seconds / hour})$$

Theoretical minimum number of work stations

$$TM=\left(\frac{\sum t}{c}\right)$$

Idle time (in seconds)

$$=nc-\sum t$$

Efficiency (%)

$$=\left(\frac{\sum t}{nc}\right)(100\%)$$

Balance delay (%)

$$=100\%-\text{Efficiency }(\%)$$

Chapter Ten — Forecasting

Linear regression

$$Y=a+bX$$

where

$$a=\overline{Y}-b\overline{X}$$

$$\overline{Y}=\frac{\sum Y}{n},\ \overline{X}=\frac{\sum X}{n}$$

$$b=\frac{\sum XY-n\overline{X}\overline{Y}}{\sum X^2-n\overline{X}^2}$$

Correlation coefficient

$$r=\frac{n\sum XY-\sum X\sum Y}{\sqrt{\left[n\sum X^2-(\sum X)^2\right]\left[n\sum Y^2-(\sum Y)^2\right]}}$$

Chapter Ten, continued

Coefficient of determination

$$r^2=\frac{a\sum Y+b\sum XY-n\overline{Y}^2}{\sum Y^2-n\overline{Y}^2}$$

Standard deviation of the estimate

$$\sigma_{yx}=\sqrt{\frac{\sum Y^2-a\sum Y-b\sum XY}{n-2}}$$

Naive forecasting

$$\text{Forecast}=D_t$$

Estimating the average

$$\text{Forecast}=A_t$$

Simple moving average

$$A_t=\frac{D_t+D_{t-1}+D_{t-2}+\ldots+D_{t-n+1}}{n}$$

Weighted moving average

$$A_t=W_1D_t+W_2D_{t-1}+\ldots+W_nD_{t-n+1}$$

Exponential smoothing

$$A_t=\alpha D_t+(1-\alpha)A_{t-1}$$

Trend-adjusted exponential smoothing

$$\text{Forecast}=A_t+T_t$$

$$A_t=\alpha D_t+(1-\alpha)(A_{t-1}+T_{t-1})$$

$$T_t=\beta(A_t-A_{t-1})+(1-\beta)T_{t-1}$$

Forecast error

$$E_t=D_t-A_t$$

$$\text{CFE}=\sum E_t$$

$$\text{MSE}=\frac{\sum E_t^2}{n}$$

$$\sigma=\sqrt{\text{MSE}}$$

$$\text{MAD}=\frac{\sum|E_t|}{n}$$

Exponentially smoothed error

$$\text{MAD}_t=\alpha|E_t|+(1-\alpha)MAD_{t-1}$$

Mean Absolute Percent error

$$\text{MAPE}=\frac{\sum\frac{|E_t|}{D_t}(100\%)}{n}$$

Tracking signal

$$\text{Tracking Signal}=\frac{\text{CFE}}{\text{MAD}},\ \text{or}\ \frac{\text{CFE}}{\text{MAD}_t}$$

Chapter 12 — Independent-Demand

Cycle inventory $= \dfrac{Q}{2}$

Pipeline inventory $= dL$

Weeks of supply

$$= \frac{\text{Average aggregate inventory value}}{\text{Weekly sales (at cost)}}$$

Inventory turnover

$$= \frac{\text{Annual sales (at cost)}}{\text{Average aggregate inventory value}}$$

Total annual cost, $C = \dfrac{Q}{2}(H) + \dfrac{D}{Q}(S)$

Economic order quantity, $EOQ = \sqrt{\dfrac{2DS}{H}}$

Inventory position, $IP = OH + SR - BO$

Continuous review system:

Reorder point (R) = Average demand during the protection interval + Safety stock

Protection interval = Lead time = L

Safety stock $= z\sigma_L$

Standard deviation of demand during the protection interval, $\sigma_L = \sigma_t\sqrt{L}$

Periodic review system:

Target inventory (T) = Average demand during the protection interval + Safety stock

Protection interval = $P + L$

where $P = EOQ/D$

Safety stock $= z\sigma_{P+L}$

Standard deviation of demand during the protection interval, $\sigma_{P+L} = \sigma_t\sqrt{P+L}$

Order quantity = $T - IP$

Supplement H — Inventory Models

Non instantaneous replenishment:

Economic production lot size

$$ELS = \sqrt{\frac{2DS}{H}}\sqrt{\frac{p}{p-d}}$$

Maximum inventory, $I_{max} = Q\left(\dfrac{p-d}{p}\right)$

Total cost

$$C = \left[\left(\frac{Q}{2}\right)(H)\right] + \left[\frac{D}{Q}(S)\right]$$

Time between orders

$$TBO_{ELS} = \frac{ELS}{D}$$

Quantity Discounts:

Total annual cost:

$$C = \left[\left(\frac{Q}{2}\right)(H)\right] + \left[\frac{D}{Q}(S)\right] + PD$$

One-Period Decisions:

Payoff matrix:

$$\text{Payoff} = \begin{cases} pQ, & \text{if } Q \le D \\ pD - l(Q-D) & \text{if } Q > D \end{cases}$$

Chapter Fifteen — Just-In-Time

Number of kanban card sets:

$$k = \frac{\text{Average demand during lead time } \textit{plus} \text{ safety stock}}{\text{size of container}}$$

$$k = \frac{d(\overline{w} + \overline{p})(1+\alpha)}{c}$$

Chapter Sixteen — Scheduling

Critical ratio:

$$CR = \frac{\text{Due date} - \text{today's date}}{\text{Total shop time remaining}}$$

Slack per remaining operation:

$$S/RO = \frac{(\text{Due date} - \text{today's date}) - \text{Remaining work}}{\text{Number of operations remaining}}$$

Chapter Seventeen — Projects

Start and finish times

ES = max [*EF* time of all activities immediately preceding activity]

EF = *ES* + *t*

LS = *LF* – *t*

LF = min [*LS* times of all activities immediately following activity]

Activity slack

S = LS – ES or = LF – EF

Expected activity time:

$$t_e = \frac{a + 4m + b}{6}$$

Variance

$$\sigma^2 = \left(\frac{b-a}{6}\right)^2$$

z-transformation formula

$$z = \frac{T - TE}{\sqrt{\sigma^2}}$$

Project costs

$$\text{Crash cost per unit of time} = \frac{\text{Crash cost} - \text{Normal cost}}{\text{Normal time} - \text{Crash time}} = \frac{CC - NC}{NT - CT}$$